THE *DECAMERON* SIXTH DAY IN PERSPECTIVE

The *Decameron* Sixth Day in Perspective

Volume Six of the Lectura Boccaccii

EDITED BY DAVID LUMMUS

UNIVERSITY OF TORONTO PRESS
Toronto Buffalo London

Toronto Buffalo London
utorontopress.com

ISBN 978-1-4875-0871-5 (cloth)
ISBN 978-1-4875-0870-8 (EPUB)
ISBN 978-1-4875-0869-2 (PDF)

Library and Archives Canada Cataloguing in Publication

Title: The Decameron sixth day in perspective / edited by David Lummus.
Names: Lummus, David, editor.
Series: Toronto Italian studies. | Toronto Italian studies. Lectura Boccaccii ; v. 6.
Description: Series statement: Toronto Italian studies | Lectura Boccacci ; volume 6 | Includes bibliographical references and index.
Identifiers: Canadiana (print) 20210146559 | Canadiana (ebook) 20210146583 | ISBN 9781487508715 (cloth) | ISBN 9781487508708 (EPUB) | ISBN 9781487508692 (PDF)
Subjects: LCSH: Boccaccio, Giovanni, 1313–1375. Decamerone.
Classification: LCC PQ4287 .D4258 2021 | DDC 853/.1–dc23

University of Toronto Press acknowledges the financial assistance to its publishing program of the Canada Council for the Arts and the Ontario Arts Council, an agency of the Government of Ontario.

Canada Council for the Arts | Conseil des Arts du Canada

Funded by the Government of Canada | Financé par le gouvernement du Canada | Canada

Contents

THE *DECAMERON* SIXTH DAY IN PERSPECTIVE

Introduction

DAVID LUMMUS

Incomincia la sesta, nella quale, sotto il reggimento d'Elissa, si ragiona di chi con alcun leggiadro motto, tentato, si riscotesse, o con pronta risposta o avvedimento fuggì perdita o pericolo o scorno.

(VI.Intro.1)

[The Sixth Day begins, in which, under the regime of Elissa, stories are told about those who redeemed themselves with an elegant saying when provoked or those who with a quick response or stratagem escaped loss or danger or scorn.][1]

The Sixth Day of the *Decameron* marks a new beginning.[2] Its first story is the structural centre of the one hundred tales and is accordingly a reflection on storytelling and, more generally, on the power of the word. The stories of Day Six – each in some way a meditation on language, narration, or meaning – are the shortest in the entire work. The theme that governs the day, both as recorded in the rubric and as pronounced

1 I cite the text of the *Decameron* from Branca's 1976 edition for *Tutte le opere*. Translations of Boccaccio and others are my own unless otherwise noted.

2 The structural place of Day Six is considered important from several different perspectives, not least its central position and the connotations of the number six (the six days of creation, the *Hexameron*, etc.). See Meier, "Day Six" 289; and Kriesel, "The Marvelous" 222–3 and 252 for a review. My reading is informed primarily by Fido, "Boccaccio's *Ars Narrandi*"; Stewart, "La novella di Madonna Oretta"; Barolini, "Wheel," esp. 527–30; and Picone, "Leggiadri motti." See also Van der Voort for a discussion of the interrelation of Days One and Six. For general overviews of Day Six, see Fido, "Boccaccio's *Ars Narrandi*"; Picone, "Leggiadri motti"; Alfano, "Giornata VI"; Andrei, "*Motto*"; Martinez, "*Scienze della Cittade*"; and Meier, "Day Six."

at the end of Day Five (V.Concl.3),[3] also indicates a return to the word as the fundamental building block not only of the *novella*, but also of human communication in the function of self-preservation. The art of speaking was codified in Boccaccio's time by numerous manuals deriving in one way or another from classical rhetorical treatises, such as Cicero's *De oratore* or *De inventione*.[4] Like Cicero, Boccaccio understood right-headed and properly oriented speech to be fundamental to ethical and civic rectitude. In Boccaccio's Christian world, however, the words that make up human communication are indelibly linked with truth.[5] The word in the Sixth Day – the *motto* or quick-witted response – could be considered the worldly version of the *Verbum* at the beginning of the Gospel of John, the healing word of Christ, the *verbum salutis omnium*.[6]

---

3 In the Conclusion to Day Five, the topic appears as follows: "di chi, con alcun leggiadro motto tentato, si riscotesse, o con pronta risposta o avvedimento fuggì perdita o pericolo o scorno." As Zygmunt G. Barański pointed out in an earlier version of his contribution to this volume, there is a discrepancy in the punctuation between the two versions of the rubric in modern editions. In VI.Intro.1, "tentato" is bracketed off by commas, while in V.Concl.3 it is only separated from "si riscotesse." This editorial inconsistency would seem to lead to two different interpretations of the first half of the sentence that describes the day's theme: "those who redeemed themselves with an elegant saying when provoked" (VI.Intro.1) and "those who redeemed themselves, when provoked with an elegant saying" (V.Concl.3). In my view, the version that appears in the rubric to Day Six is the correct understanding of the phrase's meaning. These phrases are not punctuated in Boccaccio's autograph of the *Decameron*, Berlin, Staatsbibliothek, MS Hamilton 90. I leave it to Barański to explore further the significance of this editorial, but ultimately interpretative, problem.

4 On Ciceronian rhetoric in this period, see the essays in Cox and Ward.

5 On the early adaptation of Cicero's rhetoric by Christian writers see Copeland.

6 The opening of the Gospel of John is: "in principio erat Verbum et Verbum erat apud Deum et Deus erat Verbum" [John 1:1; in the beginning was the Word and the Word was with God and God was the Word]. The rubric to Day Six calques the Christian commonplace of the healing or redemptive (*sanum*) Word of God. Some biblical loci for this concept are Paul's epistle to Titus: "verbum sanum inreprehensibilem" [Titus 2:8; the irreproachable healing word]; Paul's second epistle to Timothy: "formam habe sanorum verborum quae a me audisti in fide et dilectione in Christo Iesu" [2 Timothy 1:13; have the form of healing words which you heard from me in faith and love Jesus Christ]; and the Gospel of Matthew: "et respondens centurio ait Domine non sum dignus ut intres sub tectum meum sed tantum dic verbo et sanabitur puer meus [Matthew 8:8; and in response the Centurion said, "Lord, I am not worthy for you to enter my home, but just say the word and my servant will be healed"]. In a tenth-century hymn for Vespers during Advent, this concept can be seen in a more popular form: "Verbum salutis omnium, Patris ab ore prodiens, Virgo beata, suscipe casto, Maria, viscere" ["Florilegium Casinense" 235; The Word of salvation for all, which comes from the mouth of the Father, O blessed Virgin Mary, receive it in your chaste womb]. For the text of the Vulgate Bible, I have used Weber and Gryson's *Biblia Sacra Vulgata*.

The salvific Word of God may seem to be parodied in this debasement of its redemptive powers into quotidian and individualistic self-serving contexts. It is more likely, however, as several of the essays herein testify, that Boccaccio saw a continuum – albeit precarious – between the Word and the stories people tell.

This continuum was a part of Boccaccio's ideas about poetry, which he expressed in more theoretical terms later in his life.[7] In his defence of poetry at the end of the treatise on myth, *Genealogie deorum gentilium libri*, Boccaccio links the term for story, *fabula*, to human speech and specifically to the conversations of Christ's disciples on the road to Emmaus:

> Fabula igitur ante alia *for faris* honestam sumit originem, et ab ea *confabulatio*, que nil aliud quam *collocutio* sonat; quod satis per Lucam in *Evangelio* demonstrantur, dum dicit de duobus discipulis post Christi passionem euntibus in castellum cui nomen Emaus sic aiens: "Et ipsi loquebantur ad invicem de his omnibus, que acciderant, et factum est, dum *confabularentur* et secum quererent, et ipse Christus appropinquans ibat cum illis" etc. Et si *confabulari* santis hominibus non imputatur in vicium, non erit fabulas composuisse peccatum. (XIV.ix.3–4)

> [The term for story, *fabula*, honestly originates, above all, from *for faris* (to speak), from which also derives *confabulatio* (conversation), which means nothing other than *collocutio* (speaking together). Luke, in the Gospel, demonstrates this clearly enough, when he writes about the two disciples, after Christ's passion, who are going to a castle called Emmaus. He writes: "And these men were speaking to one another [*loquebantur ad invicem*] about all the things that had occurred, and it happened that, while they were conversing [*confabularentur*] and asking each other questions, Christ himself came near and walked with them" and so on. And so if conversing [*confabulari*] is not to be attributed as a vice for holy men, it will not be a sin to have composed stories.][8]

7 Some critics see Boccaccio's ideology of language as indeterminate, and might disagree with this statement. See, e.g., Marcus, *Allegory of Form*; Mazzotta, *World at Play*; and Milner, "Boccaccio's *Decameron*." Although it is clear that Boccaccio understood the relationship between everyday speech and the Word as complex and often ambiguous, I do not think he viewed language as entirely indeterminate. See Lummus, "The *Decameron*." For a more extensive reading of Boccaccio's ideas on language and meaning, reconstructed in their medieval context, see Kriesel, *Boccaccio's Corpus*.

8 For the text of the *Genealogie* I cite from Zaccaria's 1998 edition for *Tutte le opere*. The text of the Latin Vulgate is quoted almost verbatim by Boccaccio here: "et ecce duo ex illis ibant ipsa die in castellum quod erat in spatio stadiorum sexaginta ab Hierusalem

In light of Boccaccio's reference to the Gospel of Luke, we should consider these cognates of *fabula* in contrast to the words of Christ (*verba eius*) that the disciples doubted – that is, the promise of resurrection and redemption.[9] The questions and conversation on the road to Emmaus emerged from a sense of wonder and bewilderment at the apparent death of Christ. The disciples' wonder distracted them so much that they did not recognize him until they had broken bread with him at Emmaus. As a defence of human storytelling, then, Boccaccio is signalling that the *fabula* (*μῦθος*) emerges as a means of communally seeking the truth when faced by wonder – as a path to achieving true discourse (*Λόγος* or *Verbum*).[10] For the *Decameron*, we may use this etymology as a way of understanding how Boccaccio would have viewed the relationship between his stories about the power of words and the Word of Scripture.[11] Unlike for the disciples on the road to Emmaus, who later

---

nomine Emmaus et ipsi loquebantur ad invicem de his omnibus quae acciderant et factum est dum fabularentur et secum quaererent et ipse Iesus adpropinquans ibat cum illis" [Luke 24:13–15; And now two of them were going that day to a castle that was sixty *stadia* from Jerusalem and was called Emmaus, and they were speaking to each other about all the things which had taken place and it happened that, while they were conversing and asking each other questions, Jesus himself came near and walked with them].

9 Earlier in the same chapter of Luke, the women who find Christ's tomb empty are said to remember Christ's words when they are confronted by angels: "et factum est dum mente consternatae essent de isto ecce duo viri steterunt secus illas in veste fulgenti cum timerent autem et declinarent vultum in terram dixerunt ad illas quid quaeritis viventem cum mortuis non est hic sed surrexit recordamini qualiter locutus est vobis cum adhuc in Galilaea esset dicens quia oportet Filium hominis tradi in manus hominum peccatorum et crucifigi et die tertia resurgere et recordatae sunt verborum eius" [Luke 24:4–8; and it happened that, while they were mentally confounded by this [i.e., the empty tomb], two men in gleaming dress suddenly stood beside them. Since they were frightened, the women bowed their heads to the ground, and the men said to them: "Why do you seek the living man among the dead? He is not here but he has risen. Remember how he spoke to you when he was still with you in Galilee and said: 'It is necessary that the Son of man be given over to the hands of sinners and be crucified and on the third day rise again.'" And they remembered his words.]

10 On the marvellous in Boccaccio, see Kriesel, "Marvelous."

11 Boccaccio invokes this connection in very similar terms in his defence of the *Decameron* in the Author's Conclusion. See paragraph 11: "Niuna corrotta mente intese mai sanamente parola: e così come le oneste a quella non giovano, così quelle che tanto oneste non sono la ben disposta non posson contaminare, se non come il loto i solari raggi o le terrene brutture le bellezze del cielo. Quali libri, quali parole, quali lettere son più sante, più degne, più reverende, che quelle della divina Scrittura? E sì sono egli stati assai che, quelle perversamente intendendo, sé e altrui a perdizione hanno tratto" [No corrupt mind has ever interpreted with a sane mind

encounter the Word made flesh as a miracle after the resurrection, the everyday search for truth can only happen through an imperfect language that is at once an interpretation of the world and an element of the world that requires interpretation. The distillation of the *fabula* to a *motto* – or at most a short *parabola* (parable) – signals Boccaccio's interest in excavating the core elements of language and of the production of meaning, which could lead to a new ethics and civics in the aftermath of the plague.

As Ronald Martinez has argued, Boccaccio's interest in the connections between politics and rhetoric may have been inspired by his reading of ancient rhetorical treatises, such as Cicero's *De inventione*.[12] Thirteenth- and fourteenth-century writers, from Brunetto Latini onward, found in Cicero's treatise a defence of the use of ornamented speech for the creation and maintenance of a healthy body politic. Brunetto Latini states in his *volgarizzamento* of Cicero's treatise: "Poi li savi parladori astutaro le battaglie, et apresso gli uomini fecero compagnie usando e mercatando insieme; e di queste compagnie cuminciaro a ffare ferme amicizie per eloquenzia e per sapienzia" [Latini, *Rettorica* II.2; Then the wise orators stopped the battles and made relations among men by frequenting each other and trading among one another; and from these relations grew friendships through eloquence and wisdom]. Eloquence was thought to have a civilizing effect in the history of human political development. This kind of wise orator appears frequently in Boccaccio's retelling of the myths of foundation across the *Genealogie*, figuring into the characterization of gods and heroes like Jupiter, Mercury, Prometheus, Orpheus, and Ulysses, among others.[13] Following the research of Virginia Cox and John Ward, Stephen Milner has argued that the "increasing complexity of the bureaucratic structure of these city-states [of central and northern Italy] in the late medieval period" led to the instrumentalization of the spoken word within diverse civic contexts,

any word. And just as honest words will not help a corrupt mind, so those words which are not so honest cannot contaminate a well-ordered mind, just like mud does not contaminate the rays of the sun or the filth of the earth the beauties of heaven. What books, what words, what letters are holier, worthier, more reverend than those of Holy Scripture? And yet there have been many people who have interpreted them perversely and who have earned perdition for themselves and others].

12 See Martinez, "*Scienze della Cittade*."

13 On the culture hero in Boccaccio's works, see Gittes, *Boccaccio's Naked Muse* 24–140, esp. 55–6 (on Ulysses), 63–5 (on Jupiter), and 66–8 (on Prometheus). On Jupiter as culture hero, see Lummus, "Boccaccio's Poetic Anthropology" 755–65. See also Cherchi, "Inventors of Things."

both as a tool for the securing of consensus and as weapon for asserting dominion ("Communication" 370).[14] Boccaccio's stories of eloquent culture heroes in the *Genealogie* and of performative speech acts across the *Decameron* engage with this re-emergence of the civic importance of language. He is more interested, however, in documenting how wise and ethical uses of language can foster civil society than he is in showing how rhetoric and poetics can be politically weaponized, a practice which he generally condemns.[15]

Stories, too, were held to be fundamental to political well-being and stability. In the same chapter of the *Genealogie* cited above, in which he defends the usefulness of storytelling, Boccaccio notes that two forms of *fabula* are seen both in the works of ancient writers and in the Bible: the stories of ancient myth and the Old Testament, he says, both contain a mixture of the true and the fantastic; and classical epic and comedy, like Christ's parables, present primarily historical-realistic elements in their narratives. After noting that a knowledgeable person would never call the Holy Spirit or Christ a "fabulonem" or "teller of falsehoods,"[16] Boccaccio again attempts to show the utility of storytelling by mentioning the famous episode of Menenius Agrippa from Livy's *Ab urbe condita,* in which Agrippa tells a group of plebeian soldiers a political allegory of how the parts of the body once revolted against the stomach because they did not feel like serving a single, idle unity:[17]

> Fabulis quippe ... non nunquam legimus incitatos insano fervore animos fuisse sedatos et in mansuetudinem redactos pristinam; ut-puta-dum a Memnio Agrippa gravissimo viro, romana plebs a patribus dissidens, e Sacro monte in patriam per fabulam revocata est. (XIV.ix.12)

---

14 See Cox, "Ciceronian Rhetoric"; Cox, "Ciceronian Rhetorical Theory"; Ward, *Ciceronian Rhetoric;* and Ward, "Rhetorical Theory."

15 See Lummus, "Boccaccio's Poetic Anthropology" 762–3.

16 Boccaccio is here defending poets against those who called them "fabulones," typically translated as "charlatans" or "quacks," and by some considered to have been invented by Boccaccio. The term is, however, taken from Augustine, who uses it in his treatise on heretics: "Illi autem, ut ita dixerim, fabulones, id est, qui fabulas vanas easdemque longas perplexasque contexunt, tam multis falsis dogmatibus pleni ut ipsi quoque illa numerare non possint, aut difficillime possint [*De Haeresibus*, Epilogue, 30 (126–7); But those, if I may call them so, spinners of fantastic fables, that is, men who weave empty, long, and confused stories, are full of so many false teachings that they themselves cannot even enumerate them, or can only do so with the greatest difficulty].

17 See Livy, *Ab urbe condita* 2.32.

> [Truly, by means of fables … we read often that minds incited with mad rage have been calmed and restored to their pristine mildness; such as when the Roman plebs was in dissension with the patricians and was called back to the city from the Sacred Mount by means of a fable [recounted] by Menenius Agrippa, a man of much gravity.]

Boccaccio cites a political parable as the clearest example of how stories can be useful. He follows this example with Apuleius's story of Cupid and Psyche, which demonstrates the power of stories, even those told by the most humble of storytellers, to uplift and stir the spirits of even the most important of listeners. For Boccaccio, the civic and ethical uses of storytelling originated in the classical and medieval rhetorical traditions. Yet, he constantly reminds his reader that the same rhetorical and poetic functions were present in the Bible. The alternation between classical and biblical sources in Boccaccio's defence of storytelling indicates that he sees a continuum not only between the classical and the Christian, but also between the sacred and the profane more generally. Boccaccio's belief in this continuum prompted him to downplay the precepts of classical rhetorical theory, which prescribed that an orator should select a low, middle, or high style based on the relative nobility of the subject matter. For Boccaccio, choices of register were instead determined by the relative needs and abilities of the reader. They indicated, furthermore, styles not only in Latin, but also in the vernacular. The everyday speech of commoners, for Boccaccio, is capable of communicating truths in a fundamentally similar way to the noblest writings of antiquity and to the holiest of scriptures.

The reduction of the *novella* to its shortest possible form also highlights technical aspects of storytelling, such as elements of structure, characterization, and signification,[18] and betrays a metaliterary self-reflexivity that readers have not encountered since the first three stories of Day One.[19] The metaliterary aspects of these *novelle*, however,

18 Structuralist critics, such as Todorov and his followers (e.g., Bosetti and Van der Voort), but also his critics (e.g., Edoardo Sanguineti), have been particularly drawn to Day Six. See the discussion in Fido, "Boccaccio's *Ars Narrandi*" 225–7.

19 On the metaliterary aspects of I.1 in particular, see Almansi, *Writer as Liar*, esp. 29–30; Marcus, *Allegory of Form* 11–26; Ó Cuilleanáin, *Religion and the Clergy* 148–77; Mazzotta, *World at Play* 47–74; and on I.2, see Marcus, "Faith's Fiction." On the metaliterary aspects of the stories in Day Six, see, e.g., on VI.1, Almansi, "Lettura"; and Stewart, "La novella di Madonna Oretta"; on VI.10, Marcus, *Allegory of Form* 64–78. See also Ascoli, "Auerbach."

which are discussed in several of the essays herein, are not an end in themselves. Rather, the discourses about language, style, narration, and meaning generated by these stories are reflected back onto the social world from which they emerge. The social world of the Sixth Day, in fact, after the geographical and chronological diversity of the first five days, is radically constrained to a primarily Florentine world of the recent past that would have been recognizable not only to the members of the fictional *brigata* but also to Boccaccio's Florentine readership.[20]

Within the frame narrative, the moment that signals the Sixth Day's novelty and indicates a turn back towards the realities of city life, as Barolini has shown, is the eruption of a quarrel among the servants of the *brigata*: "cosa che ancora adivenuta non v'era" [VI.Intro.4; something that had not yet happened].[21] After having spent the morning, beneath the rays of the sun, discussing the stories that had been told already and diverting themselves with games and songs – Dioneo and Lauretta sing of Troilus and Cressida – the group begins to gather for their usual storytelling pastime. As the queen, Elissa, is about to assign the first story to one of the *brigata*, "fu un gran romore udito che per le fanti e' famigliari si faceva in cucina" [VI.Intro.4; a loud noise was heard being made by maids and manservants in the kitchen]. In a scene taken from the Roman comedic and satirical tradition,[22] two servants – Licisca and Tindaro – argue over the question of whether or not women are still virgins on their wedding night. Licisca, whose speech dominates the report of the discussion, says it is ridiculous to think they are, while Tindaro disagrees. This *quaestio*, performed in the veiled sexualized language of the lower classes that has been often employed by Dioneo,[23] is handed over to the black sheep of the *brigata* for adjudication: "Dioneo, questa

20 Cf. Fido, "Boccaccio's *Ars Narrandi*" 230; and Barolini, "Wheel" 527–30.

21 See Barolini, "Wheel" 528–9 and 521.

22 On the sources for these characters, see Richardson; and Filosa, "'Decameron' 7" 317–19.

23 See VI.Intro.8: "Madonna, costui mi vuol far conoscere la moglie di Sicofante e … mi vuol dare a vedere che la notte prima che Sicofante giacque con lei messer Mazza entrasse in Monte Nero per forza e con ispargimento di sangue; e io dico che non è vero, anzi v'entrò paceficamente e con gran piacer di quei d'entro" [My lady, he wants to introduce me to Sicofante's wife and he wants to convince me that the first night Sicofante lay with her, Lord Stick entered Mount Black by force and with the shedding of blood; and I say that it is not true, rather he entered there peacefully and to the great pleasure of those inside]. See also the Author's Conclusion (4–6), where the author defends the use of such veiled sexual language, and for Dioneo's stories, see, e.g., III.10, V.10, and IX.10. On the connection between veiled language and allegory, see Mazzotta, *World at Play* 105–30.

è quistion da te" [VI.Intro.12; Dioneo, this is a dispute for you]. Dioneo quickly rules in favour of Licisca, whose empowerment over her rival in the kitchen leads her to pose a potential threat to Elissa's rule. The queen, however, quickly eliminates the plebeian distraction: "se non fosse che la reina con un mal viso le 'mpose silenzio e comandolle che più parola né romor facesse se esser non volesse scopata e lei e Tindaro mandò via, niuna altra cosa avrebbero avuta a fare in tutto quel giorno che attendere a lei" [VI.Intro.15; if the queen hadn't imposed silence on Licisca with a bad look and commanded her not to say another word or make further ruckus, unless she wanted to be whipped, and sent her and Tindaro away, they would have spent that entire day dealing with her]. The irruption of the petty concerns of the plebs into the more refined and leisurely atmosphere of the *brigata* threatens to bring about an end to the urbane *divertissement* of their escape by undermining the rule of order represented by the queen.[24]

At the end of the Sixth Day, this episode will inform the choice of Dioneo – king of Day Seven – regarding the topic of the next day's stories: the tricks women play on their husbands (VI.Concl.6). But its effect is more immediately perceptible in the quotidian settings and characters of the stories of Day Six. Franco Fido has noticed how the stories of Day Six are closer historically and geographically to the Florentine reality of the *brigata* ("Boccaccio's *Ars Narrandi*" 229–30). This contributes, in his view, to the effect of "diminish[ing] the distance ... between the universe of the tales ... and the universe of the frame" (230). The dispute between Tindaro and Licisca also foreshadows several of the themes that will direct the narrative action of the stories of the Sixth Day. This episode indicates that the day deals centrally with the tensions between members of different social classes (VI.2 and 4), and with questions of sociability and socio-intellectual hierarchies (VI.5, 6, 9, and 10), gender, sexuality, and the threat of violence (VI.1, 3, 7, and 8), some of which are embedded in considerations of the law and adjudication (VI.3, 5, and 7). In Day Six Boccaccio does not address how language can promote the *salus omnium* in abstract theoretical terms, but in the "concrete experience of life," to use Fido's words ("Boccaccio's *Ars Narrandi*" 227).

The turn back to city life is also related to Boccaccio's metaliterary reflection throughout the day. If it is Boccaccio's concern to understand the basic form of human communication – the word – and its redemptive potential, then the only theatre in which such an inquiry is valid is the city as the "normative human community," as Catherine Keen

24 See Martinez, "*Scienze della Cittade*" 68; and Meier, "Day Six" 295–7.

has described the value of the city in Dante's thought (15).[25] Since the employment of the tools of rhetoric and poetic representation is the primary means to achieving redemption in these stories, it is to be expected that Boccaccio would simultaneously turn his reflection on language inward as a kind of self-commentary on his own enterprise in the *Decameron*.[26] This double turn – the inward meditation on poetic language and the outward examination of language as a tool in society – emerges in every story, as we shall see:

1. The story of Madonna Oretta recounts an episode of poor storytelling within the context of a leisurely retreat of aristocrats, with a literary subtext that evokes the threat of violence against women;
2. The story of Cisti the baker presents a meditation on noble meanings hidden within simple containers, while the surface-level narration is entirely social, pitting the virtues of a noble-hearted baker against a nobleman;
3. The third tale, a rarely commented story about Monna Nonna, represents the threat of sexual violence, but also contains a powerful reflection on gendered reading;
4. The fourth tale shows how a lowly cook can best his noble lord, but also comments on the hybrid nature of the literary vernacular;
5. The fifth story, about Giotto's repartee to his lawyer friend, Forese da Rabatta, has long been recognized for its engagement with issues of artistic representation and interpretation, yet it is situated in a verisimilar context that highlights the social standing of the artist and lawyer and questions the ethics of their respective fields;
6. The sixth tale is ostensibly about a social *brigata* of young men who discuss the nature of nobility, but it is also a critique of syllogistic logic and an appraisal of the power of rhetoric;
7. The seventh story concerns the adulteress Filippa's escape from the death penalty in Prato and interrogates the language of the law by putting into question the ability of language to represent those it affects;
8. The eighth tale situates a critique of the *donna angelicata* of the *dolce stil novo* within a verisimilar representation of a Florentine woman's lifestyle;

---

25 See also Honess, *From Florence* 5.

26 Self-commentary was a part of Boccaccio's literary toolkit from early on. See, e.g., Schnapp. It is worth mentioning that diverse characters in Day Six could be (and have been) considered as representations of the author. Among them are Giotto (VI.5), Michele Scalza (VI.6), and Frate Cipolla (VI.10).

9. The ninth tale is famously about the intellectual hierarchy and the negative sociability of intellectuals like Guido Cavalcanti, whose final *motto* opens up questions of interpretability and probes the ethical limits of philosophical inquiry;
10. The final story is a tour de force of deceptive rhetoric that pushes to the limits the commonplace of the writer as liar, set in Boccaccio's hometown of Certaldo in a comically verisimilar representation of a small-town holy day.

While some stories are more self-reflexive than others, they all generally deal with the power of language, and specifically that of the vernacular, to represent and form the social and moral values that bring order (and sometimes its opposite) to communal life, but also its potential to bring to bear on that life the abstract considerations of philosophy and theology. In the Sixth Day, this aspect of Boccaccio's project in the *Decameron* rises closer to the surface than in any other moment of the work that is not a direct intervention of the author (e.g., the Introductions to Days One and Four and the Author's Conclusion).

At the other end of Day Six, in the Conclusion, after Dioneo becomes king and defends his choice of theme – which the women think "male a lor convenisse" [VI.Concl.7; would be unbecoming of them] – the *brigata* is able to enjoy leisure time, since the stories were so brief (VI. Concl.17). While the men play at dice, Elissa leads the women to what will become the new location of their storytelling activities in Day Seven: "la Valle delle Donne" [VI.Concl.18; the Valley of the Ladies].[27] A large part of the day's concluding section is dedicated to the description of this paradigmatic *locus amoenus* (VI.Concl.20–9). The valley is circular and is surrounded by six hills, each with a small castle on top, whose slopes flatten out towards the centre where there is a pond fed by a small stream. In the Valley, oppressed by the hot sun, the women undress and bathe in the transparent waters of the pond, "senza alcun sospetto d'esser vedute" [VI.Concl.29; with no suspicion of being seen]. This ultimate *locus amoenus*, described by Boccaccio as "ritondo come se a sesta fosse stato fatto, quantunque artificio della natura e non manual paresse" [VI.Concl.20; circular as if it had been made with a compass, even if it seemed natural and not manufactured], is, in Tobias Gittes's view, an artifact that combines the archetypical "loci of rape: the theatre,

27 On the Valley of the Ladies, see Bàrberi-Squarotti; Cerisola; Filosa, "'Decameron' 7"; Getto 1–33; Gittes, "Boccaccio's Valley of Women"; Güntert 13–43; Petrini, *Ragionare* 145–54; and Stillinger, "Language of Gardens." On Dioneo's rule, see Ascoli, "Pyrrhus' Rules."

the wooded tarn, and the pleasance" ("Boccaccio's 'Valley of Women'" 149). The threat of sexual violence, which emerges several times in the Sixth Day, is transformed into an aestheticized voyeurism within the theatre of the Valley. After the young men make their own trip to see the Valley, Dioneo moves the entire group there temporarily. As Gittes convincingly argues, the telling of the next day's stories in the Valley indicates that "Boccaccio is proposing a radical shift away from carnal intercourse to erotic discourse and voyeurism" whereby "[e]rotic titillation through image and text ... triumphs over erotic consummation through act" ("Boccaccio's 'Valley of Women'" 149).[28] The complete aestheticization of the erotic, which is implied by the Valley and which indicates art's greatest attempt to sublimate human experience, will be only temporary. The *brigata* will return at the beginning of Day Eight to the walled garden and then to the city at the end of Day Ten.[29]

The bookends of the Sixth Day demonstrate the tension between the lived theatres of everyday experience – the streets of the city and their chaotic multiplicity – and the imagined theatres of poetic representation – the *locus amoenus* of aestheticized nature and its ideal ordering of chaos. The new beginning signalled by Day Six regards the potential resolution of this tension. In Days Two through Five, the *brigata* explored the forces that govern human life – Nature, Fortune, and Love – without confronting directly the life (and death) that they had left behind in the city. Day Six throws the *brigata* and the readers of the *Decameron* back into the mix of familiar experience and challenges them to devise a language that can redeem and to create a form of representation that is both philosophically introspective and inclusive of the multiplicity of human experience.

~

This book is a collection of readings of each of the ten stories of Day Six. It is not meant to pronounce a unified interpretation of the day or even the final word on each of the stories. The model of the *lectura* may be flawed in the way it inevitably gives less weight to the *Decameron*'s complex structural architecture. It does, however, offer at least two advantages: first, it reflects the piecemeal way the work has been

28 Gittes further opines on how the erotic fits into Boccaccio's ideology in *Boccaccio's Naked Muse*. See, more recently, Kriesel, *Boccaccio's Corpus*, esp. chapter 4 on the *Decameron*.

29 On the relation between place and representation in the structure of the frame of the Decameron, see Barolini, "Wheel," esp. 534 and 538 in reference to the Valley of the Ladies.

received since the very beginning, in translations of individual tales, in anthologies, and in abbreviated, frameless versions of the *Decameron* itself; second, it guarantees a critical space to those stories that have been overlooked by readers and critics precisely because they were deemed not paradigmatic enough for anthologization or translation. Some of the tales have received ample attention from critics (VI.1, 5, 9, and 10) and in anthologies of Italian literature (VI.2 and 4), while others have been all but ignored (VI.3, 6, 7, 8). Rather, by bringing together a diverse group of critical readers, whose expertise is not limited to Boccaccio, the book also offers a plurality of individual perspectives on the tales, which (it is our hope) may become crucial points of reference for other critics and for students or general readers who would like a place to start in their engagement with these stories.

While these are all readings of the tales in their singularity, each also makes abundantly clear the relation of a given tale to others, both in Day Six and across the work. Many of these readings also show how Boccaccio engaged in rethinking or elaborating on the great patrimony of Western literature and thought, including the Bible, the Roman literary, rhetorical, and legal heritage, the works of the Church Fathers, and the ideas of scholastic theologians, but also more recent works such as the poetry of the *dolce stil novo*, Dante's *Vita nova* and *Commedia*, and Boccaccio's own early writings. The result is more than just a miscellany; these *lecturae* are united by methodologies that account for both historical and theoretical concerns and by the seriousness with which they approach Boccaccio's poetic and ethical project in the *Decameron*.

In her reading of Madonna Oretta's playful and witty rebuke in first story of Day Six, Teresa Kennedy investigates from a feminist perspective, informed by Kristeva's ideas on the abject, the darker side to the story recounted by Filomena. She brings to bear an analysis of the complex and systematic use of intertextual allusions in the tale and in the Introduction to the day. Specifically, Kennedy analyses the significance of Filomena as narrator of this tale, ostensibly on the pleasures of reading, in relation to Ovid's "tongueless" Filomena and to Cressida, whose story is sung by Dioneo and Lauretta in the Introduction to Day Six. Kennedy suggests that Cressida, Licisca, Filomena, and other women in the *Decameron*, especially women readers, risk being transformed into the transgressive image of the gaping mouth.

Giulia Cardillo reads the tale of Cisti the baker (VI.2) in the light of Boccaccio's considerations on poetry in the *Genealogie* and in the Author's Conclusion to the *Decameron*. Her *lectura* draws out several analogies regarding allegory and the metaliterary elements of the tale, showing how the story represents a continuation of the first *novella*'s concern with the form of storytelling. Cardillo argues that Cisti's combination of a humble form with a noble heart is analogous to the way allegorical discourse, especially in the vernacular, hides sublime meanings within a humble outer shell. In this way, the social and the poetic are bound up with Boccaccio's ideas about language, ethics, and meaning.

The reading of the third tale given by Guyda Armstrong takes a historicist-feminist approach to understanding the import of Monna Nonna's refusal to bed a Catalan nobleman. She takes special account of the experience of a young wife whom the nobleman rapes, a rarely commented on minor character in the tale. Armstrong reads Nonna's tale in terms of the historic condition of women in fourteenth-century Italy, contending that the protagonist should be considered one of the iconic female characters of the *Decameron*. Important to her analysis is the examination of the spaces of urban life and the gender norms that govern them. Nonna expertly navigates the urban landscape, becoming a model on par with those praiseworthy women of Boccaccio's Latin treatise *De mulieribus claris*.

James Kriesel's interpretation of the story of Chichibio (IV.4) focuses on the metalinguistic aspects of the story by examining how the famous crane with one leg is related to ideas about cranes and other birds in the Middle Ages, which were often a part of reflections on language and writing. He links the social status of the cook, Chichibio, and his wealthy master, Currado Gianfigliazzi, to debates on vernacular poetics. Kriesel shows how the tale dramatizes a vernacular poetics of congruence, a term for harmony that is etymologically related to the Latin word for crane, or *grus*. The interplay of Venetian and Florentine speech in VI.4, Kriesel argues, is a part of Boccaccio's own poetics of congruence, according to which different types of vernacular culture are harmoniously incorporated in the *Decameron*. In so doing, Kriesel furthermore indicates, Boccaccio was engaging with and challenging Dante's ideas about vernacularity.

In his analysis of the tale of Giotto and Forese Rabatta (VI.5), Zygmunt G. Barański distances himself from readings of the meta-artistic implications of the figure of Giotto, focusing instead on the structural and ideological tensions of the tale. In order to tease out these tensions, he highlights the story's system of allusion and citation, which takes advantage of works of Roman oratory, the Bible and its exegeses, works of scholastic theology and philosophy, and – of course – the works of Dante. This system of allusion is employed in key points in the characterization of Giotto and his travelling companion, but also in the more theoretical Proem to the tale. Barański argues that the story has more than merely metaliterary aims, inasmuch as it also presents a rigorous treatment of interpretation, which for Boccaccio was the other side of a single coin. The tale, for Barański, brings together Boccaccio's socio-political and ethical concerns with his ideas on language, representation, and interpretation.

The reading that Peter Carravetta provides of the often overlooked tale of Michele Scalza and his band of young Florentine men (VI.6) shows how Scalza's parody of syllogistic logic impacts the representational strategies that Boccaccio employs in the *Decameron*. In his demonstration that the Baronci are the oldest and noblest family of Florence because they are the ugliest, Scalza represents scholastic modes of thought as semiotic constructions that can deviate from the truth just as much as rhetorical ones can. Together with the previous *novella*, this story completes a diptych on deceptive appearances and perceptions of the world. As Carravetta argues, in this *novella* Boccaccio employs "serious humour" both as a form of critique and as a way of exploring philosophically the crisis of the human condition brought about by the plague.

Bernardo Piciché interprets the story of Madonna Filippa's trial for adultery (VI.7), which was punishable by death in Prato, in the context of the legal statutes of medieval Tuscany. He sees two polemical discourses at work in the *novella*. The first is against laws that unnecessarily abuse the citizenry. The other is against Dante's treatment of the famous adulteress, Francesca da Rimini. For Piciché, the two polemics must also be understood in the context of Florentine propaganda against Prato and of the tensions between Boccaccio and the Neapolitan nobility. Piciché ultimately sees Madonna Filippa's retuning of the law against adultery as a move that redeems the fate of Francesca da Rimini and as a demand that the law be equal for those whom it affects.

Aileen Feng's *lectura* of the story of Cesca and the mirror (VI.8) situates the narrative within Boccaccio's broader engagement with the question of female exemplarity in the *Filostrato*, *Corbaccio*, and *De mulieribus claris*. Her close reading of the tale shows how Fresco da Celatico's attempt to correct the vice of vanity in his niece, Cesca, plays on notions of binaries through what Feng calls "gendered mirrorings." Beginning with an examination of the doubling of their names – Fr(anc)esco/(Fran)Cesca – Feng draws out how their worldviews are presented as polar opposites through the symbolic function of the mirror. While the *novella* closes claiming that Cesca did not learn the intended lesson, Feng argues that this story, analysed within Boccaccio's history of writings on women and their vices, critiques stilnovistic and Dantesque models of female exemplarity.

In her essay on Cavalcanti's discussion with Betto Brunelleschi's *brigata* and his subsequent *motto* and leap over the tombstones (VI.9), Maria Lettiero reads the tale in the light of Italo Calvino's famous words on Cavalcanti in his memo on lightness, as well as in reference to the story's import for poets and critics such as Ezra Pound and André Jolles. The *lectura* contextualizes the brief tale in terms of Cavalcanti's intellectual ethos in *Donna me prega* and of Petrarch's anecdote about Dino del Garbo in the *Rerum memorandarum libri*, but also of Francesco Pandolfini's fifteenth-century Latin translation of the tale. She shows how Cavalcanti's enigmatic response and haughty behaviour signal the profound difference between intellectuals and the masses. In the end, Lettiero understands that Boccaccio uses Cavalcanti as an example of knowledge and wisdom in a pointed contrast between the death of the body and that of the soul.

Cormac Ó Cuilleanáin provides a *lectura* of the tale of Frate Cipolla's rhetorical tour de force (VI.10) that examines, through a lively reflection on translation, the translatability of linguistic performances for diverse audiences. He examines the story in relation to others in Day Six and in the *Decameron*, but also indicates how the story engages Dante's *Inferno* and *Paradiso*. If the tale has consistently been interpreted as a celebration of the creative power of eloquence, Ó Cuilleanáin argues that the rhetoric of the story itself is strangely "tongue-tied." Furthermore, he shows that if the tale is successful as a meditation on the art of storytelling (like its companion piece I.1), it is thanks to the wilful separation of audiences into two groups: the ignorant and the knowledgeable. It encapsulates the potential audiences that Boccaccio imagined for his work.

1 The Tale of Madonna Oretta (VI.1)

TERESA KENNEDY

The Sixth Day of the *Decameron* is routinely recognized as a microcosm of the larger rhetorical concerns of Boccaccio's narrative, framed by the theme of those, "chi con alcun leggiadro motto, tentato, si rescotesse, o con pronta resposta o avvedimento fuggí perdita o pericolo o scorno" [VI.Intro.1; Who, on being provoked by some verbal pleasantry, have returned like for like, or who, by a prompt retort or shrewd manoeuvre, have avoided danger, discomfiture or ridicule; 444].[1] At first glance this topic appears to be benign, but experienced readers will recognize that there are multiple implications embedded in this topic that crystallize how many of Boccaccio's narratives reveal the anxiety created through the revelation of knowledge that is conventionally repressed, often by constrictions of class or gender. In other words, the veil of comic witticism functions as a stylistic strategy that paradoxically allows the reader to perceive the violent potential of discourse while maintaining an aesthetic distance. The first tale is exemplary in this respect, focusing on the power of feminine discourse to exploit figurative language and sustained metaphor to express potentially illicit sexual knowledge. Oretta's *motto* is frequently read as a playful and witty rebuke to her *cavaliere*'s stylistic incompetence, focusing the reader's attention on questions of class, female sexuality, and rhetorical motive.[2] This strategy simultaneously exposes implicit connections between the pleasures

1 All references to the text of the *Decameron* are from Vittore Branca's 1967 edition of *Tutte le opere*. Translations, unless otherwise noted, are from McWilliam's revised Penguin edition.

2 See, for example, Freedman; Fido, "Silenze e cavalli"; Migiel 123–8; Olson, "Language of Women"; Psaki, "Women in the *Decameron*"; Serafini-Sauli; Usher, "'Desultorietà' nella novella portante di Madonna Oretta"; and Wallace 68–70.

of reading and the pleasures of the flesh through a sustained analogy between failed storytelling and poor horsemanship. There is a darker side to Filomena's story, however, one that can only be developed through an analysis of the larger context of the complex and systematic use of intertextual allusions in the narratological strategies incorporated in the *Decameron*.

Boccaccio's choice of Filomena as the narrator for the first story of the Sixth Day is significant precisely because of the multiple figurative associations that connect to her name on the one hand, and the way these associations create a specific narratological effect on the other.[3] To understand Filomena's rhetorical function in the *Decameron*, two subtexts must intrude and subsequently merge into the reader's consciousness: the horrific metonym of Filomena's tongueless gaping mouth and her transformation into a nightingale from *Metamorphoses* VI, and her literary figuration of cruel inconstancy in the *Filostrato*.[4] These allusions account in some way for scholarly assessments of Filomena's character: as part of the "densely woven polyphony of voices" in the *Decameron*; e.g., as Pampinea's satellite, as Licisca's mistress, and as the target of and passive-aggressive respondent to the theatrics engendered by the interplay among all of its characters.[5] Filomena's insistence on rhetorical discretion, brevity, and oblique critique that appears to defer to masculine authority conceals her hidden motive; that is, to mask her own figurative trauma, accessible to the reader only through the larger

3 The importance of the allegorical and figurative importance of names in Boccaccio is well recognized. See, for example, Ascoli, "Pyrrhus' Rules" 19; see also note 12 below for additional bibliography.

4 Ovid, *Metamorphoses* 241–8. Although some scholars point out that the words "nightingale" and "swallow" do not appear in the Ovidian text, Boccaccio surely was aware of the tradition connecting Filomena to the nightingale. See his gloss to *Teseida*, IV.54: "Progne … e avendo nell'animo di fare un gran vendetta di questa cosa, e non sappiendo di che farsela maggiore, uccise uno picciolo figliuolo che avea nome Iti, che avuto aveva di Tereo, e cosselo e diedelo mangiare a Tereo. Di che quando Tereo s'accorse, correndo loro dietro per ucciderle, Progne diventò rondine e Filomena usignuolo e Iti diventò pettorosso e Tereo becchipuzzola" [Procne then planned a terrible vengeance, and not able to imagine anything worse, killed her little son she had named Itys, whom she had borne to Tereus, and cooked him and gave the dish to Tereus to eat. When Tereus discovered this, he ran after her to kill her, Procne became a swallow and Filomena a nightingale, Iti a robin, and Tereus a hoopoe]. The tensions between Filostrato and Filomena will be further discussed below.

5 Psaki, "Women in the *Decameron*" 80. For extensive discussion of Filomena's oblique rhetorical approaches and its effect on the dynamic among the other women characters, see Migiel 109–13; 147–59.

knowledge of the texts that the allusions trigger. The narratological effect of these allusions is to force the reader into metaleptic awareness at certain points in the text, especially in the Introduction and first tale of Day Six.[6]

It is important to underscore that Boccaccio's narrative technique throughout the *Decameron* focuses on the notion of developing an ideal reader who can understand and appreciate a secular vernacular poetics.[7] In addition to creating specific relationships between literary tradition and the immediacy of his historical present, he is deeply committed to exposing the rhetorical and figural strategies that create literary fictions. One of the key ways that he achieves this is through the manipulation of diegetic and tropological typologies, in order to amplify and complicate levels of meaning. This results in an "ambiguity created by the multiple diegetic levels [that] causes a crisis of interpretative authority, which calls into question the effectiveness of all external hermeneutic systems and gives the text authority" (Lummus, "The *Decameron*" 78). The stylistic effect of this strategy is to force the reader to insert himself into the construction of meaning as a figure that consciously exerts a reader's interpretive authority in the narrative, an effect that is at the heart of metalepsis, or a transgression of the limits that separate the levels of a narration. This is especially notable in Boccaccio's structural approach to Oretta's tale, as he builds the thematic affinities that destabilize and ironize the authority of his text.

The Prologue to Day Six, for example, focuses attention on the lyrical aesthetic function of the familiar *locus amoenus* for the garden, a typical framing strategy for the *Decameron*, which "separates the world of pleasure and beauty from the world of utility and work" (Lummus, "The *Decameron*" 80). It begins:

> Aveva la luna, essendo nel mezzo del cielo, perduti i raggi suoi, e già per la nuova luce vegnente ogni parte del nostro mondo era chiara, quando la

6 The notion of metalepsis and its effects has been extended from classical rhetoric by Gérard Genette: "the most troubling thing about metalepsis indeed lies in this unacceptable and insistent hypothesis, that the extradiegetic is perhaps always diegetic, and that the narrator and his narratees – you and I – perhaps belong to some narrative" (236). See Cohn; and Gobyn.

7 Much of the scholarship on Boccaccio's understanding of poetics develops from applying close readings of the *Geneaology of the Gentile Gods* to his vernacular works. See, for example, the classic study by Marcus, *Allegory of Form*, and recent work by Kriesel, "Genealogy" and *Boccaccio's Corpus*; and Lummus, "Boccaccio's Poetic Anthropology" and "The *Decameron*." See also Mazzotta, "Boccaccio."

reina levatasi, fatta la sua compagnia chiamare, alquanto con lento passo dal bel palagio, su per la rugiada spaziandosi, s'allontanarono, d'una e d'altra cosa varii ragionamenti tegnendo e della piú bellezza e della meno delle raccontate novelle disputando e ancora de' varii casi recitati in quelle rinnovando le risa, infino a tanto che, già piú alzandosi il sole e cominciandosi a riscaldare, a tutti parve di dover verso casa tornare: per che, voltati i passi, là se ne vennero.

E quivi, essendo già le tavole messe e ogni cosa d'erbucce odorose e di be' fiori seminata, avanti che il caldo surgesse piú, per comandamento della reina si misero a mangiare. E questo con festa fornito, avanti che altro facessero, alquante canzonette belle e leggiadre cantate, chi andò a dormire e chi a giucare a scacchi e chi a tavole; *e Dioneo insieme con Lauretta di Troilo e di Criseida cominciarono a cantare.* (VI.Intro.2–3, emphasis added)

[The moon, poised in the centre of the heavens, had lost her radiance, and the whole of our hemisphere was already suffused with the fresh light of dawn, when the queen arose and summoned her companions. Leaving their fair abode, they sauntered over the dew, conversing together on one subject after another, and discussing the merits and demerits of the stories so far narrated, at the same time laughing anew over the various adventures therein related, until as the sun rose higher and the air grew warmer, they decided with one accord to retrace their steps, whereupon they turned about and came back to the house. The tables being already laid, with fragrant herbs and lovely flowers strewn all around, they followed the queen's bidding and addressed themselves to their breakfast before the heat of the day should become too oppressive. And after making a merry meal of it, they first of all sang some gay and charming songs, after which some of their number retired to sleep, whilst others played chess or threw dice. *And Dioneo, along with Lauretta, began to sing a song about Troilus and Cressida.*] (444, emphasis added)

The Introduction extends the mythopoetic context for the *brigata*'s escape from Florence to Fiesole, including its emphasis on a new social order, centred on the myth of a recovered Eden.[8] The setting is benign, and the idealized reading community is figured by pastoral language. The community of readers is united through the breaking of bread, and the illusion of paradisal harmony is stabilized through the primary level of narration.

8 The literary contexts for this argument are extensively explored in Gittes, *Boccaccio's Naked Muse* 22–6.

A hint of potential disruption, however, is introduced by the metonymic allusions to Troilus and Cressida that Lauretta and Dioneo begin to sing, figuratively embedding the *Filostrato*, a text illustrating Boccaccio's theory of the intersubjective relationship of myth to vernacular poetics, and not incidentally a gesture to his own poetic authority. The allusion functions to emphasize the intersubjectivity of multiple reading communities. The conventional personae of the *brigata* and the larger reading audience should understand the allusion as a multivalent extended metaphor, polemically provoking the roles of Filomena and Filostrato as recurring characters both in the *Decameron* and in their earlier representation in the *Filostrato*. Certainly Filostrato is aware of the performative nature of his own fictive status as betrayed lover; he reinscribes his fictive "betrayal" frequently in the *Decameron*.[9] In the immediately preceding day, for example, his story of Ricciardo and Caterina in V.4 obscenely figures the capture of the nightingale as a metaphor for the female desire for the phallus and – whatever else it represents – appears intended to taunt Filomena in her Ovidian context noted above.[10] Is the song of Troilus and Cressida a parodic goad directed at Filostrato, or is beleaguered Filomena also a target of the spoof? Either way, the reader should not be surprised by Filomena's lack of direct retort, but her thematic figuration suggests an awareness of and resistance to her role as faithless betrayer in the *Filostrato* and as the mutilated rape victim in the *Metamorphoses*.[11] As Victoria Kirkham

9 As Thomas Stillinger notes, "Filostrato is the only storyteller who seems to have any grasp of his own status as a fictional character" (*Song* 130). See also Ascoli, "Pyrrhus's Rules," who notes: "The full title of the *Filostrato* includes this gloss on the narrator's name: 'Filostrato tanto viene a dire quanto uomo vinto e abbattuto d'amore.' The character Filostrato in the *Decameron* alludes explicitly to this meaning in III.Concl., par. 6: 'né per altro [that is his unhappiness in love] il nome, per lo quale voi mi chiamate, da tale bene seppe che si dire mi fu imposto.' … 'Tale' is, of course, Boccaccio [see I Intro., par. 76], despite Filostrato's apparent implication that it is his unyielding beloved" (20n12).

10 For Boccaccio's use of sexual doublespeak, see Psaki, "'Women Make All Things Lose Their Power'" 20; Migiel views the metaphor as exemplary of the prerogative of masculine discourse (126–39).

11 See, for example, Zinevra's protests when she is falsely accused of adultery and nearly put to death at II.9.39: "A cui la donna piagnendo disse: 'Ahi! mercé per Dio! non volere divenire micidiale di chi mai non t'offese, per servire altrui. Idio, che tutto conosce, sa che io non feci mai cosa per la quale io dal mio marito debbia cosí fatto merito ricevere'" [The lady began to weep. "Oh, for the love of God, have mercy" she said. "Don't allow yourself to murder someone who never did you any harm just for the sake of obeying an order. As God is my witness, I have never given my husband the slightest cause for taking my life"; 214]. For Dioneo's critique of Filomena's conservatism with respect to adultery, see DeCoste.

has argued, one framework for understanding Filomena's role is as a metaphor for one of the cardinal virtues, fortitude, paired antithetically with the irascible Filostrato. Further, Filomena explicitly engages the theme of constancy (Kirkham, "Allegorically" 12). This suggests the idea that Boccaccio wishes to remind the reader that Filomena, as much as Filostrato, continually reprises her fictional literary history, constantly aware of her ironic literary positions as they are juxtaposed between faithlessness and constancy in the two separate texts. However, the allusion to Ovid's "tongueless" Filomena as it operates in the *Decameron* suggests that she apparently cannot speak directly in her own defence.

One could argue that the reference to the *Filostrato* is complementary and anticipatory of the disruption created by the content of the argument Licisca forces into the world of the *brigata*. Moreover, Licisca erupts into the idyllic setting:

> Madonna, costui mi vuol far conoscere la moglie di Sicofante e, né piú né meno come se io con lei usata non fossi, mi vuol dare a vedere che la notte prima che Sicofante giacque con lei messer Mazza entrasse in Monte Nero per forza e con ispargimento di sangue; e io dico che non è vero, anzi v'entrò paceficamente e con gran piacer di quei d'entro. E è ben sí bestia costui, che egli si crede troppo bene che le giovani sieno sí sciocche, che elle stieno a perdere il tempo loro stando alla bada del padre e de' fratelli, che delle sette volte le sei soprastanno tre o quatro anni piú che non debbono a maritarle. Frate, bene starebbono se elle s'indugiasser tanto! Alla fé di Cristo, ché debbo sapere quello che io mi dico quando io giuro: io non ho vicina che pulcella ne sia andata a marito, e anche delle maritate so io ben quante e quali beffe elle fanno a' mariti: e questo pecorone mi vuol far conoscer le femine, come se io fossi nata ieri! (VI.Intro.8–10)

> [Madam, this fellow thinks he knows Sicofante's wife better than I do. I've known her for years, and yet he has the audacity to try and convince me that on the first night Sicofante slept with her, John Thomas had to force an entry into Castle Dusk, shedding blood in the process; but I say it is not true, on the contrary he made his way in with the greatest of ease, to the general pleasure of the garrison. The man is such a natural idiot that he firmly believes young girls are foolish enough to squander their opportunities whilst they are waiting for the fathers and brothers to marry them off, which in nine cases out of ten takes them three or four years longer than it should. God in Heaven, they'd be in a pretty plight if they waited all that long! I swear to Christ (which means that I know what I'm saying) that not a single one of the girls from my district went to her husband a

virgin, and as for the married ones, I could tell you a thing or two about the clever tricks they play upon their husbands. Yet this great oaf tries to teach me about women, as though I were born yesterday.] (445)

Many scholars have focused readings of the Sixth Day on issues of class and gender, and on the structural arrangement that informs the larger context of the work.[12] Marilyn Migiel, for example, provides a fascinating reading for this passage, highlighting the key questions: "Will the lower classes no longer remain hushed and orderly? Does Licisca speak not only for herself and her consort, but for all women? Of these two questions, the more threatening for the group of storytellers is the second: Is Licisca's women's discourse?" (111). In order to answer these questions, Migiel focuses attention on the reaction of female members of the *brigata* to the maid's discourse, citing "Mentre la Licisca parlava, facevan le donne sí gran risa, che tutti i denti si sarebbero loro potuti trarre" [VI.Intro.11; While Licisca was talking, the ladies were laughing so heartily that you could have pulled all their teeth out; 445]. Migiel juxtaposes the nature of Licisca's speech to the reaction of the ladies of the *brigata*, and connects the two passages hermeneutically to the image of the gaping mouth as a way to represent truth.[13] Finally, Migiel emphasizes the intertextual reference between the content of Licisca's speech and the parallel language in the *Ninfale fiesolano* and in the *Corbaccio* noted by Branca, to illustrate the irony of masculine authority speaking the truth about women "habillé en dame," as it were.[14] Of course, this is exactly what is at issue for women's voices; that is, apparently female subjectivity cannot be represented in direct discourse, but only subliminally at the level of the image.[15]

12 For further work on structural questions, see, for example, Stewart, "La novella di Madonna Oretta"; and Hollander, *Boccaccio's Dante* 128–33. The debate over Boccaccio's attitude towards women has a staggering bibliography. A short list might include Gittes, "Boccaccio's 'Valley of Women'"; Psaki, "Giving Them the Bird" 207–23; Psaki, "'Women Make All Things Lose Their Power'"; Barolini, "'Le Parole son femmine e i fatti sono maschi'"; and Serafini-Sauli. For class and gender especially, see Migiel 109–13; Martinez, "*Scienze della Cittade*" 69; and Gaylard.

13 Migiel 112–33; Migiel draws on Spackman 19–34, 22–4 for the theoretical foundation of the image.

14 Migiel 112. Branca in Boccaccio, *Decameron* (1976), 1529n4.

15 As de Lauretis notes, "If Nietzsche and Derrida can occupy and speak from the position of woman, it is because that position is vacant and, what is more, cannot be claimed by women … I simply want to suggest that while the question of woman for the male philosophers is a question of style (of discourse, language, writing – of philosophy), for Salomé, as in most present-day feminist thinking, it

The stylistic effect of the figural pattern is disturbing extradiegetically to the reader, not to the members of the *brigata* – an effect one might describe as a metalepsis of the narrate – because the *reader* is forced to recognize that Licisca's transgressive speech in fact suggests a potential defence of Filomena's position as Cressida, even as her rhetorical strategy is bounded by masculine authority. In the maid's mimetically masculinized view, Cressida's betrayal simply illustrates the natural order of female sexuality, a view that short-changes feminine subjectivity, only tangentially exposed on the narrative level. It is the image of the gaping mouth that forcefully reminds the reader of Ovid's maimed Filomena and intimates a relation between rhetoric and violence.[16] It is precisely the ability of the reader to grasp the reciprocal ironies of the metaphoric sequence that creates anxiety for the reader, and exposes the disjunctive starting point of an accretion of multiple metalepses beginning with the allusion to Troilus and Cressida that appears early in the day's Prologue and continuing through to the metanovella of the first story of Day Six that creates the illusion of mise en abyme – the sense of vertigo experienced by a reader who "faces the disconcerting sight of a configuration that suggests an infinite repetition of the read text" (Cohn 109). In other words, within the figurative hall of mirrors the multi-layered literary context creates, the reader begins to glimpse a potential interpretation: that Cressida, Licisca, Filomena, and perhaps all women who appear in the *Decameron* have coalesced

---

is a question of gender – of the social construction of 'woman' and 'man,' and the semiotic production of subjectivity" (32). In the context of Filomena, the antithetical effect of these different subjective representations might be found in the contrast between her stories of Lisabetta and the pot of basil (IV.5) and that of Nastagio at V.8. In the former, the pot of basil must be read in its metaliterary context to become comprehensible, and as such is a collocative partner in semantic affiliation with the image of the gaping mouth. For bibliography on the sources of Lisabetta's tale, see Marcus, "Cross-Fertilizations"; Baratto, "Struttura narrativa" 41–4; and Getto 125–30. The latter tale, as Wofford points out, shows "the ways in which a patriarchal system masking an unacknowledged misogyny makes the novella into a man's story (in spite of its fictional narrator) that ends appropriately enough with a man's joke. In this account of the novella the cultural writing on the body of the woman – her disfigurement – is defined by the fiction as a sacrifice necessary to guarantee the continuation of society, and the novella is shown to put forward a myth about marriage" that simultaneously posits a "second reading, [that] opposes this emphasis on the patriarchy's informing pressure with a study of the ways in which the novella structure itself resists its own too-neat closure, providing a supplemental interpretation that allows the woman's voice to be heard, and returns the narration rightly to a Trecento Filomena" (204–5).

16 De Lauretis 34–6; and Cahill 84–5.

into the transgressive image of the gaping mouth, and that all represent the traumatic metamorphosis of the enchantress refigured into literal hag, suggesting the reversal of the aesthetic into the abject. Boccaccio's metaleptic narrative strategy is created in this context by the multiple metonymies the history of the literary characterization Filomena represents – from Ovid to the *Filostrato* to the *Decameron*.[17] The toothless mouth of the hag figures the abject truth: the grotesque of death. The intertextual elements combine to create a reader's awareness of the artificial quality of the text through the crudity of Licisca's transgressive speech – culminating in the rhetorical intersection of female sexuality and the abomination of the "wounded" corpse that in fact subliminally intimates the knowledge of death. This is the psychological effect of the metaleptic narrative strategy; the encounter with the truth of death foreshadows the *brigata*'s anxious response as they anticipate a return to plague-ridden Florence, and forces a temporary collapse of meaning and an intimation of the abyss of death.

It is in this context that Boccaccio's choice of Filomena to restore the aesthetic veil over this trauma can be interpreted as consistent with the internal logic of the *Decameron*. The aesthetic boundaries breached by Licisca's transgression are tentatively redrawn by Oretta's tale. Moreover, because Licisca is her servant, it is Filomena's responsibility to regain control over the narrative, an action that Elissa, the queen of Day Six, fails to do until she threatens the maid with a beating (VI.Intro.11). It is Filomena's story that restores rhetorical and aesthetic order to control the potential violence.

Before focusing on an interpretation of Oretta's tale that begins Day Six, the larger structural context of the narrative needs some exploration. Many scholars have long appreciated that the stories of Day Six focus on the relationship of language and narrative to the larger social world of Florence that the *brigata* inhabits. Barolini notes, for example, that the *novelle* are "situated in Tuscany, for the most part in Florence," and that they "involve characters whose lives and histories are known to the *brigata*, with the result that the plague – and reality – must finally intrude" (Barolini, "Wheel" 529). Martinez creates an explicit connection among the political, commerce, and eloquence: "the novelle of the

17 For the topos of the enchantress turned hag and its connection to abjection, see Spackman 22–4; she notes, "Refiguring woman is tantamount to refiguring truth" (23). For the relationship of the intersection of the aesthetic and the abject in a specifically Boccaccian context, see Civitarese. On abjection, see Kristeva 40–62; and Creed.

Sixth Day, with an almost percussive consistency, offer snapshots of effective, usually reactive speech that sometimes mediates, sometimes lays bare the *tencioni* of gender, class, rank, occupation, party, and faction which make up the fabric of the city" (Martinez, "*Scienze della Cittade*" 64).[18] Significantly, this impulse to give "a local habitation and a name" to the stories of the Sixth Day appears to be anticipated by Licisca's metaleptic intrusion in the Prologue, exemplifying Boccaccio's approach to narrative strategy.[19] Further, the use of the *motto* as the rhetorical figure that frames the day's return to the social reality of Florence invokes a specific formal discursive strategy. The intelligent quip rescues the protagonist from danger and violence.[20]

Central to this argument is the problematic question of how best to interpret Oretta's *motto*, and its function within the text. It is more than forty years since Guido Almansi first established that Oretta's tale functions as a meta-novella, a story designed to comment on the nature of storytelling itself.[21] Precisely because of this emphasis on narrative style over content in the tale, the enigmatic nature of her *motto*, or witticism, remains resistant to conventional interpretation. The entire narrative sequence develops a superficially

18 See also Mazzotta, "The *Decameron*," who notes that "the sixth day, in general, is very important in terms of our discussion because its declared focus is the uses of language; the tales gravitate around the concept of literary taste and literature as part of human leisure" (66). See also his *World at Play* 1–15. Martinez notes that Day Six is a "mercurial day" ("*Scienze della Cittade*" 57). See further Kirkham, *Sign of Reason* 73–4; Getto 40–52; and Wallace 67–77.

19 I am thinking here of Ascoli's point: "What concerns me most … is the question of what it means when literature (and literary modes of thought and representation – narrative and figure above all) provides a 'local habitation and a name' both for that which is identifiably 'historical' and for that which seemingly stands apart from history" (*Local Habitation and a Name* 4). See also Barolini: "If Licisca operates as a kind of reality principle, whose function it is to introduce aperture where there was closure, severing the *brigata*'s isolationism and turning them back toward Florence, her effect should be felt at once, even before her argument inspires the theme for the following day" ("Wheel" 528–9).

20 For this point, see Andrei, "*Motto*" 32. For the history of the enigma as trope, see Cook, esp. 4–32. Filomena has already demonstrated the imaginative value of the *motto;* she uses one to stage the rescue of Melchisedech from Saladin (I.3.16). For Boccaccio's rhetorical motive for the tale, see Marcus, "Faith's Fiction" 48–52.

21 Almansi, *Writer as Liar* 44. For the tale as mise en abyme in the *Decameron*, see Andrei, "*Motto*" 29–32. An important distinction between metalepsis and mise en abyme should be noted, however. Metalepsis is the rhetorical effect of transgression across narrative boundaries, or merging diegetic levels. Mise en abyme, or what Cohn calls "pure" mise en abyme, creates a disorientation for the reader through repetition. See note 6 above.

comic exposition of how storytelling connects to horsemanship: "disse uno de' cavalierei della brigata: 'Madonna Oretta, quando voi vogliate, io vi porterò, gran parte della via che a andare abbiamo, a cavallo con una delle belle novelle del mondo'" [VI.1.7; one of the knights ... said: "Madonna Oretta, if you like I shall take you riding along a goodly stretch of our journey by telling you one of the finest tales in the world"; 447]. The relation of the metaphor's tenor "belle novelle" to its vehicle "a cavallo," created through the verb "vi porterò," can technically be classified as a zeugma – the use of one word to modify two words that is appropriate to each in a different way – and the logic of the connection of horseback riding to storytelling is in fact comically purposeful and appears frequently in the *Decameron*.[22] More importantly, it is difficult to draw a sexual inference from the metaphor as it is voiced by the *cavaliere*. The more obvious explanation is that storytelling is like horseback riding in as much as it speeds up a journey that can become tedious without distraction. It is Filomena's critique of the *cavaliere*'s rhetorical eloquence that introduces the sexualized innuendo:

> Messer lo cavaliere, al quale forse non stava meglio la spada allato che 'l novellar nella lingua, udito questo, cominciò una sua novella, la quale nel vero da sé era bellissima, ma egli or tre e quatro e sei volte replicando una medesima parola e ora indietro tornando e talvolta dicendo: "Io non dissi bene" e spesso ne' nomi errando, un per un altro ponendone, fieramente la guastava: senza che egli pessimamente, secondo le qualità delle persone e gli atti che accadevano, profereva. (VI.1.9)

> [Whereupon this worthy knight, whose swordplay was doubtless on a par with his storytelling, began to recite his tale, which in itself was excellent. But by constantly repeating the same phrases, and recapitulating sections of the plot, and every so often declaring that he had "made a mess of that bit," and regularly confusing the names of the characters, he ruined it completely. Moreover, his mode of delivery was totally out of keeping with the characters and the incidents he was describing.] (447)

The suppression of the content of the *cavaliere*'s tale in favour of its failures of style forms the basis, of course, for the scholarly appreciation

22 See Gaylard 36: "The metaphor of a horse for a novella, of a knight beguiling a lady with a tale so that she feels as though she were riding, recalls the prevalent use of riding and horse lexicon to describe intercourse elsewhere in the *Decameron* (III, 2; III, 4, 25; VII, 2, 34; VIII, 4, 32; IX, 10)."

of this tale as a metanovella.[23] Less emphasized is the figurative shift Filomena introduces by her conflation of poor rhetorical skills with poor sexual performance, "forse non stava meglio la spada allato che 'l novellar nella lingua." Any reader familiar with Boccaccio will recognize this formula as one of his favourite techniques, the sexualized double entendre, and as a departure from Filomena's usually more oblique strategies of critique.[24] Although it certainly does not rise to the level of discursive violence that appears elsewhere in the *Decameron*, there is a level of contempt or hostility directed towards the incompetent narrator that is unusual for Filomena's rhetorical strategy that insists on deferring to male authority (Migiel 116.) Moreover, what is the reader to make of her claim that the story "nel vero da sé era bellissima"? Certainly, the reader must now speculate first as to the thematic content of the tale, and second as to whether this statement is an effort to temper the potential emasculation of her critique of the *cavaliere*'s "swordplay."[25] A third reading also obtrudes: should her praise of the tale in fact be taken ironically? If ironic, what is the rhetorical motive that inspires the ambiguity?

To answer these questions, the reader must make some interpretive choices suggested by the allusions invoked in the Prologue; that is, Filomena's narrative in Day Six depends on awareness of her fictional status, and her identity as the character Cressida and as Ovidian Filomena is necessarily framed by masculine subjectivity. Her oblique critique then suggests that the suppressed content of the bad story is in fact one like those told at her expense by Filostrato, reduced to absence yet

---

23 See Almansi, *Writer as Liar* 44–6; Andrei "*Motto*" 22; Fido, "Silenzi e cavalli" 80–3; Freedman; Usher, "'Desultorietà'"; and, especially, Migiel 114–18.

24 As Migiel points out, Filomena frequently resorts to oblique strategies both to critique both other narrators in the *Decameron* and in her stories (93–6; 123–6). Filomena routinely defers to masculine superiority, and insists in the Introduction that men must accompany them on their journey outside of Florence; as Kristina Olson has suggested to me, it is ironic that in this tale, at least, this *cavaliere* does not travel well.

25 Gaylard argues that "[t]he storytelling *cavalcare* of the knight in VI, 1 is a verbal gesture that never leads to real sex but only to a formless flow of words, endless stories without resolution, parole never leading to the satisfaction of *fatti*. Unlike the sodomites Cepparello and Cipolla – both of whom are adept storytellers – the knight is incapable of imposing verbal form on even the most receptive content; metaphorical and actual sexual power to *cavalcare* are simultaneously denied to him. His title *cavaliere* is as ironic as Cepparello's sainthood and Brunetto's metaphorical generation of Dante in *Inferno* XV" (42). For Filomena's story as concerned with gender rather than class, see Wallace 67–70.

present in its erasure because neither tongueless Filomena nor Cressida can speak as an authentic female subject. The reticent, indirect rhetorical strategy and the insistence on deferring to masculine authority that informs the Filomena of the *brigata* could, therefore, be understood as an expedient method to protect herself from the rhetorical violence that surrounds her literary context and defines her sense of trauma and her fear of rape (Wofford 189–92).

At a minimum, the poor narrative performance creates enough anxiety to manifest itself in Madonna Oretta's somatic response that precedes her *motto*, and the witticism itself:

> Di che a madonna Oretta, udendolo, spesse volte veniva un sudore e uno sfinimento di cuore, come se inferma fosse stata per terminare; la qual cosa poi che piú sofferir non poté, conoscendo che il cavaliere era entrato nel pecoreccio né era per riuscirne, piacevolemente disse: "Messer, questo vostro cavallo ha troppo duro trotto, per che io vi priego che vi piaccia di pormi a piè." (VI.1.10)
>
> [it was painful for Madonna Oretta to listen to him. She began to perspire freely, and her heart missed several beats, as though she had fallen ill and was about to give up the ghost. And in the end, when she could endure it no longer, having perceived that the knight had tied himself inextricably in knots, she said to him in affable tones: "Sir, you have taken me riding on a horse that trots very jerkily. Pray be good enough to set me down."] (447)

Filomena's description of Oretta's physical response extends the ironic characterization of the *cavaliere*'s ineptitude in an interesting set of images that exemplify the use of indirect discourse to represent a non-verbal communicative act.[26] If, as Fido suggests, Oretta's reaction mimics a false orgasm, Filomena could deliver no more devastating critique of masculine authority while simultaneously exposing the limits to expressing female agency within the boundaries of masculine discourse. The story results in ethical as well as physical violence since Boccaccio appears to suggest that deceit is a necessary condition of

26 As Albers points out: "The novella about Madonna Oretta shows both the close relation between bodily and linguistic gestures and the poetological dimension of the theme, since it refers to the bodily and emotional impact of storytelling, which was already a subject of ancient rhetoric. As a 'metanovella' that thematizes novella telling, the story which Boccaccio places at the exact center of his *Decameron* hints at a poetics of the bodily emotions that will remain specific to the genre of the novella until the seventeenth century" (26–7). For Oretta's somatic response as an "anti-orgasm," see Fido, "Silenzi e cavalli" 82. See also Cahill 82–4.

female subjectivity, because an articulation of the truth would engender a potentially violent response.

Oretta's *motto* formally represents the brevity that Filomena insists improves feminine discourse: "cosí de' laudevoli costumi e de' ragionamenti belli sono i leggiadri motti; li quali, per ciò che brievi sono, tanto stanno meglio alle donne che agli uomini quanto piú alle donne che agli uomini il molto parlar si disdice" [VI.1.2; so likewise are graceful manners and polite discourse enriched by shafts of wit. These, being brief, are much better suited to women than to men, since it is more unseemly for a woman to make long speeches that it is for a man; 446]. Indeed, its brevity interferes with its comprehensibility. How is the reader to understand what Oretta means when she says "Messer, questo vostro cavallo ha troppo duro trotto, per che io vi priego che vi piaccia di pormi a piè"? It is interesting to note, as Andrei points out, that the tradition of the *motto* invariably demands a "shift from ignorance to knowledge" as a function of the dialectic and "is a device that hides knowledge by virtue of its rhetorical form and needs to be explained by someone else in the narrative" ("*Motto*" 33). Such explicatory guidance is only partially provided in Oretta's story. The *cavaliere* clearly does not understand the insult to his sexual prowess, only that to his narrative ineptitude:

> Il cavaliere, il quale per avventura era molto migliore intenditor che novellatore, inteso il motto e quello in festa e in gabbo preso, mise mano in altre novelle e quella che cominciata aveva e mal seguita senza finita lasciò stare. (VI.1.12)

> [The knight, who was apparently far more capable of taking a hint than of telling a tale, saw the joke and took it in the cheerfullest of spirits. Leaving aside the story he had begun and so ineptly handled, he turned his attention to telling her tales of quite another sort.] (447)

Taken together with Oretta's somatic response to his narrative, the *cavaliere*'s egotism verges on the comic sublime. Of course, the reader recognizes the connection to sexual competence in the metaphoric "duro trotto" as a substitution for copulation, or to borrow Filomena's term "swordplay," in a way that the *cavaliere* evidently does not, or he would not be able to "[mettere] mano in altre novelle."[27] Significantly, the

27 Freedman suggests that the *cavaliere*'s response illustrates the profound irony that concludes the tale (236–8); Gaylard notes that the *cavaliere* "underinterpret[s] her words, excluding himself as the brunt of the joke. Thus the male figure demonstrates the interpretative obtuseness that Filomena regrets" (36).

content of these "other tales" is, like his failed preliminary attempt, also suppressed, leaving the reader to wonder if the *cavaliere* has learned anything about what constitutes the pleasure of the text. More importantly, he hears no threat to his empowered masculine position because his intellect has failed him and thus is free to "[mettere] mano," to "take in hand," a phrase that suggests a heteronormative and patriarchal metaphor of control. At any rate, the success of the *motto* depends on its ironic incomprehensibility. What remains is for the reader to understand the formal demands of the *motto* as a verbal duel that has as its stakes an escape from potential physical harm or other violence, as the frame for the day decrees. The gendered power struggle figured by the "duro trotto" is masked by the double entendre that connects sexuality to storytelling. The subtext embedded in the "duro trotto" that needs to be deciphered is the tenor of the zeugmatic metaphor connecting horseback riding to both storytelling and sexuality, the reciprocal implication of which could be crudely put as "who is riding whom?" The critique of masculine performance in connection to sexuality potentially extends a threat to male dominance that could result in violence, or in terms of the *motto*, the danger is that the rider could become the unwilling ridden. The ironic "duro trotto" is necessarily ambiguous because the riposte simultaneously constructs this threat even as its wit offers a passive-aggressive refuge for the female subject. The reading community understands the semantic paradox even as the *cavaliere* apparently cannot.

Boccaccio, then, uses the first story of the Sixth Day of the *Decameron* to synthesize several elements of his theory of vernacular poetics, especially his appreciation of the unstable relationship between knowledge and its rhetorical construction in the literary imagination. At the centre of this poetics is the notion that the reader's ability to comprehend tropological language in its broadest definition depends upon a capacity to remember and superimpose multiple metonymies as part of the typology of reading. In turn, literary knowledge creates a reciprocal matrix that allows the reader to negotiate experience, even as such knowledge may not be authoritative. Boccaccio limits Filomena's "knowledge," for example, to a very specific set of intertextual allusions that contextualize her rhetorical strategies in the larger narrative. She is one among the polyphony of voices that define Boccaccio's encyclopedia of Florentine society. Ultimately, his narratological approach highlights ethical problems. Boccaccio appears to encourage readers to consider the aesthetic value of literary tradition and its construction of humane values, especially myth, as it is translated into popular culture. This strategy, in turn, suggests a didactic agenda that insists on the development of empathy as the appropriate response to the ethical demand placed on the reader. The second half of the *Decameron* begins by once more interrogating the notion that it is a human virtue to have compassion for others. Filomena stands as a fulcrum across the literary tradition that encapsulates an important aspect of how readers can achieve an imaginative and sympathetic construction of gendered experience. Because the reader is aware of her status as metonymic artifact, Boccaccio creates a narrative that allows for a reconsideration of the justice of her ontological position. In short, he shows the reader how to give Filomena a voice.

2 The Tale of Cisti the Baker (VI.2)

GIULIA CARDILLO

In the Author's Conclusion to the *Decameron*, Giovanni Boccaccio compares tales to wine. Delightful for many, wine can be harmful for the feverish. This unhealthy effect, however, is not intrinsic to its nature, but rather incidental, due to the physical state of those who drink it. In the same way, depending on those who savour them, tales can have either a favourable or detrimental impact. This oenological analogy allows the author to draw together wine and tales on an aesthetic level and to reflect on the relation between the role of the readers and the function of literary narration. In Cisti's tale, a similar analogy emerges between his luscious wine, served in an "orcioletto" [small flagon], and the "sola parola" [single sentence] the baker pronounces in order to illuminate Geri Spina's understanding about a neglectful request. Cisti maintains that his wine is not a "vin da famiglia" [wine for servants], of low quality and, as such, to be consumed in large quantities, but one that only a sophisticated palate can appreciate (VI.2.29; 451).[1] In the same way, he knows that his few words will remain obscure to the servant, leaving only Geri Spina to decipher their true meaning. The "novelletta," like the "orcioletto," shows that the quality of the object is as important as the taste of those who enjoy it. In the tale, wine and words are both part of an aesthetic and intellectual experience that requires a refinement of the perceiver.

The *novella*, narrated by Pampinea, tells the story of Cisti, a rich Florentine baker unfairly penalized by Fortune, who assigned to him a humble trade, even if Nature endowed him with remarkable ingenuity. His intelligence, nonetheless, lies hidden beneath his modest craft like

1 All citations of the *Decameron* are from Branca's 1992 Einaudi edition reprint. The English translations, unless otherwise indicated, are from McWilliam.

a precious object, until the moment to shine presents itself during the papal ambassadors' visit to Florence. As they walk by Cisti's bakery every day, together with the Florentine banker Geri Spina, the baker realizes that it would be an act of courtesy to offer them one his best wines. He does not, however, deem it appropriate to make such a direct invitation to those of a higher social status. Thus, Cisti designs a way to induce Geri Spina to invite himself: sitting in front of his bakery and wearing white clothes, Cisti displays the great enjoyment that sipping his fresh wine provides on a hot day. Lured by the spectacle, the banker and the ambassadors stop to taste and appreciate the wine. Later, when Geri Spina organizes a banquet and invites the baker, Cisti declines, prompting Geri Spina to send one of his servants to fill one flask of the wine. Desiring some of it, the servant fetches a very large flask. Seeing this, Cisti tells the servant that Geri Spina directed him to the wrong place. As he receives the message, Geri Spina asks where he is sending his servant then. Cisti's short but effective answer "To the Arno," the humour of which is lost on the oblivious servant, opens the eyes of the intellect of Geri Spina, who scolds the servant and sends a smaller flagon. Cisti finally fills it and, later that day, donates all his precious wine to Geri Spina for his banquet, explaining that his intention was not to withhold his stock, but rather to prevent the servant from stealing it. From that moment on, Geri Spina regards Cisti as a good friend.

Similar to other tales of Day Six dedicated to the power of words, Cisti's *novella* reveals a metaliterary feature, a reflection on the function and reception of verbal creation.[2] The *novelle* about Madonna Oretta (VI.1),[3] Giotto (VI.5),[4] and Fra Cipolla (VI.10)[5] are all in strategic positions[6] within the structure of the Sixth Day (which itself inaugurates the

2 On the metaliterary aspects of the of the Sixth Day *novelle*, see Fido, "Boccaccio's *Ars Narrandi*."

3 The metaliterary quality of Madonna Oretta's story, also discussed in the previous chapter, has received much attention. I indicate here a limited number of studies: Barilli; Almansi, "Lettura della novella di Madonna Oretta," esp. 142, where Almansi defines the tale a "metanovella"; Stewart, "La novella di Madonna Oretta"; Baratto, *Realtà e stile* 75; and Confalonieri.

4 Many studies concentrate on the parallelism that Boccaccio builds between painting and poetry, and on painters such as Giotto as figures of Boccaccio himself. See Marcus, *Allegory of Form* 79–94; Baratto, *Realtà e stile* 410; Watson, "Cement of Fiction" 43–64; Mazzotta, *World at Play*, 192–200 and 237–40; Martinez, "Calandrino and the Powers of the Stone"; and Ricketts, *Visualizing Boccaccio* 91–100.

5 On the metaliterary importance of Frate Cipolla's tale, see Marcus, *Allegory of Form* 64–78.

6 On the importance of Madonna Oretta's location within the text, see Almansi, "Lettura della novella di Madonna Oretta" 140.

second half of the *Decameron*) and share the common topic about the tension between substance and appearance, content and form, meaning and sign. This question on the role and nature of poetic fiction returns, in different ways, in each of the author's interventions throughout the *Decameron* (in the Prologue, the Introduction to Day Four, and the Conclusion). Boccaccio explores these issues further in the fourteenth and fifteenth books of his *Genealogie deorum gentilium libri*, dedicated to the defence of poetry,[7] an artistic category that for him is not restricted to writing in verse, but that includes prose as well. In book XIV, in particular, he claims that "poesis est, quicquid sub velamento componimus et exponitur exquisite" [XIV.7.8; whatever is composed as under a veil, and thus exquisitely wrought is poetry; 42].[8] Such a definition of poetry yokes together two components: the concealing of an "other sense" under the veil of allegory and the aesthetic refinement of its literary fabric.[9]

By analysing the analogies between VI.2 and the considerations on poetry in the *Genealogie*, this essay aims to uncover the metaliterary elements present in the tale. After an overview of the tale's critical reception, I show, through a close textual reading, that Cisti's story alludes to the nature and function of the *novella*'s form. First, I investigate how Boccaccio's theory of allegory, developed in the *Genealogie*, echoes the opening reflection of VI.2 on how Fortune and Nature conceal a noble soul under the shadow of humble "arti." This leads to a comparison of the uses of the expression "eye of the intellect," which appears both in Cisti's tale and in the *Genealogie*. My analysis then moves to the analogy between the "orcioletto" and the "novelletta," in order to expose the contiguity between the rhetoric of *parvitas* and *brevitas*. In the context of this poetics of humility, I suggest that the vernacular prose of the *novella* itself represents for Boccaccio the humble veil under which he hides his poetic truths, thus mirroring the very premise of Cisti's tale. Finally, the connection between VI.2 and the Author's Epilogue shows

---

7 On the connection between Boccaccio's poetics in the *Decameron* and his theory of poetry in the *Genealogie*, see Lummus, "The *Decameron*."

8 Citations in Latin of the *Genealogie* are from Zaccaria's 1998 text for *Tutte le opere*. English translations from the first book are from Solomon's 2011 edition for Harvard's I Tatti Renaissance Library. Because the full translation of the *Geneaologie* is in preparation at the time of this article, the translations of excerpts from books XIV and XV are from Osgood (in Boccaccio, *Boccaccio on Poetry*).

9 In a previous passage, Boccaccio erroneously claims that *poesis* etymologically derives from the Greek *poetes*, which he translates into "exquisita locutio" [XIV.7.2; exquisite discourse; 24].

that, like Cisti's wine, appreciation of the *Decameron*'s *novelle* needs a sophisticated palate.

Scholars have developed different perspectives and approaches in the study of this tale, in large part exploring its social, civic, and political facets. Notwithstanding the extensive metaliterary component of the Sixth Day, the social dynamics performed by the characters on the Florentine stage of VI.2, together with the introductory reflection on Fortune and Nature, have received most of the scholarly attention. Giovanni Getto saw in Cisti's attention to decorum, good manners, and form the possibility of creating an environment where different social classes can coexist. Good taste makes Cisti an "artista della vita" [artist of life], able to create with his aesthetic care a splendid picture enticing Geri Spina and the ambassadors, and prepared to use words elegantly (Getto 143–6). Vittore Branca, in *Boccaccio Medievale*, briefly claims that Cisti's witticism, and more in general his *ingegno* (one of the three forces that drive the human world "quasi strumenti della Provvidenza divina" [16; like instruments of divine Providence]), elevate him beyond his position as a humble merchant.[10] In *Realtà e stile nel "Decameron,"* Mario Baratto interprets VI.2 as a "lezione di carattere sia morale (il rapporto tra Fortuna e Natura) sia sociale (il rapporto tra individui di classi diverse)" [86; a lesson both moral (the relationship between Fortune and Nature) and social (the relationship between individuals from different social classes]. In Baratto's reading, the two foci of the tale are inextricably woven together: on the one hand, the role of Fortune and Nature, and on the other, the social interaction between Cisti and Geri Spina. According to Baratto, the narrative structure of the "contrasto" characterizing the *novella* allows the encounter and the comparison between contrasting values and principles, within the controlled and civilized setting prepared by Cisti. His virtues are exemplary because he does not belong to the social class that his wit deserves. This injustice, due to the workings of Fortune, has been balanced by Nature, who has given Cisti the same *ingegno* as Geri Spina, and by Fortune herself, who made Cisti rich. Social differences do not represent an obstacle to the friendship between the two, because social rules are broken only on an individual level.

Similarly, but with a greater emphasis on the role played by language, Giuseppe Mazzotta in *The World at Play in Boccaccio's "Decameron"* states

---

10 According to Branca, *ingegno* governs the actions of Days Six, Seven, and Eight. For the brief remark on this tale, see *Boccaccio Medievale* 151.

that in VI.2 "language is endowed with efficacy to redeem Cisti in the social hierarchy in the sense that the language he uses with Geri levels the social differences between them" (63). Nevertheless, language can be the instrument to overcome the social gap, because Boccaccio depicts "Fortune not as the random, blind chance of the pagans, but as an intelligence of God. The world is given a metaphysical coherence, in other words, and within this context, language has its efficacy" (ibid.). As an instrument of divine Providence, Fortune provides the conditions which allow Cisti to bridge, through language, the social disparity that separates him from Geri Spina.

In her investigation of the meaning of *cortesia* in Boccaccio's oeuvre, Kristina Olson analyses the manner in which Cisti redirects the inexpert Geri Spina – a prominent member of the Black Guelphs and part of the *gente nuova* of Florence in Boccaccio's time – towards the "principle of *cortesia* as the code of conduct" (*Courtesy Lost* 86). In this context, *cortesia* represents the civic ethic that is being lost with the *gente nuova*, the new elite of Florence. Providing a detailed social and political background for the two protagonists, Olson shows that Cisti's "'pronta risposta' conveys the discontent and growing political power of the *popolo minuto*" (*Courtesy Lost* 91). With his witticism, Cisti shows the social awareness that Geri Spina lacks. In "La misura del privilegio: il vino di Cisti Fornaio," Giulio Savelli combines the idea of Cisti's social awareness with the concept of "giusta misura": moderation and good taste regulate his behaviour towards both the consumption of wine and social hierarchy. The idea that excellence moves from the product to the consumer, that it can be transmitted, constitutes the similarity between offering exquisite food and producing a work of art, a notion implied by Panfilo when he recalls Cisti's tale in introducing the story of Giotto and Forese (VI.5.3). Cisti's wine is also at the centre of Salvatore Musumeci's socio-historical analysis, which focuses on the culture of wine consumption in Boccaccio's time and illustrates references to the Eucharist as well as the Christological metaphors throughout the tale. Musumeci identifies wine as the element that facilitates, through sharing, the building of a friendship beyond the constraints of social difference and etiquette.

In the *novella*'s critical reception, Cisti's social status constitutes the fulcrum of the tale, around which questions on societal dynamics, civic decorum, language, ingenuity, and taste simultaneously unfold. In what follows, I suggest that there is a further layer of interpretation which deserves consideration, but which scholarship has only briefly examined: Cisti's tale represents a continuation of Madonna Oretta's reflection on the form of the *novella* itself, on the relation between form and content, and on the tension between the literal and the allegorical. Pampinea's Introduction, with its description of the value hidden in the "arti," foreshadows Boccaccio's own theory of the poetic veil and its function in the poet's *fabulae*, which he develops and articulates in the *Genealogie*.

As Vittore Branca emphasizes, Cisti's tale is almost completely new, and it is possible to find only a few analogies with two tales from the *Novellino* and with one from the *Panciatichiano*.[11] The distance between the *Decameron*'s *novelle* and the earlier tales, mainly featuring denied requests of wine, does not lie merely in the difference of plots, but more substantially in the preface to the tale, which functions as a gloss that guides the reader to the central issue of the story: the unfair contrast between Cisti's trade and his noble soul, between his social appearance and his virtue. Even if the rubric provides the basic storyline, Pampinea warns the listeners and the readers about the meaning of the story.

As alluded to earlier, Boccaccio employs in VI.2 words and expressions similar to those that he will later use in his *Genealogie* in order to refer to poetry and its usefulness. The idea of hiding treasured items to be revealed at a later time constitutes the first analogy between the tale and Boccaccio's considerations on poetic fiction. In the *novella*, Pampinea begins her storytelling with a chiastic parallelism on the workings of Nature and Fortune, the first demeaning a noble soul by bestowing upon it an inferior body, the second giving an unsuitable profession to a noble soul. As Giuseppe Velli demonstrated, Pampinea's considerations on Nature, Fortune, and the nobility of the soul, echoed by Panfilo in the Introduction to VI.5, derive in part from Seneca's *Ad Lucilium epistulae morales*, and in particular from letters 44 (three excerpts of which are copied in one of Boccaccio's notebooks, the Zibaldone Magliabechiano) and 66.[12] In these letters, Seneca reflects on how the noble soul is able to overcome the circumstances imposed by Fortune. Nonetheless, as Velli noticed, the second part of Pampinea's meditation differs from Seneca's text, which argues that Nature and Fortune are negative forces. In the *Decameron*, instead, Pampinea presents Nature and Fortune as prudent forces, comparing

---

11 See Branca's note in Boccaccio, *Decameron* (1992) 720n2. For the relationship between the *novelle* of the Sixth Day of the *Decameron* and the *Novellino*, including a comparison between the tale of Cisti and the story of Iacopino Rangoni, see Cuomo.

12 See Velli. On the connection between Seneca's letters, Pampinea's Introduction, and III.2, see Filosa, "Tale of the King and the Groom."

them to human beings who store and bury their dearest possessions in the humblest parts of their houses:

> E certo io maladicerei e la natura e parimenti la fortuna, se io non conoscessi la natura esser discretissima e la fortuna aver mille occhi, come che gli sciocchi lei cieca figurino. Le quali io avviso che, sì come molto *avvedute*, fanno quello che i mortali spesse volte fanno, li quali, incerti de' futuri casi, per le loro opportunità le loro *più care cose* ne' più vili luoghi delle lor case, sì come meno sospetti, *sepelliscono*, e quindi ne' maggior bisogni le traggono, avendole il vil luogo più sicuramente servate che la bella camera non avrebbe. E così le due ministre del mondo spesso le lor cose più care *nascondono* sotto l'ombra dell'*arti* reputate più *vili*, acciò che di quelle alle necessità traendole più *chiaro* appaia il loro splendore. (VI.2.5–6, emphasis added)

> [I would assuredly curse Nature and Fortune alike, if I did not know for a fact that Nature is very discerning, and that Fortune has a thousand eyes, even though fools represent her as blind. Indeed, it is my conviction that Nature and Fortune, being very *shrewd*, follow the practice so common among mortals, who, uncertain of what the future will bring, make provision for emergencies by *burying* their *most precious possessions* in the least imposing (and therefore least suspect) part of their houses, whence they bring them forth in the hour of their greatest need, their treasure having been more securely preserved in a humble hiding place than if it had been kept in a sumptuous chamber. In the same way, the two fair arbiters of the world's affairs frequently *hide* their greatest treasure beneath the shadow of the *humblest of trades*, so that when the need arises for it to be brought forth, its *splendour* will be all the more *apparent*.] (448)

Unsure about the future, mortals bury ("sepelliscono") their most valued ("care") belongings in places that appear less conspicuous, and are consequently safer than a beautiful room. Then, at the moment of greatest need they unearth their valuables. Pampinea claims that in a similar way Fortune and Nature, who are discerning agencies (contrarily to what is believed), conceal their most precious things in the shadow of the humblest "arti," so that they will shine even more brightly when taken out for necessity.

After the Senecan beginning about the difficulties posed by Fortune, Pampinea changes the course of her argument in the second part of her Introduction, and reveals allusions to the arts in general, to rhetoric, to ideas of beauty, and to poetry. Because of the opening statement about those possessing noble souls but unbefitting trades, the term "arti" refers here to guilds, and in particular to Cisti's minor guild, the Arte dei Fornai. Nonetheless, it also alludes to the arts, which in the medieval educational system were traditionally divided into liberal (*trivium* and *quadrivium*) and mechanical. Thus, the sentence opens itself to an interpretation on what the arts may hide and then reveal in a brighter way. The term "chiaro" can have multiple meanings and alludes to ideas of clarity, beauty, and renown. First, it hints at the language of rhetoric, one of the arts of the *trivium*, where *claritas* (as opposed to *obscuritas*) refers to a quality of style that makes the discourse intelligible.[13] Second, *claritas* also constitutes one of the elements of beauty in Thomas Aquinas's thought, together with *integritas* and *proportion*.[14] Umberto Eco notices that, notwithstanding the multiple ways in which Aquinas employs the word *claritas* and its derivatives – including "(1) light and physical color; (2) the light of reason … (3) the shining forth of earthly renown; (4) the celestial glory of the glorified bodies" – the concept of clarity is always connected to that of beauty (*Aesthetics* 104).[15] According to Eco, in Aquinas the actualization of beauty occurs in the relationship between the perceiving intellect and the object observed.[16] In other words, it is the encounter of the object with sight (*visio*) that confers the aesthetic quality to the object itself. Similarly, in VI.2, which so closely

13 In the *Convivio*, when Dante speaks about the two characteristics that rhetoric shares with the Heaven of Venus, he asserts that the first is the clarity of its image ("la chiarezza del suo aspetto") and the second its appearance ("la sua apparenza, or da mane or da sera") (*Conv.* II.xiii.13). I have used Vasoli's 1979 edition of the *Convivio*. For the debated issue of the influence of Dante's *Convivio* on the *Decameron*, see Ferreri; Forni, "Boccaccio tra Dante e Cino"; and Arduini. In the *Institutio oratoria*, Quintilian defines *claritas orationis* as the power of eloquence to move the listeners' minds to virtue (2.16.10). See Quintilian, *Institutio oratoria* 323 (trans. Butler). On Boccaccio and Quintilian, see Coulter. On Quintilian in the Middle Ages, see Boskoff.

14 Ruggiero Stefanelli notices that these same three components are, in Boccaccio's thought, the means through which one can develop an aesthetic perception (153n63). On Boccaccio and Aquinas, see Mazzotta, *World at Play* 126–7; Grossvogel 132–9; Kirkham, *Sign of Reason* 11–12; Bausi; and Andrei, *Boccaccio the Philosopher* 199–204.

15 More in general on *claritas* in Aquinas, see Eco, *Aesthetics* 114–21.

16 Discussing Aquinas's aesthetics of form, Eco thus defines *claritas*: on an ontological level it is "the one principle of expressiveness in medieval times which could fill the place occupied nowadays by such concepts as the lyricism or symbolism or the iconicity of form. An organism which is fully perceived and grasped reveals its organic nature, and the intellect can enjoy the beauty of its discipline and order … it becomes real and manifest when the *visio* focuses upon it, a form of disinterested observation which regards the object under the aspect of its formal cause … Ontologically, *claritas* is clarity 'in itself', and it becomes aesthetic clarity or clarity 'for us' in a specific perception of it" (*Art and Beauty* 81–2). See more in general *Art and Beauty* 75–83.

follows Boccaccio's theory of poetry, it is only when Geri Spina sees with his intellect the concealed meaning of Cisti's message that clarity follows, displaying an aesthetic nuance deriving from the appreciation of the allegorical veil of the word. Finally, in the *Decameron* the adjective "chiaro" also refers to the classical idea of renown, fame, and illustriousness, which Cisti reaches when his story is told.[17] As a result of these subtle references, the last sentence of Pampinea's preface casts a new light on the whole passage and invites the readers to look beneath the shadow of the "arti" – in this case the *arte della parola* – and discover what lies hidden.

The description of such a process can be found in the *Genealogie*, where Boccaccio describes the poets' task of hiding truths under the veil of poetry in ways that resemble Fortune's and Nature's actions as depicted by Pampinea. In the fourteenth book, two passages illustrate the poetic process of concealing the truth *sub cortice fabularum*, under the outer layer (cortex) of fables.[18] In the first excerpt, Boccaccio affirms that it is contrary to the poet's task to leave the meaning uncovered, because the poetic truths need to be buried and kept away from the eyes of sluggish minds ("oculis torpentium"), since this would diminish their value: "Verum non ob id, ut isti volunt, iure damnanda, cum inter alia poete officia sit non eviscerare fictionibus palliata, quin imo, si in propatulo posita sint memoratu et veneratione digna, ne vilescant familiaritate nimia, quanta possunt industria *tegere* et ab oculis torpentium auferre" [XIV.xii.8; Yet not by this token is it fair to condemn them; for surely it is not one of the poet's various functions to rip up and lay bare the meaning which lies hidden in his inventions. Rather where matters truly solemn and memorable are too much exposed, it is the office by every effort to protect as well as he can and remove them from the gaze of the irreverent, that they cheapen not by too common familiarity; 59]. Excessive familiarity with poetic truths devalues those that merit remembrance and veneration. In the *Genealogie*, the poets veil their truths just as mortals conceal their prized possessions, and as Nature and Fortune disguise noble souls in Pampinea's Introduction. In the tale, Cisti's wine is kept away from the "famiglia," or servants, and his words hide a witticism from the unaware servant, opening only the eyes of the intellect of the desired interlocutor.

---

17 On the idea of *claritas* as renown in Boccaccio, see Boitani 172 and 37–9 on classical ideas of *claritas*. For the concept of *claritas* connected to women, see Jordan, "Boccaccio's In-Famous Women."

18 On Boccaccio's defence of poetry, see Osgood's introduction to Boccaccio, *Boccaccio on Poetry* xi–xlix; Gullace; Stone 145–54; Cerbo 13–29; and Pastore Stocchi.

In the ensuing paragraph of the *Genealogie*, Boccaccio explains the reason for the poet's *obscuritas*, which has the sole purpose of making poetic truths more valuable:

> Nec sit quis existimet a poetis veritates fictionibus invidia conditas, aut ut velint omnino absconditorum sensum negare lectoribus, aut ut artificiosiores appareant, sed ut, que apposita viluissent, labore ingeniorum quesita et diversimode intellecta comperta tandem faciant *cariora* (XIV.xii.9, emphasis added)
>
> [Surely no one can believe that poets invidiously veil the truth with fiction, either to deprive the reader of hidden sense, or to appear more clever; but rather to make truths which would otherwise cheapen by exposure the object of strong intellectual effort and various interpretation, that in ultimate discovery they shall be *more precious*] (60, emphasis added)

The veil of poetry is intended to sharpen the reader's intellect, not deny access to the inner meaning of the *fabulae* or to signal the poet's craftiness. Ultimately, the intellectual effort renders the discovered truths dearer ("cariora"), which coincides with the effect achieved by Nature and Fortune in concealing a noble soul in a humble tradesman.

As a consequence, there is an implicit analogy between the workings of Nature and Fortune and the poets' activity. Beverly Joseph Layman, in "Boccaccio's Paradigm of the Artist and His Art," identifies in the two ministers of the world a paradigm of the artist that, like the poets described by Boccaccio in the *Genealogie*, conceals and reveals wonders (19–21). The term used to define Nature and Fortune, "avvedute," corroborates this similarity. This adjective echoes the noun "avvedimento" found in the rubric of Day Six, which means, *in sensu stricto*, ingenious action or stratagem. The shared etymology of these words indicates a view and consideration of things ahead, which extends to the idea of worldly prudence and wisdom.[19] In the *Decameron*, both expressions describe an

19 See *TLIO*, s.v. "avvedimento." Hastings records the different terms employed by Boccaccio related to Reason; among them he lists "Avvedimento": "*Avvedimento* may mean a number of things: shrewdness, perspicacity and discernment; resourcefulness and ingenuity; or an expedient, ruse, stratagem" (74n). Hastings also claims that "avvedimento" in the *Decameron* can overlap with words like "discrezione," "ingegno," and "senno." The words "prudenza" and "prudente" do not appear in the *Decameron*. However, Victoria Kirkham in *The Sign of Reason in Boccaccio's Fiction* identifies Pampinea, the storyteller of this tale, with Prudence itself, since she shares with the Christian virtue the same leading role in appealing to the rational faculty (in the case of Pampinea, that of the *brigata*). In the same book, Kirkham demonstrates the significance and marked presence of Prudence in Boccaccio's fictional production.

attitude that resembles that of the poets as described in the *Genealogie*. In the Proem, the author addresses King Hugh IV of Cyprus, who asked him to write on the genealogies of the pagan gods and heroes, and to explain what the poets hid under the *cortex* of their *fabulae*, in order to reveal their true meaning: "Addebas preterea ut explicarem quid sub ridiculo cortice fabularum abscondisset *prudentes viri*" [I.Proem.16; You added in addition that I should explain the meaning *wise men* had hidden under the outer layers of these inane fables; 9, emphasis added]. The author here calls the poets "prudentes viri," a definition that he clarifies in a later passage, when describing his method of reconstructing the pagan gods' genealogies through the commentary of ancient poets' texts:

> et hoc faciens, primo, que ab antiquis hausisse potero scribam; inde, ubi defecerint seu minus iudicio meo plene dixerint, meam apponam sententiam; et hoc libentissimo faciam animo ut, quibusdam ignaris atque fastidiose detestantibus poetas, a se minime intellectos appareat; eos, etsi non catholicos, tanta fuisse *prudentia* preditor, ut nil artificiosus humani ingenii fictione velatum sit, nec verborum cultu pulchrius exornatum ... Ex quibus enucleationibus, preter artificium fingentium poetarum et futilium deorum consaguinitates et affiniates explicitas, naturalia quedam videbis tanto occultata misterio, ut mireris. (I.Proem.44–5)

> [My plan is, first, to write what I have extracted from the ancients, and then I will offer my interpretation where they have offered none or have done so that the text deserves. I do this most readily so that those who in ignorance fastidiously detest poets hardly known to them will see clearly that these ancient poets, despite not being Christians, were gifted with such *prudence* that no creation of human genius was ever veiled in fiction more cleverly, nor adorned more beautifully in the splendor of words ... Once the outer layer is peeled back for you, beyond the artifice of the poets who fashion them and the relationships and affinities of the meaningless gods you will see aspects of nature, once shrouded in mystery, that will amaze you]. (21)

The poets' prudence consists in employing their ingenuity in order to veil poetic truths through the ornament of words. Thereby, the author's task consists not only of putting together the pieces of information he finds in the ancient poets (an operation that later he compares to that of Prometheus,[20] and of Aesculapius recomposing Hippolytus's body),

20 On the figure of Prometheus in the *Genealogie* and the *Decameron*, see Marino; Barsella, "Myth"; and Gittes, *Boccaccio's Naked Muse* 155–7.

but also of adding his commentary.[21] Boccaccio thus presents glossing texts as a necessary practice, designed to uncover what lies under the poetic *velamen*. In the *Genealogie*, this practice serves to show that even poetry written by pagan authors contains truths. As David Lummus has pointed out, "The authority of the ancient and that of the Christian are intricately interwoven. The Christians are literally 'more prudent,' and thus hold religious authority, but the poetic authority of the name is not based on this prudence" ("Boccaccio's Poetic Anthropology" 758). What distinguishes poetry from rhetoric and philosophy is indeed not prudence, but allegory.[22]

Drawing together the passages about the "avvedute" Fortune and Nature and the prudent poets demonstrates that both these terms define the cautious planning of hiding precious items, with the anticipation that they will increase in value once revealed.[23] Is Boccaccio suggesting an analogy between the working of the two ministers and the artistic endeavour of the poets? As mentioned before, Layman claims that "a realm where built into the very nature and fortune of things is a love of deft concealment and revelation is a very Boccaccian realm indeed; and the thrust of his charming metaphor is such that the ethereal ministers threaten to emerge as two clever Florentines" (20). I would add to this statement that the parallelism finds its specific roots in Boccaccio's own theory of poetry as formulated in the *Genealogie*. Both the ministers and the poets provide order, the former to the world, the latter to words.[24] The term "apparecchiare," employed by Pampinea to outline the workings of Nature and Fortune, contains the idea of organizing and setting things up, and it implies finding a match or "pari" (something equal). The two "ministre" appear to be mismatching souls and trades, but later the apparent incongruity of their choices reveals its invisible order, its inner coherence.

---

21 The connection between prudence and the actions of writing, reading, and interpreting is developed during the early phases of humanism. As pointed out by Victoria Kahn in *Rhetoric, Prudence, and Skepticism in the Renaissance*, for early humanists "the prudence that is the intellectual virtue of right judgment about our actions applies to the author's and reader's acts of interpretation as well" (21).

22 On the theory of allegory in Boccaccio's *Genealogie*, see Kriesel, "Genealogy of Boccaccio's Theory of Allegory" and, more recently, *Boccaccio's Corpus*.

23 For the depiction of Fortune in this specific passage, see Russo, *Novelle scelte* 160; Branca, *Boccaccio Medievale* 16; and Mazzotta, *World at Play* 63. For the topic of Fortune in the Decameron, see also Cioffari; Marcus, *Allegory of Form* 27–44; and Barolini, "Wheel."

24 On the analogy between poetic creation and Nature in Boccaccio, see Lummus, "The *Decameron*" 66.

Nonetheless, "avvedimento" and prudence do not coincide. In Christian moral thought, prudence is considered one of the cardinal virtues (together with fortitude, justice, and temperance),[25] designated by Dante as the "conduttrice de le morali virtù," the guide of moral virtues (*Conv.* IV.xvii.8). Thomas Aquinas defines it as the right "reason in actions to be done" (*Summa Theologiae* II, 2, q. 47, art. 2; 153),[26] quoting Aristotle's *Nicomachean Ethics* (VI.5).[27] Aquinas also cites Isidore of Seville, who highlights that "prudent," coming from "porro videns" (seeing from afar), is connected with the idea of foreseeing "the outcome of uncertain things ahead" (*Etym.* X.201; 225).[28] "Avvedimento," on the other hand, has a secular connotation and indicates the ability to discern an advantageous arrangement.

The second parallel between Cisti's tale and Boccaccio's poetic defence in the *Genealogie* consists of the power of words to awaken and open "the eyes of the intellect." This expression returns twice in VI.2, at the beginning of the tale and the end, thus framing the entire narrative. After the Introduction, Pampinea anticipates the story's end by saying that Cisti shows the validity of her premise about Fortune, Nature, and noble souls, "gli occhi dello 'ntelletto rimettendo a messer Geri Spina" (VI.2.7), which literally means by "putting the eyes of the intellect back into Geri Spina." The second occurrence appears immediately after Cisti's witty reply, "A Arno" [To the Arno]: "Il che rapportando il famigliare a messer Geri, subito gli occhi gli s'apersero dello 'ntelletto" [VI.2.26; When the servant reported this conversation to Messer Geri, his eyes were immediately opened to the truth; 451]. The metaphor of the opening of the mind's eye describes in terms of sight (*visio*) Geri's comprehension of Cisti's layered answer, which leads to the banker's immediate measure against the servant. Once seen by the intellect, both the hidden sense of his reply and Cisti's disguised eloquence become clear.

With its roots in Neoplatonic and Augustinian tradition,[29] the expression "gli occhi dell'intelletto" describes the uncovering of meaning and

25 For the medieval history of prudence as one of the cardinal virtues, see Bejczy.

26 For Aquinas's *Summa Theologiae* here I have used the translation by Gilby et al.

27 For pre-Christian authors, especially within the tradition including Aristotle's notion of *phronesis* and Cicero's understanding of *prudentia*, prudence represented practical wisdom and was deeply connected with rhetoric and politics. For the idea of *phronesis* in Aristotle's works, see Garver 232–48. For the concept of *prudentia* in Cicero, see Cape.

28 For Isidore's *Etymologies*, I have used the translation by Barney et al.

29 On the use of this trope in the *Decameron* to describe the process of cognition, its origin in Neoplatonism, and its use by Franciscan theologians, see Andrei, *Boccaccio the Philosopher* 15–17.

the unveiling of truth, which correspond to acquiring a new intellectual vision and as a consequence also imagination.[30] Metaphorical language stimulates Geri Spina's (and the reader's) imaginative faculty because it demands that each recreate the hidden meaning of the literal surface of the word.

In the *Genealogie*, Boccaccio employs the same expression, "oculos intellectus" [eyes of the intellect], when defending the poets' *obscuritas*. Detractors of poets accuse them of being untruthful, because they do not lay the literal truth bare on the surface of their *fabulae*, but the author argues that poets are free from such obligation. As those detractors would not accuse the prophets and the authors of the Scriptures of lying, they should not accuse the poets, since also in parts of the Bible, like the Book of Revelation, the truths do not rest on the surface. Claiming the opposite is a lie that veils the eyes of the intellect: "Sed in hoc minus questionis sit: figure sunt; nunquid habeant in licterali cortice veritatem exprimant, queso. Si me hoc velint credere, nil aliud erit quam mendacio velare michi *oculos intellectus*, uti illa velant suppositam veritatem" [XIV.xiii.6; Then, let me ask, does the truth which they express lie on their surface? If they wish me to think it does, what else is it but a lie thus to veil the *eyes of my understanding*, as they also veil the truth beneath?; 64, emphasis added]. Real lies obfuscate both our intellect and the true meaning beneath the literal sense.

Poetry and its *velamen*, instead, have the opposite goal, that of stimulating the understanding of the readers. Through a layered text, *fabulae* can please and spark the *ingenium* of different kinds of readers: "Tanti quidem sunt fabule, ut earum primo contextu oblectentur indocti, et circa abscondita doctorum exerceantur ingenia, et sic una et eadem lectione proficiunt et delectant" [XIV.ix.15; Such then is the power of fiction that it pleases the unlearned by its external appearance, and exercises the minds of the learned with its hidden truth; and thus both are edified and delighted with one and the same perusal; 51]. Boccaccio elaborates this concept further in a later passage quoting Petrarch's *Contra Medicum*, where he emphasizes the idea of the "sweet labour," implying that difficulty and pleasure are part of the same aesthetic and intellectual experience of the reader: as for the majesty and dignity of Petrarch's poetry, "Nec, ut ipsi arbitrari videntur, carpere nequentibus invidetur 'sed, *dulci labore* preposito, delectationi simul memorique

30 On the eye of the mind as *oculus imaginationis* in the *Genealogie*, see Lummus, "Boccaccio's Poetic Anthropology" 731.

consulitur; cariora sunt enim, que cum difficultate quesivimus, accuratiusque servantur'" [XIV.xii.15; Such majesty and dignity are not intended to hinder those who wish to understand, "but rather propose a *delightful task,* and are designed to enhance the reader's pleasure and support his memory. What we acquire with difficulty and keep with care is always dearer to us"; 61]. The intellectual effort to understand poetry leads the readers to both aesthetic appreciation and long-lasting memory.

Boccaccio adds another consideration that underscores the role of the reader. The obscurity of a text can come from the poets' desire to veil their truths under the ornaments of words, or from the depth and difficulty of the texts' content, but it can also derive from the beholder's blindness:

> Debuerant hi vidisse non nulla obscura videri, cum clarissima sint, intuentis vicio (lusco quidem illucescente sole, qui limpidus est, nebulosus videtur aer); quedam alia de natura sui adeo profunda esse, ut non absque difficultate acies etiam egregii intellectus possit in earum abditum penetrare, uti in solis globo, antequam eum possit contingere, non nunquam perspicacissimi retunduntur oculi. Quedam vero, etsi natura sui forsan sint lucida, tanto sunt fingentium palliata artificio, ut egre etiam quis possit ingenio verum ex illis excerpere sensum. (XIV.xii.6–7)

> [They should have realized that when things perfectly clear seem obscure, it is the beholder's fault. To a half-blind man, even when the sun is shining its brightest, the sky looks cloudy. Some things are naturally so profound that not without difficulty can the most exceptional keenness in intellect sound their depths; like the sun's globe, by which, before they can clearly discern it, strong eyes are sometimes repelled. On the other hand, some things, though naturally clear perhaps, are so veiled by the artist's skill that scarcely anyone could by mental effort derive sense from them.] (59)

The readers' refinement is as important as the content of the text. The aesthetic experience derives from both the splendour of the object observed and the beholders' sight. A sound intellect can access and decipher any text, no matter how opaque: "Et ideo, ut iam dictum est, fateor illos non numquam obscuros esse, sed extricabiles semper, si sanus ad eos accesserit intellectus" [XIV.xii.9; Wherefore I again grant that poets are at times obscure, but invariably explicable if approached by a sane mind; 60]. This concept returns in the *Decameron*'s Epilogue, where the author points out that the tales do not have the same effect on all readers, just as wine does not cause the same reaction in all those who drink it. In the same way, the metaphorical aspect of Cisti's *motto* remains obscure to the literal-minded servant, while it unfolds in front of the eyes of Geri Spina's intellect.

The third correspondence between Cisti's tale and the defence of poetry in the *Genealogie* is in the idea that brevity can spur the readers' intellect. The rubric of VI.2, as mentioned earlier, has at its centre the "sola parola" that the baker pronounces prompting the banker to mend his ways: "Cisti fornaio con una sola parola fa raveder messer Geri Spina d'una sua trascutata domanda" [VI.2.rubric; By means of a single phrase, Cisti the Baker shows Geri Spina that he is being unreasonable; 448]. The rubric, in its brevity, juxtaposes Cisti's illuminating single sentence with Geri Spina's thoughtless demand. Pampinea coherently shows the power of *brevitas* through a "novelletta assai piccola" [VI.2.7; a very small short story], in order to demonstrate how "in poca cosa," in an episode of little importance, it is possible to observe that Fortune and Nature hide valuable things in the humblest of places. Pampinea thus presents the topic of *brevitas* strictly connected to the topic of humility. Later in the tale, a laconic sentence introduces the "sola parola": "Rispose Cisti: 'A Arno'" [VI.2.25; "To the Arno," replied Cisti; 451]. The introductory sentence contains only the subject and the verb, while the direct speech has an elliptical construction. The ellipsis hides the unspoken truth that the large flask is an unbefitting request. Boccaccio follows here one of the suggestions of Geoffrey of Vinsauf, in his *Poetria Nova*,[31] which advises those desiring to be brief to "let the skill of your expression signify what is not said in what is said" (58). One method of *abbreviatio*,[32] then, consists in relying on the allusiveness of words, but also in the tension between the said and the unsaid, which is part of allegory. *Brevitas* amplifies the humorous effect of Cisti's witticism. Like the "orcioletto," the short sentence becomes the fitting container for a "motto" that can be appreciated by a refined mind.

In the *Genealogie* Boccaccio briefly investigates the benefits of *brevitas* in *fabulae*,[33] by remarking that a small effort generates a greater pleasure and observation:

> Preterea, ut exerceantur ingenia, non adeo plene scribenda sunt omnia; na, que labore aliquo quesita sunt, placere magis consueverunt, et cum

31 The *Poetria Nova* by Geoffrey of Visnauf is among the texts that probably belonged to Boccaccio. See Mazza.

32 Geoffrey of Vinsauf compares the choice between the two stylistic principles of *amplificatio* and *abbreviatio* to choosing between a "river or a rivulet" (41), a simile that finds a contrasting echo in Cisti's reply "A Arno."

33 For *brevitas* as a topos and element of style in medieval literature, see Curtius 487–94.

> maiori diligentia conservari, quam que sponte sua in intellectum legentis accedunt. (XV.xii.3)
>
> [Besides, that the reader's mind may exert itself, one book should not be too full; whatever is got at the cost of a little labor is both more pleasing and more carefully observed than that which gets to the reader's mind of itself.] (136)

Moreover, Boccaccio explains, a brief text stimulates the minds of learned readers in a more effective way: "Uti brevia habent intelligentium exercere ingenia, sic et ampliora minus intelligentium revocare" [XV.xii.5; In short, as a condensed account exercises the educated mind, so a fuller appeals to the less educated; 136]. In this excerpt, Boccaccio suggests a direct correlation between the *brevitas* and a sophisticated mind. In the *Decameron*'s Epilogue, when dismissing the accusation that some stories are too long, the author states that while lengthy tales are a good pastime for the ladies, who have time to spare, brevity befits the students, who, on the other hand, employ their time profitably and have "negli studi gl'ingegni assottigliati" [Concl.21; sharpened their wits with the aid of their studies; 801] in the schools of Athens, Bologna, or Paris. Boccaccio here further explores the link between narrative form and refined wits, this time connecting it with the schools of philosophers. The mention of Bologna, as the place for philosophical studies, constitutes a remarkable connection with Cisti's wine, which is stored in a "piccolo orcioletto bolognese."

Cisti's crafty answer, "A Arno," thus contains a contrast between its conciseness and the *magnitudo* of the river, the *parvitas* of words and the *copiositas* of water supplied by the Arno. The baker expresses the distance between the "orcioletto" he has used so far to serve Geri Spina and his guests and the large flask presented by the servant. In Cisti's answer, Boccaccio condenses the analogy that there is between *brevitas* and *parvitas*, which hinges on both an intellectual and aesthetic appreciation.

In VI.2, Cisti's "arte," his guild, represents the humble veil that conceals his noble soul, which nonetheless emerges through his generous gesture of donating the wine. The real focus of the story, however, as suggested by the rubric, resides in the words that reveal his fine intellect, allowing him to send a message to Geri Spina consequently exposing the servant's deceit.

The topos of humility returns at the end of Pampinea's Introduction, where the storyteller, through the rhetoric of modesty, smallness, and brevity, presents her tale as a "novelletta assai piccola" that demonstrates the moral of the story in "poca cosa." Boccaccio draws together the discourse on the humble arts with that of the tale's modest length and content. Moreover, the humility of the *novelle* appears as a theme in the author's Introduction to Day Four, where he defends his poetic endeavour. In order to avoid the envy that usually targets the "alte torri o le più elevate cime degli alberi" [IV.Intro.2; lofty towers and the highest summits of trees; 284], the author states that he decided to dwell in deep valleys, a metaphor that signifies his choice of humility: "il che assai manifesto può apparire a chi le presenti novellette riguarda, le quali non solamente in fiorentin volgare e in prosa scritte per me sono e senza titolo, a ancora in istilo umilissimo e rimesso quanto il più si possono" [IV.Intro.3; This can very easily be confirmed by anyone casting an eye over these little stories of mine, which bear no title and which I have written, not only in the Florentine vernacular and in prose, but in the most homely and unassuming style it is possible to imagine; 284]. The choice of humility invests the content, the language, the form, and the style of the "novellette."[34] The passage echoes Boccaccio's *Accessus* to the *Esposizioni sopra la Comedia di Dante*, in which he describes Dante's style in the *Commedia* as "umile e rimesso" [Accessus.19; humble and unassuming; 42].[35] However, as in the Introduction to Day Four, the poetics of humility concerns the choice of the Florentine vernacular language as well. In the *Esposizioni*, Boccaccio claims that, while Petrarch "con la dottrina poetica riempiuta ogni parte, dove la lettera latina è conosciuta" [15.lit.96; has filled through his poetic teaching every place where the Latin language is known; 570], the light of Dante's genius "per alquanto tempo stata nascosa sotto la caligine del volgar materno" [15.lit.97; was for some time hidden in the shadows of the mother tongue; 570]. Dante's value is a light hidden under the soot ("caligine") of the vernacular, whereas Latin has contributed to the "maravigliosa e splendida fama" [15.lit.96; marvelous and splendid fame; 570] of Petrarch. Martin Eisner has pointed out that, in Boccaccio's interpretation, "Dante's use of the vernacular thus contributes to further a layer of allegory, because the vernacular text contains hidden meanings. The popular, vulgar quality of the vernacular becomes an allegory of allegory" (*Boccaccio and the Invention* 114). As a consequence, since vernacular poetry – and even more so prose – does not enjoy the same status bestowed on Latin poetry, it functions like the humblest place in the house described by Pampinea, where value is hidden and preserved.

---

34 See Lummus, "The *Decameron*," who finds in the defence of poetry in the *Genealogie* a theorization of the *Decameron*'s humble poetics, based on "the verisimilar narrations of events in a corresponding realistic language" (79).

35 For the text of Boccaccio's *Esposizioni*, I have used Padoan's 1965 edition for *Tutte le opere* and Papio's 2009 translation for Toronto's Lorenzo da Ponte Italian Library.

To conclude, Cisti's tale contains numerous metaliterary aspects that emerge when the tale is read in a joint analysis with Boccaccio's *Genealogie*. The analogies between the humble arts and the *novella* in vernacular, the noble soul and the hidden poetic truth, appear through the figures of Cisti and his wine. The Conclusion of the *Decameron* shows the final correlation between wine and *novelle*:

> nuocere e giovare possono, sì come possono tutte l'altre cose, avendo riguardo allo ascoltatore. Chi non sa ch'è il vino ottima cosa a' viventi, secondo Cinciglione e Scolaio e assai altri, e a colui che ha la febbre è nocivo? Direm noi, per ciò che nuoce a' febbricitanti, che sia malvagio? (Concl.9)
>
> [Like all other things in this world, stories, whatever their nature, may be harmful or useful, depending on the listener. Who will deny that wine, as Tosspot and Bibber and a great many others affirm, is an excellent thing for those who are hale and hearty, but harmful to people suffering from a fever?] (799)

The effect caused by the tales depends not only on the content of the stories themselves, but also on the reader. In a similar vein, Boccaccio writes in the *Genealogie*, as we saw above, "poets are at times obscure, but invariably explicable if approached by a sane mind" (60). The understanding of the poets' work is contingent also on the mind of the reader and its wholesomeness.

The reflection on tales and wine focuses on the presumed dangers posed by literature. Tales possess the potential of being an advantage or a risk, which the author first compares to wine, then to fire, and finally to weapons. In his argument, even if fire may present a hazard for the houses, it is still necessary in human beings' lives. In the same way, arms can offer defence or be the means of murder. The threefold parallelism hinges on the threat supposedly inherent to *fabulae*, which constitutes a fundamental component of the author's defence of his literary enterprise in the Epilogue and the Introduction to Day Four and again in the *Genealogie deorum gentilium*. Nonetheless, the analogy between tales and wine contains an aesthetic implication that the other two parallelisms do not hold. The connection between appreciation of wine and listening to stories – but also any act of aesthetic engagement, such as viewing a painting – pivots on the aesthetic practice and experience of the perceiver, rather than on the object itself.

By emphasizing the role of the listener, this consideration is part of the author's transferral of responsibility onto the readers. They are accountable for their response to the tales, as much as for their reading choices.

The readers can pick the stories to read like flowers in a meadow: "Niun campo fu mai sì ben coltivato, che in esso o ortica o triboli o alcun pruno non si trovasse mescolato tra l'erbe migliori … Tuttavia che va tra queste leggendo, lasci star quelle che pungono e quelle che dilettano legga" [Concl.18; No field was ever so carefully tended that neither nettles nor brambles nor thistles were found in it, along with all the better grass … And the fact remains that anyone perusing these tales is free to ignore the ones that give offence, and read only those that are pleasing; 800]. By intertwining the oenological simile with the garden metaphor, Boccaccio meditates on the role of readers in their own aesthetic experience.

Their common healing aspect reinforces the identification of tale and wine. As Giovanni Spani points out, the *Decameron* presents multiple instances where wine serves as a remedy, in line with the medical treatises of the time.[36] In comparing wine and tales, and their beneficial effects, Boccaccio draws together the curative properties of wine with the therapeutic efficacy of storytelling, as presented in the Proem and the Introduction.[37] To the censors concerned with the dangers of literature, Boccaccio replies by defending both its aesthetic and remedial legitimacy.

In light of the analogies between Cisti's tale and Boccaccio's theory of poetry, the story provides the fitting continuation of Madonna Oretta's *novella*. If VI.1 as a metanovella reflects on the rules of good storytelling, VI.2 represents a meditation on the nature of the *ars narrandi*, by indicating two of its most salient features: its ability to conceal truths and to awaken the intellect of its listeners (and readers). The fact that the protagonists of VI.1 and VI.2 are wife and husband invites the readers to peruse these two tales together, as in a metaliterary diptych. At the same time, a third link between VI.2 and VI.5 suggests that Cisti's and Giotto's stories, united by the topic of humble appearances, gloss each other, by focusing on different roles involved in the aesthetic experience. In VI.5, Giotto, as a painter, is "the maker of appearances" (Mazzotta, *World at Play* 239), but by pointing out the illusory nature of appearances themselves, he exposes Forese's literal-mindedness. In VI.2, instead, the concealing or revealing power of language is determined by the listener's abilities to perceive.

Cisti's tale, as promised by Pampinea, is a story about appearances and hidden treasures. His humble trade as a baker conceals his noble

36 See Spani 79–98.
37 See Marcus, *Allegory of Form* 112–15.

soul; his "orcioletto" contains a delicious wine; the literal sense of his *motto* veils the metaphorical meaning of his answer. It is a story for the non-literal-minded, who, like Geri Spina, can open the eyes of their intellect and enjoy what this "novelletta assai piccola" has to offer.

3 The Tale of Nonna de' Pulci (VI.3)

GUYDA ARMSTRONG

With its narrative focus on speech and gender, socially sanctioned behaviours, and the power and limitations of wordplay, the tale of Nonna de' Pulci exemplifies the fundamental themes and tensions of Boccaccio's *Decameron*. In only twelve short paragraphs – less than four pages in the most recent critical edition, and less than a column and a half of script in the autograph Hamilton manuscript – Boccaccio provides a compelling snapshot of a brief conversational exchange in a Florentine street that travels far beyond the narrative moment.[1] Read simply for its *motto*, this tale offers arguably the best example of a consummate female comeback in the *Decameron*, when Nonna returns fire on the toxic masculinity of her upper-class male interlocutors with a targeted riposte, an episode that still resonates across the centuries for its realistic characterization and continued relevance. But the art of the story, and the key to its effectiveness, lies in its formal qualities and hidden layers, which are economically signalled with Boccaccio's customary precision: the deployment of the pithy *motto* performing one aspect of the wider discussion of discourse that animates the text as a whole, and especially that of the relative capacities of men and women for "bel parlare" (the art of speaking well); a demonstration of contemporary sexual mores and the unequal social consequences of sexually transgressive behaviour for men and women; the question of fraud, both legal and moral; and the ever-present memory of the plague that rages still in the city.

It is therefore surprising that this tale has been so little discussed, and this essay will seek to explore some of the reasons for this critical

1 The tale can be found on fol. 74r–74v (i.e., a single leaf) of the Hamilton manuscript (Berlin Staatsbibliothek zu Berlin, Preußischer Kulturbesitz, Hamilton 90). The most recent critical edition, which I use throughout this essay, is in the BUR edition of the *Decameron* edited by Quondam, Fiorilla, and Alfano, 991–4.

absence. I will argue that, at heart, this is a story about rape and the societal sexual control of women, which to date is not an angle to be much noted in the literature.[2] We have lost sight of (or perhaps have never even seen) the actuality of the interpersonal interactions represented here: one woman, raped by an acquaintance of her complicit husband (and who is never mentioned in the literature about this tale, except as a plot point relating to the rapist); a second woman, subsequently sexually harassed on the street by a family friend in the company of the rapist himself. Nonna's verbal prowess and quick-wittedness is certainly to be celebrated, but what is less (if ever) acknowledged is the culture of toxic masculinity that produces both the harassment and her carefully modulated response. Perhaps the historical scholarly focus on the Sixth Day's themes of language and cleverness and the art of storytelling has calcified one particular academic reading of this narrative, and thereby rendered less visible the female experiences and subject positions articulated within and beyond it. The female protagonist, Nonna, is shown to demonstrate her prowess with archetypal male discourse, thereby making the reader think that the tale is primarily about language (and perhaps even, in the most progressive interpretations, offering a possible example of proto-feminism). However, in the critical concentration on her verbal prowess to the exclusion of all other considerations, this reading actually displaces female-oriented perspectives and subject positions, as well as materially displacing the other female protagonist of the tale, the rarely mentioned young wife who is subjected to sexual violence as a result of the avariciousness of her husband.

This essay will therefore direct an explicitly feminist gaze onto the tale and, for the first time, reflect on the situation of the *two* women, and on the historic condition of women in Trecento Italy that the tale exposes. Rather than simply saluting Nonna de' Pulci as a proficient wordsmith, who can more than hold her own with the other figures of Day Six, I will go further and will contend that she can and should be read as one of the iconic female characters of the *Decameron*, who stands for and beside the other female protagonist of the tale and the women of the *brigata*, becoming a resistant female reader in her own right. Using approaches deriving from

2 This peculiar oversight may be a manifestation of what Violet Jeffries has termed "manly delicacy," when addressing the remarkable lack of critical engagement with the description of the woman's body in the *Corbaccio*: cited in Armstrong, "Boccaccio and the Infernal Body" 84n2. The lack of close scholarly engagement with the tale is astonishing. The story is briefly discussed in Muscetta, *Ritratti e letture* 201–2; and Wallace 72–3, and at more length in Alonzo; and Stoppino 103–7. One brief but important feminist contribution can be found in Migiel 119–22.

cultural geography and spatial theory, I will likewise reflect on the ways in which this story navigates urban spaces, both past and present, and celebrates Nonna as an accomplished female actor in the storied streets of the city, again like the women of the *brigata*, and future readers.

The *Motto* and the Art of Female *Bel Parlare*

The tale of Nonna de' Pulci is the third of the Sixth Day, and the second of three on that day which have female protagonists, the other two being Madonna Oretta (VI.1) and Madonna Filippa (VI.7).[3] Like the other tales in this day, the tale is concerned with the theme of the *motto*, that is, of speech and especially "bel parlare," and importantly, Boccaccio makes it clear this skill is not one that is restricted by gender.[4] The *Decameron* itself, of course, is wholly concerned with the language arts, both in the delineations of its architectural superstructure (that is, the authorial metatextual frame and *cornice*) and in the stories themselves, but within this, there is a small group of characters who are designated as especially skilled in this area by the use of this phrase, and Nonna is named as one of these particularly gifted interlocutors.[5] Nonna's tale is formally the fifty-third of the whole book, and as such is situated very near to the centripetal fulcrum of the text as a whole, that of Madonna Oretta (VI.1, that is, story 51).[6] It is therefore tightly bound to

3 The best recent introduction to this *novella* (in Italian) can be found in the 2013 BUR edition, which includes a "Scheda introduttiva" to each day with a summary of each individual *novella*. For VI.3, see Alfano, "Giornata VI."

4 On the importance in the *Decameron* of speaking well, and thereby conducting oneself appropriately for the circumstances, see Quondam 18–20. Pamela Stewart defines the theme of the Sixth Day thus: "Argomento della giornata è, quindi, senza dubbio un tema strettamente legato all'arte oratoria, all'arte cioè del ben parlare, dell'esprimersi con abilità e efficacia"; indeed, the day "offre una specie di poetica, o meglio di *ars narrandi per exempla*" (*Retorica e mimica* 20).

5 Quondam describes the "ben parlanti" as "un gruppo folto e rappresentativo, di donne e uomini," comprising Coppo Domenichi (V.9); Madonna Oretta (VI.1); Bergamino (1.7); Guglielmo Borsieri (I.8); Nonna de' Pulci (VI.3); Giotto (VI.5); Guido Cavalcanti (VI.9); frate Cipolla, (VI.10); Niccoluccio Caccianimico (X.4); la Niccolosa (IX.5); and Torello (X.9) (19). No less than five of them are found in the Sixth Day, the day of the *motto*.

6 Following Stewart, among others, Quondam favours the model "a baricentro" of the *Decameron*'s textual architecture, in which the structural centrality of Oretta's tale reflects its thematic centrality "in quanto novella che affronta la questione del saper ben novellare" (73). Almansi likewise notes that this tale is "proprio nel centro geometrico della sua superficie testuale" (cited in Stewart, *Retorica e mimica* 24). Note that I am not counting the "extra" tale in the Introduction to Day Four in this count.

the discursively focused and narratively activated critical superstructure of the text, simultaneously progressing Oretta's demonstration that less is more when it comes to making a point and, as the third story of the day, intensifying this lesson with a more savage retort than the two which have preceded it.

But to situate the specifically female valences of the *motto* in this tale, i.e., the capacities of *women* in particular for such verbal prowess, we need to move back in the text and into the frame tale between Days Five and Six (that is, into the very structural fulcrum of the frame tale), where the theme for Day Six is first introduced. The discussion of women's verbal prowess and the necessity of their mastering brevity of speech is staged via a sequence of no fewer than six discrete narrative moments in this transitional *cornice* space between the days and tales. It begins with Elissa's statement of the next storytelling theme as she assumes her queenship at the Conclusion of the Fifth Day (V.Concl.3), which is followed by Dioneo's relentless suggestions of sexually explicit songs to conclude the day, suggestions which are increasingly impatiently closed down by the queen (V.Concl.7–14). The theme is picked up again with the argument between Tindaro and Licisca the next morning, which interrupts the *brigata* just as they are about to begin their storytelling for the day (again characterized with suggestive language [VI.Intro.4–11]), and skilfully handled by Elissa, who refers the business over to Dioneo and asks him to pronounce on it at the end of the day (VI.Intro.12). Filomena revisits the theme again in her Introduction to the first tale of the day (Madonna Oretta; VI.1.2–4), referring herself back to Pampinea's words introducing her concluding tale of Day One, and finally, this intratextual nexus is referred to directly by Lauretta as she embarks on her telling of the third story (VI.3.3). The interactions among the characters in the frame thus introduce and play out elements of the theme of the day, which are then reprised (often intratextually) in the individual *novelle*.

It is worth reviewing these textual moments in sequence so as to set Nonna's tale within this wider debate. At the conclusion of Dioneo's tale at the end of Day Five, the new Queen Elissa announces the theme, saying:

> Noi abbiamo già molte volte udito che con be' motti o con risposte pronte o con avvedimenti presti molti hanno già saputo con debito morso rintuzzare gli altrui denti o i sopravegnenti pericoli cacciar via; e per ciò che la materia è bella e può essere utile, voglio che domane con l'aiuto di Dio infra questi termini si ragioni, cioè di chi, con alcun leggiadro motto

tentato, si riscotesse, o con pronta risposta o avvedimento fuggì perdita o pericolo o scorno. (V.Concl.3)

[Already we have heard many times how various people, with some clever remark or ready retort, or some quick piece of thinking, have been able, by striking at the right moment, to draw the teeth of their antagonists or avert impending dangers. This being so splendid a topic, and one which may also be useful, I desire that with God's help our discussion on the morrow should confine itself to the following: those who, on being provoked by some verbal pleasantry, have returned like for like, or who, by a prompt retort or shrewd manoeuvre, have avoided danger, discomfiture or ridicule.] (441)[7]

In her first words as queen, Elissa highlights here the ability of mottoes, or "risposte pronte" [ready retorts], to deflect the bites of others with appropriately sized bites of their own ("debito morso"), or to escape danger.[8] The action of biting, and biting *back*, is thus introduced immediately as a remedy against verbal (or physical) attacks from others, a point reiterated by Elissa in the second part of her speech, where she carefully outlines the formal theme of the day, expanding on the "sopravegnenti pericoli" to show that these may encompass "loss, peril, or scorn" ("perdita, pericolo o scorno").[9] In most interpretations of this tale, Nonna's accomplished verbal performance is usually read merely to emphasize the wit and aptness of her riposte over any explicit social or political interpretation.[10] But her words are very much more than this; following Elissa's directive, we can read them for their speech act function, as a means of escape and self-preservation, and a tool of social and retributive justice. In this way, we can move from a merely rhetorical debate into the social world outside the text, with an analysis which considers the very real physical dangers of sexual and reputational violence to a woman in elite Trecento Florentine society.[11]

7 English translations are taken from McWilliam, although in places I offer alternatives.

8 Note that, for example, J.M. Rigg's translation of this phrase gives more of a sense of the meaning: "how to repugn with apt checks the bites of others."

9 My phrasing here cites that of Rigg's translation, accessed via the Decameron Web.

10 One exception to this is Forni, who observes a similarity between this tale and I.9, in that both women are in conflict with a social superior, and that "the greatness of the victory is in proportion to the prestige of the interlocutor" ("Tale of the King" 218).

11 In fact, Milner has argued that the whole *Decameron* should be seen as "an extended speech act" ("Boccaccio's *Decameron*" 84).

Once the theme of the day is established, the *brigata* engage in their usual post-storytelling pursuits, but the courtly tone of their after-dinner entertainment is disrupted by Dioneo's choice of a sexually suggestive song (V.Concl.7). The song at first makes the women, and especially the queen, laugh ("Di che tutte le donne cominciarono a ridere, e massimamente la reina" [V.Concl.8; Whereupon all the ladies began to laugh, especially the queen; 441–2]) but she asks him to choose another, to which command he responds by suggesting no fewer than eight more in the same vein. Elissa's amusement begins to wane, although the others continue to laugh, and after two polite interventions ("No, dinne un'altra" [V.Concl.10; No … sing us another; 442]; and then, "Deh in malora! dinne una bella, se tu vuogli, ché noi non voglian cotesta" [V.Concl.12; Oh, confound you … if you're going to sing, choose something nice. We don't want to hear that one; 442]), she firmly asks him to stop his jesting (with the very loaded word "motteggiare"), else he will provoke her anger: "La reina allora un poco turbata, quantunque tutte le altre ridessero, disse: – Dioneo, lascia stare il motteggiare e dinne una bella; e se no, tu potresti provare come io mi so adirare" [V.Concl.14; All the ladies laughed except the queen, who was beginning to grow impatient with him. "No more of your nonsense, Dioneo," she said. "Sing us something pleasant, or you'll learn what it means to provoke my anger"; 442]. We should not forget the subject matter of the *novella* immediately preceding this one, also told by Dioneo – *novella* V.10, the tale of Pietro di Vinciolo and his sexual liaisons, which, with its allusions to homosexuality, sails close to the obscene. Elissa's response as queen can therefore be read as an attempt to restore decorum and bring the tale-telling back into the realms of the licit.[12] But, reading this passage in a more feminist key, and in anticipation of the tale to come, it is very striking that we see a male speaker making the women around him – and especially the female authority figure, Elissa – uncomfortable with his sexualized language, and refusing to stop, even when politely asked. Elissa, for her part, laughs along for a while, before firmly putting a stop to this line of joking; the banter is not so far from what Nonna de' Pulci is subjected to in the third tale, as we shall see.

The Sixth Day famously begins with the interruption from below stairs, when Licisca and Tindaro's off-stage argument breaks into the harmonious gathering. The subject matter is ribald in the extreme: the question of extramarital sexual relations and the likelihood of young

12 See Alfano, "Giornata V" 807.

brides still possessing their virginity on marriage.[13] This lively, not to say virulent, argument is presented in a lower register, thereby not only demonstrating the servants' vulgar disrespect of conversational conventions in terms of subject matter, speech volume, and interlocutory turn-taking, but also serving in itself as a comic inversion of the *brigata*'s more elevated discussion of these themes in the days of storytelling.[14] The scandalized women of the *brigata* laugh: "Mentre la Licisca parlava, facevan le donne sì gran risa, che tutti i denti si sarebbero loro potuti trarre" [VI.Intro.11; While Licisca was talking, the ladies were laughing so heartily that you could have pulled all their teeth out; 445], a striking loss of self-control in comparison to their usual modest demeanour. Muscetta has suggested that, rather than an instance of coarseness on their part, this instead might indicate "una nervosa dissimulazione d'imbarazzo e sorpresa" [a nervous dissimulation of embarrassment and surprise] a near-involuntary shocked response to the sexualized discourse of the servants inflicted upon them.[15] It is the mention of the teeth which startles even now, an image which occurs only once elsewhere when describing immoderate laughter in the *Decameron*, in IX.3.25, when the doctor Master Simone roars with laughter, mouth agape, at Calandrino's ascription of his pregnancy to an unnatural sexual position.[16] While sexually explicit comments are thus shown to produce literal open-mouthed affective behaviours in the intradiegetic and hypodiegetic auditors, it is also important to note here that the teeth motif (first broached in Elissa's presentation of the theme, in V.Concl.3) will return again at the start of Lauretta's tale of Nonna de' Pulci.

The uses and abuses of words, then, are the subject of this day, and Filomena makes it clear that this is a subject of particular concern to women, as she introduces the first tale of Day Six (VI.1.2–4). In her preamble, Filomena underlines how brief and witty speech is especially desirable for women, since it is better for women not to speak at length ("quanto piú alle donne che agli uomini il molto parlar si disdice"); but alas, few women remain who are able to either produce a ready witticism or understand one, to the general shame of them all ("general vergogna di tutte noi" – a phrase which is curiously left untranslated in the

13 The following discussion is indebted to Alfano, "Giornata VI" 949–51.

14 See Alfano, "Giornata VI" 949.

15 Cited in Alfano, "Giornata VI" 949.

16 "il maestro Scimmione rideva sì squaccheratamente, che tutti i denti gli si sarebber potuti trarre" (IX.3.25). Cf. Alfano, "Giornata VI" 950.

Penguin translation).[17] Filomena here echoes the words of Queen Pampinea as she introduces her concluding tale to the First Day (I.10.3–5), an echo which proceeds virtually word for word until Filomena stops, and notes that Pampinea has said all this already. This verbal cue sends us back to the end of the First Day, and we note that Pampinea actually goes much further than Filomena and extends her criticism beyond the women gathered in the group ("tutte noi") to all women alive ("general vergogna è di noi e di tutte quelle che si vivono"; I.10.4), continuing on to lambaste modern women for their lack of virtue, their attentiveness to superficial ornament and self-beautification, and, most importantly, their inability to converse (I.10.6–7). There is much to note in this abrupt turn to misogyny: the association of women's intellectual capacities and verbal prowess in speech with their supposed predilection for ornament, and their self-deception as to their virtuousness, will be reprised elsewhere in Boccaccio's works, most obviously in the *Corbaccio*. The word-for-word reprisal of this theme by Filomena in the opening tale of the second half of the *Decameron* – with a cue to the intradiegetic auditors and external readers that this has previously been expanded on by Pampinea – underlines the importance of this framing both to the text as a whole and specifically to the matter of women's speech in the Sixth Day.[18] And operating on Boccaccio's common rule of threes, the narrator of the third story of the Sixth Day, Lauretta, herself makes the thematic link to both these prior discussions of this theme, when she says "Piacevoli donne, prima Pampinea e ora Filomena assai del vero toccarono della nostra poca vertù e della bellezza de' motti" [VI.3.3; Lovesome ladies, there is much truth in what both Pampinea and Filomena have been saying about the beauty of repartee and our own lack of skill in its use; 452]. From the very first words of its narrator, Nonna's tale is therefore framed as the next narrative contribution to the ongoing debate about women and language.

17 Filomena here emphasizes a seemly brevity of speech as a desirable quality in women, that is, in their own authorial production. However, note that brevity is not such a concern for female literary *consumption* when receiving male-authored texts, according to the Author's Conclusion, since they have plenty of time on their hands (Concl.21).

18 Stewart was the first to identify the significance of this repetition to the underpinning narrative structures of the *Decameron*, noting the strong similarities between the First and Sixth Days, and thus the continuities of this theme, of women's verbal capacities and their "onestà" (*Retorica e mimica* 28–33). See also Cottino-Jones, *Order from Chaos* 103–4.

Florence, Dante, Boccaccino, and the Memories of the City

It is well known that the tales of the Sixth Day have explicit Florentine and Tuscan connections, and this story is one of four of this day which are located inside the city, the others being the second, sixth, and ninth tales.[19] The physical location of the narrative action within the city walls unites this tale to the frame setting of the *brigata*'s tale-telling, and thus to Boccaccio's wider intellectual project and his characterization of a peculiarly Florentine attribute of "ben parlare." Likewise the relative closeness in time of the tales on this day – all of which take place within some fifty years of the narrative "present day" in 1348 – reinforces the narrative realism with a highly localized intimacy with the inhabitants of the city, and its artistic and literary traditions.[20] Indeed, the main protagonist, Monna Nonna de' Pulci, is already personally known to the *brigata*, as the narrator, Lauretta, points out, in what is famously the first point in the diegesis where the plague intrudes into the storytelling space:[21]

> una giovane la quale questa pistolenzia presente ci ha tolta donna, il cui nome fu monna Nonna de' Pulci, cugina di messere Alesso Rinucci e cui voi tutte doveste conoscere: la quale essendo allora una fresca e bella giovane e parlante e di gran cuore, di poco tempo avanti in Porta San Piero a marito venutane. (VI.3.8–9)

> a young woman (now, alas, no longer with us, having died in middle age during this present epidemic), whose name was Monna Nonna de' Pulci. You all know the person I mean – she was the cousin of Messer Alesso Rinucci, and at the time of which I am speaking she was a fine-looking girl in the flower of youth, well-spoken and full of spirit, who had recently been married and set up house in the Porta San Piero quarter. (453)

The main protagonists mentioned in the tale are all documented Florentine figures, closely embedded in the tight networks and territorial spaces of the city. First of all we have Nonna herself, a daughter of

19 On the Florentinity of the day, see in the first instance the Introduction to this volume, and also Alfano, "Giornata VI" 953–4.

20 See Alfano, "Giornata VI" 954.

21 The only other mention of the plague to occur within the days of storytelling is by Dioneo, at the conclusion to this day, when he refers to "la perversità di questa stagione" (VI.Concl.9). Cf. Alfano, "Giornata VI" 960.

the noble Pulci family, and her (unnamed) newlywed husband, who the archival record suggests was Passa Passavanti, an associate of the Pazzi family. A "Lady Lapa, called Nonna, once daughter of Uberti de' Pulci, then wife of Passa Passavanti, and later wife of Master Manni de' Donati" is mentioned in a notarial act of 1340.[22] There is also her cousin Alesso Rinucci, a Florentine politician, named here as one of her relations, and, most prominently for the action, another distant relative of hers, Antonio degli Orsi, the bishop of Florence. In the first part of the tale, the bishop Antonio degli Orsi takes primary place, on the occasion of his hosting his friend the Catalan captain Dego della Ratta, marshal of King Robert of Naples, on a diplomatic visit to Florence, which is thought to have taken place in either 1310 or (more likely, according to Branca) 1317–18, either way some thirty or forty years before the time of the supposed telling of this tale.[23] We do not know exactly when the second part of the tale takes place, when Nonna meets the bishop and Dego della Ratta in the street, but we are told that it is the feast day of St John, that is, 24 June, the feast day of the patron saint of the city, and thus a time and place of immense significance for its inhabitants.

The cityscape and the precise geolocation of its inhabitants are similarly critical to Boccaccio's narrative worldbuilding. Nonna is a daughter of the Pulci, whose historic family residence was close to the river, near the Piazza della Signoria, and Lauretta tells us that she had moved across town to the house of her new husband, in the Porta San Piero district, as would be usual on marriage. Indeed, the location for the second part of the tale is specified right down to the street, "la via onde il palio si corre" [the street where the palio is run], in the sestiere just to the east of the cathedral.[24] This whole area was controlled by the Donati

22 MS Magliabechiano XXV 591, fol. 404. "Domina Lapa vocata Domina Nonna filia quondam Uberti de Pulcis uxor quondam Passe Passavantis et postea uxor Domini Manni de Donatis" (Boccaccio, *Decameron* [1992] 2:728n7). Antonio degli Orsi was bishop of Florence between 1309 and his death in 1322 (Boccaccio, *Decameron* [1992] 2:727n1). On Florentine kinship and neighbourhood relations, see Eckstein, "Neighborhood."

23 See Boccaccio, *Decameron* [1992] 2:727n2.

24 The *palio* was run from Porta al Prato to Porta alla Croce, via Borgo degli Albizi and Porta San Pier Maggiore, where Nonna lived (Boccaccio, *Decameron* [1992] 2:728n5). For an excellent summary of the lives and spaces of the Florentine elite families, see Najemy, "Florentine Politics" 19–54. Lauretta's location of Nonna within her neighbourhood here is an example of what Eckstein has called a "prepositional relationship with the urban environment, whereby Florentines instinctively positioned themselves in relation to places that they knew firsthand and the people who filled them" ("Prepositional City" 1235–6).

family, and in fact one hitherto unremarked implication of this notarial document (if it does in fact refer to the historic Nonna) is its mention of the fact of her second marriage, to one Manni de' Donati (a marriage which links her explicitly to the family of Dante, who married Gemma Donati sometime between c. 1290 and 1295).[25]

The importance of the streets of Florence to several of the tales of the Sixth Day has been well noted (e.g., in relation to VI.2 and VI.9), but this is not an aspect which has been particularly highlighted for this tale.[26] Yet the emphasis on Nonna's residence in Porta San Piero is hugely significant in activating an intimate and very personal evocation of family histories and literary genealogies of this so recently lost world, as well as allowing us to reconstruct the gendered spatial dynamics of this tale. Strikingly, Boccaccio's father, Boccaccio di Chellino or Ghellino, is recorded as living in the quartiere San Pier Maggiore from 1314, having moved there from the quartiere San Frediano, and thus he would have been living there (with his young son) at the time of this supposed encounter in 1317/18.[27] While the future second marriage of Nonna de' Pulci is not germane to the tale being told at the time of this encounter, it can of course be presumed to be known by the *brigata* members who know her. In this way the ritualistic naming of her family and home subtly also draws the historical author into this particular time and place, effecting a breaking of the fourth wall in this moment of memory and memorialization. Nonna's life, and death, thus trigger a matrix of Dantean associations – of kin, in the Donati family, and via co-location in space, with her home in the historic city walls, that is, the "picciol cerchio" (*Par.* 16.125) mentioned by Dante's own ancestor Cacciaguida in his extended memorialization of the great families of Florence of yore.[28] But more than that, she represents a call back to Boccaccio's own youth in the city, and his own personal bereavements of the plague, which saw the loss of his own father and his second wife. As ever in Boccaccio, as we will see, Dante is the catalyst for his combinatory strategies, interwoven into the layering of personal biography, intertextual reference, and narrative incident.

---

25 See Najemy, "Florentine Politics" 22, and Eckstein, "Neighborhood."

26 E.g., see Alfano, "Giornata VI" 954.

27 On Boccaccino's residence in San Pier Maggiore, see Zafarana; and Sapegno. We know, too, that Boccaccino's second wife, Bice dei Bostichi, was distantly related to the historical Beatrice Portinari and note that Beatrice's father, Folco Portinari, was elected prior of the sestiere di San Piero in 1282, 1285, and 1287.

28 All quotations and translations from the *Commedia* are taken from Hollander's facing-page translations.

Perhaps it is for this reason that the plague rips through the narrative veil at this point for the first time since the Introduction to Day One. The city of Florence is the setting and the catalyst for the two narrative events related in this tale, inasmuch as Dego della Ratta has come there for diplomatic business. And in both episodes, grand geopolitics and the lives of men collide violently (in the first instance) and humiliatingly (in the second) with the domestic lives of women, in their personal spaces. For the first young wife, the intimate home space is violated through a betrayal, while for the second, the resources of the city, her birthright, and the public spectatorship of the street and piazza, her home ground, mean that she is able to take a measure of action against the routine male invasion of her personal space. With Boccaccio underlining that all of the women of the *brigata* know this woman – "voi tutte doveste conoscere" (VI.3.8) – he makes her one of them. The Nonna they knew, in their narrative reality of the late 1340s, was an older woman, but she is remembered here as she was in her youth, young and beautiful, quick-witted and good-hearted, a woman who walked the same streets that they did, and who has experienced the same grotesquely gendered power imbalances that they have. The warm and intimate characterization of Nonna as part of their social world (now destroyed for all of them by the plague, which killed her), unparalleled anywhere else in the *Decameron*, signals a tacit solidarity among these women, based in a universalizing subjectivity in their condition as women, with all the constraints upon them. This female solidarity is not necessarily visible to the men of the *brigata*, or indeed to external readers, but it is coded into the text for those who choose to see it. And we know that at the tale's conclusion, there is a general satisfaction with her retort from all the listeners: "Tacevasi già la Lauretta e da tutti era stata sommamente commendata la Nonna" [VI.4.2; When Lauretta was silent, and they had all paid glowing tribute to Monna Nonna; 454]. As Alfano has noted, "la Narratrice riprende così un piccolo aneddoto reso piccante dal pettegolezze locale e lo trasforma nell'esemplare illustrazione di un codice condiviso (e cittadino) che regola la retorica e il comportamento" [Alfano, "Giornata VI" 960; the Narrator thus takes up a brief anecdote that has been made spicy by local gossip and transforms it into an exemplary illustration of a shared (civic) code that regulates both rhetoric and behaviour]. Nonna's skilful and witty riposte pleases all the listeners, but there just might be a degree more satisfaction from those who identify more strongly with her harassment.

Structures of the Tale

As previously noted, the tale itself is very short (twelve paragraphs in total in the modern editions), and can be divided narratively and structurally into four main sections. The first section (VI.3.1–5) contains the introductory formulas of the tale: the rubric (VI.3.1), the frame narrative detailing the positive response of the listeners to the previous tale (that of Cisti the baker), the transition between storytellers from Pampinea to Lauretta (VI.3.2), and the opening part of Lauretta's direct speech, where she addresses her audience and outlines the relationship of her tale to the theme of the day. The second section (VI.3.6–7), only two paragraphs in length, is the first of the two narratives within this tale, what we might even think of as the back story, since narrative focus is drawn to Nonna in the rubric. At the time when Antonio degli Orsi was bishop of Florence, the Catalan nobleman and notorious womanizer Dego della Ratta paid a visit to the city and took a fancy to one unnamed young noblewoman who was a niece of the bishop's brother (VI.3.6); having heard that the woman's husband was avaricious and a very nasty piece of work, despite his noble birth, Dego conspired with him to pay him five hundred gold florins if he would let him sleep with his wife. Dego forged the payment, by gilding silver coins of lower value, then forced himself on the wife against her will, and paid the husband. When this tale became known to everyone, the avaricious husband became the target of ridicule and jokes, while the bishop pretended to know nothing about it (VI.3.7).

The third section moves the narrative to an unspecified later time period, again in Florence. The bishop and the captain are riding together through the streets of Florence eyeing up women, when the bishop recognizes Nonna and points her out to his friend. Putting his arm around Dego's shoulders, he asks Nonna what she thinks of him, and whether she could make a conquest of him (VI.3.8–9). Nonna, knowing these words discredit her chaste reputation in front of a large crowd of onlookers, returns the jibe blow for blow, saying that, actually, in the event that he conquered her, she would want to be paid in good coin (VI.3.10). The fourth and final section (VI.3.11–12) is the resolution of the story, relating the two men's reaction to this public barb: they slink off, shamed and not looking at each other, without saying anything else to her that day. The narrative formula is repeated with the next tale, where we learn in the *cornice* that the *brigata* thoroughly approves of Nonna's retort.

Part 1: Opening Formulas and the Art of the Apposite Bite (VI.3.1–5)

The first part of the tale contains the conventional opening structures of rubric, *cornice* narrative, and the introductory speech by the narrator, Lauretta, setting out the theme. The rubric floats in the narrative space between the tales, serving as a referent for the reader, rather than as a feature of the internal diegesis, but in its prefatory, privileged position on the page, it offers a parallel line of argument and thematic framing above that articulated by the characters in the *cornice*.[29] It reads: "Monna Nonna de' Pulci con una presta risposta al meno che onesto motteggiare del vescovo di Firenze silenzio impone" [VI.3.1; With a quick retort, Monna Nonna de' Pulci put a stop to the unseemly banter of the bishop of Florence; 452]. Nonna is introduced as the focal point of the *novella*, one of only two woman in the book to be designated with the contracted title "Monna" in the rubrics (the other being Monna Belcolore, VIII.2), while the other two female protagonists of Day Six, Oretta and Filippa, are both referred to as Madonna in their rubrics.[30] The rubric underlines the theme of *motteggiare* above all else, introducing the "meno che onesto" [less than honest] words of the bishop of Florence, and counterbalancing them with her concluding imposition of silence. The gracious storytelling conventions of the *brigata* then follow, with everyone commending both Cisti's riposte to Messer Geri Spina and his subsequent generous gift of the wine at the conclusion of Pampinea's tale, and the queen (Elissa) requesting that Lauretta go next, a request to which she accedes "lietamente" (VI.3.2). Directing her storytelling to the "Piacevol

29 On the peculiar narrative and paratextual functions of the *Decameron* rubric, see Daniels, "Where Does the Decameron Begin?"

30 Titles are not very much used in the rubrics, especially for women: in addition to Oretta and Filippa, we find only Madama Beritola (II.6) and Madonna Isabella (VII.6); Madonna Beatrice (VII.7), Monna Belcolore (VIII.2); Madonna Francesca (IX.1); Madonna Dianora (X.5); also Ser (I.1), Maestro (I.10; VI.5; VIII.9; IX.3), Frate (IV.2; V.10; VII.2), Messer (VI.2; IV.8; VI.5; VII.6; X.4; X.5); Re (X.6; X.7; X.9). It seems clear that titles of this sort are mainly used for women when their respectable married status is relevant to the narrative. Interestingly, in VIII.2, Monna Belcolore is also sexually importuned by a cleric, and agrees to sleep with him for the price of his fine woollen cloak; the cleric then manages to have his payment returned by the agency of her husband. The adulterous sexual encounter is played for laughs in the later tale, with the husband facilitating the repayment of the fee rather than facilitating the sexual encounter, but the reworking of key narrative elements between them is none the less striking.

donne" (a conventional opener for virtually all the narrated tales in the *Decameron*),[31] she reminds her audience (mixed-sex, but coded female in the address) of the ongoing debates they have been having about women's diminished capacity for accomplished wordplay, first in the Introduction to the First Day by Pampinea, and earlier on the Sixth Day, in the Introduction to the first tale by Filomena (VI.1.3). As previously discussed, the mention of these key interventions cues the readers (via the fictional internal auditors) to remember or consult these debates without having to rehearse them again. One point, however, is worth reiterating:

> oltre a quello che de' motti è stato detto, vi voglio ricordare essere la natura de' motti cotale, che essi, come la pecora morde, deono così mordere l'uditore e non come 'l cane: per ciò che, se come il cane mordesse il motto, non sarebbe motto ma villania. (VI.3.3)[32]
>
> [but I should like to remind you that apart from what has already been said on this subject, the nature of wit is such that its bite must be like that of a sheep rather than a dog, for if it were to bite the listener like a dog, it would no longer be wit but abuse.] (452)

By reprising the biting metaphor, first introduced by Elissa in her designation of the theme of the Sixth Day, Lauretta firmly locates her tale in this theme, and indeed, it is striking to note how far the rubric echoes this, thematically and in its reprisal of key words ("Noi abbiamo già molte volte udito che con be' *motti* o con *risposte* pronte o con avvedimenti *presti* molti hanno già saputo con debito morso rintuzzare gli altrui denti o i sopravegnenti pericoli cacciar via" [V.Concl.3; Already we have heard many times how various people, with some clever remark or ready retort, or some quick piece of thinking, have been able, by striking at the right moment, to draw the teeth of their antagonists or avert impending dangers; 441, emphasis added]). Lauretta notes (very politely) that comic rhetoric is aggressive, and therefore it is appropriate that the comeback should bite, but not mortally wound,

31 Only VII.1 begins "Signor mio," and even in this case, shifts to the female audience with "carissime donne" in the second sentence.

32 This point will be underlined once more when the keywords "mordere" and "motto" recur in the last sentence of the tale. Lauretta is explicitly teaching the *brigata* a lesson about women and speech management, and by extension, the external audience as well.

the aggressor, so that the proprieties of social interactions are respected. And she commends both Oretta and Cisti for having done this "ottimamente." But, she proceeds, sometimes it is in fact appropriate to bite back like a dog, if you have been attacked, and therefore, rhetorically, one should always be sensitive to the context and regulate one's speech accordingly:

> È il vero che, se per risposta si dice e il risponditore morda come cane, essendo come da cane prima stato morso, non par da riprender come, se ciò avvenuto non fosse, sarebbe: e per ciò è da guardare e come e quando e con cui e similmente dove si motteggia. (VI.3.4)

> [It is of course true, in the case of repartee, that when someone bites like a dog after having, so to speak, been bitten by a dog in the first place, his reaction does not seem as reprehensible as it would have been had he not been provoked; and one therefore has to be careful over how, when, on whom, and likewise where one exercises one's wit.] (452)

There are therefore circumstances which justify what might be considered an excessive response in other contexts, and which might allow the usual social conventions of gender and rank to be disregarded if there are more compelling moral reasons. The presentation of the dilemma is very carefully handled by Lauretta, but reading in the feminist key, we cannot but remember all the gendered dialogic interactions which have come before, from Dioneo's dishonourable intervention forcing the women of the *brigata* into compliance at the Conclusion to Day Five, through Oretta's skilful management of the male ego in VI.1, and now, a new example of an abuse of power by a high-status cleric, who forgot to observe the unwritten social rules of *motteggiare* and paid the price:

> Alle quali cose poco guardando già un nostro prelato, non minor morso ricevette che 'l desse: il che io una piccola novella vi voglio mostrare. (VI.3.5)

> [To these matters, one of our prelates paid so little attention on one occasion, that he received no less painful a bite than he administered; and I should now like to tell you, in a few words, how this came about.] (452)

The use of "nostro" for the cleric reiterates the particularly Florentine dimension of the tale to come, a setting in line with the previous two of the day, which will be underlined repeatedly throughout this tale.

Part 2: Masculine Sociability and Covert Crimes (VI.3.6–7)

Following this economical introduction, the second part of the tale moves back into a more distant time frame, although this is not immediately apparent to the listeners (and readers): the occasion of the Catalan marshal Dego della Ratta's diplomatic visit to Florence, at the time when Antonio degli Orsi was bishop. The locating of this first narrative episode on the occasion of this diplomatic visit to Florence quickly establishes the political importance and social standing of these two male protagonists, as they confidently traverse the masculine social and political spaces of the city as powerful agents of its internal and external relations.[33] Florence is the backdrop to their public and private business, a city which is naturally and uncontroversially made by and for men, and animated by what Guido Ruggiero has termed "a regime of masculine sociability" (Ruggiero 296). In the man's world of Florence, "masculine sociability" was the primary means of performance of self, and a preeminent way therefore of demonstrating one's own prowess in social behaviour, that is, *virtù*. Verbal quick-wittedness and a sensitivity to social appropriateness are the Florentine male values par excellence, which is why, of course, this tale is framed around the question of whether women can exceptionally also possess these qualities.

Both the bishop and his friend are presented by Boccaccio in laudatory terms which indicate their high social rank and supposedly similarly elevated characters: the bishop is a "valoroso e savio prelato," while Dego is "un gentile uom catalano ... maliscalco per lo re Ruberto" [VI.3.6; a wise and worthy prelate; a Catalan nobleman ... Marshal to King Robert of Naples; 452]. Yet we readers already know from the rubric that the bishop has an honesty problem, while the internal Florentine auditors of the *brigata* (and the characters within the *novella*) might be expected to be aware of a more serious moral failing, that is, that the bishop is an infamous corrupt cleric. Dino Compagni condemns him as a simoniac and "non di santa vita" [not of a holy life] in his *Cronica* of c. 1310–12, a text which either was roughly contemporaneous with, or possibly preceded, this visit.[34]

33 See Trexler for the ritualized social interactions of the Florentine city and body politic, especially the chapter "The Ritual of Foreign Relations," on how foreign dignitaries were welcomed into the city by high-ranking citizens (279–330, esp. 306–15).

34 Qtd. in Boccaccio, *Decameron* [1992], 2:727n1. Alonzo writes that Compagni makes the bishop "un modello di quell'uso distorto della moneta," by noting his corrupt political and financial dealings, and suggests that Boccaccio, some decades later, then transfers the notorious fraudulent qualities of the bishop onto the character of Dego (87–8 [88]).

These ironically presented attributes will be undermined further even by the end of the sentence, when we learn that the diplomatic visitor is a very handsome man, and a more than prolific womanizer, with a predatory eye for women, and in particular for a young relative of his friend the bishop: "il quale essendo del corpo bellissimo e vie più che grande vagheggiatore, avvenne che fra l'altre donne fiorentine una ne gli piacque, la quale era assai bella donna e era nepote d'un fratello del detto vescovo" [VI.3.6; being a fine figure of a man, and inordinately fond of women, Messer Dego pursued a number of the Florentine ladies, for one of whom, a ravishing beauty, he conceived a particular liking, and she happened to be the niece of the Bishop's brother; 452]. One might wonder exactly when Dego della Ratta would have had an opportunity to view this young woman, since Trecento Florence was a city in which young middle- and upper-class women lived in conditions of virtual enclosure, emerging from the family home (either that of their fathers, or if married, of their husband's family) very rarely, and generally then only when chaperoned.[35] Women would attend church and emerge onto the streets for ritual festivities or to travel to events in private houses, but the patrician women of Florence (that is, the class of women depicted in – and telling – this story) lived lives of enforced seclusion for much of the time.[36] The circumstances of his seeing her are not specified, but it is safe to surmise that he would have viewed her (perhaps not even speaking to her) either in a private house belonging to the extended family or perhaps in church, both of which are social spaces which might be expected to be a safe environment for a young married woman.

35 There have been many important studies of the lives of women in Renaissance Italy. See in the first instance the seminal studies of Klapisch-Zuber on Florentine women living within traditional kinship structures, such as "La femme et la lignage florentin (xive–xvie siècles)" and *La maison et le nom*. English versions of some of these works are found in her *Women, Family and Ritual in Renaissance Italy*. See also King.

36 In an important essay, Tomas notes, however, that upper-class women could travel around the city and even beyond, in certain conditions, and their ability to do so increased as they grew older (324). The conditions of the social confinement of women are highly visible in Boccaccio's works, for those who care to see them, and indeed he often locates his women in spaces where their confinement and the navigation thereof becomes a plot device in itself (e.g., Fiammetta's adulterous sexual transgression is much easier to manage in the external leisure space of the thermal baths, rather than if it took place in the closely controlled surveillance society of the patrician inner-city family complex).

An iniquitous plan is thus devised, with the connivance of the men concerned:

> E avendo sentito che il marito di lei, quantunque di buona famiglia fosse, era avarissimo e cattivo, con lui compose di dovergli dare cinquencento fiorin d'oro, e egli una notte con la moglie il laciasse giacere. (VI.3.7)
>
> [Having learnt that the lady's husband, though he came of a good family, was very greedy and corrupt, he came to an arrangement with him whereby he would give him five hundred gold florins for allowing him to sleep for one night with his wife.] (453)

Once again Boccaccio sets up the contrast between social position and character, noting that the husband is avaricious and wicked, despite his coming from a prominent family; the irony is, of course, that he is the only person formally to be designated as "cattivo" in the tale (that is, in contrast to the glowing descriptions of the bishop and Dego), although his faithless betrayal of his wife and their socially sanctioned marital bond comes about entirely as a result of his deal with Dego and, implicitly, the bishop. The constant Florentine background soundtrack of gossip, rumour, and reputation-policing, one of the key themes of this tale, is also functional to this plot point, with Dego "avendo sentito" [having heard] of the husband's avariciousness and thus able to exploit his potential for corruption with the promise of a handsome payment in gold florins, the iconic coin of the city.[37]

However, just as the husband is corruptible, so is Dego corrupt, and instead of honouring his verbal contract with the payment of five hundred florins, he instead gilds five hundred coins of lower value, then pays them to the husband after having forced his wife to have sex with him:

> per che, fatti dorare popolini d'ariento, che allora si spendevano, giaciuto con la moglie, come che al contro al piacer di lei fosse, gliele diede. (VI.3.7)
>
> [But what he actually did was to gild five hundred coins of silver, called *popolini*, which were in everyday use at that period, and having slept with the man's wife against her will, he handed these over to the husband.] (453)

---

37 For a detailed discussion of the florin and *popolino*, including a discussion of the dates the *popolino* was in use and the bearing on the dating of this supposed event, see Alonzo, esp. 95–104.

The actual sexual assault is treated only in passing in a couple of clauses embedded within the main clause about the forging of the florins and their payment; the woman's resistance marginalized in a single phrase, noting simply that this was against her will ("come che al contro al piacer di lei fosse"). Can this be the reason why her experience and subject position have been for so long overlooked in the literature, the unsavoury details of the assault politely glossed over in favour of an analysis of the mechanics of the fraudulent transaction? Or is there a wider critical unwillingness to see and acknowledge the realities of the female condition, which have been so effectively erased here? The narrative in this first story is entirely concerned with the male figures, and focalized primarily on Dego, who sees a woman, cuts the deal, forges the coins, rapes her, and pays the husband. But this narrative erasure should not be at all surprising, since the account we have here is entirely representative of the power dynamic and legal status of wives in wider Florentine society, where a married woman was subject in every way to the will of her husband. In a passage which could have been coined especially for this particular tale, Margaret King has noted that "husbands exercised over their wives in private, and male authorities defended in public, a supremacy that was enhanced by age, backed by force, and rationalized by words" (38).[38] Thus in a conspiracy between a husband and a sexual aggressor invited into the home, as we see related here, a young married woman would be literally and physically overpowered, with very little redress left to her, apart from public opinion (which could in no way be relied on to take her side, such was the stigma of sexual dishonour).[39] The wife is legally and socially the property of her husband, a reality which is underlined in the most stark terms when Dego pays him for the use of her body.

In the telling here, the marital betrayal and implied sexual violence are of much less consequence than the forging of the money and the

38 On the social history of wives, see King 36–56 (esp. 40–2, for sexual directives within marriage).

39 Within the "honour"-based society of elite Trecento Florence, masculine control of women was intended to protect family honour, and thereby property rights, from the corruption and contamination from illicit sexual activity – especially before marriage, but also within it (the taboo of adultery), and even afterwards, as patriarchal family structures sought to control the property of widows and their dowries after the death of a spouse. Violent abuse in marriage could sometimes be used to justify a wife leaving her husband (King 42–3), but in general, in the legal record, rape and sexual exploitation were things that happened to lower-class women.

fraudulent transaction. Forgery in this period in Florence was a capital crime, that is, punishable by death, and so Dego della Ratta would be risking far more than his good standing in undertaking this criminal activity. Even more so than violence against the body, which we already know Dego is guilty of, the forging or counterfeiting of coins is a crime with a profound ethical dimension, which goes beyond the monetary value of the deception to the heart of issues of trust and honour and the social compact of citizens. And of course, the dishonour is all the greater when the coins in question are considered to symbolically embody the value system and financial worth of a territory, as the iconic florin did for Florence: it is nothing less than a crime against the state. It is for this reason that Dante's counterfeiter Maestro Adamo (like Dego della Ratta a counterfeiter of the florin and high-ranking practitioner of white-collar crime) is located in the tenth bolgia of the eighth circle of hell, that of the *falsatori di moneta*, and whose contrapasso is to have his aerial body distended and weighed down by dropsy (*Inf.* 30.49–129).[40] Adamo himself signals the peculiarly Florentine dimensions of his crime to Dante-*personaggio* through reference to the image of the patron saint which the coin bears: "io falsai / la lega suggellata del Batista; per ch'io il corpo sù arso lasciai" [*Inf.* 30.73–5; I forged / the coinage stamped with John the Baptist. / For that I left my body burned above]. Burning at the stake was the usual method of punishment for forgers in Tuscany,[41] but while the public penalties for counterfeiting coins were heavy indeed, in this tale (in the first narrative sequence, at least) the penalty falls only on the husband who sold the sexual use of his wife to the visiting dignitary:

> Il che poi sappiendosi per tutto, rimasero al cattivo uomo il danno e le beffe; e il vescovo, come savio, s'infinse di queste cose niente sentire. (VI.3.7)

> [Subsequently the story became common knowledge, so that the scoundrelly husband was not only cheated but held up to ridicule. And the Bishop, being a wise man, feigned complete ignorance of the whole affair.] (453)[42]

---

40 See Alonzo 105–7, for a discussion of Maestro Adamo.

41 For other punishments, see Alonzo 105–6.

42 We might consider whether the choices of some English translators (such as McWilliam's "scoundrelly") have given enough moral weight to the crimes of the husband, and what the effect of this might have been on the critical history of this tale in the anglophone world. In his 1930 translation of the *Decameron*, Aldington went even further in taking the side of the men, suggesting that Dego "happened to be specially in love with a very pretty Florentine woman … He had penny pieces

The episode reflects badly on all the men concerned, although only the husband pays a social price, being subjected to public scorn, as much for his gullibility in being cheated in the payment as for the societal taboo of having permitted his wife's sexual honour (and therefore his own and his kin's honour) to be corrupted in this way. The peculiarly Florentine codes of speaking and silence are operationalized here, with the town's rumour mill and verbal codes effectively policing the social behaviour of its inhabitants, with the husband mocked, and the complicit bishop observing the proprieties to protect himself. While there is no mention here of the wife's fate, she herself has been violated and dishonoured, and worse, with the complicity of her husband. In the worst-case scenario, she could herself be considered at risk of criminal proceedings as a woman having sex outside marriage (we need only think of the example of Madonna Filippa, in the seventh tale of this day, who is on trial for her life for taking a lover).[43]

The gendered social spaces of the city shape its narrative interactions. We start in the male public space in the first sequence of this section, when Dego and his fellow high-ranking politicians move through the city and into and out of its social spaces, where he is able to identify a specific young married woman he wants to sleep with. The narrative then moves into the private realm in the second part of this sequence, for the various illicit activities (the deal with the husband; the forging of the coins; the rape; the payment), and concludes back out in the public arena, where the events become known and widely discussed, with the public shaming of the husband, and the bishop's performance of ignorance. Interior space is implicitly gendered female, with women's confinement and enclosure within their family homes, but the incursion of the predatory Dego della Ratta disrupts the domestic space, and brings the aggressively masculine homosocial culture of the streets indoors into the safe family refuge. But the binaries are not so simple as that,

---

gilded and, after lying with the wife against her will, gave the husband this false money. This became known to everyone, and the harm and the joke were on the bad husband" (II. 24). An older anonymous translation, printed in 1904, by contrast, was highly condemning of the husband, even amplifying the condemnation: he is "abominably sordid and covetous"; Dego "obtained his desire contrary to her will and knowledge," and "the wretch became the common jest and scorn of mankind" (310–11).

43 The historical likelihood of Madonna Filippa's situation is discussed elsewhere in this volume; we should also note that there is evidence of Italian courts showing some sympathy for raped women and ill-treated wives. See King. As Nonna will show, while there is no guarantee of legal recourse, there is a less observed but still effective female rough justice in the verbal economy, as well.

since, as Ruggiero has noted, "how space is used ... can transform it profoundly, and ... the gendered use of space breaks down the modern concept of public and private that seems to turn around the home" (299).[44] The home is generally the space of women, but is breached and violently repurposed here by masculine conspiracy. But in the same way, the public street, generally the domain of men, can also be disrupted by a determined female actor on a mission.[45] Space, and narratives, can be overwritten, as Nonna is about to show.

Part 3: Gender and Justice in the Streets (VI.3.8–10)

The narrative now moves to an unspecified time after this iniquitous event; we do not know how much later (it could be weeks, or even years), but we are told it is "il dì di San Giovanni," the day of St John the Baptist, that is, the day of the patron saint of Florence, 24 June.[46] Boccaccio's situating of this culminating narrative event of this story on this particular day is by no means accidental: the feast of St John is the day when the city itself expresses its civic values with highly choreographed and semiotically charged display. More pragmatically for the plot, it is a day when the whole town, including its women, is out in the streets seeing and being seen. The bishop and his friend are out and about taking advantage of this in their usual sexually predatory way:

> usando molto insieme il vescovo e 'l maliscalco, avvenne che il dì di San Giovanni, cavalcando l'uno allato all'altro veggendo le donne per le vie onde il palio si corre. (VI.3.8)

> [The Bishop and the Marshal were frequently to be seen in one another's company, and one day, it being the feast of St John, they happened to be riding side by side down the street along which the *palio* is run, casting an eye over the ladies.] (453)

---

44 See also Eckstein, "Prepositional City" 1244, for a warning against the simple categorization of binary spaces as "public" or "private" in the premodern context.

45 Attentiveness to the multidimensional dynamics of space has had a profound effect on post-structuralist premodern cultural studies. In addition to the specific works on Florence cited here, see the fundamental studies by Gaston Bachelard, Michel de Certeau, and André Lefebvre; for a wider overview of the field and recent scholarship, see Armstrong, "Towards a Spatial Early Modern Translation Studies."

46 On the extended rituals around St John's Day, which included processions, feasts, celebratory masses, the formal display of shopkeepers' goods in the streets, ritualized civic offerings to the saint, and the concluding horse race, the *palio*, see Trexler 240–78.

The scene is all too easy to imagine in spatial terms: the two elite men, riding high above the pedestrians in an easy display of social and gender superiority, moving through the crowded streets as privileged masculine actors in the urban space, and looking at – and down on – the women walking or standing at the edges of the road. Their confidence and potential for aggression is amplified by the fact that they are on horseback, an acknowledged statement of virility in a city where courtship (and martial) rituals were often expressed by equestrian prowess.[47] As mature men of secure professional standing, the bishop and the marshal should be supposedly past the age of ostentatious masculine display on horseback, but in fact they continue to use it (albeit in a more sedate way) as would less mature *giovani*; this too may be an indication of their poor judgment and failure to observe the unwritten social norms of the city. Faced with a man on a horse, a woman's resources can be severely limited, as Oretta herself showed in VI.1 with her skilful dismount from an unpleasant metaphorical ride.

Riding alongside his friend, the bishop sees Nonna, points her out to his friend, and speaks to her:

> il vescovo vide una giovane la quale questa pistolenzia presente ci ha tolta donna, il cui nome fu monna Nonna de' Pulci, cugina di messere Alesso Rinucci e cui voi tutte doveste conoscere: la quale essendo allora una fresca e bella giovane e parlante e di gran cuore, di poco tempo avanti in Porta San Piero a marito venutane, la mostrò al maliscalco; e poi, essendole presso, posta la mano sopra la spalla del maliscalco, disse, "Nonna, che ti par di costui? crederestil vincere?" (VI.3.8–9)

> [the Bishop spotted a young woman (now, alas, no longer with us, having died in middle age during this present epidemic), whose name was Monna Nonna de' Pulci. You all know the person I mean – she was the cousin of Messer Alesso Rinucci, and at the time of which I am speaking she was a fine-looking girl in the flower of youth, well-spoken and full of spirit, who had recently been married and set up house in the Porta San Piero quarter. The Bishop pointed her out to the Marshal, then he rode up

47 Strocchia discusses how horsemanship served a performance of upper-class masculinity by the young men of the Florentine patriciate ("Theaters" 71–2). Young men would participate in public displays such as jousting and the famous horse race, but equestrian prowess was also central to day-to-day courtship rituals; for example, when "a Florentine youth rode past the house of his lady, he paused to strike the wall with his lance, with obvious symbolic implications for his manhood" (72).

beside her, clapped his hand on the Marshal's shoulder, and said: "How do you like this fellow, Nonna? Do you think you could make a conquest of him?"] (453)

While the action as recounted here takes just a few seconds, the first sentence above in fact encompasses decades of narrative time. Nonna's personal history (her kinship ties to the Rinucci family, the circumstances of her marriage, her recent move to Porta San Pietro), and her tragic future fate to die of the plague (which is unbeknownst to her at the time of this tale) are all given here in an extended ellipsis spliced in between the bishop's seeing her and – fatally – showing her to his friend. In one complex sentence, the plague and the horrific realities of the *brigata*'s present-day existence briefly break through into the frame, only for Boccaccio to swiftly return the auditors and readers back into the more reassuring and safely bounded space of the story. It is so subtly done that a casual reader might not even notice the vertiginous time travelled in these few lines, but this disorienting rupture gives the same brief and destabilizing glimpse into lived social realities as we have seen in the bland delineation of the sexual violence in the first sequence of the tale.[48]

The easy masculine homosociality and overall threatening dynamic are expressed spatially and now gesturally: the men are close enough to Nonna to speak to her (but on horseback, remember), "essendole presso," and their complicity and combined societal dominance are physically expressed by the bishop putting his arm around the marshal's shoulder. The encounter is verbally encoded as an apparent courtly appeal, but the aggression is clear: "Nonna, che ti par costui? crederestil vincere?" While the men might hide behind the defence of banter, Nonna immediately recognizes the very real danger of these words (and indeed, the dangerous record of these two particular men) and the threat which they pose to her. In a remarkable focalization shift at the start of paragraph 10, we are suddenly transported from the standard, third-person, male-identified perspective into Nonna's internal monologue and her awareness of the space and people around her:

> Alla Nonna parve che quelle parole alquanto mordessero la sua onestà o la dovesser contaminare negli animi di coloro, che molti v'erano, che l'udirono. (VI.3.10)

48 On the narrative mechanisms of time in the *Decameron*, see Cirilli.

> [It seemed to Monna Nonna that the Bishop's words made her out to be less than virtuous, or that they were bound to damage her reputation in the eyes of those people, by no means few in number, in whose hearing they were spoken.] (453)

The urban street space, so comfortable and visually stimulating for the men on horseback, offers very different meanings and experiences to a female pedestrian, even one on her marital home ground.[49] Space is not static, but dynamic; its meanings are not fixed, but mutate according to the people and things which pass through it, and narratives have perspectives, even if these are not all equally represented in their recording. Feast days were some of the few occasions when respectable Florentine upper-class women could be out unchaperoned in the streets, but the street was still a potentially dangerous space for them.[50] For Nonna, publicly visible and under threat from this uninvited interaction, the risks are both physical and reputational, just as they were for the young wife in the first narrative sequence. As Strocchia has noted, "The threat to personal and familial honor was especially acute for unsupervised women as they moved along the city's gendered pathways" ("Theaters" 61), and Nonna is put in the invidious position of being insulted at close range by a high-ranking cleric who had infamously facilitated, and then ignored, the rape of a married female family member and the subsequent defrauding of her husband, while now being in the company of the unpunished rapist and forger himself. The language used to describe her interior perspective on these words is striking: the insulting words have *bitten* at her modesty ("mordessero la sua onestà") and cannot but contaminate her ("la dovesser contaminare") in the opinion of the audience of bystanders.[51] The reprise here

49 See Strocchia, "Theaters" 56: "For urban dwellers open spaces brimmed with layered meanings and clusters of associations. The particular character of urban space at any moment depended on two interdependent features: first, on the people or objects moving through a space, charging it with symbolism and energy; second, on an audience of spectators – visual consumers – who viewed and evaluated these shifting scenes."

50 See Strocchia, "Theaters" 61. We can assume that Nonna was unchaperoned, since the bishop would presumably not have made his remark if she had been accompanied by her husband – although we have seen already in this tale that husbands are not necessarily reliable protectors of their wives' honour.

51 For an excellent discussion of the notion of contamination in the *Decameron*, including extensive analysis of VI.3, see Stoppino, who notes that Boccaccio uses "contaminazione" in two ways in the text: "in the physical sense, for the plague, and in the moral sense of 'staining of the honour' of someone" (103), noticing that the word is also used in this latter way in III.2, and in the Author's Conclusion (§11).

of the lexis of biting and purity links back to the earlier pre-signalled instances of this theme.[52] Social and sexual propriety are figured here in terms of hygiene and contagion; Nonna's good reputation as a married woman of high social standing in Florence is nonetheless vulnerable enough that it can be infected by the words – and being in the presence – of these two men who have themselves transgressed social proprieties and violated marital and kinship norms and spaces. Both valences of the word "contaminare" are thus in play here as Nonna reacts to the improper words of the bishop – as is, of course, the ever-present threat of the plague, which we readers know will kill Nonna herself several decades into the future.

Nonna's only recourse – and it too is one facilitated by the urban space and its closely pressed actors – is therefore to bite back, not so much to erase the stain or purge the contamination as to wound in equal measure:

> per che, non intendendo a purgar questa contaminazione ma a render colpo per colpo, prestamente rispose: "Messere, e' forse non vincerebbe me; ma vorrei buona moneta." (VI.3.10)

> [So that, less intent upon vindicating her honour than upon returning blow for blow, she swiftly retorted: "In the unlikely event, my lord, of his making a conquest of me, I should want to be paid in good coin."] (453)

In her outrage, Nonna, too, is able to draw on the power dynamics afforded by the streetscape; just as the traffic flow and transport options facilitate the male abuse of power which we have just witnessed (i.e., men on horseback in a crowded thoroughfare), so she can savvily exploit the material resources at hand, that is, the crowd around her in the streets on this feast day, that ever-present Florentine audience watching and policing social interactions.

Nonna's words are still as startling in their directness today as they must have been at their time of writing in the Trecento. She is asked, in public, by the bishop what she thinks of his friend, and whether she would conquer him, with clear sexual insinuations. (Indeed, to ask the question alone dishonours her as a young married woman.) Nonna bites

52 Elissa's invocation of the "debito morso" the night before; the exposed teeth of the scandalized women of the *brigata* gasping at Licisca's vulgarity in describing the morals of married women earlier that day; and most importantly, Lauretta's framing of the tale, as an example of when it is appropriate to bite like a dog, and not a sheep (VI.3.3).

back with a riposte which turns the tables on them both by publically exposing their complicity in Dego's crimes, while asserting her own honour, wit, and personal worth as a commodity. Alluding explicitly to Dego's rape of her Florentine compatriot, she points out that this would be an unlikely event, since he would be more likely to conquer her (that is, given his past record in forced sexual encounters), but if this were to come to pass, she would prefer to be paid in good coin. Her *battuta* is meticulous in its construction: high-register and exquisitely polite in its conditional voice (she addresses the men respectfully as "Messere"), yet with the insolent implications of the taboo subject matter, and perhaps a dash of the self-assuredness of the unashamed prostitute which the bishop has just accused her of being. Her words draw their power from the urban space, and the other uses of it by other women.

Surprising as it may seem to us now, the Florentine public space was flexible enough to encompass disruptive interventions of this type by women, precisely because of their powerlessness elsewhere in their social spheres, and the safeguarding afforded by the audience. Florentine society in this period had a highly ritualized system of rhetorical insults and slurs through which to parlay social interactions, and this was by no means only limited to masculine discourse:[53]

> Ritualized verbal assaults were particularly important for woman in premodern communities. Insults and gossip gave women of virtually all classes "a major, albeit highly informal, means of influencing or shaping 'public opinion' in a society where males controlled all formal political activity." *Injurious words, or retorts provided an especially powerful tool for women seeking to defend their honour, given their problematic relationship to physical violence in the early modern period.* (Strocchia, "Gender" 53–4, emphasis added)

Cornered in the street and with her honour threatened by men she knows are capable of the worst violence against women, Nonna resorts to a drastic but still socially sanctioned strategy. Her words are immodest, but the street gives them legitimacy; her self-control and verbal command as "bella giovane e parlante" move her discourse out of the lower registers (and away from the lower orders, always a danger in the unruly urban thoroughfares), although she inhabits all those registers as a woman speaking out in public, indeed, as one who has just been

53 On insults within this "rhetoric of honour" (52), see Strocchia, "Gender and the Rites of Honor," esp. 52–60.

indirectly invited to sexual misbehaviour in the street; with her answer suggesting that if she is going to be forced to act as a prostitute, she should at least be paid properly.[54] In this moment she speaks for more than herself, and represents all the women who are ill treated in that specific patriarchal society – whatever their rank, since society is not necessarily safer for high-ranking wives than it is for common prostitutes, as we now know.[55]

The text gives no details of those who are around her, only that there are a lot of them and they are listening, and, as we might put it, witnessing. Her reply, with its polite but devastating insistence on a fair transaction (even more so than on her own sexual honour), cuts to the business of the day: the civic celebration of St John, the patron saint of the city, through whose agency its extraordinary wealth had been created and continued to be protected. On the saint's day, above all other days of the year, great emphasis was placed on honesty in contract-setting, and deals were held to be especially binding if made on that day before witnesses; it was also the occasion for social bonds and alliances to be ritually reaffirmed annually.[56] Nonna's jibe at the dishonourable conduct of these two men, witnessed in front of the crowd just as honourable contracts would be, therefore exposes the profound deceits of this pair of upper-class criminals for what they are: an immoral deal to enact an iniquitous sexual assault, a contract broken by a fraudulent payment in bad coin, and a fundamental insult to the city's own signature coinage, the florin, and its honour codes. By contrast, she positions herself as the arbiter and merchant of her own sexual and financial affairs.

Part 4: Shame and Authority in a Storied Place (VI.3.11–12)

The effect of Nonna's words on the bishop and the marshal is electric and instantaneous, cutting through the hubbub of the street and piercing them both equally ("trafitti"), a deft and female-authored verbal reversal of a combat manoeuvre:

---

54 See Tomas 322: "Prostitutes were, in effect 'public women', women of the street, by definition immodest, loquacious, and dishonourable."

55 There is also a curious and implicit correspondence in this day between the Tuscan punishment for forgers and what Boccaccio claims to be the historic Prato penalty for adulterous women and prostitutes, with which Madonna Filippa is threatened in VI.7, that is, burning at the stake (VI.7.4). By publicly denouncing Dego's forgery, Nonna is able to condemn him in terms of the penalty specifically mentioned later this day as applied to women who are paid for sex.

56 See Trexler 265.

La qual parola udita il maliscalco e 'l vescovo, sentendosi parimente trafitti, l'uno sì come facitore della disonesta cosa nella nepote del fratel del vescovo e l'altro sì come ricevitore nella nepote del proprio fratello, senza guardar l'un l'altro vergognosi e taciti se n'andarono, senza più quel giorno dirle alcuna cosa. (VI.3.11)

[These words stung both the Marshal and the Bishop to the quick, the former as the author of the dishonest deed involving the niece of the bishop's brother, and the latter as its victim, inasmuch as she was one of his own relatives. And without so much as looking at one another, they rode away silent and shamefaced, and said no more to Monna Nonna on that day.] (453–4)

Nonna's words spoken, the narrative focalization moves back to the two men, and this time we see their reaction to this public articulation of their guilt, feeling themselves "parimente trafitti" for their respective parts in the crime. Dego is the doer of the dirty deed ("facitore della disonesta cosa"), but the bishop is equally condemned as the willing accomplice who covered up the rape, even though the victim was a member of his own family.[57] Nonna skewers them there and then for their sexual harassment and previous crimes on the most holy civic day. There is literally nothing left to say, once they have heard her words: the two men cannot even look at each other, and ride away, shamefaced, without saying another word to Nonna that day. Silence has been imposed, just as it was by Elissa on Dioneo, and by Oretta on the knight.

The description of the public shaming of the two men by the righteous words of a woman recalls in its situation and phrasing one of Boccaccio's key Dantean loci, the meeting of Dante-*personaggio* with Beatrice in the Earthly Paradise, where the humbled Dante casts his eyes down to the ground like a scolded schoolboy: "Quali fanciulli, vergognando, muti / con li occhi a terra stannosi, ascoltando / e sé riconoscendo e ripentuti, / tal mi stav'io" [*Purg*. 31.64–7; As children in their shame stand mute, their eyes / upon the ground, listening / acknowledging their fault, repentant, / just so I stood].[58]

57 The bishop is sometimes interpreted as one of the victims, because of the dishonour to his family by the violation of the young wife (e.g., Cottino-Jones, *Order from Chaos* 108), but Quondam's edition offers a more nuanced reading in Fiorilla's notes to this tale: "'il vescovo in quanto l'aveva accettata (*ricevitore:* #) anche se fatta contro la nipote di suo fratello' (contro una donna di famiglia, dunque)" (Boccaccio, *Decameron* [2013], 994n11).

58 I have written extensively elsewhere about Boccaccio's intertextual deployment of Dante in strategically marked places. For discussion of other instances of this particular *dantismo*, see Armstrong, "Heavenly Bodies" 6 and 6n22. For a general overview of his techniques, see Armstrong, "Boccaccio and Dante," esp. 128–36.

While some of the Dantean resonances of this tale have already been noted (e.g., by Alonzo), the wider ramifications of this, and its relation to Boccaccio's specific use of Dante in relation to questions of gender and social decay, have, to the best of my knowledge, not been explored to date. By invoking the textual memory of Beatrice here, Boccaccio is able to align Nonna de' Pulci with a tradition of authoritative female speech, itself framed within a Dante-inflected Cacciaguida-esque memorialization of another long-gone Florence, disappeared with the plague.[59] This tale, perhaps more than any other in the *Decameron*, serves as a nostalgic and affective re-evocation of the Florence the *brigata* have lost, as it articulates their personal acquaintance with its whip-smart protagonist, recently taken by the plague. The listing of Nonna's kinship ties in VI.3.8–9, and her deliberate location in the Donati family-controlled zone of the old city, within the walls, parallel Cacciaguida's ritualistic invoking of the ancient families of Florence who live "dentro da la cerchia antica" [*Par.* 15.97; within the circle of her ancient walls]; Dante, in conversation with his *avo*, also specifically defines the city as under the protection of St John ("l'ovil di San Giovanni" [*Par.* 16.25; the sheepfold of St John]), and, of course, the Cacciaguida episode is intimately concerned with the management of women's behaviour, the city itself personified as a modest and unadorned matron, unlike the painted and sexually disorderly women of today.[60]

There is a doubled nostalgia at play here, which is arguably even more densely signifying in this tale than Boccaccio's usual *dantismo*: Dante-*personaggio*, in the fictionalized year 1300, asks the blessed soul of his great-great-grandfather, a Florentine citizen-knight, to tell him about the Florence of the twelfth century. Their deeply nostalgic and heartfelt conversation invokes the places and experiences of a shared childhood, separated by the generations: Dante asks: "Ditemi dunque, cara mia primizia, / quai fuor li vostri antichi e quai fuor li anni / che si segnaro in vostra püerizia" [*Par.* 16.22–4; Tell me then, belovèd stock

59 Allusions to the Cacciaguida cantos also occur elsewhere in Boccaccio; e.g., the reference to the notoriously immodest Florentine widow la Cianghella in the *Corbaccio* (§§259–62), named alongside the equally dishonest jurist and poet Lapo Salterello by Cacciaguida as examples of the degraded moral compass of modern Florence (*Par.* 15.128), or in his late sonnet CXXIV on Dante. On the latter see Armstrong, "Boccaccio and Dante" 132.

60 There is a vast literature on Cacciaguida and the social regulation of women; see in the first instance Keen 203–33; and Honess, "Feminine Virtues." I discuss this at more length in Armstrong, "Fat Is a Feminist Issue," esp. 18n3.

from which I spring, / who were Your ancestors, and say what were the years / written in the record of Your childhood]. Overlaid on the exiled Dante's nostalgia for his own city at the time of writing of the *Paradiso*, expressed via the invented memories of his great-great-grandfather, we find a similar mechanism in Boccaccio: an evocation of the streets and people of a recently lost city, retold through Lauretta's narration of a small interpersonal interaction three decades earlier. Just as Dante-*personaggio* returns to the city of his and his *avo*'s infancy in this heavenly conversation, the tale of Nonna transports us back to the child Boccaccio's time, inhabiting the very same places and spaces around the Porta San Pietro. Cacciaguida, Dante, Beatrice, Giovanni, Nonna, the fictional young people of the *brigata*: all have travelled along the same streets, and all come together briefly, out of time, in this tale. If further proof be needed of the intentionality and meaningfulness of these vertical stratifications echoing through time, then the locating information supplied by both Dante and Boccaccio provides it: Nonna's run-in with the bishop and his friend happens "per la via onde il palio si corre" (VI.3.8), in her neighbourhood, while Cacciaguida locates his family and the place of his birth "nel loco / dove si truova pria l'ultimo sesto / da quei che corre il vostro annüal gioco" [*Par*. 16.40–2; just where / the horsemen in your yearly race / first come upon the farthest district], that is, the place where the Florentine *palio* ends, the sestiere of Porta San Pietro, the home of both Nonna and the young Boccaccio.[61]

Boccaccio's familiar nexus of Dantean references, which cluster so often in his discussions of gender and morality, thus opens here to a slightly different world: more deeply hidden in the narrative than his other more noted and familiar citations, these references point to the literary pasts of his city, to the cycles of mourning and remembrance and the community of women in the *Vita nuova*, and the rage of Dante (via Cacciaguida) at the social, moral, and political corruption which now infuse the Florentine body politic. While I hesitate to push the textual correspondences too far between the Cacciaguida canti and this tale, it can surely be no coincidence that Cacciaguida singles out for specific contempt the activities of corrupt Florentines who fraudulently profit from the bishopric (either by taking the church income when the seat

61 Indeed, just a few lines later, Cacciaguida attacks the future incomers from the Florentine countryside, who would invade the city and dilute its pure Florentine population, naming among them those "di Certaldo" (*Par*. 16.49–51). There may well be some irony in using Cacciaguida in this way, inasmuch as this was of course Boccaccio's own family's journey to the city.

was vacant, or for selling clerical office, that is simony):[62] "Così facieno i padri di coloro / che, sempre che la vostra chiesa vaca, / si fanno grassi stando a consistoro" [*Par.* 16.112–14; Thus did the fathers of those who now, / whenever your church needs to fill the bishop's seat, / fatten themselves by sitting long in council]. Even more strikingly, he goes on to attack those iniquitous wretches who terrorize those who are fearful of them, but placate those like a lamb who bare their teeth, or pay them ("L'oltracotata schiatta che s'indraca / dietro a chi fugge, e a chi mostra 'l dente / o ver la borsa, com' agnel si placa" [*Par.* 16.115–17; The proud and insolent race, playing the dragon / at the back of him who flees, but mild as a lamb / to him who shows his teeth – or else his purse]). While Cacciaguida here is referring obliquely to the Adimari faction of nobles, the striking references to the teeth, the purse, and the sheep, which immediately follow the condemnation of the abuses of the bishopric in this passage, find themselves picked up as key motifs in this tale, and indeed, in the guiding theme of the day.[63] It is yet another example of Boccaccio's remarkable facility of intertextual accumulation, woven deep into the threads of his material.

With her "presta risposta," then, Nonna shows herself to be an exemplary practitioner of Florentine quick-wittedness, biting her assailant with a pitch-perfect comeback: "Così adunque, essendo la giovane stata morsa, non le si disdisse il mordere altrui motteggiando" [VI.3.12; In this case, therefore, since the girl was bitten first, it was not appropriate that she should make an equally biting retort; 454]. With these final words, Lauretta returns once again to the theme of the day and her opening Introduction, where she framed the art of "motteggiare" in terms of animal bite (VI.3.3–4): in socially sanctioned wordplay, one should ideally bite lightly like a sheep, so as not to wound, but in certain circumstances, after extreme provocation, it is none the less permissible to bite back like a dog. In Dante's "ovil di San Giovanni," one aims to bite like a sheep, precisely like the two Florentine protagonists of the first two tales of the day, commended by Lauretta ("La qual cosa ottimamente fecero le parole di madonna Oretta e la risposta di Cisti" [VI.3.4; The remark

62 While Dante and Cacciaguida's conversation ostensibly takes place in the year 1300, Antonio degli Orsi was the bishop of Florence at the time that Dante was writing the *Paradiso*, and so this condemnation of the abuses of the Florentine bishopric could even refer specifically to him.

63 In the Due- and Trecento, the Adimari were held to be *nouveaux riches* among the Florentine magnate families, and thus, for Cacciaguida, part of that corrupt horde of ignoble incomers characterized by their dirty dealings. See d'Addario.

made by Madonna Oretta, and Cisti's retort, were excellent examples of the genre; 452]). But sometimes the sheepfold needs a sheepdog to restore order, and Nonna's sharp words, uttered in the public street and witnessed by her fellow citizens, ring out clearly as a denunciation of the fraudulent conspiracy and criminal acts of the two men.

Nonna is a woman of considerable personal and familial resources, yet, in this unwelcome encounter with the bishop and his friend, she knows this has been no protection for the unnamed wife raped in the first sequence. But in the heat of the moment, on this particular day, and on this particular street, in front of this particular audience, she is able to leverage the coercive power of the urban space and the people and fight back against her aggressors. With the full weight of the city and the patron saint behind her, she is thus a woman who is finally and unusually allowed to get the better of a male authority figure, and live to be praised for it. In the day-to-day way of things, Antonio degli Orsi and Dego della Ratta command the street as high-ranking noblemen and office-holders, but command of the urban space is held by consent, and Nonna's demolition of their impolite approach to her, in publicly exposing their moral and financial corruption, drives them away in shame on this day. Nonna thus succeeds in overwriting their dominant narrative and reclaims the street for herself and all the others who have been personally or institutionally abused by the behaviour of these men. It is a moment of subversive resistance, yet one which is expressed in perfectly appropriate and licit terms.

We have seen that the urban city space is not a static or fixed site through which its inhabitants move passively; instead, meaning is generated afresh by the people who move through it, and it mutates and accretes over time. Sharon Strocchia has noted that "the Renaissance city functioned as a set of connected stages, backdrops, and viewing frames that permitted many different venues for social actors, which in turn afforded various angles of vision for their audiences" ("Theaters" 56); but, as we have seen, the perspective on the streets is very different when one is mounted on a horse or stood on the pavement, when one is inside looking out through a window, or outside in the crowd. Just as the meaning of the spaces of the city is produced by and is particular to its different inhabitants, so this tale can be shown to offer multiple points of view and competing (unresolved) interpretations, enacted through the nesting of narrators and narrative levels, and – crucially – by a focalization on different characters and subject positions as the narrative progresses and the reader is taken through the different spaces and plot moments to its resolution.

In this way, the standard view of this tale can be challenged by a new perspective. For too long it has been read as a simple example of Florentine accomplishment in *motteggiare*, with very little account taken of the female subject position, and this despite the fact that the female subject position and perspective is overtly articulated at every turn. In this *lectura* I have thus tried to give equal weight to the two narratives within the tale, and the *two* women who feature, the raped young wife and the wife who fights back, and to situate it within a wider historical framework of the lived experience of women in Trecento Florence. This historicizing lens is then able to magnify the local, and the specifically biographical and familial ties of its author Boccaccio to this part of the city, and by extension to the terrible losses of the plague, which break through the diegesis for the only time here in any of the tales told.

In conclusion, a historicized close reading of the tale of Nonna de' Pulci offers an opportunity to contemporary twenty-first-century readers to read against the grain of the critical tradition, and thereby propose a more subversive and explicitly feminist take on the tale, even in a highly patriarchal setting. By approaching this story in part in terms of its account of gendered actions in space, we see that resistance can coexist alongside the dominant form, for its characters and its readers, just as the people of the city can use its official spaces for their own purposes.[64] And Boccaccio's account of this tale, and its framing, leaves enough space for a specifically feminist interpretation to flourish alongside those others which have previously dominated. The tale of Nonna de' Pulci, overlooked for too long, deserves to take its place as one of the great metatextual performances of the book, like that of Madonna Oretta but concerned with readership rather than authorship. Nonna herself breaches the narrative frames: at once a character and a real-life acquaintance of the *brigata* women, a woman who is simultaneously a young woman of Florence like them and a mature woman who has died of the plague, like their own family members. She exists entirely within the female narrative and social space; narrated by Lauretta, on a day governed by Elissa, who is herself responding to comments by

64 Writing about past trends in Florentine historiography, Milner rejects those interpretations which focus solely on the political motivations of the elite, valorizing instead the "agency implicit ... with the semiotics of the everyday ... By shifting attention to the conditions of reception, the possibility of resistance, or reappropriation, is presented on account of the manner in which symbols, with their multiple associations, permi[t] ... alternative visions of social ordering to coexist alongside the dominant form" ("Florentine Piazza della Signoria" 85).

Pampinea in the Day One frame. And, like Nonna, the *brigata* women are resistant actors in their own social group, who have themselves been crudely reminded of the power imbalance and masculine sexual domination by Dioneo in his comments of the day before. This tale offers us a moment in the *Decameron* where the veil falls away and the workings are shown, while at the same time giving us a deeply situated vignette of pre-plague Florentine daily life, where for once the social order is overturned and the victims win through Nonna's righteous words. And if Dioneo can be understood as an author-figure in the text, then Nonna should stand equally as an exemplar of the accomplished, resistant reader.

4 The Tale of Chichibio and the Crane (VI.4)

JAMES C. KRIESEL

I. Introduction

The fourth story of Day Six, that which dramatizes how a "leggiadro motto" [V.Concl.3; graceful saying] can ameliorate a dangerous situation, is exceptional in the context of the day.[1] The *novelle* of Day Six prominently feature Florentine protagonists and settings. Neifile's tale instead concerns the Venetian cook Chichibio. He is the only protagonist of the day to speak in a non-Florentine vernacular (VI.4.8). A secondary theme of the day concerns appearances of a potentially vexing nature. Pampinea's story reveals that Cisti, though a humble baker, nevertheless has a noble soul (VI.2.3). Panfilo's story about the painter Giotto demonstrates that "maravigliosi ingegni" [marvellous geniuses] can be found "sotto turpissime forme d'uomini" [VI.5.3; under the most disgusting forms of men]. And Dioneo's story about Frate Cipolla highlights that even a man "niuna scienza avendo" [having no science] can be an influential orator (VI.10.7). With respect to these protagonists, Chichibio is presented as the most uninformed of the day's speakers (VI.4.3 and 6).[2] Neifile contributes to the day's subtheme by telling a story about a man who apparently does not possess any hidden dignity or genius. Rather, the cook's graceful saying is inspired by fortune (VI.4.3).

---

1 I would like to thank Jesse Flavin of Villanova University and Elizabeth Dunn of Duke University for their help with bibliography related to VI.4. I am also grateful to David Lummus and Caroline Wilky, who offered suggestions on an earlier version of this chapter. For the text of the *Decameron* I have used Branca's 1992 Einaudi edition. Translations are my own unless otherwise noted. The English translations have occasionally been modified to draw out the meaning of the original more accurately. In Latin quotations, i/j, u/v, and f/s have been standardized.

2 Cesca appears to be the most ignorant listener of the day (VI.8.4–6 and 10).

Neifile's tale dramatizes a dispute between Chichibio and the Florentine noble Currado Gianfigliazzi. After killing a crane, Currado asks Chichibio to cook it for his guests. While Chichibio prepares the bird, a woman named Brunetta asks him for a piece. Chichibio, who is "forte innamorato" [VI.4.7; strongly in love], reluctantly cuts off a leg of the crane to appease her. When Currado asks about the missing piece, the cook declares that cranes have only one foot. Angered by this reply, Currado demands that he and Chichibio ascertain the next day how many feet the birds have. They travel to a river where cranes are standing on one foot "sí come quando dormono sogliono fare" [VI.4.16; as they are wont to do when they sleep]. However, Currado creates a ruckus so that the cranes put down their other foot. Then Chichibio, "non sappiendo egli stesso donde si venisse" [VI.4.18; he himself not knowing from whence it came], answers that, had someone yelled at the table, the cooked crane would have done the same thing. The response pleases Currado so much that "la sua ira si convertí in festa e riso" [VI.4.19; his anger was converted into joy and laughter].

Scholars have proposed Latin, French, and Tuscan antecedents for Neifile's story about a missing piece of food. In Apuleius's *Metamorphoses* (c. 160–c. 175), a dog steals the leg of a deer that a cook was preparing for his master (VIII.31–IX.3).[3] The cook's wife then observes that they have a remedy for their bad fortune: the ass Lucius, who can supply a leg (VIII.31). Lucius avoids being butchered because of his cunning "consilium" [thinking] and the confusion created by a dog (VIII.31 and IX.1). A Latin fable by Avianus (c. 400) about a farmer and a pig may also have inspired Boccaccio's story (*Fab. Av.* XXX).[4] After a pig repeatedly raids a farm, a peasant captures the beast, butchers it, and serves it without its heart to his lord. When asked about the organ, the man calms his master's "iustam ... iram" [just anger] by noting that the pig was stupid and never had a heart (ll. 13–14). The French fabliau *Les Perdrix* (pre-1300) may also have inspired the narrative of VI.4.[5] A gluttonous wife eats two partridges that were being prepared for her husband and a priest (her secret lover). She diffuses her husband's anger

3 For Apuleius's *Metamorphoses* I have used the Loeb edition and translation by Hanson. On parallels between this episode in the *Metamorphoses* and VI.4, see Fiorilla xxxviii–xxxix; and Bisanti, "Una fonte" 49–50.

4 For the *Fabulae Aviani* I have used the Loeb edition and translation by Duff and Duff. On similarities between this fable and VI.4, see Bisanti, "Una fonte."

5 For the text of the *Les Perdrix*, see *Fabliaux du Moyen âge*. On the general themes and circulation of the *Perdrix*, see Brown 12–14 and 126–8. For a discussion of thematic parallels between the anonymous French and Boccaccio's narratives, see Picone, "Dal fabliau."

about the missing food by recounting an elaborate lie. First, she makes the priest flee by telling him that her husband wants to castrate him (ll. 83–9). Then she tells her husband that the cleric stole the birds, which prompts the husband to chase him (ll. 108–14). Finally, in the Tuscan *Novellino* (c. 1280–c. 1300), a courtier buys a goat for his lord, but he eats the kidneys before serving it (LXXV).[6] When his lord asks about them, the courtier replies with a vulgar double entendre: "E' non ànno ernioni quelli di questo paese" [126; They don't have kidneys, those of this country].

From the Renaissance to modern times, VI.4 has interested diverse writers and visual artists.[7] The story has been considered one of the most emblematic of the *Decameron*. Textbooks and anthologies propose that the story features elements of Boccaccio's so-called realist poetics.[8] Traits of his realism supposedly include the depiction of plebeian speech (Chichibio's), Tuscan settings (Peretola), and historical contemporaries (Currado). Didactic texts note that VI.4 dramatizes in a comedic manner one of the *Decameron*'s primary ideological concerns, namely how speech impacts reality. Though VI.4 has been considered one of the *Decameron*'s key *novelle*, scholars have not dedicated much attention to the story. Studies of VI.4 have highlighted the etymological resonances of Chichibio's name, and explored whether the subaltern is characterized positively.[9] In analyses of the entire Day Six, scholars mention in passing that the tale depicts how language can resolve social, economic, or epistemological tensions.[10] Finally, scholars of animals and food have

---

6 See *Il Novellino* 126–8. On the similarities between the two narratives, see Muscetta, "Introduzione" 205; Cuomo 258; and Bisanti, "Una fonte" 50.

7 For references to the story in Renaissance and early modern texts, see Bisanti, "Una fonte" 47–9. For visual depictions of the tale in these periods, see Branca, ed. *Boccaccio visualizzato* 2:25, 3:208, 216, 220, 227, 262, 305, 314, et passim.

8 For examples of anthologies that include VI.4, see Luperini et al., eds. 1:541–4; and Panebianco et al., eds. 1:T10 (online.scuola.zanichelli.it/letterautori-files/volume-1/pdf-online/10-boccaccio.pdf, accessed 19 July 2017).

9 The etymology of Chichibio's name was a topic of discussion in the 1930s and 1940s. For bibliography on the issue, see Fanini; and Boccaccio, *Decameron* [1992], 731n5. For discussions of Chichibio's dignity, see Picone, "Dal fabliau" 121–2 (he also notes that the story concerns the power of language, 111–12); Russo, *Letture critiche* 209–11; and Baratto, *Realtà e stile* 50–1 and 370–1.

10 On ideas about speech in the story, see Van der Voort 212–13 and 218; Getto 143 and 148 (who also notes that VI.4 and Day Six dramatize a celebration of Florentine culture); Giusti, "La novella" 328–31; Mineo 50, 52, 64–5, and 68–9; and Muscetta, "Introduzione" 204–6 and 211. On ideas about acquiring knowledge through language in VI.4, see Andrei, "*Motto*" 19–20, 28–9, and 31; Meier, "Day Six" 299–304 and 306; Giusti, "La novella" 330–1; Cuomo 257–8; and Fido, "Boccaccio's *ars narrandi*" 77–8, 81–3, and 85–6. See also Testaferri 228–30.

focused on the role of the crane in the plot.[11] Such generalizing studies are partially due to the fact that the symbolic import of the crane – an animal frequently discussed in bestiaries, histories, and encyclopedias – has not been considered. Modern scholars have even suggested that Boccaccio did not draw on the allegorical resonances of non-human animals in his writings.[12] For decades Boccaccio was characterized as a proto-modernist realist, who eschewed medieval allegorical and symbolic modes of writing.[13]

What follows refines interpretations of VI.4 by suggesting that the tale is inspired by the metaliterary connotations of cranes in the Middle Ages. Boccaccio modified a narrative tradition about missing food by featuring a crane in VI.4. Scholars have documented that birds of all types were often evoked in reflections on language and writing.[14] Medieval authors may have reflected on metaliterary issues in narratives about birds because their feathers (*pennae* in Latin or *penne* in Tuscan) were often used as writing instruments.[15] In ancient times, birds were also associated with semiotic issues because they were employed in augury, namely the interpretation of avian flight for ideas about reality.[16]

A consideration of the crane in VI.4 reveals that Neifile's tale dramatizes what is characterized as a vernacular poetics of congruence. In the Middle Ages, the etymology of congruence (in Latin *congruentia, congruo*) was thought to be related to the word for cranes (*grus*).[17] By featuring Venetian and Florentine speech in VI.4, Boccaccio strove to incorporate in the *Decameron* – harmoniously and congruently – different types of vernacular culture. Boccaccio thus engaged contentious discussions about vernacularity. Late medieval writers reflected on the relative dignity of various vernacular cultures, especially those of a plebeian nature.[18] In the Conclusion to Day Five, Dioneo recalls

---

11 For studies of non-human animals in the *Decameron* that discuss VI.4, see Mouchet, "Anguille"; Mouchet, "Asini"; and Sanguineti-White 114–18.

12 For example, see Picone, "Dal fabliau" 121; and Ó Cuilleanáin, "Man and Beast" 87.

13 For these historiographical paradigms, see Kriesel, *Boccaccio's Corpus* 4–5, and 276–7nn17–25.

14 On the symbolic import of cranes in the *Comedy*, see Conte; della Cagna; Fioretti; Gorni, "'Gru' di Dante"; and Martinez, "Pilgrim's Answer."

15 See *A Latin Dictionary*, s.v. *penna* (II.C, 1330); and *TLIO*, s.v. *penna*. On the types of feathers used as quills, see de Hamel 27–9.

16 See *A Latin Dictionary*, s.v. *avis* (II, 215).

17 On medieval ideas about the etymology of *congruentia*, see Fioretti 87–9; and *A Latin Dictionary*, s.v. *congruentia* and *congruo* (420–1). The topic is addressed in section III below.

18 On debates about vernacular and plebeian cultures in Florence, see Tavoni 245–6 and 251–4; Cherchi, "Vernacular Literatures"; and Robins 1–5.

these cultures when he cites popular poems with erotic and vulgar elements (V.Concl.6–14). Moreover, Boccaccio's peers debated the dignity of non-Florentine languages and culture in comparison to local literary traditions.[19] The present chapter suggests that, in VI.4, Boccaccio was inspired by but also modifying Dante's own ideas about vernacularity and literary congruence. It suggests that Boccaccio expanded upon Dante's attempt to congruently incorporate diverse vernacular cultures in the *Comedy*.

II. Vernacularity and Cranes

Neifile's Proem foregrounds that her story concerns vernacular speech. She introduces the subject by repeating a term for speaker (*dicitore*) with vernacular and rhetorical connotations:

> Quantunque il pronto ingegno, amorose donne, spesso parole presti e utili e belle, secondo gli accidenti, a' *dicitori*, la fortuna ancora, alcuna volta aiutatrice de' paurosi, sopra la lor lingua subitamente di quelle pone che mai a animo riposato per lo *dicitore* si sareber sapute trovare: il che io per la mia novella intendo di dimostrarvi. (VI.4.3, emphasis added)
>
> [Though, loving ladies, a quick mind can often provide speakers [*dicitori*] appropriate, useful, and beautiful words according to the circumstances, sometimes Fortune, occasionally assisting the fearful, can put words on the tongue of a speaker [*dicitore*] who never would have found them in a calm moment. This I intend to show you in my short story.]

In the thirteenth century, the term *dicitore* appeared in Brunetto Latini's *Rettorica* (c. 1260–1), a translation of the opening chapters of Cicero's treatise on rhetoric *De inventione* (c. 85 BCE).[20] It also appeared in Bono Giamboni's *Fiore di rettorica* (1292), a vernacular reworking of sections of the Pseudo-Ciceronian *Rhetorica ad Herennium* and Cicero's *De inventione*. In the *Vita nova* (c. 1293), Dante used the term in the chapter dedicated to a defence of personification in vernacular writing. Dante justifies his decision to speak of Love as an embodied figure by specifying that love is not actually a "sustanzia corporale" [bodily substance], but an

19 See note 18 above.

20 Search conducted through the *Gattoweb* database of medieval vernacular texts. With respect to texts composed prior to or around the time of Dante's *Vita nova*, the term appears almost exclusively in Latini's *Rhetorica* and Giamboni's *Fiore*.

"accidente in sustanzia" [XXV.1 (16.1); accident in a substance].[21] He argues that vernacular "dicitori d'amore" [love poets] should be able to use the trope because ancient Greek and Latin poets employed it (XXV.3 and 7 [16.3 and 7]). He concludes that a "dicitori per rima" [vernacular poet] can personify concepts because the ancients imagined many types of "accidenti" [accidents] in bodily form (XXV.8–9 [16.8–9]). In the mid-fourteenth century, the word typically referred to a sophisticated orator, writer, or ambassador.[22]

Boccaccio employed the term in accord with its technical resonances. In the *Decameron*, the word is present in two stories in addition to VI.4. In I.9, Elissa uses the word while introducing a story with thematic concerns resembling those of Neifile's tale. Her story shows that "una parola molte volte, per accidente non che *ex proposito* detta" [a word many times said by accident rather than *ex proposito*] can prove useful no matter who the "dicitore" [speaker] is (I.9.3). In a tale about the efficacy of unrefined speech, the Latin phrase *ex proposito* nevertheless recalls the technical connotations of the term. In X.7, Pampinea uses the word when discussing Mico da Siena, who is called a "buon dicitore in rima" [X.7.18; good vernacular poet].[23] Given the resonances of *dicitore*, Neifile's remarks signal that the tale concerns theoretical issues about vernacular speech and poetics.

At the same time, the Proem recalls ideas about unsophisticated vernacular speech. Neifile employs the term when speaking about a person who is not, in reality, rhetorically or theoretically trained. Her tale features a speaker who requires the assistance of fortune, since Chichibio would not have, of his own accord, been able to speak *ex proposito*. In the *Decameron*, Neifile had previously reflected on matters related to unintentional or unrefined speech. In her contribution to Day Four, she expressed concern about those who believe themselves to be exceptionally intelligent. She introduced a story about the dangers of suppressing eros by arguing that clever persons, sometimes unwittingly, adopt unnatural behaviours:

> Alcuni, al mio giudicio, valorose donne, sono li quali piú che l'altre genti si credon sapere e sanno meno; e per questo non solamente a' consigli degli

21 For the text of the *Vita nova*, I have used Barbi's edition. Parenthetical citation indicates both numbering systems.

22 See *TLIO*, s.v. *dicitore*.

23 For information about the identity of this writer, see Boccaccio, *Decameron* [1992] 1171–2n7.

> uomini ma ancora contra la natura delle cose presummono d'opporre il senno loro; della quale presunzione già grandissimi mali sono avvenuti e alcun bene non se ne vide giammai. (IV.8.3)
>
> [There are some, worthy ladies, in my opinion who believe they know more than other people but know less. And for this not only do they presuppose to oppose their wisdom to the advice of men but even go against the nature of things. From their presumption, evil things have happened, and no good has ever come of it.]

Her contribution to Day Six similarly addresses matters concerning the natural or instinctual versus the artificial or refined.

Neifile's preface intimates that her tale highlights the potential dignity of unrefined speech (unrefined because guided by fortune). In medieval culture, that which was unintentional or that which was motivated by instinct was related to specific types of vernacular discourse. In the *De vulgari eloquentia* (1304–6), Dante discussed the instinctual and natural resonances of the vernacular.[24] He explains that Latin is an artificial language with fixed rules, which is learned though study, while the vernacular is a natural language without fixed rules, which is acquired by means of a child's natural capacity to imitate (I.1.2–4).[25] In addition, the evocation of non-intentional speech would have reminded contemporaries of another category of communicators: non-human animals. Writers from Augustine to Aquinas acknowledged that non-human animals communicated with verbal signs. However, they hypothesized that they did not fully comprehend the significance of their actions.[26] In *De doctrina christiana* (397–426), Augustine wonders whether non-human creatures signify instinctually or intentionally:

> Habent etiam bestiae quaedam inter se signa, quibus produnt appetitum animi sui. Nam et gallus gallinaceus reperto cibo dat signum vocis gallinae, ut accurrat; et columbus gemitu columbam vocat, vel ab ea vicissim vocatur; et multa huiusmodi animadverti solent. Quae utrum, sicut vultus aut dolentis clamor sine voluntate significandi sequantur motum animi,

24 For a summary of Dante's ideas about Latin and vernacular speech, see Tavoni 253–4.

25 For the text and translation of Dante's *De vulgari eloquentia*, I have used Botterill's 1996 edition.

26 For a summary of medieval ideas about non-human animals and speech, see Eco et al., "On Animal Language."

an vere ad significandum dentur, alia quaestio est et ad rem, quae agitur, non pertinet. (II.2.3)[27]

[Some beasts also employ signs among themselves by which they communicate the desires in their mind. For example, when food has been found, the cock signals with his voice for the hen to come. The dove calls his mate with a cooing sound, or he is called by her. We can observe many signs of the same kind. However, whether these signs, like the expression or cry of one in pain, follow the movement of the mind without a true intention of signifying, or whether they are emitted for the purpose of signification, is another question, and does not pertain to the current discussion.]

Medieval writers generally agreed that non-human animals signify with a minimal or negligible degree of intentionality. These creatures were thought to signify non-conventionally or naturally (*naturaliter*) in comparison to (adult) humans, who were said to signify conventionally and on account of common accord (*ad placitum; ex institutione*; or *ex impositione*).[28] Therefore, Neifile's Proem recalls different types of vernacular speech and writing. More specifically, her remarks conflate ideas associated with a refined, an elite, and a classicizing tradition with notions related to an unrefined, a plebeian, and a natural tradition. VI.4 then clarifies the confusion potentially engendered by characterizing Chichibio, an uninformed speaker, as a *dicitore*.

The story's two protagonists have symbolic resonances that suggest they personify different types of vernacular culture. Neifile first introduces Currado, who lived in Florence in the early to mid-fourteenth century:[29]

Currado Gianfigliazzi, sí come ciascuna di voi se udito e veduto puote avere, sempre della nostra città è notabile cittadino, liberale e magnifico, e vita cavalleresca tenendo continuamente in cani e in uccelli s'è dilettato, le sue opere maggiori al presente lasciando stare. (VI.4.4)

27 For the text of Augustine's *De doctrina christiana* I have used Martin's 1962 edition.

28 This sentence summarizes the taxonomies of medieval ideas about human and non-human speech discussed by Eco et al.

29 For biographical information about Currado Gianfigliazzi, see Boccaccio, *Decameron* [1992] 730–1n5; and Arrighi. The family appears among the usurers damned for sins against nature (*Inf.* 17.58–60). On Boccaccio's knowledge of Dante's attitude toward the family, see Olson, *Courtesy Lost* 134–7. It may, therefore, be significant that Currado appears in a story about natural signs and signifying in the *Decameron*. Boccaccio's engagement with Dante's ideas about this subject will be addressed in section IV below.

> [Currado Gianfigliazzi, as each of you women could have heard and seen, has always been a notable figure of our city, liberal and magnificent, and, maintaining a knightly manner of living, he continually found delight in hunting with his dogs and birds, not to mention his pre-eminent works.]

Being a noble and genteel man, Currado partakes in cultural activities, like hunting with a falcon (VI.4.5), that were the hallmarks of the late medieval elites.[30] In the Middle Ages, the practice of hunting (with a falcon) was also a common metaphor for erotic courtship.[31] In the *Decameron*'s *Proemio,* the narrator draws on this metaphor when describing how men attenuate their erotic desires by hunting (Prologue.11–12). In V.9, a falcon also plays a central role in the noble Federigo degli Alberighi's courtship of his beloved (V.9.5–6, 10–15, and 24–7). In addition, the meta-artistic resonances of Currado are signalled by Neifile's decision (not) to mention Currado's "opere maggiori" [VI.4.4; pre-eminent works]. In late medieval Italy, the term *opera* was commonly used for architectural, artistic, and literary creations (for example, see *Dec.* I.Intro.2 and Concl.1). As a noble Florentine with elitist, erotic, and literary overtones, Currado personifies the "pre-eminent works" of Florentine culture, especially the *stilnovo* tradition. Indeed, *stilnovo* poets partially defined their conception of love by reference to ideas about gentility and birds. In the poem "Al cor gentil rempaira sempre amore," Guido Guinizzelli (1235–1276) begins with the declaration that "Al cor gentil rempaira sempre amore / come l'ausello in selva a la verdura" [ll. 1–2; Love always returns to the gentle heart / as the bird to its verdant abode in the woods].[32] In the *Vita nova,* Dante drew on Guinizzelli's ideas while theorizing that "Amore e 'l cor gentil sono una cosa" [XX.3.1 (11.3.1); Love and the gentle heart are one]. By introducing an embodiment of *stilnovo* culture, the tale complements another reflection on Florentine poetic traditions in Day Six. Like Currado, the poet Guido Cavalcanti is described as a "leggiadrissimo" [most graceful], "costumato" [courteous], and "gentile uom" [genteel man] (VI.9.8).

---

30 On the socio-economic connotations of hunting with falcons, see Gualtieri 1–2 and 6–8.

31 See Gualtieri 34–43.

32 For the text of Guinizzelli's *canzone,* I have used the edition in Contini's *Poeti del duecento* 2:460–4.

Chichibio instead has plebeian and Venetian cultural resonances. Scholars have suggested that his name has etymological connotations in Venetian ranging from simpleton to good-for-nothing.[33] Neifile highlights his non-Tuscan language and plebeian origins by calling him a *bergolo*, a Venetian term meaning fool, windbag, or vacuous.[34] The name Chichibio has onomatopoetic resonances related to the call of a finch. Chichibio sings like a bird when he intones a line with truncated words for Brunetta.[35] He sings a verse that features post-tonic apocope characteristics of Venetian and other northern Gallo-Italic vernaculars: "Voi non l'avrì da mi, donna Brunetta, voi non l'avrì da mi" [VI.4.8; You will not have it from me, Lady Brunetta, you will not have it from me].[36] His name and truncated verse conceptually associate him with the crane that has a cut-off leg (when cooked) or a hidden foot (while standing). These resonances of Chichibio imply that he personifies an unrefined, instinctual vernacular speech. The trope *onomatopoeia* was conventionally defined as human words that imitate sounds, like non-human animal calls, in the natural world. In the *Institutio oratoria* (c. 90–6), the theorist of oratory Quintillian stated:

> *Onomatopoeia* quidem, id est fictio nominis, Graecis inter maximas habita virtutes, nobis vix permittitur. Et sunt plurima ita posita ab iis qui sermonem primi fecerunt, aptantes adfectibus vocem: nam "mugitus" et "sibilus" et "murmur" inde venerunt. (*Inst.* VIII.6.31)[37]

> [*Onomatopoeia*, that is the creation of words, is regarded as one of the major virtues by the Greeks, but is hardly allowed us at all. Yet many words were created in this way by the originators of the language, who suited sound to sensation. *Mugitus*, *sibilus*, and *murmur* (bellowing, hiss, murmur) came to us in this way.]

33 For scholarship on the etymological resonances of Chichibio's name, see note 9 above.

34 For scholarship on the term *bergolo*, see note 9 above.

35 On Chichibio's speech, in addition to the bibliography in note 9, see Cottino-Jones, "Hiccuping Rhythm" 89–90. She notes that the language of the whole story has sing-song elements.

36 On the linguistic characteristics of northern vernaculars present in Chichibio's song, see Boccaccio, *Decameron* [1992] 732nn5, 6, and 9.

37 For the text of Quintilian's *Institutio oratoria*, I have used the Loeb edition and translation by Russell.

In his *Eytmologiae* (c. 600–25), Isidore of Seville defined the trope as speech that imitates natural sounds.[38]

While Currado embodies the sublime Florentine amatory culture, the Venetian Chichibio also personifies base bodily matters. He is, in virtue of his culinary profession, concerned with the appeasement of carnal desires. The cook satisfies Brunetta's hunger after she taunts him with erotically ambiguous remarks: "In fé di Dio, se tu non la mi dai, tu non avrai mai da me cosa che ti piaccia" [VI.4.9; Swear to God, if you don't give it to me, then you will not have from me what you like]. In addition, the narrator highlights the superficial nature of Chichibio's character and behaviour: "come nuovo bergolo era cosí pareva" [VI.4.6; as he was a new *bergolo*, so he seemed].

Finally, Currado and Chichibio have gendered connotations that were associated with different types of vernacularity. On the one hand, vernacular speech and literature were associated with women. Medieval writers thought that vernacular poetry was invented by a man who wanted to speak to a woman who did not know Latin (Dante, *Vita nova* XXV.6 [16.6]).[39] On the other hand, the *stilnovo* tradition was characterized by masculine and homoerotic overtones.[40] In *Purgatorio* 26, the masculine resonances of *stilnovo* poetry are highlighted when the pilgrim meets Guido Guinizzelli. He is named the "padre" [father] of the "rime … dolci e leggiadre" [97–9; sweet and graceful rhymes]. Boccaccio was aware of the gendered connotations of vernacular culture. In the *Esposizioni*, he downplayed the feminine resonances of the *Comedy* by arguing that the poem's language is not feminine: "quantunque in volgare scritto sia, nel quale pare che comunichino le feminette, egli è nondimeno ornato e leggiadro e sublime, delle quali cose nulla sente il volgare delle femine" [Accessus 19; although it is written in the vernacular, in which it seems that women communicate, it is nevertheless ornate, graceful, and sublime, which in no way is characteristic of the vernacular spoken by women].[41] In VI.4, Boccaccio recalls these ideas about the masculine resonances of elitist vernacular culture. A man with a patrilineal

38 See Isidore of Seville, *Etym.* I.37.14: "Onomatopoeia est nomen adfictum ad imitandum sonum vocis confusae, ut 'stridor valvarum', 'hinnitus equorum', 'mugitus boum', 'blatus ovium'" [Onomatopoeia is a word that imitates the sound of a vexing noise, such as the "creaking of hinges," the "whinnying of horses," the "mooing of cows," and the "bleating of sheep"]. For the text of the *Etymologiae* I have used the 1989 reprint of Lindsay's edition.

39 On the feminine resonances of the vernacular, see Olson, "Language of Women."

40 On the masculine resonances of certain types of vernacular culture (in Dante's works), see Ascoli, *Dante and the Making* 140–2; and Cornish 145–57. See also Barolini, "Sociology of the 'Brigata.'"

41 For the text of Boccaccio's *Esposizioni*, I have used Padoan's 1965 edition for *Tutte le opere*.

pedigree represents the Florentine *stilnovo* tradition: Gianfigliazzi (Gian + figli [sons] + azzi [suffix]). By contrast, Chichibio, who embodies a Venetian plebeian culture, has no masculine pedigree. He lacks any pedigree, since his surname is not mentioned. Moreover, his name has resonances related to anonymity and ubiquity: Chichibio (Who who I? or Who who I go?; *bio* perhaps being related to the infinitive *ire* – "to go").[42] Finally, he embodies feminine desires in virtue of his feelings for Brunetta. Like Chichibio, she is not identified by a patrilineal surname. Therefore, the tale juxtaposes a tradition with a noble and an elitist patrimony to one that is plebeian, anonymous, shifting, and feminine. The story thus develops ideas about the gendered connotations of language and genre that had been introduced in VI.1. In VI.1, vernacular literature, especially the vernacular *novella,* was coded as feminine in virtue of being associated with Madonna Oretta; VI.4 refines the literary connotations of gender in the *Decameron* by highlighting that the feminine genre encompasses many types of vernacular speech, stories, and narrators.

Therefore, the opening sections of Neifile's tale highlight that the text deals with matters related to the literal sense of a vernacular text (language, etymology of words, etc.). These introductory passages also signal that the tale treats matters associated with the superficial dimension of bodies (external appearances, erotic desires, etc.). The story addresses these issues in a tale about two protagonists who debate the physical, or superficial, form of a crane. A survey of medieval ideas about cranes clarifies the symbolic connection between these ideological concerns and the crane's body. These ideas would have alerted Boccaccio's contemporaries to the analogic connection in the story between text and bird.

Cranes were thought to have inspired the birth of writing, especially the formation of letters.[43] Medieval writers noted that Lucan discussed cranes and the form of letters in his Latin epic *Pharsalia,* a text that circulated widely with a Latin gloss and in vernacular translation:[44]

Strymona sic gelidum bruma pellente relinquunt
Poturae te, Nile, grues, primoque volatu

42 See *TLIO,* s.v. *ire,* accessed 24 July 2017.

43 On the recollection of cranes and the birth of writing in the *Comedy* (*Inf.* 5.46–8; *Purg.* 24.64–9 and 26.64–69; *Par.* 18.73–81), see della Cagna 73–5; and Conte.

44 On the gloss that circulated with the *Pharsalia,* see della Cagna 70–2. On the circulation of the text in vernacular translation, see Lorenzi. When commenting on the similitude of cranes in *Inferno* 5 (46–8), the Dante commentator Guido da Pisa recalled ideas about cranes in Lucan's *Pharsalia,* Ambrose's *Hexaemeron,* and Isidore's *Etymologiae.* See Guido da Pisa 354.

Effingunt varias casu monstrante figuras;
Mox, ubi percussit tensas Notus altior alas,
Confusos temere inmixtae glomerantur in orbes,
Et turbata perit dispersis littera pinnis. (*Phars.* 5.71–6)[45]

[Thus, when cranes are driven by winter from the frozen Strymon to drink the water of the Nile, at the beginning of their flight they describe various chance-taught figures; but later, when a loftier wind beats on their outspread wings, they combine at random and form disordered packs, until the letter is broken and disappears as the birds are scattered.]

In the *Etymologiae*, Isidore recalled Lucan's verses while discussing cranes and the alphabet (XII.7.14). Authors evoked these ideas about cranes to create enigmas about writing. In his *Epigrammata*, in the book titled *Xenia* (presents for dinner guests), Martial wrote about the Greek Palamedes. He had supposedly invented letters by tracing the forms of cranes in flight: "Turbabis versus nec littera tota volabit, / unam perdidieris si Palamedis avem" [*Ep.* 75; You will disturb the lines and the writing will not fly complete, if you lose one of Palamedes's birds].[46] Therefore, in medieval culture, cranes were emblematic of the spelling and formation of words, aspects of a text's literal sense. In VI.4, Boccaccio evinced these ideas about cranes and letters by depicting a debate about language by reference to a crane's shifting shape. The story might also recall Martial's verses about the disfigured forms of cranes, which symbolized "disfigured" writing.[47] In Martial's text, the epigram appeared in the section dedicated to dinner gifts. In VI.4, Chichibio presents the crane at a dinner in an altered, or a dis*figured*, form (VI.4.10–11). The fact that Currado feels "turbato" [VI.4.11; disturbed] at the sight of the crane may recall Martial's remarks about disturbing the lines of a text.

Cranes also supposedly possessed characteristics that were considered typical of vernacular languages. Although authors of bestiaries or didactic texts did not state that the crane symbolized the vernacular, they did discuss the linguistic resonances of the birds in general terms.

45 For the text and translation of Lucan's *Pharsalia*, I have used the Loeb edition by Henderson and Duff.

46 For the text and translation of Martial's *Epigrams*, I have used the Loeb edition by Bailey.

47 Boccaccio copied the *Epigrammata* either between 1361 and 1362 or between 1370 and 1371 (Milan, Biblioteca Ambrosiana, C 67 sup.). However, he could have encountered sections of the work before these dates. On Boccaccio's Martial and the manuscript tradition of the *Epigrammata*, see Petoletti.

Indeed, cranes were seen to have traits that came to be associated with the vernacular. These traits may have prompted late medieval writers of literary texts to employ the birds to symbolize ideas about the vernacular, notably Dante in his *Comedy* (see subsection IV, below). As the vernacular was generally classified as a natural language, so cranes were thought to be emblematic of natural signifying. The Latin name for cranes was considered onomatopoetic. Medieval writers hypothesized that the names of diverse birds derived from various traits. The falcon, a bird mentioned in the tale, was supposedly so-called due to the curved shape of its talons: "Hunc nostri falconem vocant, quod incurvis digitis sit" [Isidore, *Etym*. XII.7.57; We call this one the falcon because its talons are curved inward]. Instead, it was thought that "[g]rues nomen de propria voce sumpserunt; tali enim sono susurrant" [Isidore, *Etym*. XII.7.14; (c)ranes took their name from their voice, for they call out with such a sound].[48] In addition, as the vernacular varied according to time and place, so the cranes were thought to migrate as the seasons changed. In his *Hexaemeron* (c. 370), Ambrose explained: "Grues, quia alta petunt, amant frequenter peregrinari" [V.14.48; Cranes, because they fly high, love to migrate frequently].[49] Finally, the popularity of animal lore in late medieval culture was partially due to vernacular texts. Writings that feature information about non-human animals were either translated from Latin into a vernacular, or they were originally written in a vernacular language (*Pharsalia*, Brunetto Latini's *Tresor*, various bestiaries and fables with cranes, etc.).[50] The Latin illiterate Chichibio voices ideas about cranes that were commonly known, such as the fact that cranes sleep on one foot (VI.4.16), because these notions were discussed in vernacular texts.[51] This tale encourages readers to appreciate that the

48 In his commentary on *Inferno* 5.46–8, Guido da Pisa cites Isidore when mentioning the etymology of cranes (354).

49 For the text of Ambrose's *Hexaemeron*, I have used the edition by Schenkl. In his commentary on *Inferno* 5, Guido da Pisa repeats Ambrose's comments (354). In his *Tresor*, Brunetto Latini also discusses the migratory patterns of cranes. See Latini, *Tresor* I.163.1–3. Latini's text circulated widely in Tuscany in both the French original and in Tuscan vernaculars. For example, the Florentine vulgarization has been edited as *I libri naturali del "Tesoro" emendati colla scorta de' codici, commentati e illustrati da Guido Battelli*. For the chapter on cranes, see V.27.

50 On the vernacularization of these texts, see notes 44 and 49 above. For an example of a Tuscan vulgarization of Aesop's fables, see Branca's edition of the *Esopo toscano dei frati e dei mercanti trecenteschi*. For the fable about the wolf and the crane, see VIII.

51 On the popular resonances of bestiaries and animal lore in the Middle Ages, see Ziolkowski, "Popular Culture" 393–4. On cranes' sleeping habits, see Latini, *Tresor* I.163.4–6; *Libri naturali del "Tesoro"* 123–4; and *Il bestiario toscano* XXII.

crane symbolizes the vernacular by foregrounding conceptual similarities between Chichibio and the bird. Both are associated with Venetian speech characteristics (truncation) and have onomatopoetic names. Neifile's Proem – about vernacular topics – would also have helped readers appreciate that the crane symbolizes types of vernacular speech.

In VI.4 the crane evokes ideas about the superficial dimension of bodies. In the Middle Ages, the peculiar bodily properties of cranes were discussed. Writers observed that the feathers of cranes turned from white to black as the birds aged, a trait of cranes that recalls the writing process (black ink on parchment).[52] The crane was also remarkable because of its unattractive physical form. In one of Avianus's fables, a peacock teases a crane for its uncomeliness (*Av. Fab.* XV.5–8). The crane responds by taking flight and then noting that the peacock's beautiful plumage is useless because it cannot fly (*Av. Fab.* XV.11–14). Finally, late medieval writers hypothesized that cranes were lustful creatures. Dante featured cranes in a simile that compared one group of lustful sinners to the birds:

> E come i gru van cantando lor lai,
> faccendo in aere di sé lunga riga,
> così vid'io venir [ombre], traendo guai (*Inf.* 5.46–8)
>
> [And as the cranes go singing their laments,
> making a long line of themselves in the air,
> so I saw [the shades] come, bearing woes]

Medieval Dante commentators noted that the poet had employed this simile because cranes were renowned for their erotic desires.[53] In VI.4 Neifile recalls ideas about the bodily connotations of cranes. As noted, she characterizes Chichibio, who speaks like a crane, as a superficial and unstable creature (VI.4.6). He struggles to be vigilant against the allures of desire. He eventually succumbs to Brunetta's erotic lures by giving her a piece of the crane. At the same time, the central ideological crux of the tale concerns the unstable form of a crane, a bird known for its shifting and ugly appearance. Finally, Neifile recalls the belief that cranes were lustful creatures when she states that Brunetta was attracted by the aroma and appearance of the cooked bird.

---

52 On the changing nature of cranes' bodies, see Isidore, *Etym.* XII.7.15; Latini, *Tresor* I.163.6; *Libri naturali del "Tesoro"* 124.

53 For example, see the gloss in the *Ottimo commento* on *Inf.* 5.46 (90.89–92).

Boccaccio's decision to dramatize matters related both to the literal sense of a text and to the superficial dimension of bodies in a story about cranes was not occasional. VI.4 draws on pervasive ideas about cranes that had both metaliterary and bodily resonances. Given that various ideas about cranes had textual connotations, medieval readers would have appreciated that in VI.4 the crane's body represents the vernacular text. By featuring a debate about the formal traits of a crane, Boccaccio encouraged readers to reflect upon the literal and superficial aspects of vernacular literature.

III. Truth and Vernacular Bodies

Neifile's tale addresses the dignity of vernacular literatures by assessing their relative capacity to be truthful. In medieval culture, writers of all stripes debated whether imaginative texts – Latin, ancient, vernacular, etc. – could signify truthfully. Critics of literature argued that fictional works were both untruthful and unnatural because they communicated meaning in a false narrative.[54] Theologians and philosophers denigrated fictional texts in comparison to God's mode of signifying in history and nature.[55] VI.4 foregrounds issues concerning truth and literature by dramatizing a debate between Chichibio and Currado. They disagree about whether the crane – a vernacular textual symbol – is naturally mono- or biped (VI.4.10–13). While describing their disagreement, the narrator calls Chichibio a "bugiardo" [VI.4.10; liar]. After dinner, Currado states that he wants to determine whether he or the cook has "mentito" [lied] about the crane; and the Florentine wants "pruova della ... bugia" [proof of the ... lie] (VI.4.14 and 15). Therefore, while reflecting on the true form of the crane (its ontology), they disagree about who has properly understood and described the crane's body (epistemology and semiotics). Neifile emphasizes that their disagreement concerns who has a proper view of the form of the crane. Currado asks Chichibio whether he has ever seen cranes, while Chichibio responds that Currado will see their true form in living birds (VI.4.11 and 12).[56] Given the metaliterary resonances of the protagonists, their

54 For medieval perceptions of literature as a fraudulent mode of discourse in comparison to God's historical signifying, see Kriesel, *Boccaccio's Corpus* 9–11.

55 Boccaccio discussed these objections in *Genealogie* XIV.xiv.2–6, 13, and 19.

56 The fact that their debate concerns seeing the crane correctly is emphasized. See *Dec.* VI.4.11, 12, 15, 16, and 17.

debate concerns the following textual and linguistic issue. The tale dramatizes whether a plebeian, Venetian, vulgar literature or a refined, Florentine, sublime textual tradition is (more) truthful. In the tale's metaphoric terms, VI.4 explores whether Chichibio's truncated, plebeian, non-Tuscan language (symbolized by the truncated crane) is less true in comparison to Currado's unabridged Florentine, noble, refined speech (symbolized by the biped form of the bird).

The tale assesses the truthfulness of each (textual) body by reference to a divine-human form that embodied truth. The theological resonances of the tale are introduced when Brunetta testifies to her truthfulness: "In fé di Dio, se tu non la mi dai, tu non avrai mai da me cosa che ti piaccia" [VI.4.9; Swear to God, if you don't give it to me, then you will not have from me what you like]. Currado instead swears on the truthfulness of his words by invoking the Incarnation, the Word-Made-Flesh: "io ti guiro in sul corpo di Cristo che, se altramenti sarà, che io ti farò conciare in maniera, che tu con tuo danno ti ricorderai, sempre che tu ci viverai, del nome mio" [VI.4.13; I swear to you on the body of Christ that if it is otherwise [i.e., that the crane does not have one foot], I will reduce you to such a state, that on account of the pain inflicted you will remember my name as long as you live]. The remarks about Christ's body and remembering Currado's name evoke the Eucharist: "accepto pane gratias egit et fregit et dedit eis dicens: 'hoc est corpus meum quo pro vobis datur: hoc facite in meam commemerationem'" [Luke 22:19; Taking bread, He gave thanks, broke it, and gave it to them saying: "This is my body which has been given to you: do this in memory of me"].[57] The references to truth and Christ's body encourage readers to consider human (vernacular) textual bodies in relation to God's bodily mode of signification.

Furthermore, medieval readers might have thought about Christ in relation to cranes because the birds had theological connotations. Many creatures supposedly expressed Christological or providential traits, and cranes were no exception.[58] This interpretation of the birds was inspired by the fact that they seemingly sacrificed themselves willingly; took turns leading each other in flight; and shared the burden of guarding the flock.[59] Writers noted that cranes take turns remaining vigilant

57 For the text of the Vulgate Bible, I have used Weber and Gryson's *Biblia Sacra Vulgata*.

58 For example, see *Il bestiario toscano* 43–4; and the *Aberdeen Bestiary* (c. 1200; Aberdeen University Library MS 24), 45v–46v. For a discussion of the providential and Christological resonances of cranes, see Charbonneau-Lassay 593–8.

59 For example, see Guido da Pisa 354; *Il bestiario toscano* 43–4; Isidore, *Etym.* XII.7.14; and Ambrose, *Hexaemeron* V.14.49–52.

when they sleep. They explained that one crane remains vigilant by holding a rock in an elevated foot. If the vigilant crane falls asleep, the rock will fall into the water and the noise will wake the flock. The rock itself was occasionally interpreted as a *figura Christi*. The author of the so-called *Aberdeen Bestiary* (c. 1200) interprets the crane holding the rock as an example of how an individual should keep Christ in mind.[60] Finally, in VI.4, the cranes have apostolic resonances. The protagonists observe a flock of twelve cranes (VI.4.16), the number of disciples charged with disseminating the Word in the Bible. Writings about cranes do not state that cranes typically travel in flocks of a specific number, a fact that suggests the number twelve in VI.4 is meaningful.

The import of reflecting on vernacular textuality in relation to divine signification emerges when Chichibio and Currado observe the cranes. When they see the cranes on one foot, Chichibio affirms that he is correct, that cranes have a monoped form. In response, Currado yells "[h]o, ho!" [[o]h, oh!], which causes the cranes to put down their other foot (VI.4.17). The Florentine noble then proclaims that they are biped creatures. The story thus highlights that cranes, by nature, have different forms and assume various shapes. The two protagonists make peace (VI.4.20) because each of them is being truthful (whether intentionally or not). The Christological, Eucharistic, and Apostolic allusions in the story would have prompted readers to consider the cranes' bodies in relation to the embodied *Logos*. In particular, the *novella* – by alluding to Christ's body and the Eucharist – recalls that Christ presented and presents himself in various forms. As the crane's body migrates and assumes multiple shapes, so Christ's body is manifest in different places and changes forms. Christ assumed different forms in part because of his age and in part because he presents himself in the Eucharist. In medieval philosophical terms, his accidents change (his physical exterior) but his essence does not.[61] Niefile obliquely signalled the pertinence of ideas about accidents in the tale by discussing "accidenti" [VI.4.3; accidents] in her Proem. By recalling Christ's evolving physical presence, VI.4 suggests that various types of vernacular texts can be truthful even though they have different forms and properties. The story thereby recalls the fact that vernacular textual traditions are related to one another. Boccaccio reminds readers that though vernacular literatures change through

60 See *Aberdeen Bestiary* 46r.

61 On the distinctions between accident, essence, and substance in medieval culture, see Macy; and Wippel.

time and place (accidents), they nevertheless share similar basic linguistic and signifying properties (substance).

Moreover, VI.4 dramatizes the import of reflecting on matters related to the literal, or superficial, sense of a literary work. In medieval culture, it was thought that readers needed to understand the literal sense of a text before they could profitably consider its allegorical meaning.[62] In VI.4, Currado and Chichibio investigate the superficial form of the crane's body, a symbol for the literal sense of a vernacular text. And regarding the literal sense, they are not only debating ideas about vernacularity. They are also engaging with issues concerning versification and prosody (does the text have one or two metrical feet?).[63] They eventually discover that the poetic body can comprise a different number of feet, thus resolving their epistemological and hermeneutic disagreement. The point is that both a plebeian Venetian text (with a truncated foot) and a refined Florentine one (with two feet) can have natural and truthful properties.

The tale addresses the nature of non-Tuscan, municipal, plebeian vernacular traditions. At the same time, Neifile's story invites readers to consider the dignity of other textual *corpora*. Other literary forms featured various types of metrical feet, and had controversial plebeian or vulgar connotations. Elegiac writings, like Ovid's erotic poems, were comprised of verses of different feet, a hexameter and pentameter. The literary theorist Matthew of Vendôme (1100–1185) stated that elegiac poems are written in distichs "inequalitate pedum" [*Ars versificatoria* II.8; with unequal feet]. Ovid's poems influenced diverse ideas about poetics and ethics in the *Decameron*.[64] Moreover, the Introduction to Day Six may have been inspired by the medieval genre of elegiac comedy.[65] These licentious poems typically featured couplets comprising a hexameter and pentameter, and they circulated widely in both Latin and peninsular vernaculars. Like these poems, the Introduction features servants and concerns ideas related to (female) sexuality and infidelity. Various fables were also composed in Latin elegiac couplets; as noted, these works often circulated in vernacular translation. The story about

62 On the import of studying the literal sense of a text, see Dante, *Convivio* II.i.8–15. I have used Ageno's edition of the work.

63 Beginning in antiquity, verses were described in terms of metrical feet. See *A Latin Dictionary*, s.v. *pes* (II.K, 1362–1).

64 For a survey of Boccaccio's engagement with Ovid, see Kriesel, *Boccaccio's Corpus* 157–201.

65 On the genre of elegiac comedy, see Bertini. On Boccaccio's engagement with Latin elegiac comedy (in *Dec.* VII.9), see Ascoli, "Pyrrhus's Rules" 83–90 and 108–9.

animals and missing body parts would have reminded readers of Avianus's fable, a short narrative that inspired VI.4.[66] Finally, many of Martial's epigrams, and all of book XIII dedicated to dinner gifts (a potential source for VI.4), were composed in elegiac couplets. By highlighting the naturalness of a body with different lengths of feet, VI.4 shows that texts with varying forms and properties can be truthful. The story suggests that though types of literary bodies appear disfigured, they may have natural properties and be truth-bearing.

Finally, VI.4 suggests that a writer can incorporate diverse vernacular traditions – with apparently contradictory connotations – congruently in one literary *corpus*. Currado, who embodies a refined Florentine literature, forms a harmonious relationship with Chichibio, who personifies a non-Tuscan, plebeian tradition. By depicting a synthesis of vernacular writings, Boccaccio may have again been inspired by ideas about cranes. Writers from Ambrose to Brunetto Latini observed that cranes share leadership roles, respect one another, and present a model order for society.[67] On account of these notions, late medieval writers thought that the term *congruentia* was derived from the Latin word for crane (*grus*):[68]

> *Grus-is* a sono vocis dicitur, unde ... *gruo-is*, convenire, concordare ... et inde *congruus-a-um*, id est conveniens ... unde *congrue* et *congruenter* adverbia et hec *congruitas*, idem quod *congruentia*. (Uguccione da Pisa, *Derivationes* 2:547)

> [*Grus-is* gets its name from the sound of its voice, which ... is related to the verb *gruo-is*, namely to be suitable, or to accord ... and also the adjective *congruous-a-um*, meaning agreeable ... from whence we get the adverbs *congrue* and *congruenter* and the noun *congruitas*, or *congruentia*.]

During the tale, Chichibio and Currado become members of one "flock" as differences between them are attenuated. Despite Neifile's initial remarks about Chichibio's intellect, he possesses a degree of artistic ability. Chichibio is presented as a "buon cuoco" [VI.4.5; good cook], a profession that had artistic overtones. In his scholarship, Boccaccio noted that contemporary cooks should be considered artists:

> arte è quella intorno alla quale non solamente l'opera manuale, ma ancora lo 'ngegno e la 'ndustria dell'artefice s'adopera ... e sì come è il cuocere

66 On Avianus's fables in the Middle Ages, see Bisanti, *Le favole di Aviano*.

67 On the flock of cranes as a model for society, see note 58 above.

68 On the etymology of *congruentia*, see also note 17 above.

> oggi, al quale non basta far bollir la caldaia, ma vi si richiede l'artificio del cuoco in fare che quel che si cuoce sia saporito, sia odorifero, sia bello all'occhio. (*Espos.* VI.2.14)
>
> [art does not only involve manual work, but also the genius and industry of the artist ... take for example cooking today, which does not merely require the boiling of the pot, but also requires the artifice of the cook so that what is cooked tastes good, has an appealing odour, and appears pleasing to the eye.]

In accord with these ideas, Neifile highlights Chichibio's creativity by describing how Brunetta is attracted by the aroma and visual presentation of the cooked bird (VI.4.5–7). Though guided by instinct and circumstance, Chichibio also teaches Currado scientific ideas about cranes. Finally, as the crane alters its shape, so Chichibio modifies his speech and register in accord with the social status of his interlocutor. After speaking to Brunetta in his plebeian Venetian vernacular, the cook addresses Currado in grammatically correct Florentine:

> Messer sí, ma voi non gridaste "ho, ho!" a quella d'iersera; ché se cosí gridato aveste ella avrebbe cosí l'altra coscia e l'altro piè fuor mandata, come hanno fatto queste. (VI.4.18)
>
> [Yes sir, but you did not yell "oh, oh!" to that [bird] last night; for if you had yelled like this, it would have put down its other thigh and other foot, as these have done.]

Chichibio's discourse features various tenses and a hypothetical clause. By contrast, Currado adopts a simple mode of signifying by employing the interjection "oh, oh!" to rouse the cranes. As cranes supposedly shared governing roles, so he allows Chichibio to lead him by accepting the cook's explanation. In the metaphoric terms of the tale, they, like cranes, mutually guide one another. They thus resolve their differences, and form a congruent literary society.

IV. Boccaccio's and Dante's Literary Congruence

When reflecting on textual congruence in VI.4, Boccaccio engaged with Dante's views about this subject. Neifile's story may have been inspired by ideas expressed in Dante's *De vulgari eloquentia*.[69] Boccaccio initially

69 For a synthesis of the primary concepts of the *De vulgari eloquentia*, especially those pertinent to this chapter, see Scott 35–7, 41–4, and 46–52.

read the work while living in Naples, and he may have reread the text while composing the *Decameron* (c. 1348–c. 1360).[70] In the treatise, Dante recognizes that vernacular languages change as a result of what is termed "congruitas" [congruence]: "humanis beneplacitis localique congruitate nascuntur" [1.9.10; they arise from people's preferences and geographical congruence]. However, he did not approve of vernacular writers who employed linguistic expressions that had local or pedestrian connotations. Types of such speech are categorized as rustic ("rusticanus"; I.11.6), plebeian ("plebeius"; I.12.3), mediocre ("mediocris"; I.12.6), municipal ("municipalis"; I.13.1), feminine ("feminus"; I.14.2), unrefined ("rudis"; I.14.4), bitter ("acerbus"; I.15.4), and not pure ("purus"; I.15.7). By contrast, Dante promotes texts written in a so-called "vulgare illustre" [I.17.1; illustrious vernacular], which is characterized by aulic words and a sublime register (II.6–7). Dante specifies that this vernacular is not composed of words that are infantile like "babbo" [daddy], feminine like "placevole" [pleasing], bestial like "greggia" [herd], urban, smooth, or rough like "femina" [female] or "corpo" [body] (II.7.3–5).

Dante revised these ideas by including a range of speech and registers in the *Comedy*.[71] However, Boccaccio did not think that the poem was a plurilingual text.[72] He argued that the *Comedy* was written in a sublime style that did not have extensive instances of plebeian or feminine speech. In contrast to this view of Dante's writing, VI.4 features – overtly and centrally – examples of municipal, popular, and unrefined Venetian idioms. The story has the words "Chichibio," "bergolo," "feminetta," and "corpo," the types of infantile, municipal, and plebeian words denigrated in Dante's treatise (for example, VI.4.6, 7, and 13). Whereas Boccaccio thought Dante did not approve of these expressions, the Florentine Currado symbolically makes peace with them in VI.4. The personification of *stilnovismo* thereby endorses non-Florentine and plebeian

70 A passage of Dante's treatise probably inspired Boccaccio to compose the *Teseida delle nozze d'Emilia*. Dante noted that no one had written an epic poem about arms in the vernacular (*De vulgari eloquentia* II.2.8). Boccaccio's Florentine epic-romance hybrid deals centrally with this topic (*Tes*. XII.84–6). On the *De vulgari* and *Teseida*, see Coleman 89. For other echoes of Dante's treatise in Boccaccio's works, see Pistolesi 163–7. She also notes that the Venetian word *plaghe* mentioned in the treatise (I.14.6) appears at *Dec*. IV.2.43, a story set in Venice (165). On Boccaccio's engagement with the treatise in the 1350s, see Nussmeier.

71 On the vernacular idioms and registers depicted in the *Comedy*, see Scott 262–9.

72 Boccaccio did not think that Dante had rejected the ideas developed in his treatise. Rather, he thought Dante's death prevented him from completing the work (see Boccaccio, *Tratt*. §200 [Toledano redaction; c. 1351–5]; and Nussmeier 251–2).

traits in vernacular writing. Moreover, Neifile's tale dramatizes how geographical *congruitas* engenders a plurilingual (con)text. The story refers to the presence of "forestieri" [foreigners] in Florence on two separate occasions (VI.4.10 and 13). Neifile's story does not only involve the Venetian Chichibio, but it concerns guests from another unspecified city.

While VI.4 addresses Dante's theoretical ideas about vernacularity, it also engages with his vernacular poetics as expressed in the *Comedy*. Throughout the poem, Dante developed views about the vernacular by reference to cranes.[73] In *Inferno* 5, the poet mentions cranes in a simile that characterizes one type of vernacular writing ambiguously (cited above in section II).[74] In his commentary on Dante's poem, Boccaccio discussed both the spiritual and literary resonances of the simile:

> Qui per un'altra comparazione ne discrive una brigata di quegli spiriti dannati aver veduti venire verso quella parte dove esso e Virgilio erano; e dice quegli esser da quel vento menati in quella forma che volano per aere i gru; *cantando lor lai,* cioè lor versi. Ed è questo vocabolo preso, cioè "lai," dal parlar francesco, nel quale si chiamano "lai" certi versi in forma di lamentazione nel lor volgare composti. (*Espos.* V.1.49)

> [Here with another simile he states that he saw a group of the damned come towards where he and Virgil were; and he says they were buffeted by the wind in that form that cranes fly in the air; *singing their lai,* namely their verses. And this word *lai* comes from French; it is a type of poem composed in their vernacular in the form of a lament.]

Like his peers, Boccaccio understood that the francophone *lai* tradition was potentially damned by association with the lustful.[75]

In *Purgatorio* 24, the pilgrim meets the poet Bonagiunta da Lucca (c. 1220–1290) among the souls purifying the sin of gluttony. After their encounter, these penitents are compared to birds that "in aere fanno schiera" [make a flock in the air] and form "un fil" [a line] (65–6). The phrases recall the description of cranes in *Inferno* 5. In Dante's treatise on the vernacular, Bonaguinta was criticized along with Guittone d'Arezzo (c. 1230–1294) as a municipal writer (*De vulgari eloquentia*

---

73 For bibliography related to cranes and vernacularity in the *Comedy*, see note 14 above.

74 On the symbolic import of cranes in relation to francophone *lai* in *Inferno* 5, see Conte; and Fioretti 75–82.

75 See note 53 above.

I.13.1 and II.6.8). In the *Comedy*, Bonagiunta acknowledges the dignity of the *stilnovo* tradition:

> "O frate, issa vegg'io," diss'elli, "il nodo
> che 'l Notaro e Guittone e me ritenne
> di qua dal dolce stil novo ch'i odo!" (*Purg*. 24.55–7)
>
> ["O brother, now I see," he said, "the knot
> that kept the Notary and Guittone and me
> from the sweet new style that I hear!"]

However, he also uses the municipal word "issa" [now], a fact that highlights how the *Comedy* – crucially – incorporates municipal words and expressions.[76] In *Purgatorio* 26, the homosexual and heterosexual penitents are compared to cranes that migrate in different directions (43–8).[77] In this canto, the pilgrim meets the Provençal poet Arnaut Daniel (c. 1150–c. 1210), who speaks in his native vernacular (a unique occurrence in the poem). He identifies himself as a writer of erotic verse and prose romances, and repents of his former sin (140–7). Finally, ideas about cranes are recalled in the *Paradiso*. In *Paradiso* 17, Cacciaguida criticizes the Florentine factionalism that will result in Dante's exile (36–69). In the next canto, the pilgrim sees the souls of just rulers fly together, "come augelli" [like birds], to form the letters of the opening words of the book of Wisdom: "Diligite iustitiam, qui iudicatis terram" [Love justice, you who rule the earth] (*Par*. 18.73–93). One implication of these passages about cranes is that Dante's vernacular poem recognizes yet harmonizes political and cultural divisions.[78] By repeatedly referring to a symbol of congruence and vernacularity, Dante signalled that *congruentia* characterizes the poetics of the *Comedy*.[79] These verses highlight that the vernacular poem incorporates both Florentine and non-Florentine cultures as well as diverse municipal, plebeian, and aulic expressions.

In VI.4, Boccaccio engaged with one passage related to Dante's notion of *congruentia*. Boccaccio reflects on *Inferno* 5 by recalling the simile

76 On the import of Bonagiunta's words for ideas about language in the *Comedy*, see Martinez, "Pilgrim's Answer" 54–63; and Fioretti 68–75 and 82–6.

77 On cranes and vernacularity in *Purgatorio* 26, see Fioretti 86–93; and Gorni, "'Gru' di Dante."

78 On the symbolic import of the cranes in relation to the divine skywriting, see Conte 121–2; della Cagna 73–80; Ledda 109–14.

79 For the relevance of cranes in relation to Dante's poetics of congruence, see Fioretti 86–93; and Ledda 109–14.

about cranes singing *lai* (*Inf.* 5.46–8). Chichibio, who speaks like a crane, responds to Brunetta in song: "Chihibio le rispose *cantando* e disse: 'Voi non l'avrí da mi, madonna Brunetta, voi non l'avrí da mi'" [VI.4.8; Chichibio answered her *by singing* and said: "You will not have it from me, lady Brunetta, you will not have it from me"; emphasis added]. Moreover, the cook intones a verse from a northern *lai* called *Donna Lombarda,* which was perhaps transmitted in oral form: "Ameme mi, dona Lombarda, ameme mi" [Love me, lady Lombarda, love me].[80] In several redactions of the poem, this verse begins the popular song. In the poem, the male narrator asks a woman to betray her husband. Therefore, the crane-like Chichibio goes "cantando" [singing] an adulterous love lament (*lai*) in a northern vernacular. Boccaccio thereby recalls the languages and cultures associated with cranes in *Inferno* 5. Though *Donna Lombarda* is not a French poem, it is a northern vernacular *lai.* In the medieval period, northern vernaculars were geographically and conceptually intertwined with francophone culture. The Veneto was permeated by French linguistic forms and texts (for example, Arthurian and erotic romance poems).[81]

The echoes of *Inferno* 5 in VI.4 prompt comparison of Dante's and Boccaccio's poetics of congruence. In the *Esposizioni,* Boccaccio noted that certain municipal and erotic literatures were characterized ambiguously in *Inferno* 5. In Boccaccio's view, they are not clearly incorporated in the poetics of the *Comedy.* In VI.4, Boccaccio recalls the type of *lai* described ambiguously in *Inferno* 5, and then incorporates it in his text. By having Chichibio and Currado make peace, Boccaccio signalled that the Franco-Venetian poem should not be damned or denigrated. Moreover, by writing about a *lai,* Boccaccio was by extension reflecting on other types of municipal poems. He was prompting readers to remember those verses intoned by Dioneo in the Conclusion to Day Five (6–13). Like Chichibio's Franco-Venetian *lai,* these municipal songs feature vulgar, adulterous, and plebeian content. Boccaccio thus suggested that, in comparison to Dante, he was more clearly incorporating – in a congruent fashion – types of writing with controversial municipal, plebeian, feminine traits.

80 For the verse and a discussion of the poem in VI.4, see Petrolini, who suggests that Boccaccio cited the poem to create a realistic depiction of a Venetian and to parody non-Florentine speech (712).

81 On French culture in Italy and on Franco-Venetian culture, see Cherchi, "Vernacular Literatures" 371–6; and Tavoni 256–8.

V. Conclusion

Dante inspired Boccaccio to consider matters concerning vernacular congruence. He offered a model for how to incorporate in one text vernacular cultures with divergent connotations. However, Dante – in Boccaccio's opinion – had not clearly incorporated in the *Comedy* several cultures that were considered controversial.[82] In the *Esposizioni*, Boccaccio also explained that the poem did not feature vulgar elements that were typical of comedy. He states that the *Comedy* does not depict rustic persons talking about animal husbandry or their "bassi e rozi inamoramenti" [Accessus 18; low and rustic love affairs]. In VI.4, Boccaccio dramatized that he was incorporating these plebeian, rustic, and vulgar traditions in the *Decameron*. Therefore, VI.4 is emblematic of key aspects of the *Decameron*'s ideology. Its metatextual significance pertains to cultural forms that were occasionally – according to Boccaccio – ignored by late medieval authors. On the one hand, VI.4 reminds readers that the *novelle* draw upon the Tuscan cultures of Guido Cavalcanti, Dante, and Cino da Pistoia (writers who are mentioned in the Introduction to Day Four [33–4]).[83] On the other hand, the tale emphasizes that the story collection is informed by non-Tuscan oral, popular, and vulgar traditions.[84] VI.4 thus, in a day dedicated to metaliterary issues, programmatically highlights the range of cultures that inspire the *Decameron*.

Regarding the day's subtheme, VI.4 encourages readers to not be fooled by superficial or unconventional appearances. By depicting Currado's reaction to Chichibio, Boccaccio offers readers a hermeneutic lesson. The story emphasizes that readers, like Currado, might learn from speakers and (textual) *corpora* that seem to have deformed or superficial traits. In fact, VI.4 implies that even providential concepts might be communicated by such orators and texts. In VI.4, Boccaccio highlighted this issue by writing about cranes, which were thought to behave in a providential manner. Moreover, one of the tale's clearest antecedents treats ideas about fortune and divine providence. Though Lucius in the

---

82 For a modern view of the types of popular culture that are depicted in the *Comedy*, see Ziolkowski, "Popular Culture."

83 On the import of the Introduction to Day Four for creating a canon of Tuscan writers, see Eisner, *Boccaccio and the Invention* 4–9.

84 Robins suggests that Boccaccio, like his peers, reacted ambiguously to itinerant singers and performers (4–5). He also notes that the *Decameron* "tries to strike the right balance between popular forms of storytelling … and forms of courtly refinement" (28).

Metamorphoses thinks that one cannot contradict these forces, they conspire to help him escape danger. By modelling VI.4 on Apuleius's story about beasts, Boccaccio prompted readers to consider similar themes in his tale about a crane. Boccaccio was encouraging readers to look for the workings of providence in various situations and contexts. Finally, VI.4 dramatizes a biblical lesson about speech. Neifile explains that her specific contribution to the day's theme concerns how a "leggiadro motto" [graceful saying] might diffuse anger (VI.4.1; compare VI.4.14, 15, and 19). These concepts recall a biblical proverb: "responsio mollis frangit iram sermo durus suscitat furorem" [Prov. 15:1; a gentle response diffuses anger, harsh speech engenders fury].[85] VI.4 depicts how a gentle discourse – even when spoken instinctually by "foreigners" – can ameliorate ideological tensions. Yet it also encourages "locals" to react kindly to their speech to promote social and cultural congruence.

85 Both the Tuscan *leggiardo* and the Latin *mollis* have resonances ranging from graceful and comely to delicate and pleasant. See *A Latin Dictionary*, s.v. *mollis* (1159).

5 The Tale of Forese da Rabatta and Giotto (VI.5)

ZYGMUNT G. BARAŃSKI

[V]idi quod de rebus per apparentia naturalia quasi nulla certitudo potest metiri [I saw that almost no certainty about things can be assessed through natural appearances]

(Nicholas of Autremont, *Exigit* 181)[1]

I. Problems of Structure and Rubrication

Decameron VI.5 is a perplexing tale. Indeed, given its sharp division into two generically distinct yet equal parts (on which more anon), "tale"[2] would seem to be a somewhat reductive designation for the text that may be read under the rubric "Messer Forese da Rabatta e maestro Giotto dipintore, venendo di Mugello, l'uno la sparuta apparenza dell'altro motteggiando morde" [VI.5.1; Messer Forese da Rabatta and maestro Giotto painter, coming from Mugello, each, quipping, bites the other's shabby appearance]. On reaching VI.5's *explicit*, the rubric too is a wellspring, perhaps emblematically, of perplexity. Thus, while the header's closing phrase announces that both Forese and Giotto utter a *motto* regarding the other's look, the problem arises to what extent, in its form and intent, the lawyer's laborious question can actually be

1 I should warmly like to thank James Kriesel, David Lummus, and Justin Steinberg for their comments on an earlier version of this chapter. All quotations from the *Decameron* are from Branca's 1985 Mondadori-Meridiani edition. Unless indicated otherwise, all translations are my own. In translating, my aim is literal accuracy rather than idiomatic elegance.

2 Despite my reservations regarding the designation "tale" to describe VI.5, as a matter of convenience and respect for a critical convention, I shall continue to use the term whenever I refer to VI.5 in its entirety.

described as a case of *motteggiare*: "Giotto, a che ora venendo di qua alla 'ncontro di noi un forestiere che mai veduto non t'avesse, credi tu che egli credesse che tu fossi il migliore dipintore del mondo, come tu se'?" [VI.5.14; Giotto, if right now a stranger were to come towards us who had never seen you before, do you believe that he would believe that you are the best painter in the world, as you are?]. Connected to this, a broader and more substantial difficulty arises. How might the lawyer's inquiry (and equally the painter's reaction) conform to the day's appointed theme: "si ragiona di chi, con alcun leggiadro motto, tentato, si riscotesse, o con pronta risposta o avvedimento fuggì perdita o pericolo o scorno" [VI.Intro.1; to discuss those who, with a charming quip, having been provoked, got their own back, or with a ready reply or with expediency evaded a loss or a danger or a humiliation]?

In truth, Day Six's general rubric confirms and accentuates VI.5's puzzling slipperiness. It leaves unanswered the question of whether or not Forese's baiting is a *motto*, while at the same time complicating the status of Giotto's reaction, as well as the relationship between Day Six's rubric and that of the tale itself. Rather than a *motto*, the painter's retort is a "ready reply," the second type of rejoinder posited in the Introduction: "A cui Giotto prestamente rispose" [VI.5.15; To whom Giotto readily replied]. The tale thus raises suggestive questions about what precisely might constitute a *motto*[3] – an issue to which I shall need to return. Furthermore, in light of Day Six's preordained narrating parameters, the *novella*'s resolution is also baffling. How, in practice, might Forese's seemingly playful question – "cominciò a ridere" [VI.5.13; he began to laugh] – a private joke between two professionally and socially well affirmed individuals, be considered as menacing "a loss or a danger or a humiliation"? VI.5, or better, its "novella" (VI.5.8), namely its second part, relates awkwardly to the theme of the day of which it is a part, as it does, albeit to a lesser extent, to its rubric. Accordingly, one cannot but wonder, on the one hand, about the "novella"'s status within the narrating macrostructure of Day Six and, on the other, about its standing and function in VI.5's microstructure.[4]

In any case, as is the norm for the *Decameron*'s rubrics,[5] VI.5's header only provides a précis of that section of the tale which straightforwardly

3 On the *motto*, see Andrei, "*Motto*"; Cuomo; Fido, *Il regime* 83–5; Meier, "Day Six" 292–3; Oesch-Serra; and Palumbo.

4 The same two questions also bear upon VI.5's first part; for a fuller discussion of the issues raised here, see below, pp. 124–32.

5 On these see D'Andrea 98–119; Milanese; and Usher, "Le rubriche del *Decameron*."

can be designated a "novella" (VI.5.8). It does not offer even a hint of the most structurally striking and innovative feature of *Decameron* VI.5, namely, its precise division into two almost equal halves, whose discrete textual status Panfilo underscores when he declares: "Ma alla novella venendo, dico" [8; But coming to the *novella*, I say].[6] This arresting balanced partition, without precedent in the *Decameron*[7] – and yet, for all its ostensible importance, essentially overlooked by Boccaccio scholarship[8] – is yet another conundrum which, as with so much else in the tale, proliferates questions. What might the reasons be for VI.5's peculiar organization? Given that the second section is conventionally labelled a "novella," how might the first section be defined? What might be the relationship between the two parts? Are there implications for the genre of the *novella* of being so closely associated with another, strikingly distinct, textual form? To what extent might VI.5's divided structure be connected to its thematic, ideological, and meta-artistic concerns? Like the vagaries of fortune, nature, and even the weather,

6 If I were editing *Decameron* VI.5, I would be tempted to treat this sentence as a self-standing paragraph. It has no connection with the remainder of the current eighth paragraph, functioning both as a marker of transition to the "novella" and as a sign of the separation between the text's two parts. *Decameron* VI.5 is 701 words long. The rubric is made up of 20 words, the first section (paragraphs 2–8) of 350, and the second (paragraphs 9–16) of 331. Indeed, since paragraph 2 constitutes a typical "preamble" that conventionally prepares for Panfilo's bifurcated presentation, then the two halves are almost identical in length: 329 and 331 words respectively.

7 The tale that comes closest to mirroring the structure of VI.5 is I.10. In the latter, paragraphs 3–8 (approximately 40 per cent of the text) examine the relationship between women, virtue, and *motteggiare*, and reflect on the nature and purpose of the *motto*; while paragraphs 9–20 (the remaining 60 per cent) tell of Maestro Alberto and Madonna Malgherida. Although, as is well known, there are several striking correspondences between VI.5 and I.10, it is important to note as regards their respective first parts that, unlike the wide-ranging variety and formal autonomy of VI.5's initial section, I.10's is clearly focused on a single question that is closely connected to the *novella* that ensues, as paragraphs 7 and 8 make evident: "acciò che voi vi sappiate guardare [resorting inappropriately to *motti*] … questa ultima novella di quelle d'oggi … voglio ve ne renda ammaestrate" [8; so that you might know to avoid … this last tale of those of today … I want that it will make you aware of this].

8 I have consulted the following analyses of VI.5: Baratto, *Realtà e stile* 409–13; Mazzotta, *World at Play* 238–40; Ruffini; Schaber; Stewart, *Retorica e mimica* 83–92; Veglia, *"La vita lieta"* 235–7. See also the studies on Boccaccio and Giotto listed in note 11. On Day Six, see Alfano, "Giornata VI"; Andrei, *"Motto"*; Ascoli, "Auerbach"; Bosetti; Cuomo 252–65; Fido, *Il regime* 73–89; Getto 140–64; Gittes, "Boccaccio's 'Valley of Women'"; Giusti, "La novella di Cesca"; Mineo; Muscetta, *Boccaccio* 245–50; Martinez, *"Scienze della Cittade"*; Meier, "Day Six"; Oesch-Serra; Palumbo; Petrini, *Nel giardino* 77–90; Picone, "Leggiadri motti"; Van der Voort; and Wallace 67–77. All these studies pass comment on VI.5.

Decameron VI.5 paratextually and in its organization creates difficulties: its "apparenza" [VI.5.1; appearance] refuses easy access to what might be found "sotto" [VI.5.3; beneath]. Attempting to reconcile its two parts, as well as rubric(s) and text, recalls, *mutatis mutandis*, the effort to *believe* (VI.5.14 and 15) that "turpissime forme" [most ugly forms] can "nascond*ere* ... maravigliosi ingegni" [VI.5.3; conceal marvellous intellects]. Thus, in both its formal and intellectual substance, VI.5 highlights difference and the relational and perceptual problems that (seeming) divergence might pose. Finally, Panfilo's introductory appeal to recognize what lies "beneath" immediately recalls the most basic tenet of medieval allegoresis: the need to recognize and then assess the dissimilarities, yet also the interconnections, between exterior and interior.[9] Our tale deliberately and systematically engenders problems – problems that, as the nod to allegoresis indicates, demand interpretation. Like Giotto's art, its aim is "compiacere allo 'ntelletto de' savi" [VI.5.6; to please the intelligence of the wise].

Whatever other functions part one of VI.5 may have, it unquestionably offers a wealth, even if "brievemente" [VI.5.4; briefly], of historical, cultural, social, biographical, and ideological – both loosely philosophical and theological – matter. Given VI.5's unusual structure, it is not illegitimate to treat this section, at least in a first instance, as a "self-sufficient" text that, as we shall see, touches on a host of important and, in some instances, controversial contemporary questions. Although, thanks to the figures of Forese and Giotto, it has obvious links with the "novella" that follows, its overall tone is generalizing and expositional. Thus, its presentation of VI.5's protagonists involves broad issues, such as the workings of fortune and of nature; the role of sight; the relationship between appearance and reality; the rapport between the human and the divine; the status of the body; the social standing of the artist; the purposes, effects, and audiences of painting; civic pride and identity; cultural renewal; and the implications of humility. These were all topics of considerable import in the late medieval (Italian communal) world, and it is thus unsurprising that they should be associated with persons of the intellectual and public prestige of a highly respected judge and politician[10] and of a famous painter who was "meritamente una delle

9 On allegory in Boccaccio, see Kriesel's fundamental monograph, *Boccaccio's Corpus*. See also Lummus, "Boccaccio's Poetic Anthropology"; Kirkham "Allegorically Tempered *Decameron*."

10 Boccaccio scholarship has ignored the implications of Forese da Rabatta's substantial standing in Florence and his many legal and political accomplishments during the first half of the Trecento (on which see Ciappelli, "Forese da Rabatta").

luci della fiorentina gloria" [VI.5.6; deservedly one of the lights of Florentine glory]. What is problematic, however, is, first, the possible interconnections between the various questions adumbrated in part one, and second, the nature of their relationship to the substance of the "novella." Indeed, complicating matters further, there would seem to be a major disjuncture between the cultural and intellectual gravity of the issues alluded to in the first half of VI.5 and the trivialness of its concluding section: visits to country estates, the quality of horses, unpreparedness for changes in the weather, shabby dress, travelling in the rain – all of which serve, if somewhat perfunctorily, to prepare for the "novella"'s resolution in a commonplace situation: the ready wit of a wise man.

II. Giotto *Orator*

Obsessed by the figure of Giotto and, consequently, by VI.5's metaliterary and meta-artistic implications, scholarly attention has firmly been fixed on the nature and functions of the painter's art, and, by extension, on the connections between the *novelliere* and the artist, "bellissim*i* favellator*i*" [VI.5.13; most beautiful speakers] and consummate "realists" both.[11] My analysis, on the other hand, normally eschews discussion of the tale's metaliterary features to focus instead on the breadth of the text's interests and on its structural and ideological tensions – matters that Boccaccio studies have generally ignored. In particular, by highlighting VI.5's rich system of culturally sensitive allusion, which brings together classical oratory, Scripture and its exegesis, as well as scholastic philosophy and theology, I lay stress on how Boccaccio intimates that correct interpretation of and reaction to not just language and art but also reality in general, coupled to virtuous behaviour, serves as the basis for an ethical Christian way of life, whether individual or communal. From this perspective, rather than straightforwardly metaliterary, VI.5 would seem to engage with matters that might be termed meta-interpretive. More broadly, and in line with a growing trend in *Decameron* criticism, my *lectura* endeavours to suggest that it is probably unhelpful to draw sharp distinctions between the collection's socio-political and ethical interests and its linguistic, literary, and exegetical consequences, not least because the two sets of concerns appear to be strictly interconnected in Boccaccio's poetics.

11 See Bartuschat 93–6; Ciccuto, "Il novelliere 'en artiste'" 773–83 and "Un'antica canzone"; Falaschi; Gilbert; Grassi; Ladis; Larner 274–82; Stewart, *Retorica e mimica* 249–77; Watson, "Cement of Fiction."

In keeping with the narrow priorities of the critical tradition on VI.5, what historical and cultural contextualization has so far been attempted with regard to our tale has been restricted to a relatively limited set of artistic and literary concerns. Equally, scholars have failed to pinpoint possible textual borrowings in VI.5 beyond Boccaccio's presentation of Giotto in part one. The sources indicated are four: Dante's *Purgatorio* 10, 11, and 12;[12] Pliny's account of Zeuxis and Parrhasius, ancient artists whose paintings were so lifelike that they deceived "il visivo senso" [VI.5.5; the visual sense; cf. *Naturalis historia* XXXV.61–6]; classical accounts of ugly artists who created beautiful art (for example, Macrobius, *Saturnalia* II.2.10); and Quintilian's maxim "docti rationem componendi intellegunt, etiam indocti voluptatem" [*Institutio oratoria* IX.4.116; the learned understand the logic of composition, but even the unlearned perceive its pleasure], which Boccaccio reworks as "più a dilettar gli occhi degl'ignoranti che a compiacere allo 'ntelletto de' savi dipignendo" [VI.5.6; more to delight the eyes of the ignorant than to please the intelligence of the wise].[13] Yet, there are other important quotations in the first section's portrait of Giotto – quotations that point to the text's ideological breadth and the richness of its remit; and the remainder of VI.5 too depends on a significant array of citations. Indeed, this complex of allusions constitutes a single system that establishes secure connections between VI.5's two halves.

The tale has an impressive pedigree. As far as I am aware, no source that might embrace VI.5 as a whole has hitherto been proposed. Carlo Muscetta has suggested a couple of possible precedents for the "novella," specifically Macrobius, *Saturnalia* VII.3.20 and Quintilian, *Institutio oratoria* VI.3.31–2 (*Boccaccio* 250). The passage from the *Saturnalia* is certainly suggestive: "Commendat scomma et conditio dicentis, si in eadem causa sit: ut si alium de paupertate pauper inrideat, si obscure natum natus obscure" [A jibe too is agreeable if the condition of the speaker is the same as that of the person being addressed: as, for example, if a poor person were to joke about another's poverty, or if someone of obscure birth were to make fun of someone's obscure birth]. Although the extract is too limited as a source for the "novella," since it primarily pertains to the latter's dénouement, the social stress that Macrobius gives to the exemplum fits well with the social dimension

12 See in particular Ascoli, "Auerbach."

13 Quintilian is referring to the reception of music and speech, and, unlike Boccaccio, is not making a polemical distinction between different types of listeners. For the text of Quintillian's *Institutio oratoria*, I have used the edition by Winterbottom.

that Boccaccio introduces into his story. By describing a situation that overturns Macrobius's advice that for a "scomma" to be *commendable* it needs to be directed at a social equal – in the late Middle Ages, the "condition" of lawyers and that of painters were not on a par – Boccaccio raises delicate questions regarding Forese's ethical behaviour and his status as a lawyer.

For the moment, however, I must set these fascinating matters of social standing and propriety to one side and return to VI.5's genealogy, especially as Muscetta's reference to the *Institutio oratoria* deserves closer scrutiny. Like Quintilian's physically unattractive and intellectually obtuse Sulpicius Longus, Forese belongs to those "qui ne id [iocum] quidem quod in ipsos recidere possit evitent" [*Institutio oratoria* VI.3.32; who do not even avoid a joke that can rebound against them], since, like his Roman predecessor, he speaks "senza avere a sé niuna considerazione" [VI.5.13; without giving any consideration about himself]. Once more Forese's reputation and lawyerly standing seem to be in doubt. Quintilian's description introduces Longus's gaffe that triggers Afer's cutting riposte, both of which are included in a long chapter on laughter, whose connections with our tale, and in particular with its second part, are conspicuous. Rather than depend on the anecdote of Longus and Afer, the "novella" originally and accurately illustrates, while also highlighting its relevance for the present, Quintilian's generalization: "[Risus] habet ... sedem in deformitate aliqua et turpitudine: quae cum in aliis demonstrantur, urbanitas, cum in ipsos dicentis reccidunt, stultitia vocantur" [7–8; Laughter has its seat in a certain deformity and ugliness: which when they are indicated in others is termed urbanity, but when it rebounds against those speaking, is termed stupidity]. In addition, Boccaccio lays stress on two other elements highlighted by Quintilian: the differences in natural ability when it comes to fashioning witticisms and the difference between "dicendi ac respondendi" [45; making a point and replying to it]. Finally, some of the "novella"'s key narrative details are already present in *Institutio oratoria* VI.3. We thus find someone "ab equo luto ... adspersus" [90; spattered with mud by a horse], as well as someone, who, despite the inclement weather, and unlike our two travellers, is refused a *paenula* (64 and 66), a cloak used on journeys and in the rain. Even the pecuniary metaphor – "videsi di tal moneta pagato" (VI.5.16) – to describe the effects on Forese of Giotto's quick response may have a distant precedent in the ending of Quintilian's chapter: "dictum est ... de actore facile dicente ex tempore, ingenium eum in numerato habere" [111; it was said about a pleader who was a fluent off-the-cuff speaker that he held his intellect in ready cash]. Just as interesting is the fact that *Institutio oratoria* VI.3 includes important elements – the effects of nature (11–12) and of fortune (28), the "indocti" (the unlearned who are Boccaccio's "ignoranti"; 6), and different social classes (28) – that structure part one of VI.5. Although Quintilian's chapter cannot be considered a source for the tale as a whole, it certainly appreciably affects its two sections and establishes a link between them, while firmly rooting both parts in classical culture.[14]

The impact of Quintilian's influence on VI.5 is reinforced by Cicero. *De oratore*'s discussion of "iocus et facetiae" [II.54.216–71.289; jokes and witticisms], an obvious source for *Institutio oratoria* VI.3, almost certainly also exercised an influence on our tale, not least because Boccaccio was very likely familiar with both rhetorical texts.[15] Specifically, rather more energetically than the *Institutio*, and closer to Boccaccio, Cicero stressed that quick-wittedness is a gift of nature (216, 219, and 233); that the retort is the true mark of witty intelligence (219, 230, 236; 255);[16] and that joking and ugliness are intimately entwined (236, 239, and 266), which, together with illustrating that "beneath most ugly forms are concealed marvellous intellects" (3), is a key nub of our "novella." Cicero thus further augments the tale's classicizing tenor. Indeed, both Latin rhetorical works, with their discussion of different types of humorous modes, which they exemplify with anecdotes of more or less successful contemporary verbal jousters, set a precedent, even a textual model, for Boccaccio's own assessment of different types of *motti* in Day Six (but also in Day One). The quick-witted Florentine speakers of VI.5, just as those of Day Six in general, "bring back to the light,"[17] as Giotto had done with his painting, the "art" of pithy and humorous repartee that, as Quintilian documents, had been a typical feature of ancient Rome (103). Florence is thus not simply the centre of a classicizing artistic renewal but is also a city whose citizens are the heirs to Roman intelligence, which

14 It would be fruitful to explore the relationship between Day Six and Quintilian's chapter in light of the orator's stress on the opportunities, relating to circumstance and a previous speaker's utterance, that allow the unlearned and "rustics" to utter witticisms (*Institutio oratoria* VI.3.13).

15 On Quintilian, see Coulter; and Mazza 50–1.

16 By reprising Forese's repetition of "credere" and turning the issue of belief against his challenger (VI.5.14–15), Giotto makes concrete Cicero's observation that repeating an opponent's word can be a most effective way of attacking an antagonist (*De oratore* 255).

17 "Avendo egli [Giotto] quell'arte ritornata in luce, che molti secoli … era stata sepulta" (VI.5.6).

finds expression in a revival of Roman rhetorical *brevitas* – a veritable *translatio urbis*.[18]

III. *Humilis* Giotto

Once more we find classical culture serving as a bridge between VI.5's two parts. And yet, the tale's most obvious – and I would contend, most substantial – source is not classical. Boccaccio begins to bring his appreciation of Giotto to a close by highlighting his humility.[19] The painter "meritamente una delle luci della fiorentina gloria dir si puote; e tanto più, quanto con maggiore umiltà, maestro degli altri in ciò, vivendo quella acquistò, sempre rifiutando d'esser chiamato maestro" [VI.5.6; deservedly can be called one of the lights of Florentine glory; and all the more so, in so far as with greater humility, master of others in this, while alive he gained that [glory], always refusing to be called master]. The final clause of the encomium alludes to and reworks "nec vocemini magistri quia magister vester unus est Christus" [Matthew 23:10; nor be called masters because Christ is your only master].[20] However much Giotto may recall and even revive classical achievement, his moral compass is unquestionably scriptural. Indeed, while his classically evocative reply to Forese's provocation is a spontaneous, and hence limited, act of intelligence – "cum ante illud facete dictum emissum haerere debeat, quam cogitari potuisse videatur" [Cicero, *De oratore* II.54.219; whereby the witty saying ought to be uttered and fixed in the listener's mind, before it seems possible to have been thought] – his humility constitutes a deliberate Christian ethical choice: "il qual titolo [maestro] rifiutato da lui" [VI.5.7; which title was refused by him], a decision that is clearly in line with "quid est esse humilem? Nolle in se laudari" [Augustine, *Enarrationes* XXXIII(2).5; what constitutes being humble? Refusing to

18 See Andrei, "*Motto*" 37. Martinez suggests a Horatian substratum for VI.5, specifically *Ars poetica* 1–5 ("*Scienze della Cittade*" 65). I also wonder whether there may not be a trace in VI.5 of Ovid, *Metamorphoses* VIII.611–724, the tale of poor Philemon and Baucis, who, not unlike Boccaccio's "lavoratore" [VI.5.10; peasant], offer shelter, food, and old drapery (640, 657–9) to Jupiter and Mercury disguised as human travellers. Like VI.5, the myth deals with reality and appearance. Furthermore, Aristotle (*Nicomachean Ethics* X.9) addresses topics close to VI.5 such as the law; being a *magister*; the role of painters, including as teachers; and correct and incorrect ways of judging a painting.

19 On Boccaccio's views on humility, see Kirkham, *Sign of Reason* 249–65.

20 The scriptural verse is especially memorable because the same point is made in similar terms in the preceding two verses (8–9).

be praised in oneself].[21] To put it somewhat differently, while Giotto's response is evidence of his natural intelligence, his humility, like his painting, is evidence of the remarkable ways in which he puts his gift to work.

The circumstances that Boccaccio evokes in paragraphs 6 and 7 – the humble master whose "title" "con maggior disidero ... era cupidamente usurpato" (VI.5.7; with greater desire was greedily usurped)[22] by others – are overtly biblical. In particular, they establish suggestive links with the exegetical tradition on Matthew 23.[23] Thus, in glossing the chapter's fifth verse – "omnia vero opera sua faciunt ut videantur ab hominibus dilatant enim phylacteria sua et magnificant fimbrias" [And all their works they do to be seen by men. For they broaden their phylacteries and enlarge their fringes] – Thomas Aquinas clarifies and condemns behaviour that recalls the avidity of those who wish to "usurp" Giotto's "glory": "Causa autem quare homo sit difficilis ad corrigendum vel incorrigibilis, est quaerere gloriam propriam" [*Super Evangelium S. Matthaei lectura* XXIII.1; the reason, however, why man is difficult to correct or incorrigible is his seeking his own glory]. Furthermore, the Angelic Doctor's comments on the first clause of Matthew's sixth verse accurately anticipate the conditions and effects of Giotto's reputation and humility: "*amant autem primos recubitus in cenis* ... Et dicit *amant*, quia non reprehenditur auctoritas, sed inordinatus appetitus. Quidam enim sunt in primo loco corporaliter, qui tamen in corde sedent in novissimo" [XXIII.1; *however they* [the Pharisees] *love the first places at feasts* ... And he says *they love*, because authority is not to be rebuked, but the inordinate desire for it. For certain people are in the first place bodily, who for all that in their hearts sit in the last place]. Giotto's humbleness and the immorality of the reaction that his behaviour and success engender effectively illuminate Jesus's monitory maxim later in the chapter: "qui autem se exaltaverit humiliabitur et qui se humiliaverit exaltabitur" [Matthew 23:12; and who will exalt himself will be humbled, and who will humble himself will be exalted]. Equally, Giotto's humble attitude towards "gloria" closely conforms to Augustine's dictum: "Humilitas, claritatis est meritum; claritas, humilitatis est praemium" [*Iohannis*

21 See Mazza 18–19, for Boccaccio's knowledge of the *Enarrationes*.

22 Ziolkowski notes, in the later Middle Ages, "as the standing of the *magister* soared the honorific became coveted" ("Mastering Authors" 102). See also Congar.

23 I use as my main source of evidence Thomas's commentary on Matthew, since it draws extensively on earlier interpretations, thereby making it a good record of the exegetical tradition on the evangelist.

evangelium tractatus CXXIV CIV.3; humility is the merit of glory, glory is the reward of humility]. The painter is the very embodiment, as is Guido Cavalcanti in VI.9,[24] of the ideal Florentine luminary of the generation before the plague: intelligent, artistically refined, sensitive to the accomplishments of classical culture, ethically upright, and most of all an exemplary Christian.

In fact, it would be more precise to state that Boccaccio's Giotto takes on distinctly Christological lineaments. Jesus's humility is of course proverbial, finding its most obvious affirmation, as Paul wrote, in his willingness to embrace our human state: "formam servi accipiens in similitudinem hominum factus et habitu inventus ut homo humiliavit semet ipsum" [Philippians 2:7–8; taking the form of a servant, being made in the likeness of men, and in habit found as a man. He humbled himself].[25] Christ's submission was apparent not just in his humanity but also in his physical appearance. Thus, even though the predominant view had long held that Jesus was extraordinarily beautiful, a tradition, with its roots in the Church Fathers, also maintained that he was ugly, a strikingly visible mark of his humility.[26] Indeed, this current of thought had been granted a new impetus in the thirteenth and fourteenth centuries with the ever-increasing mendicant emphasis, in both art and literature, on Christ's passion.[27] In its turn, this perspective had evident connections to the renewed interest in humility, a consequence of mendicant piety and of unease with ecclesiastical power, as well as a counter to intellectual self-importance and social elitism – attitudes these last that Boccaccio too, as I shall soon have cause to examine, felt compelled to criticize through his treatment of physically unseemly *humilis* Giotto. While, in passion narratives, Jesus's ugliness is a direct result of the terrible tortures that ravage and debase his normal beauty, the ancient tradition insisted on his actual bodily unsightliness on the basis of Isaiah's prophecy: "non est species ei neque decor … et desideravimus eum despectum et novissimum virorum virum dolorum et scientem infirmitatem et quasi absconditus vultus eius et despectus" [53:2–3; there is no beauty in him, nor comeliness that we should be desirous of him. Despised and the most abject of men, a man of sorrows, and acquainted with infirmity: and his look was as if hidden and despised]. Isaiah had already referred to the condition of the "man of

24 See Barański, "Alquanto tenea."
25 For the text of the Vulgate Bible, I have used Weber and Gryson's *Biblia Sacra Vulgata*.
26 See von Dobschütz. See also Viladesau 10–12.
27 See Belting; Derbes; and McNamer.

sorrows" in the preceding chapter: "inglorius erit inter viros aspectus eius et forma eius inter filios hominum" [52:14; his look will be inglorious among men, and his form among the sons of men], a verse that may have had some sway over VI.5's first allusion to unsightly physical appearance: "turpissime forme d'uomini" [VI.5.3; most ugly forms of men]. Since the times of the Ante-Nicene Fathers, these prophetic passages were frequently cited – regularly together – reworked, and extensively glossed. Augustine offers several instances of this practice, and in terms that find a possible echo in VI.5. Specifically, "formam illam deformem carnis ostendens" [*Enarrationes* XLIII.16; revealing this deformed form of his flesh] resonates in Forese's "form*a* … isformat*a*" [VI.5.3–4; form … deformed], which is of course Giotto's outward aspect too: "né di persona né d'aspetto in niuna cosa più bello che fosse messer Forese" [VI.5.8; neither in his person nor in his appearance was he in any way more attractive than Messer Forese]. The reason why Christ "ut homo, non habebat speciem neque decorem" [as man was neither seemly nor beautiful] was most commonly explained in terms of the need to ensure that "fides nostra … ad invisibilia praeparetur" [our faith might be made ready for invisible things], since "videtis formam servi, occulta est forma Dei" [*Enarrationes* XLIII.16; you see the servant's form, yet God's form is hidden]. Jesus's "beauty," like Forese's and Giotto's "intellects" (VI.5.3), was concealed "beneath a most ugly human form" (VI.5.3). The scriptural tradition and *Decameron* VI.5 thus share the same concern with the relationship between the external and the internal, between appearance and reality, between the body and the spirit – a concern that I firmly believe is at the very core of our tale.

Once again, I am not quite ready to address a matter of some importance – a fact that offers a hint of that ideological, yet also socio-ethical, complexity that I feel distinguishes VI.5, since other, more immediate issues continue to press. That, in the tale, Giotto has an exemplary function – and indeed one that goes beyond humility to touch on matters of art, rhetoric, and social status – ought, by now, to have begun to be self-evident. Nonetheless, why Boccaccio should have constructed the painter's exemplarity, at least in part, in such an obviously Christological key requires more detailed explanation. I can think of two principal reasons. First, by highlighting the fact of Christ's ugliness, Boccaccio provides definitive proof in support of Panfilo's claim regarding the misleading nature of "human forms" (VI.5.3), while at the same time legitimating the logic of his tale. Second, by portraying Giotto as following closely in Jesus's steps, Boccaccio fashions a figure whose exemplarity is beyond question. Indeed, by stressing his Christ-like humility – and we should not forget that it is this aspect of the artist's behaviour that is intertextually granted most prominence[28] – Boccaccio shifts attention away from his painterly qualities, which in any case only very few can imitate, to his practice of a virtue that all of us can attempt to replicate. Giotto thus becomes a *modello di vita* that anyone can imitate. He is the very embodiment of humility: "Umiltà è vertù per la quale soffera l'uomo di portare vile abito, e il ben che fa nasconde, acciò che non appaia di fuori a le genti" [Bono Giamboni, *Il libro dei Vizî* XXXIV.16; Humility is a virtue for which man suffers to wear poor clothing, and conceals the good that he does, so that it does not appear externally to people]. More specifically, since humility was typically deemed to lie at the root of all the other virtues and to serve as the prerequisite of faith (Anthony of Padua, *Sermones*, Sexagesima VII), it transcended rank, profession, intellectual ability, and artistic prowess. From the "lavoratore" [VI.5.10; peasant] to the lawyer, from the *magister* to the painter, everyone, if they want to live well, has to do so humbly. If the majority of the protagonists of Day Six demonstrate admirable qualities worthy of imitation, it is Giotto who represents the model of all-round virtuous living. Day Six is more than simply a celebration of Florentine achievement. It presents modes of intelligence and comportment that are vital if the city is to be restored after the ravages of the plague. Indeed, as I discuss below, thanks to the exemplary tale of Giotto and Forese, Boccaccio suggests how Florence might be "revived" in ways that would actually be an improvement on its earlier civic make-up.[29]

I am almost tempted to conclude this subsection by suggesting that Giotto, morally, culturally, and professionally, is meant to serve as a possible "salvific" model for that renewal that Florence must undertake in the wake of the plague and that would make it a worthy "daughter of Rome." However, I am not sure how appropriate such an overtly religious reading might actually be, especially as the manner in which Boccaccio fuses his sources in the figure of Giotto would imply that he is advocating a coming together of classical and Christian values. At the same time, I feel able to state with confidence that, differently from some other tales with a recognizable religious, even biblical, substratum, there is nothing parodic in Boccaccio's presentation of "the best painter in the world" (VI.5.14). The problems that he is addressing

28 "Boccaccio is the sole witness from the early Trecento" (Watson, "Cement of Fiction" 48) of Giotto's humility, a fact that underlines the importance of this attribute in VI.5.

29 On the centrality of Florence in the *Decameron*, see Baratto, *Realtà e stile* 24–42; and on its centrality in Day Six, see Fido, *Il regime* 78–9; Getto 140–64; Martinez, "*Scienze della Cittade*" 59–61; Meier, "Day Six" 297–8; and Olson, *Courtesy Lost*.

are too weighty, too closely involved with decisive contemporary concerns to sanction such a potentially light-hearted approach. Equally, the *novelliere*'s aim is firmly to establish his Giotto as a "luce," a light,[30] a title that in the Trecento was of considerable cultural and social import: *lights* were both sources of civic pride and paradigms of good conduct. Thus, with the possible exception of the reference to the Baronci, there is nothing remotely *levis* in part one; and much the same can be said of the "novella," especially in light of the heavily moralizing tone of its *explicit*: "il suo error riconobbe" [VI.5.16; he recognized his error].[31] The "error" is of course Forese's, which poses awkward questions about the nature of his exemplary status, not least because Giotto represents such a perfect instance of *imitatio Christi*,[32] that ideal towards which every person should aspire. Indeed, the deeper we drill into VI.5's bedrock, the more its Christian foundations become visible.[33]

IV. Muddy Giotto

Giotto's humility is not only signalled by his Christological ugliness but also by his muddy appearance: "tutti molli veggendosi e per gli schizzi che i ronzini fanno co' piedi in quantità zaccherosi" [VI.5.12; seeing themselves totally wet and on account of the many muddy squirts that horses make with their hooves]. The etymology of "humility," as Isidore of Seville had authoritatively established, linked it to *humus*, earth, soil: "humilis quasi humo adclinis" [*Etym.* X.115; humble as if leaning to the

30 This designation too is obviously Christological: "Iesus dicens ego sum lux mundi" [John 8:12; Jesus saying, "I am the light of the world"].

31 In light of VI.5's striking religious atmosphere (more on this below), "recognizing one's error" recalls a standard formula for repentance. (Perhaps I should have been less hasty in casting doubt on Giotto's "salvific" role.) The seriousness of the ending is further reinforced by the closing economic and mercantile metaphor (VI.5.16). Given the gravity and range of VI.5's interests, the ladies' reaction to Panfilo's *novellare* is quite inappropriate: "Ridevano ancora le donne della bella e presta risposta di Giotto" [VI.6.1; the women were still laughing at Giotto's elegant and ready riposte]. The women reveal themselves to be superficial listeners who fail to appreciate the richness of what they have heard, focusing exclusively on the pithy final witticism. More specifically, they fail to grasp what might be found "beneath" (3) the surface of the tale. They are listeners who are unable to go beyond the "appearance" of a text. The fact that the exegetical lapse is so visibly gendered is striking; unfortunately, the implications of this lie beyond the remit of the present *lectura*.

32 My reading of Giotto goes against the standard view in Boccaccio studies that deems the *novelliere*'s painters as (immoral) manipulative deceivers; see especially Legassie.

33 See Kirkham, "Morale" 263.

earth]. The association also has scriptural origins. Although, in general, mud has negative connotations in the Bible and in its exegesis,[34] there is one well-known passage that appears relevant for VI.5: "quamdiu in mundo sum lux sum mundi haec cum dixisset expuit in terram et fecit lutum ex sputo" [John 9:5–6; as long as I am in the world, I am the light of the world. When he had said this, he spat on the ground and made mud from his spittle]. Together with the reference to Jesus as "lux mundi," the exegetical tradition on the miraculous "lutum" further reinforces Giotto's *humilis* Christological traits. Thus, the mud indicates Jesus taking on bodily form: "de saliva sua lutum fecit: quia Verbum caro factum est" [Augustine, *In Iohannis evangelium tractatus CXXIV* LIV.2; with his spit he made mud: because the Word was made flesh; cf. Thomas Aquinas, *Super Evangelium S. Ioannis* IX.1]. More generally, Hugh of St Victor not only explicitly associated humility with mud, and both virtue and substance with Christ's physical appearance, but also connected these elements with another of VI.5's principal themes, the need to go beyond the surface of things to discover more profound meanings: "Noli igitur in verbo Dei despicere humilitatem, quia per humilitatem, illuminaris ad divinitatem. Quasi lutum tibi videtur totum hoc quod verbum Dei foris habet ... luto isto quod pedibus tuis conculcatur, caeci oculus ad videndum illuminatur [John IX:6]" [*De scripturis* I.5; Do not despise therefore the humility in the word of God, because thanks to humility, you will be enlightened to divinity. All this that the word of God has may seem like mud to you from the outside ... by this mud that is trodden by your feet, the eye of the blind man is enlightened to see].[35] The passage from John was also read as a reminder of our common humanity – a question that underpins Boccaccio's discussion of what criteria might be employed to assess human beings if external appearance can be so deceptive: "Lutum autem fecit ex sputo, ut ostendat se membra homini deficientia posse formare, qui formaverat totum primum hominem. Unde sicut primum hominem de luto formavit" [Thomas Aquinas, *Super Evangelium S. Ioannis* IX.1; he made mud from his spit, to reveal that he, who had made the whole first man, was able to remake man's deficient members. Just as he made the first man from

34 Mud was frequently associated with sin, earthly desires, and damnation; see, for instance, Job 9:31 and 30:19; Psalms 17:43, 39:3, and 68:3 and 15; Isaiah 10:6 and 41:25; and 2 Peter 2:22. See also Augustine, *Enarrationes* XVII.43, XXXIX.3, and LXVIII(1).5 and 18; Gregory the Great, *Moralia in Iob* II.36.56 and IV.30.60.

35 Giotto's old clothes are also Christological; see Anthony of Padua, *Sermones*, Seventeeth Sunday after Pentecost X.

mud; cf. also Anthony of Padua, *Sermones*, Quinquagesima III]. Even more significantly, as we shall see, humility was centrally involved in this matter of our common origins.

What I hope is becoming clear – and I have quite a bit more evidence to present in support of my case – is that VI.5's citational scheme *fa sistema* and effectively underpins the tale's structure and ideological concerns. For instance, Matthew 23, which, as we have seen, serves as the key to the "humble" analysis of Giotto, also casts light on the artist's muddiness. Citing pseudo-Chrysostom, the *Catena* commentary on the chapter observes that a dirty mien cannot in itself be used as a yardstick with which to measure behaviour: "Deus neque corporis munditiam laudet, neque sordes condemnet" [Thomas Aquinas, *Expositio in Matthaeum* XXIII.8; God neither praises cleanliness, nor condemns dirtiness]. And Boccaccio concurs: neither physical appearance nor other aspects of our outward show – Giotto, a paragon of virtue and artistic prowess, is ugly, dressed in old clothes, and covered in mud – have necessarily any definitive and defining value as pointers to a person's status, ability, or morals. They are primarily the effects of forces, from nature to chance – "per ciò che migliori [cloaks and hats] non v'erano" [VI.5.11; because there weren't better ones] – to the weather, that are arbitrary. Nonetheless, there may be instances when such external features, as in Giotto's case, can help us better appreciate an individual.[36] Yet, if in the here and now a muddy appearance, in the first instance, is simply that, a muddy appearance – a position that fits well with VI.5's interest in "realism" – this is not in fact the case in the afterlife. Although there is no doubt that Boccaccio's Giotto and the related issue of artistic verisimilitude are substantially dependent on *Purgatorio* 10–12, the actual verbal interconnections between the cantos and VI.5 are limited.[37] This is not so, however, as regards *Inferno* 6, where we find another Florentine soaked by rain and covered in mud.[38] The wet and muddy condition of Ciacco and his fellow gluttons is an apt symbol of their sin,

36 When I discuss the presentation of Forese below – Forese, who in appearance looks exactly the same as Giotto, but who in character could not be more different – this point ought to become clearer.

37 I have noted the following borrowings from these cantos in VI.5: unhealthy desire (7, and cf. *Purg.* 11.86–7); believing (14–15, and cf. *Purg.* 11.94); payment (16, and cf. *Purg.* 11.88).

38 VI.5 depends on *Inferno* 6 in the following instances: "Forese … fu chiamato" [VI.5.4; was called Forese, and cf. *Inf.* 6.52]; "sozzo" [VI.5.4; foul, and cf. *Inf.* 6.100]; "l'altro … ebbe uno ingegno" [the other had an intellect, and cf. *Inf.* 6.81]; "persona" (VI.5.8, and cf. *Inf.* 6.36); never seeing before (VI.5.14, and cf. *Inf.* 6.45).

and hence an appropriate means of punishment. Otherworldly mud, unlike earthly mud, has divine functions and meanings – a distinction that neatly captures the different perspectives and teleological ends of the *Commedia* and of the *Decameron*. In this regard, it is striking that Giotto's unsightly physical and outer appearance only becomes significant when, as the scriptural *sententiae* verify, it is considered in eschatological and spiritual terms, which an earthbound and superficial viewpoint can never achieve. Although the *Decameron* has undoubted earthly ends, this does not mean that it eliminates the divine from its purview. Certainly, in VI.5's heavily scriptural atmosphere, Giotto's humility, the root of faith, seems to mediate Christologically between this world and the next. In any case, it is almost definite that *Inferno* 6 was in Boccaccio's mind when he composed VI.5. Thus, his later commentary on the canto reads also like a commentary on our tale.[39] In his "literal exposition," Boccaccio discusses urban social mores (*Esposizioni sopra la Comedia di Dante* 34); those who desire the rank of others (48); God's creation of human beings with reference to Genesis (57); the way in which the body conceals our divine nature (60); the "giudicio de' volgari, li quali sempre secondo l'aparenza delle cose esteriori giudicano, senza guardare quello onde si muovono, o che importino" (69; judgment of the uneducated, who always judge according to the appearance of exterior things, without looking at that where they move, or what their importance might be); and the desire for fame (75). Furthermore, in his "allegorical exposition," the *novelliere* underscores the differences between "'l mestiere e l'arte" [13; skill and art], with the latter, as in sculpture, combining manual dexterity and intelligence (14),[40] before highlighting the rhetorical abilities of gluttons (52) and then closing by explaining how, like Giotto with Forese, the wise man knows how to silence a glutton's "offensive biting words" (60–1).

39 Book XIV of the *Genealogie* may be read in part as a "theoretical" reworking of our tale. Thus, *inter alia*, it makes reference to the learned and the unlearned (2); it witheringly criticizes lawyers who demonstrate Pharisaic qualities (4); it celebrates virtue (4) and humility (5); it condemns those who attack the "high arts" as people who fashion for themselves sinfully deceptive appearances and who, like the Pharisees in Matthew 23 (Boccaccio cites verse 7), wish to be called master (5); it celebrates Giotto and attacks poets who court popularity (6); and it praises *fabulae* that appeal to the intellect (9) and the "veiled," namely allegorical, character of poetry (12), as well as poetry's mimetic powers (17). Unfortunately, constraints of space do not allow me to explore these and other fascinating connections between VI.5 and *Genealogie* XIV. Indeed, it would be useful to examine the interplay between these two texts and the *esposizioni* on *Inferno* 6.

40 On artistic *ingegno*, see Emison 321–48.

V. Pharisaic Forese

Given Giotto's all-round excellence – he is a great intellect, a great painter, a great raconteur, who enfolds his extraordinary gifts in humility – it is easy, as scholarship largely has done, to forget Forese. Yet, in fourteenth-century Florence, the judge was considered a legal intellectual and politician of considerable status, as Boccaccio suggests: "fu di tanto sentimento nelle leggi, che da molti valenti uomini uno armario di ragione civile fu reputato" [VI.5.4; he was of such legal wisdom, that he was deemed by many worthy men a bookcase of civil law]; and socially his professional standing was higher than that of a painter, as his use of the *tu* form to address Giotto, who responds with the honorific *voi* (VI.5.14–15), reveals. Furthermore, like Giotto, he was endowed with a "marvellous intellect" (VI.5.3). Finally, since, in VI.5, Forese and his travelling companion are physically and in outward appearance almost indistinguishable, are we not to ascribe the same positive attributes to his ugliness and muddiness as we are encouraged to do with respect to Giotto's unsightliness?

In annotating Matthew 23, a chapter, as we have seen, that plays an important role in Boccaccio's treatment of the artist, Thomas Aquinas concentrates on those sinners who seek earthly glory by fashioning for themselves seemingly attractive external façades that in reality merely serve to conceal their inner corruption. This is in fact the chapter where Jesus famously compares the Pharisees to "whited sepulchres" (23:27). The learned doctor's overall reading has obvious points of contact with our tale. However, it is in the details of his exegesis that, as with Giotto, we can find suggestions that are significant for Boccaccio's portrait of Forese. Thomas observes: "Commune est quod in factis aliorum omnes sunt iudices austeri: unde si videmus aliquem peccantem, iudicamus grande peccatum, nostrum autem peccatum attenuamus ... supra VII, 5: *eiice primo trabem de oculo tuo, et tunc videbis eiicere festucam de oculo fratris tui*" [*Super Evangelium S. Matthaei* XXIII.2; It is common for all to be severe judges in the doings of others: thus, if we see someone sinning, we judge it a great sin, however we attenuate our sin ... above 7:5: *first cast out the beam from your eye, and then you will see to cast out the mote from your brother's eye*]. Jesus's warning in Matthew 7 to avoid reproaching others, especially when we lack sufficient self-awareness, memorably based on the metaphorical contrast between the "mote" and the "beam," provides the most obvious intertext for Forese's thoughtless and inappropriate goading of Giotto.[41] As Boccaccio stresses, the lawyer

41 Meier fleetingly associates this passage with Day Six in general ("Day Six" 300).

speaks "without giving any consideration about himself" (VI.5.13) – behaviour that offends both Christian and, as I discussed earlier, pagan ethics. Additionally, Thomas's reference to Matthew 7:5 in connection with Matthew 23 points to the fact that Boccaccio structures *Decameron* VI.5 according to a highly deliberate and culturally interconnected allusive system. Matthew 7 thus further refines the biblical character of our tale, especially as it is of central pertinence for the *novelliere*'s presentation of Forese – a presentation whose emphases leave little doubt as to Boccaccio's opinion of the judge.

Matthew 7 opens powerfully: "[N]olite iudicare ut non iudicemini in quo enim iudicio iudicaveritis iudicabimini … quid autem vides festucam in oculo fratris tui et trabem in oculo tuo non vides … hypocrita eice primum trabem de oculo tuo" [1–5; Judge not, that you may not be judged. For with what judgment you judge, you will be judged: And why do you see the mote in your brother's eye and don't see the beam in your eye? Hypocrite, first cast out the beam from your eye].[42] Jesus's admonition has a chilling impact on Boccaccio's portrait of Forese. He is a judge who fails to carry out his duties appropriately, and hence is in danger of lapsing into hypocrisy. In fact, scriptural exegetes regularly emphasized the legal ramifications of these verses. Several times in his commentary, Thomas Aquinas draws on the lines to condemn bad judges and to warn against bad judgments: "Unde si es in eodem peccato, vel maiori, non debes iudicare; ad Rom. II, 1: *in quo enim iudicas alterum, teipsum condemnas*" [*Super Evangelium S. Matthaei* 1.1, but see the whole of this paragraph; Thus, if you are in the same sin, or greater, you should not judge; as Romans 2:1: *For wnen you judge another, you condemn yourself.* (See also 1.3–4.)]. Such declarations impinge negatively on Forese and raise serious doubts about the commonly held view that he is "of such legal wisdom" (VI.5.4). Moreover, further damage is inflicted on him by his being associated with Christ's infamous sparring partners. As the commentary tradition stressed, Jesus's criticisms in Matthew 7 and 23 have as their target the Pharisees,[43] who, intriguingly, constitute a shadowy presence in the tale. If, thanks to Boccaccio's deft

42 I wonder whether there may be a faint echo of Matthew's pigs trampling pearls "pedibus suis" in Boccaccio's horses churning mud up "co' piedi" (VI.5.12). Furthermore, the biblical wordplay on "iudicare" seems to be replayed in Forese's and Giotto's repetition of forms of "credere" (VI.5.14–15). The most obvious source for this rhetorical flourish is of course *Inferno* 13.25.

43 John 9:5–6, our tale's other key biblical intertext, also has the Pharisees as Jesus's interlocutors.

deployment of scriptural *sententiae*, Giotto acquires Christ-like traits, those to whom he is contrasted, whether they be seekers after the title of master or imprudent lawyers, take on Pharisaic lineaments; and, consonant with their representation in the New Testament, Pharisees in medieval culture were deemed to be unreservedly bad. They were intellectually arrogant and hence prone to heresy; greedily desirous of recognition; and, on account of their blindness, unable to discriminate between exterior and interior. Most tellingly, they were both legalistic and bad interpreters of the law.[44] Indeed, by the thirteenth century, they had been transformed into venal contemporary judges, "qui procurant & amant, vt vocentur ad consistoria Principum & Praelatorum, & eadem frequentant sedentes ibi pro tribunali ad iudicandum, vel assessores existentes, vt eis litigantes reurentiam iudicialem exhibeant" [William of St Amour, *De Pharisaeo*, 12; who attend to and love being called to the consistories of princes and prelates, and frequent these sitting there before the tribunals in judgment, or appearing as assistants, so that litigants may show them judicial reverence].

I should like to be clear that I am not trying to suggest that Boccaccio inflicts upon Forese all the presumed sins of the Pharisees or even that he is fashioning him into a grimly despicable figure. The redemptive rapidity with which the lawyer recognizes his error is very much to his credit (VI.5.16). Nevertheless, it is difficult to maintain, as has been done, that there is nothing objectionable about his conduct and witticism. Boccaccio's carefully chosen biblical censure is too well aimed, too apposite, and, especially in the 1350s, too palpable. It is also too shockingly eye-catching, given Forese's prestigious reputation in contemporary Florence.

At a basic level, Forese serves as a foil for VI.5's encomium of Giotto. At the same time, his presentation, like the artist's, is absorbed into broader cultural, social, and ideological concerns,[45] whereby the pair either serve to trigger these or to embody contrasting solutions to them. The most obvious issue is that of social status and the relative value of their respective professions. On the one hand, Boccaccio recognizes that, in the contemporary world, lawyers and painters do not enjoy the same social standing; on the other hand, in a tale that calls into serious doubt the validity of using external factors as yardsticks with which to evaluate people, social rank and profession are obvious examples

44 See Elukin; Nirenberg 209–13; Szittya 34–41; and Watt.
45 See Chiappelli 110.

of elements that are quintessentially exterior, and hence arbitrary and unreliable. Indeed, as we have already seen, they offer no clue to a person's moral compass, or to their intelligence, or to the ways in which they make use of that gift. Giotto creatively revives a long-abused "art" so that it can appeal to the "intelligence of the wise" (VI.5.6); Forese aridly draws on his intelligence to turn himself into a repository of legal knowledge: "uno armario di ragione civile fu reputato" [VI.5.4; he was deemed a bookcase of civil law].[46] One works for the common good; the other is intent on assuring his own status. Finally, the painter is a living force who affects people of differing abilities; the judge is little more than an inanimate object, the preserve of an elite. Appropriately, when he addresses Giotto, Forese reveals himself to be arrogant, self-centred, and lacking self-awareness. Indeed, his question may hint at anxieties he feels as a result of looking so little like a lawyer. More drastically, his question undermines his legal authority and competence. It constitutes an obvious lapse in judgment. Although Forese's aim seems to have been to humiliate *humilis* Giotto and to validate his own cleverness, he achieves neither end. Consequently, his misstep calls into serious doubt the quality of his intelligence and the sophistication of his legal prowess, especially as it is the supposedly "inferior" artist who, in correcting his companion's "error," reveals an appreciable rhetorical mastery, an attribute that Cicero had established as essential for a lawyer.[47] Furthermore, when Giotto speaks, he cements his humble intelligence. As Thomas Aquinas explained, it is "stultitiae, si quis quodcumque abiectum assumpserit" [folly [for the humble person] to embrace any and every humiliation]. In fact, one should only passively suffer humiliation "secundum quod necessarium est" [*Summa contra gentiles* III.135.22; for a needful purpose], a circumstance that is most certainly not that described in our tale, where Giotto needs to react in order to "save" Forese.

46 Suggestively, in the *Catena* commentary on Matthew 23, the Pharisees' ostentation is also compared to *armaria*: "non intelligentibus Pharisaeis quod haec [phylacteries] in corde portanda sunt, non in corpore; alioquin et armaria et arcae habent libros, et notitiam Dei non habent" [XXIII.2; the Pharisees did not understand that these were to be worn in the heart and not on the body; similarly chests and bookcases have books, but they do not have knowledge of God].

47 On Boccaccio's largely negative views on the law and lawyers, see Battaglia Ricci, *Scrivere un libro di novelle* 116–33; Conetti; Doering; Mazzotta, *World at Play* 213–40. For an important reassessment of Boccaccio's attitude to the law, see Steinberg. See also Tang, "The Transformation of the Law," but to be read with caution. On medieval attitudes to lawyers, see Brundage "Teaching" and "Vultures"; and Green.

The conduct of and interaction between the two travellers provide compelling proof that rank and profession have no probative value. They are simply "surface": appearance and not reality. Indeed, the fact that Giotto and Forese look exactly the same when they are obviously so different as people underscores the need to assess everyone exclusively on the basis of their actions and achievements. Even in the best of cases, the external is always arbitrary. Thus, if Giotto's muddy ugliness, when considered in spiritual terms, can be read as a sign of his Christ-like *humilitas*, this is exclusively because of his behaviour. Muddy ugliness, as Forese's lifeless erudition and self-centredness verify, can never in itself be a Christological marker.

VI. Seeing and Judging Socially and Spiritually

Scholars have typically maintained that, thanks to his treatment of the two Florentines, Boccaccio marked the change in status that artists were beginning to enjoy in mid-fourteenth-century Italy,[48] while also reiterating more personal reservations about the law, especially when brought into contact with the arts. Both claims are of course correct. At the same time, they serve to corroborate the dominant Giotto-centric and metaliterary interpretations of *Decameron* VI.5. As I have endeavoured to suggest, especially given its primary dependence on a culturally interrelated web of biblical *auctoritates* whose accessibility would have been relatively straightforward for a contemporary readership – Boccaccio was overwhelmingly relying on commonplaces – there is rather more to the tale than simply those two concerns. It is in fact a major, if highly condensed, statement on contemporary reality – or, more precisely, on some key religious and socio-political aspects of this. Boccaccio appears to suggest that, as a city that was dealing both with the ravages of the plague and with rapid economic and cultural change, Florence, which is at the heart of Day Six, now had the opportunity to rethink its values and civic structures.[49] In particular, as VI.5 so adroitly demonstrates, it needed to privilege talent, virtue, and tangible positive success over rank. If the city wanted to flourish – the association between humble Giotto and "renewal" is absolutely crucial in this respect – it needed to jettison any kind of evaluative system based on incidental external factors. As the scriptural tradition made clear in the wake of Genesis 1:26–8,

48 Recourse is regularly made to Larner 264–84.
49 On this important issue, see especially Olson, *Courtesy Lost*.

the fact that we all share the same first parents means that peripheral elements, such as status, profession, and physical aspect, cannot have a bearing on how people are adjudicated[50] – that Forese is presented as an inadequate judge focused solely on external appearance is naturally telling in this regard: "nolite iudicare secundum faciem" [John 7:24; do not judge according to appearance]. Rather, as Jesus continues, we need to "judge with right judgment." An individual's true worth or worthlessness, whether spiritual, intellectual, or ethical, since these are potentialities that lie hidden, only becomes apparent when they give expression to their capacities in the world. As Paul wrote, each of us is judged "secundum opera eius" [Romans 2:6; according to their works]. By the fourteenth century, in the wake of the importance granted to the "sins of the tongue,"[51] and as evidenced by our "novella," "works" had increasingly become "words": "mores hominum pandit lingua; et qualis sermo ostenditur, talis animus comprobatur" [Humbert of Romans, *Liber de eruditione praedicatorum* VII.38; the tongue reveals men's conduct; the type of mind / soul is shown by speech]. Significantly, to accept the implications of our common humanity is a mark of humility, confirming once again the leading moral-didactic role that someone of the calibre of Giotto needs to have.

The painter and the lawyer, who tellingly are both endowed with a "marvellous intellect" (VI.5.3), emblematically represent contrasting ways of behaving. They function as metonymies for a larger social reality,[52] one in which a reductive, because superficial, system of appreciation of persons, as Panfilo intimates, continues to dominate and do damage. The problem of the tension and disjuncture between appearance and reality is not simply a Boccaccian concern that returns with

50 Boccaccio reiterates this key point elsewhere in his oeuvre; see, for instance, *Decameron* IV.1.39–40; and *Corbaccio* 503, where it is linked to a criticism of those who privilege "appearance" over "truth" (502). The emphasis on the "Creator" in these passages confirms the scriptural basis for the idea. At the same time, the notion is also classical and especially prominent in one of Boccaccio's *auctores*; see Seneca, *Epistulae Morales ad Lucilium* XLIV.3–4.

51 See Casagrande and Vecchio.

52 For a reading of aspects of Day Six in a social key, see Gittes, "Boccaccio's 'Valley of Women'"; Martinez, "*Scienze della Cittade*"; Migiel 109–13; Muscetta, *Boccaccio* 246–7; Wallace 67–77. My perspective regarding VI.5 is especially close to Martinez's: "So it is that the *novelle* of the sixth day … offer snapshots of effective, usually reactive speech that sometimes mediates, sometimes lays bare the *tencioni* of gender, class, rank, occupation, party, and faction which make up the fabric of the city" ("*Scienze della Cittade*" 64).

a degree of frequency in the *Decameron*. Since at least the thirteenth century, it had been a major theological and philosophical issue which probed questions of vision; visual error; the limitations of the senses; the nature and limits of knowledge; "how the world appears to us and … how we appear to others and to ourselves" (Denery 5); the intimate connection among sight, truth, and knowledge; and the relationship between viewer and thing viewed.[53] It is not difficult to map these issues on to our tale. Simply Forese's question, and it is thus unlikely to be a coincidence that it is a university-trained intellectual to utter it – "Giotto, if right now a stranger were to come towards us who had never seen you before, do you believe that he would believe that you are the best painter in the world, as you are?" (VI.5.14) – has obvious points of contact with several of the topics just listed, thereby calling into question its function as a simple *motto*.

Additionally, the problem of appearance and inner truth was profoundly religious, which further helps to justify the marked scriptural character of VI.5, especially as significant overlap exists between the Gospel texts that undergird our tale and spiritual-moral discussions of the ties between external and internal. Confession, which after the Fourth Lateran Council had become formally integrated into the Church's ritual, depended on the sinner recognizing, and hence externalizing, their "error,"[54] as happens with Forese. Giotto thus takes on the role of the confessor who helps the sinner/penitent "see" the reality of their sin. Given that it was not uncommon to compare the confessor to a judge and the confessional to a law court,[55] once more, Forese's lawyerly flaws are exposed and his *auctoritas* is transferred to the painter, hinting at the limitations of professional titles and qualifications. The ethical thus became closely associated with the visual, and thinkers stressed the frequency with which the Bible referred to eyes and vision.[56] Thus sin was the result of flawed exterior and spiritual vision: "In hoc autem quod visio in oculis exterius apparentibus non completur, sed in neruo communi qui interius occultatur moraliter informamur vt temerarium iudicum declinemus, nec de rebus vt apparent prima facie iudicemus, sed per deliberationem ad internum iudicium recurramus" [Peter of Limoges, *Tractatus* V.1; Given that vision is not completed in what appears to the external eyes, but in the common

53 See in particular Denery; and Tachau. See also Akbari; Crosby; and Nelson.

54 See especially Delumeau 197–8; Payen 418–22.

55 See Bériou; Denery 70–1, 110; and Goering.

56 See Roger Bacon, *Perspectiva* III.3.1; and Peter of Limoges, *Tractatus* prol.

nerve, which is hidden internally, we are informed morally that we should shun rash judgment, nor should we judge things as they first appear, but should resort with consideration to internal judgment]. In his following chapter, Peter gives two instances of flawed seeing and judging: "plerumque contingit quod pauper aliquis existens in arido paupertatis cum videt aliquem mundanis opulentiis affluentem ipsum iudicabit esse magnum ... Sed fallitur in iudicio visus eius ... Econtrario qui transitoriis huius mundi diuitiis est immersus cum videt pauperem a mundanis diuitiis elongatum reputat eum modicum cum revera sit magnus apud diuinum oculum in pauperem respicientem et in iudicio non errantem" [*Tractatus* VI.12; it often happens that a poor man living in barren poverty, when he sees a man rich in earthly wealth, will judge him to be great. But his sight is mistaken in this judgment. Conversely someone who is immersed in the fleeting riches of this world, when he sees a poor man far from worldly riches, considers him insignificant, although in truth he is great according to the divine eye that sees the poor man with infallible judgment]. The relevance of these passages for our tale, particularly in light of the reading proposed here, ought to be self-evident. That Boccaccio had notions such as these in mind as he composed VI.5 is further bolstered by Peter's claim that the humble see much more clearly than the proud (*Tractatus* XI.1).[57] And clinching evidence is provided by the fact that religious reflection on appearance and reality considered the matter, similarly to our tale, "as an intrinsically social and public affair" (Denery 71; see also 79).

VII. In Conclusion: Epistemology, Mimesis, *Compilatio*, Hermeneutics

In keeping with a cultural and intellectual environment that recognized the complexity of knowing and the threat to knowledge (and ethics) of deceptive appearance,[58] *Decameron* VI.5 deals with how we know the world, others, and ourselves. Forese and Giotto are thus ideal protagonists since, in their professions, they both rely on sight and intelligence to evaluate truth and reality. The painter's humility ensures that he "clearly sees minutely

57 I have primarily drawn on Peter for my discussion here because of the popularity and influence of *The Moral Treatise on the Eye* in late medieval culture; see Newhauser.

58 Flasch has important things to say about the relationship between seeing and knowing in Boccaccio, as well as about Boccaccio's reworking of doctrinal matter in the *Decameron*. Both he (85–93) and Muscetta (*Boccaccio* 164–5 and 248) correctly stress Panfilo's key role in presenting such information. Panfilo of course narrates VI.5.

and precisely,"[59] and this virtuous ability is at the basis of his outstanding artistic prowess. He is thus able to depict what he sees with unerring life-like accuracy: "niuna cosa dà la natura … che egli con lo stile e con la penna o col pennello non dipignesse sì simile a quella, che non simile, anzi più tosto dessa paresse" [VI.5.5; nothing given by nature that, with his stylus and with his pen or with his brush, he could not paint that was so similar to this, that not similar, but rather seemed (nature) itself].[60] However, dangers lurk in his art. Accordingly, there are those who confuse nature and Giotto, failing to realize that the painter only "seems" to be "similar" to the "madre di tutte le cose" (VI.5.5; mother of all things): "in tanto che molte volte nelle cose da lui fatte si truova che il visivo senso degli uomini vi prese errore, quello credendo esser vero che era dipinto" [VI.5.5; so that often it happened that in the things made by him the human visual sense fell into error, believing that to be true which was painted].[61] The phrase "il visivo senso degli uomini vi prese errore, quello credendo" could have come straight from one of the many works that discussed seeing and knowing, error and truth, appearance and reality. Indeed, those who are unable to distinguish between reality and Giotto's representation of reality are emblematic bad viewers who fail to discriminate between what is false and what is true.[62] According to Peter Aureol, a major contributor to the debate on seeing: "Caesar pictus denominatur a pictura; per hanc

59 "[H]umiles clarius vident subtilia et minuta" (Peter of Limoges, *Tractatus* XI.1).

60 On the medieval commonplace of art imitating nature, see Bartuschat 80–2.

61 Boccaccio's treatment of "ignorant" spectators overturns the traditional religious opinion that paintings were meant to educate the illiterate; see Barasch 64–6. At the same time, elsewhere, as Lummus ("Placing Petrarch's Legacy" 462–3) has noted with reference to *Epistola* XXIV.20–1, Boccaccio, following the standard authority of Gregory the Great (*Epistola* XI.13), did accept that art could valuably serve as the reading matter of the *ignari*. The difference in viewpoint is, of course, the result of the fact that, in VI.5, Boccaccio's concern is with deceptive appearance, while, in his last letter, he stresses the impact on a popular audience of an ornate tomb for Petrarch. Given VI.5's central concern with the need to discriminate between what is true and what is not true, I do not believe, as has been suggested to me, that Boccaccio, in line with Pliny in book XXXV of the *Naturalis historia*, is placing a positive empahasis on the relationship between ethics and supremely accurate verisimilitude. It is obviously significant that the confounded spectators of Giotto's paintings (5), the "ignorant" viewers in the past who simply treated paintings as a source of visual pleasure (6), and Forese, yet another bad observer (13), should be yoked together by the repeated use of the telling noun "errore" (5, 6, and 16) that describes the erroneous manner in which they look and behave. On Pliny's views on art, see Didi-Huberman; and Sorcha 38–78.

62 *Humilis* Giotto is the opposite of the arrogant artist who, according to myth, transgressively transcends reality with his art; see Bartuschat 88, but see 87–92; see also Freedberg. Boccaccio ensures that the fault for the confusion between what is "true" and what is "painted" lies with the spectator and not with Giotto.

enim denominationem Caesar non est praesens picturae" [*Scriptum* I.3.14; Caesar when he is painted is denominated by the painting; for through this denomination Caesar is not present in person to the painting]. Such spectators, accustomed to the works of superficial artists, ignorantly and erroneously limit the appreciation of painting to the "exterior eye," as Peter of Limoges would have put it, instead of relying on "internal judgment": "quell'arte ... che molti secoli sotto gli error d'alcuni, che più a dilettar gli occhi degl'ignoranti che a compiacere allo 'ntelletto de' savi dipignendo, era stata sepulta" [6; that art which for many centuries beneath the error of some, who painted more to delight the eyes of the ignorant than to please the intelligence of the wise, had been buried]. Such errors of seeing and believing later return in the "novella," when Forese, now an *ignorante* and not a *savio*, exaggerates the importance of appearance in respect of truth.

According to Boccaccio, Giotto restores to painting the capacity to appeal to the intellect, because it is itself the product of *ingenium*.[63] However remarkable his mimetic representational skills, a naturalistic "realism" is not the end of his art. The aim rather is for his paintings to mediate not simply between the world and the mind, but also between his "ingegno di tanta eccellenzia" [VI.5.5; intellect of great excellence] and the "intellects of the wise"; and such mediation recalls, even if obliquely, Christ's reconciliation of this world and the next, of humanity and God. Giotto's art is predicated on an aesthetic and epistemological operation and experience that moves from the outside to the inside, and that recognizes the ties and disjunctures between representation and reality. It is an art also, as I have already suggested, that has important links to contemporary allegorical thought, which was vitally concerned with the relationship between the surface of the "letter" and hidden "senses": to put it simply, Giotto's paintings demand interpretation. In view of Boccaccio's critique of treating painting as straightforwardly and exclusively mimetic, his reservation raises serious questions about the function and nature of the *Decameron*'s "realism," and about VI.5 as a sort of manifesto of this "realism." Alas, having already gone over the word limit allotted to my *lectura*, I am unable to develop this fascinating problem.[64] However, in light of VI.5's stress on the interaction between seeing and believing/knowing and on the role in this cognitive process of the interplay

63 See Ruffini 309. On the necessary link between *ars* and *ingenium*, see Coomaraswamy 85–8.

64 However, see Steinberg, who writes that, in the *Decameron*, Boccaccio, "continually questioning the very realism he employs as a poet ... puts mimesis on trial" (120) – a critique the *novelliere* undertakes in light of contemporary legal culture. The link between the law and verisimilitude in the *Decameron* would seem to be confirmed by the presence of Forese in VI.5. See, in a similar vein, Ascoli "Auerbach" and "Boccaccio's Auerbach." More generally on the poetics of the *Decameron*, see Lummus, "The *Decameron*."

between outer and inner, I would suggest that the tale is less about art and literature than about their interpretation. It is principally meta-exegetical rather than metaliterary.[65] Indeed, VI.5 itself, thanks to its allusive density and its persistent raising of questions, affirms the vital importance of interpretation. By appealing to our "intellects," it invites us to go beyond the "appearance" of its *lictera* to seek out the "truths" – the social, philosophical, religious, and cultural "realities" – that its formal surface veils. Revealingly, in the "novella," we are not presented with an example of Giotto's artistic prowess but of his interpretive intelligence: he decodes Forese's provocation in a manner that both works to his advantage and offers a timely moral lesson to his antagonist.

Unlike scholastic thinkers such as Peter Aureol, Duns Scotus, and William of Ockham, Boccaccio did not consider epistemological matters in overly theoretical terms. Indeed, his tale may serve as an implied criticism of intellectual over-elaboration and abstraction. As the moral and social tenor of VI.5 abundantly makes clear, his ideological focus is practical. Equally practical is the emphasis on the efficacy of literature to address complex abstract matters. At a quite elementary level, the tale's division into two almost equal parts mirrors the dialectical structures at the basis of medieval epistemological theory. In the same way that, philosophically, inner and outer were presented as discrete yet interconnected, VI.5's two parts share intertexts, protagonists, and ideological, cultural, and social interests, while, as Panfilo underlines, remaining distinct. For instance, part two deconstructs the first part's essentially positive portrayal of Forese. Conversely, it augments Giotto's encomium in part one with new information regarding his rhetorical and hermeneutic skills. The most striking difference between the two halves, however, is formal. As I discussed at the outset, the second part is openly termed a "novella." How, therefore, might the first part be described? Much of its subject-matter and register recall what can be found in late medieval vernacular *vitae*, sermons, chronicles, commentaries, and philosophical compendia – texts in fact whose purpose was to instruct a growing lay literate communal public. As VI.5 makes clear, it too has popularizing didactic ambitions.[66] It strives to make accessible some of the theoretical

65 On Boccaccio's introduction of interpretive structures into the *Decameron*, see ch. 4, "The Love of the Corpus: *Decameron*," in Kriesel, *Boccaccio's Corpus*; and Milner, "Boccaccio's *Decameron*," 90–7.

66 See Battaglia Ricci, "Una novella per esempio" 124. Earlier, in light of the scribal conventions that control Berlin, Staatsbibliothek, MS Hamilton 90, she points to the subordination of the *Decameron*'s narrative sections to its argumentative discourse (116). See aso Battaglia Ricci, "Leggere e scrivere;" and Alfano, "Giornata VI" 952.

intricacies of the *clerici*, and it does this by relying on the *volgare*, narrative *fictio*, allegoresis, and, importantly, a "compilatory" approach to information, namely, the same syncretic and accumulative strategy that defines the vernacular genres to which it nods.[67] In addition, as also occurs in these genres, the tale has a recognizably moralizing imperative, which, first and foremost, is an effect of its pervasive recourse to Scripture[68] – a decision that further enhances its accessibility. Part one can thus loosely be defined as a *compilatio*, integrating, as it does, a range of different topics. Indeed, its diffuse "compilatory" character stands in stark contrast to the "novella"'s tightly constrained narrative scope. Yet, it is the first part that formally classifies VI.5. Simply by bringing together parts one and two, Boccaccio was "compiling."

I am not enough of a *boccaccista* to be able to deduce the relevance for the *Decameron* of my generic and structural reading of VI.5. However, given the illustriousness of its protagonists, the sophistication of its literary operation, and the contemporary relevance of its concerns, it is hard to think that its influence on the macrostructure of the collection, itself a *compilatio*,[69] might be anything other than significant. Thus, for all its interest in exegesis, the tale does have metaliterary implications, and ones that go beyond questions of mimesis to involve the *Decameron*'s organizational principles and genre. Indeed, that complex interplay between two sets of rubrics and between these and the tale, which itself is divided in two, that serves as the starting-point for my *lectura*, can be deemed a microcosm of the structural tensions and forces that distinguish both the *Decameron*'s individual days and the collection as a whole. Although each of these interconnected short texts that bear on or constitute VI.5 has clearly delineated formal and semantic parameters, they find their resolution through their contacts with one another. Yet, despite their proximity, their connections are far from straightforward and untroubled. As we have seen, strains mark the relationship between the rubrics and between them and the tale, just as tensions distinguish the interplay between parts one and two of VI.5. This seems to be the result of the autonomy that each mini-text enjoys. For instance, if we consider part two in light of its specific and its general rubric, both seem

67 See Milner, "Boccaccio's *Decameron*" 87. On the *compilatio*, see at least Minnis, "Late-Medieval Discussions" and "*Nolens auctor*"; Parkes.

68 On the use of scriptural intertexts in Day Six, see Barański; Meier, "Day Six" 301; and Pennington. On the Bible's function in the *Decameron*, see Battaglia Ricci, *Scrivere un libro di novelle* 134–56; and Delcorno, "Appunti."

69 On the *Decameron*'s dependence on and synthesis of a range of short forms, see Gulizia 13–22. See also Orvieto.

strangely inadequate as summaries. Thus, Forese's Pharisaic comment has little of the *motto* about it,[70] while Giotto is not so much intent on mocking his companion's "sparuta apparenza" as on making serious ethical and philosophical points in a lighthearted yet rhetorically efficacious manner.[71] Equally, if Giotto is never in a position of "danger," it is Forese, the aggressor,[72] who, metatextually, ends up ironically suffering a "loss." The rubrics almost seem less like summatic introductions than as spurs to interpretation. Ultimately, it is the rich and unexpected interplay between these brief texts that generates meaning, asserting the connotative power of short texts both in themselves and when these work in unison. They are both centrifugal and centripetal: as they come together, they also push each other away, as parts one and two so proficiently demonstrate. And all this must surely have some relevance for the *Decameron*.

Perhaps, in the end, VI.5 is a metaliterary tale. Except that, by raising problem upon problem, by challenging common assumptions, by interrogating how we see and know, and by constantly drawing our attention to the need to recognize what lies "sotto," namely, the reality that transcends and corrects appearance[73] – a truth that Jesus and his "disciple" Giotto so effectively embody and elucidate – our tale constantly urges us to interpret: to discover the "grandissimi tesori" [very great treasures] that the world and it "nascond*ono*" [VI.5.3; conceal]. VI.5 is not a self-referential literary and artistic nugget but a deeply ethical appeal, integrating classical and Christian values, to see in ways that avoid "error,"[74] thereby allowing us to *credere* with a degree of

70 See Van der Voort 211.

71 Although scholars, in Boccaccio's wake, regularly refer to the importance of the *motto* in Day Six (and also in Day One), it is striking that none seems willing to offer a definition of the term. Given the flexibility of the designation in light of its usage in the *Decameron*, I wonder whether, as VI.5 implies, attention is drawn to the *motto* in order to encourage reflection on short textual forms: "intendo di raccontare cento novelle, o favole o parabole o istorie che dire le vogliamo" [*Proemio* 13; I intend to tell one hundred tales, or fables or parables or stories however we may want to call them]. See Battaglia Ricci, "*Exemplum* e novella," for an analysis of ways in which Boccaccio defines the "forma novella" (286). Oesch-Serra offers an exclusively narratological definition of the *motto* (3).

72 On the conflictual nature of Forese's question, see Bosetti 147–8.

73 Few analyses of VI.5 have focused on the tension between appearance and reality; however, see Bartuschat 95–6; Ciccuto, "Il novelliere 'en artiste'"; Cuomo 256; Ruffini 318–19; Stewart, *Retorica e mimica* 83–92. More generally, see Marcus, *Allegory of Form* 79–92. See also Ciccuto, "Un'antica canzone" 413.

74 On "error" in the Middle Ages, see Evans.

certainty – an appeal that is, of course, also relevant to all forms of language and representation. Rather than a tale straightforwardly centred on mimetic representation and the *ars narrandi*, VI.5 poses profound questions about the ways in which ethically, visually, linguistically, and socially we understand and hence interpret reality – a reality, in fact, that, as VI.5's scriptural patina reveals, is never exclusively worldly.[75]

75 My reading also distinguishes itself from ludic analyses of Day Six in general and VI.5 in particular.

6 The Tale of Michele Scalza (VI.6)

PETER CARRAVETTA

The sixth *novella* of Day Six of the *Decameron* has received little attention in Boccaccio scholarship. It is as if there were just so many other longer, more complex, more memorable stories of the over one hundred to write about that even those scholars who focused on one or more of the themes of the Sixth Day barely even mention it.[1] Tucked away in a little niche between the more famous one that precedes it, the fifth about Giotto's mordant remark to Forese da Rabatta, and the seventh, Philippa's memorable defence of her infidelity, the tale of Michele Scalza gets at best a mention in passing, a listing in a footnote. In truth, the tales about Oretta (VI.1), Cisti (VI.2), Chichibio (VI.4), and Brother Cipolla (VI.10) do lend themselves to broader, multilayered approaches, and typically yield penetrating insights into the complex world of Boccaccio's masterpiece. Assuming therefore that most readers don't have it present in their mind, let us summarize what happens in the story, before we attempt a critical reading.

Under the reign of Elissa, who entreats the storytellers to entertain by showing how "exquisite these sayings can be if proffered at the right moment," the tale is being narrated by Fiammetta, who we have learned is characterized as portraying temperance.[2] One of the cardinal virtues, temperance involves sound judgment, self-restraint; indeed prudence meant to avert excess in certain situations by directing attention to what is appropriate in given contexts. In the economy of the

1 Even in Francesco Bruni's thorough study, this tale gets less than a page (387–8). See also brief references in cited works by Petrini, *Nel giardino*; Wallace; Palumbo; Giusti, "La novella"; Olson, *Courtesy Lost*; Martinez, "*Scienze della Cittade*"; Oesch-Serra; and Picone, "Leggiadri motti." We will refer to some of them further down.

2 See Kirkham, *Sign of Reason* 169 et infra.

Sixth Day, Fiammetta sketches for us a scene wherein a group of friends is loitering in the back alleys of Florence, not too far from Santa Maria Novella, and in their playful roguishness end up bandying about which was the most noble and ancient family in the city. Some vouch for the Uberti, and some counter with the Lamberti, who were actually existing but decayed upper-crust families at the time,[3] unlike for instance the powerful clans of the Donati and the Cerchi. In the meantime, the friends end up in someone's house, Piero the Florentine, to continue their rumpus. A Michele Scalza, known to be a jolly party animal and a gossip – as "le piú nuove novelle aveva per le mani" [VI.6.4; he had any number of juicy stories up his sleeve; 395][4] – ready to jump into any boisterous gathering to draw attention and have fun, often at someone else's expense, first listens and then barges in, telling the bunch that they know not what they are talking about. He remarks with a grin that it is the Baronci[5] who are "i più gentili uomini e i più antichi, non che di Firenze ma di tutto il mondo o di Maremma" [VI.8.6; the most noble and ancient of men, not only of Florence but of the whole world and Maremma too; my trans.], a claim backed by invoking the authority of the most prestigious academics of the time, the Schoolmen. This is no small detail, as we will see.

---

3 Najemy, *History of Florence* 6 and 60–1, points out that of the great families that practically ruled Florence during the twelfth century – some listed in Cacciaguida's microhistory in *Paradiso* 16 – only a few had survived the banishment of the Ghibellines in 1267–8, and this included the powerful families of the Lamberti and the Uberti, some of whom moved on to Siena and Pisa (Olson, *Courtesy Lost* 140). However, though their reputation as noble and ancient remained in the culture, they were no longer models of ethical behaviour. We recall that Farinata degli Uberti appears in Canto 10 of the *Inferno,* whereas a Mosca dei Lamberti is presented by Dante as a sower of discord in *Inferno* 28.

4 Unless otherwise indicated, I have used the Waldman translation for the English text, but occasionally I have used the McWilliam version or my own translations, as indicated in square brackets. For the original text, I have used Branca's 1976 edition for *Tutte le opere*.

5 In Najemy's register of the old élite (the *grandi* for the Florentines of the period) – characterized by agnatic lineages, inherited wealth, and recurrent inter-family strife vying for prestige – there is no Baronci, but he attests to a Baroncelli clan in early 1300, who were part of an emerging newfangled élite (*History of Florence* 23). In *Paradiso* 16, 104, Cacciaguida lists a "Barucci" among the earlier élites in early thirteenth century. There are almost no sources on the Baronci, other than Branca's remark that they were part of an old bourgeois family (Boccaccio, *Decameron* [1976] 2:1062). In his *Ethics of Retribution*, Nissen writes: "It is evident that the Baronci of Sacchetti's generation were no more highly regarded than their ancestors who were derided in *Decameron* VI.6" (90). There are no records of the next character introduced, Michele Scalza, and a case can be made that he represents the author's critical persona.

The troop snaps back, much like a bunch of East Side Kids or Bowery Boys from the famous Samuel Goldwyn movies of the 1940s, sneering: what do you take us for? We know what you are talking about. I'll prove it to you, counters Michele, but if I win, you will treat me and six other people to supper. Sure of his hand, he further says: "io ne starò alla sentenzia di chiunque voi vorrete" [VI.6.8, I'll accept the verdict of anyone you want]. In such situations, there is always someone who immediately thinks he also can get into the wrangling to his advantage. So Neri Mannini now jumps in, plugging in Piero the Florentine, the host, as a judge, whom some of the troop immediately went to fetch.

Well, asks the newly appointed judge, "come potrai mostrare questo che tu affermi?" [VI.6.10; how are you going to prove your assertion?; 396]. The argument runs as follows:

> Voi sapete che, quanto gli uomini sono più antichi, più son gentili, e così si diceva pur testé tra costoro: e i Baronci son più antichi che niuno altro uomo, sì che son più gentili; e come essi sien più antichi mostrandovi, senza dubbio io avrò vinta la quistione. (VI.6.12)
>
> [As you know, the more ancient a family, the nobler it is – which is what we were saying a moment ago. The Baronci are a more ancient family than any other, so they must be the noblest. So once I've proved that they're the most ancient, I'm bound to win the argument.] (396)

Now in order to grasp the sense of the rest of Scalza's explanation, the reader should recall that in the previous *novella*, VI.5, featuring Giotto, a reference was made to the fact that one's talents are *not* immediately reflected in one's appearance, and to make the point Panfilo stated that, for instance, Forese da Rabatta, who will become the object of Giotto's final retort in that sketch, "essendo di persona piccolo e isformato, con viso piatto e ricagnato che a qualunque de' Baronci piú trasformato l'ebbe sarebbe stato sozzo" [VI.5.4; was a misshapen little runt of man with a moon-face and a squashed nose, compared with whom even the least favored of the Baronci would have looked an angel; 394]. In other words, in the real socio-historical context of this tale, it was common knowledge, or at least a well-known "rumour" or public embedded belief, or even, if we wish, a spontaneous association, that the Baronci family, noble though they might have been, were physically not good looking. Indeed, in plain vernacular, they were ugly, and could easily be targeted, directly or indirectly, as the butt of jokes, parody, or extemporaneous one-liners. This explains in part why the happy brigade assumes, albeit presumptively, against Michele's claim, that there could be nothing "noble" or "special" about them, other than the fact that they are powerful and socially estimable. Here then comes the key part of Scalza's little spur:

> Voi dovete sapere che i Baronci furon fatti da Domenedio al tempo che Egli aveva cominciato d'apparare a dipignere, ma gli altri uomini furon fatti poscia che Domenedio seppe dipignere. E che io dica di questo il vero, ponete mente a' Baronci e agli altri uomini: dove voi tutti gli altri vedrete co' visi ben composti e debitamente proporzionati, potrete vedere i Baronci qual col viso molto lungo e stretto, e quale averlo oltre a ogni convenienza largo, e tal v'è col naso molto lungo e tale l'ha corto, e alcuni col mento in fuori e in sú rivolto e con mascelloni che paiono d'asino; e èvvi tale che ha l'uno occhio piú grosso che l'altro, e ancora chi ha l'un piú giú che l'altro, sí come sogliono essere i visi che fanno da prima i fanciulli che apparano a disegnare. (VI.6.13–14)

> [What you have to know is that the Good Lord made the Baronci at the time He was learning to paint, while everyone else was made once He actually knew how. You'll see the truth of this if you consider the Baronci and the others. All the others, as you'll have noticed, have well made, suitably proportioned features, but take a look at the Baronci faces: some have long thin ones, others have impossibly fat ones; some have long noses, others stubby ones; some have chins that jut out to meet their noses, some have jaws the size of donkeys; you'll find some with one eye bigger than the other, some with one eye lower than the other – just like the faces children make when they're first learning to draw.] (396–7)

From these premises, which are based on several sets of assumptions, as we will see, the conclusions seem inevitable and are in fact swift:

> Per che, come già dissi, assai bene appare che Domenedio gli fece quando apparava a dipignere, sí che essi son piú antichi che gli altri e cosí piú gentili. (VI.6.15)

> [Therefore, as I said, it's obvious that the Good Lord made them when He was learning to paint, which makes them more ancient than any, and consequently more noble.] (396–7)

Piero the judge, Neri the instigator, and the amused band concur, after what we imagine a second or two to let it sink in, that Scalza is quite right and that, in fact, "per certo i Baronci erano i più gentili uomini e i più antichi che fossero, non che in Firenze ma nel mondo o in Maremma" [VI.6.16; the Baronci had to be the noblest and most ancient family not merely in Florence but in the whole wide world this side of the marshes and beyond; 397]. And this widening of the field at the end of the phrase is not an insignificant detail.

There are several levels of analysis possible to extract layers of meaning out of this little tale, and we will focus on four of them, going from the micro-text to the macro-text. The first concerns the rhetorical-logical structure of the explanation for Scalza's claim about the Baronci's nobility. The second approach links the tale to the general economy of the Sixth Day, dedicated explicitly to witticisms that "bite like a sheep," and looks at the rhetorical-social function of speech in mostly popular, non-courtly, non-literate society. Here some considerations on the role of humour and the comic are in order. In a third frame of analysis we focus on language itself, or rather the "use" of language to obtain a desired effect within a particular context, already heralded in the first level, but here elevated to the level of ideological critique. This introduces a fourth level, which concerns the question of the broader social-political import of what this and some of the other *novelle* may entail in the larger picture of Boccaccio's overall oeuvre and his role and position in the emerging secular humanism. The concluding considerations will be of a general nature about literature and society.

Let us then consider Scalza's little gem of a speech. It takes on the logical structure of a syllogism, in this fashion:

A. The more ancient a family, the nobler it is;
B. The Baronci are the most ancient;
C. The Baronci are the noblest family.

This is the standard categorical syllogism, of the form AAA 1. To make it more formal, it should be rephrased and restructured as follows:

P 1: All ancient families are the noblest families;
P 2: All Baronci are a most ancient family;
C: All Baronci are the noblest family.[6]

The reader may recall the paradigmatic example: All men are mortal, Socrates is a man, therefore Socrates is mortal.[7] But what is of interest

6 I owe this reformulation to my colleague in the philosophy department at Stony Brook, Allegra De Laurentiis.

7 See Capaldi: "in essence [this is] the basic format of all valid syllogistic arguments" (39). The preconditions for the syllogism are met insofar as each of the three terms must appear twice, and the middle term is distributed. See also Cohen and Nagel 84;

here is that Scalza's basis for pulling this apparently unassailable proof is grounded on evidence that has little to do with formal argument, relying rather on established but still circumstantial conditions, and as such it is an enthymeme, so that casting it as a syllogism is ultimately a ruse.[8] The argument is made on the basis of what everyone in that particular social sphere is predisposed to accept as a valid truth, namely, that the most ancient families must of course be the noblest, an assumption become topical on the strength of the fact that it is the upper elites who typically legitimate their status based on recorded or demonstrable genealogies. Indeed, as in the parallel case of claimed Church authority based on the Decretals, it is the documents produced, preserved, and jealously guarded that shore up the valid proof of a claim and legitimate it. This would guarantee its becoming an authority on what is called unquestioned knowledge, sort of a universal proposition, for that community or even society as a whole. The emphasis here, however, is on *that* audience, which in our tale is the fun-seeking gang of friends indubitably aware of the power and lineage of the Uberti and the Lamberti and other families in Florence.

The argument gains strength when Scalza makes a brilliant connection, based on sense evidence, that the Baronci are indeed well known

---

Broadie 174–7. Cuomo is one of the few who explores the role and use (and abuse) of the syllogism in Boccaccio, and especially in this particular *novella* (252–4), drawing attention to the fact that it employs the third mood (*darii*) of the first figure. But an argument can be made that Scalza's syllogism falls under a different mood and possibly the fourth figure. Medieval logic was a complex field, and often scholars who expound upon the major philosophers that Boccaccio is sure to have known to some degree, like Scotus, Ockham, Buridan, Peter of Spain, are not in total agreement when it comes to the evolution of the syllogistic mode, and how it was employed by non-experts. Compare Broadie, and Speca, on the much contested developments of modal syllogistic, hypothetical syllogistic, and stoic logic.

8 See Cohen and Nagel: "The fact that logic is concerned with necessary relations in the field of possibility makes it indifferent to any property of an object other than the function of the latter in a given argument" (12). In other words, *deductive* logic may by and large connect with reality, but it doesn't need reality to be formally correct. It is the propositions and the postulates that must necessarily be true on the basis of the assumed and unquestioned axioms and rules. As De Laurentiis confirmed in her email to me: "The criticism against the possible lack of soundness is irrelevant to the validity of the syllogism. Formal validity is independent of Truth or Falseness of premises or conclusion, except in one case, namely when both premises are (factually) True and the conclusion (factually) False (= unsound syllogism). This is not the case here." It is with *inference* that matters change, since this entails a temporal process (Cohen and Nagel 7) and as such bears upon empirical or factual conditions. For the long gestation of the inductive method in the Middle Ages, see Crombie 21–30.

to be unsightly or just plain ugly, and frames another shorter but efficacious syllogism:[9]

A. The Baronci are ugly, therefore not perfect looking;
B. In painting, ugly sketches are made when the artist is still learning;
C. When the Baronci were made, God was still learning.

The ending gains further conviction in the implied retrojected assumption that when God, like any artist, finally learned how to draw well, he made human beings normal, or at least not as grotesque: some with a longer nose, others with a jaw like an ass, and so on. Looking forward to the free supper, the huddle of friends look to Piero and Neri for the verdict on the "amusing argument," which they concede, for Scalza "was quite right," and confirm that, of course, everyone in the whole world knows that the "the Baronci had to be the noblest and most ancient family."

The little tale can now be subjected to further interpretive possibilities. First of all, an important textual clarification, useful when we address the comic: the troop's last witty affirmation in indirect free speech literally says "not only in Florence but in the whole wide world or in the Maremma," which was already uttered earlier in almost identical language in paragraph 6.[10] This builds on Boccaccio's penchant for subtle subversion of expected or orthodox speech patterns, for the mixing of registers is, in itself, already a convention in humour and, we will argue, an index of social critique. Technically, as Bruni points out: "after [mentioning] Florence and the world one expects that the *climax* continues with a substantive of even greater extension (such as 'universe' or something similar); instead the conclusion is no less buffonesque than the demonstration, and after world [*mondo*] the reference to Maremma … interrupts the progression of the hyperbole. The comic effect is reinforced by the disjunctive preposition 'o' (in the sense of *vel*, not *aut*), instead of the conjunction 'e' that one would expect, which suggests the interchangeability of very different signs in the meaning,

9 Cuomo claims this is a first figure syllogism, or *barbara* (254).

10 The first mention reads in Italian: "i più gentili uomini e i più antichi, non che di Firenze ma di tutto il mondo o di Maremma, sono i Baronci" (paragraph 6). The last reads: "per certo i Baronci erano i piú gentili uomini e i piú antichi che fossero, non che in Firenze ma nel mondo o in Maremma" (paragraph 16).

in themselves not interchangeable, such as world and Maremma are" (Bruni 388).[11]

Second, what passes for logic, typically associated with the learning of the, basically implied tongue-in-cheek, "Schoolmen," and therefore authoritative when searching for and demonstrating any lofty truth, is made a mockery[12] – beginning with the fact that the reference to the scholastics is introduced by the spoonerism, "fisofoli" (VI.6.6), or "phisopholers," which is rendered in English by Waldman as "what do you call 'em – schoolmen" (396).[13] For in fact the syllogistic arguments, craftily lodged one inside the other, and formally coherent though they may appear, are employed for the rhetorical purpose of confusing the little brigade to accept an off-the-wall conclusion. They reveal that the art of persuasion relies on what J.L. Austin called the "performative utterance," which is different from the "constative utterance" or the "statement," as it depends on the "appropriate circumstances" in order to trigger an

11 "Ovviamente, dopo Firenze e il mondo ci si attende che il *climax* continui con un sostantivo di estensione ancora superiore (come 'universo' o qualcosa di simile); invece la conclusion non è meno buffonesca della dimostrazione, e dopo *mondo* il riferimento alla *Maremma* (propiziato anche dall'allitterazione) rompe la progressione dell'iperbole; e il comico è rafforzato dalla disgiuntiva *o* (nel senso di *vel*, non di *aut*), invece della congiunzione *e* che ci si aspetterebbe, a suggerire l'intercambiabilità di segni diverssisimi nel significato, e di per sé non intercambiabili, come il *mondo* e la *Maremma*." The expression "che sia nel mondo o in maremma" occurs also in Frate Alberto's tale (IV.2.41), with a comical tone, and may have been a typical expression in the *contado* or implicitly of the lower unsophisticated bourgeoisie.

12 A case can be made that the dart is also aimed at the reforms being introduced in Paris by the nominalists, and the new interpretations of Aristotle that were flourishing. In particular, Leff, chapter 2, makes a case for the beginning of the religion/church divide that would inform the later humanists well into the Renaissance. This cannot be taken up here.

13 Waldman's English appropriately captures the usage of the lower register employed here, where the lectio "s'accordano tutti i fisofoli" is, according to Branca's note to the term, a "popular" way of saying "filosofi," understood as "sapienti." But I suggest translating with "phisopholers," to stay closer to the original and foreground the low-tone jab of the reference. The word was surely used purposefully by Boccaccio to suggest, sarcastically, social class distance if not, perhaps and within the universe of the tale, a thinly veiled diffidence (if contempt is too strong a word) between the actors in the episode and the literati, the intellectuals, or even the courtly establishment that often employed them.

action (5–6).[14] Moreover, the scene also demonstrates that there existed certain external contextual, and at any rate culturally unconscious, beliefs (whether based on faith or superstition or habit is not the point here) that could be leveraged to obtain a desired end. Among these, for instance, that it took six days to create the universe, as everyone in the community is presumed to know the story from Genesis.[15] What our storyteller anchors onto that cultural bedrock, which acts as a *locus communis* that, as we saw, doubles as a logical axiom, is the analogy that, just as an artist takes time to master drawing a figure, so did the Good Lord, with the added embedded analogy, again taken to be self-evident by everyone, that first sketches are infantile, and executed at an earlier age – or, say, earlier days, to stay with the time span of Genesis – so it follows therefore that our Lord drew humans like an infant, misshapen and unproportionate.[16] We will return to this topos further down.

---

14 To clarify what Austin means by performative: "The uttering of the words is, indeed, usually a, or even *the*, leading incident in the performance of the act (of betting or what not), the performance of which is also the object of the utterance, but it is far from being usually, even if it is ever, the *sole* thing necessary if the act is to be deemed to have been performed. Speaking generally, it is always necessary that the circumstances in which words are uttered should in some way, or ways, be *appropriate*, and it is very commonly necessary that either the speaker himself or other persons should also perform certain other actions, whether 'physical' or 'mental' actions or even acts of uttering further words" (8, emphasis in original). Statements may be true or false, whereas performatives are more like a pragmatic rhetorical utterances, they interact, are causative, are basically a "doing" (13), and though they may be "parasitic" (22) or used in bad faith (11), that does not impact on their function and use.

15 Martinez draws attention to this detail by pointing out the "patristic accounts of God's six-day-long fashioning of the world in Genesis" ("*Scienze della Cittade*" 59), as part of a critical analysis of the layered symbolism of the number "6" that informs the entire Sixth Day. Further down he notes that the Baronci's deformed face recalls the artistic difficulty of shaping a perfectly sculpted nose (61) as a parallel to the writer's task of framing a rhetorically perfect line, with reference to "Boccaccio's cognizance of the sixth day of the six Horation vices of composition … of the *Ars poetica*" (62).

16 A more serious elaboration of the idea that the Creator took a while to create the perfect human being reappears later in Pico della Mirandola's oration *On the Dignity of Man*. In this paradigmatic text of humanism, we read that the master architect "had adorned the supercelestial region with Intelligences, infused the heavenly globes with the life of immortal souls and set the fermenting dung-heap of the inferior world teeming with every form of animal life. But when this work was done, the Divine Artificer still longed for some creature which might comprehend the meaning of so vast an achievement, which might be moved with love at its beauty and smitten with awe at its grandeur. When, consequently, all else had been completed (as both Moses and Timaeus testify), in the very last place, He bethought

Looking at the tale in yet another and clearly related perspective, what can we say of Scalza's audience? Briefly, that they are gullible, unsophisticated, lower-class happy-go-lucky youths out to have a good time? And that they tell a humorous off-the-wall story in order to have a laugh at someone else's expense (both literally, the dinner at Piero's, and metaphorically, through the jab at the Baronci's nobility)? Yes, but there is more to it than that. Jokes are a species of utterance of which humour is the larger category. Following Freud for a moment,[17] jokes are made-up linguistic stratagems of the unconscious to release pent-up energy that self-induced inhibitions and social taboos on the vital forces, such as fear, sex, and aggression, keep in check within a society. Jokes utter the opposite of what is the case, satisfy an instinct to break through certain obstacles, and embody a way of obtaining pleasure *in spite of* distressing or unbearable feelings. Without having to make recourse to the distinct types Freud draws up, which involve condensation and unification – and of which two, the tendentious and the cynical joke, appear most frequently in the *Decameron* – what is relevant to our analysis is not solely the fact that, in the microcosm of each tale with

---

Himself of bringing forth man." However, in this case the human being, though created last, cannot be based on a "model" or archetype, and clearly God did not have to perfect his art *strada facendo* (Pico seemingly having no sense of humour!). The problem is different and will have far-ranging consequences: the "new man" cannot be created as already perfect. This introduces an uncertainty about an eternist conception of humanity as stemming from the Divine and in his image. Reading the rest of the text, we learn in fact that "all space was already filled; all things had been distributed in the highest, the middle and the lowest orders … At last, the Supreme Maker decreed that this creature, to whom He could give nothing wholly his own, should have a share in the particular endowment of every other creature. Taking man, therefore, this *creature of indeterminate image*, He set him in the middle of the world and thus spoke to him: 'We have given you, Oh Adam … no visage proper to yourself, nor any endowment properly your own, in order that whatever place, whatever form, whatever gifts you may, *with premeditation*, select, these same you may have and possess *through your own judgment and decision*. The nature of all other creatures is defined and restricted within laws which We have laid down; *you*, by contrast, impeded by no such restrictions, may, *by your own free will*, to whose custody We have assigned you, *trace for yourself the lineaments of your own nature* … It will be in your power to descend to the lower, brutish forms of life; you will be able, through your own decision, to rise again to the superior orders whose life is divine'" (5–8, emphasis added). That human beings are, even, or perhaps already, for Boccaccio, of an "undetermined nature" ("indiscretae opus imagines"), and can decide *consciously* on their fate, is part of what I am suggesting in this reading.

17 See Freud. The next three sentences basically summarize some of the main concepts in *The Joke and Its Relation to the Unconscious*.

those particular characters, the witticism permits a saving of psychical expenditure,[18] but the fact that *this is the only way they have to deal with a problem*. In other words, what may be an inhibition in the clinical sense can also be thought of by extension as a set of constraints – taboos, traditions, strong public enforcement – tantamount to repression of expression within the social order, a repression therefore whose cause is a force or forces outside the control of the actors. I believe that in our tale this external referent is clearly the upper crust, the *popolo grasso*. The hostility that belies the repression is unleashed by attacking those traits of the target, i.e., the unattractiveness of the rich family. But this cannot be done directly. Rather, it is achieved by a pseudo-logical story whereby the brigade is told that they, the Baronci, were made that way when the Lord created the universe, though because he was just learning how to make humans, he did not shape them perfectly. The absurdity of the tale gains traction with the interlocutors (*and* readers as the necessary "outside listeners" to the joke),[19] first, by a catalogue of unappealing features,[20] which rhetorically make the case by sheer *accumulatio*, and then by throwing in, to conclude and seal the *demonstratio*, a swift comparison – let us recall that this is the day dedicated to short tales, with "brevity" being a stated aim of the storytellers – that the audience could not not agree upon: just like kids when first learning how to draw. Recall that it is a crucial part of the efficacy of joke-telling that the speakers share the same (at least local) culture[21] and are also pre-prepared for

18 See Freud 114. In essence this means one of two things: I can't deal with the reality around me (because objectively I can't, I am a subaltern, so to speak, or I have to get this obstacle, this person, out of the way *now*), or: I won't deal with the reality around me (because it entails too much work, intellectual or otherwise, a larger commitment towards some resolution). Clearly we are dealing with the first instance, where the utterance lessens the tension. Specifically, we recall that Elissa had stated, at end of Day Five, that the tales were going to be about "quick-witted people resorting to a happy quip or nice repartee to slap down another person or avert some impending disaster ... people who, on being teased, give as good as they get, or who avoid danger, embarrassment, or loss by dint of a prompt rejoinder" (381).

19 Freud points out that a joke requires that a third party be present to gain the sympathy and approval of the narrator.

20 "some have long thin [faces], others have impossibly fat ones; some have long noses, others stubby ones; some have chins that jut out to meet their noses, some have jaws the size of donkeys; you'll find some with one eye bigger than the other, some with one eye lower than the other – *just like the faces children make when they're first learning to draw*" (397, emphasis added).

21 Critics have pointed out how the Sixth Day is the least multilingual or multicultural of days, suggesting that the quick-witted retorts did not have to be mediated or "translated," so to speak.

it, as the narrator typically "sets up" the ensuing story, as Scalza does. The reference to children is important in the joke because, as Freud once again argues,[22] the (unconscious) motivation behind the creation of humorous situations is the substitution of "object-associations with verbal associations and the use of absurdity" as ways to make sense out of a nonsensical story, "restoring old freedoms" and "disburdening us from the compulsion of our intellectual education." What's implied is that children do not yet have rational control of their impulses, yet we smile at their untrammelled mental freedom, and we laugh when we let down our rational defences, as when under the influence of a substance or alcohol.

The point here is that, in making sense out of the nonsensical, we are not trying to psychoanalyse the characters, but rather to look at the rhetoric of the story with the support of some mechanisms which, though they may have originated in psychology, can without much distortion be useful to orient reflections towards social and political concerns. In fact, the taboos and inhibitions of the characters, we might say of us all, derive from socially created norms, civil delimitations, laws, censure, strong traditions and rituals, fear of aggression or punishment, and so on. The social space and the condition of an unlettered populace is a recurring presence in the entire *Decameron*, and too often the ironies and parodies perpetrated upon them highlight the fact that they were regularly being taken advantage of. Not that the author cherished some sort of pious Franciscan ethos whereby we are all God's children and we shouldn't make fun of the poor, the unfortunate, the dregs of society.[23] But in order to talk about them, and in fact, to make them speak, the author had to give the whole work a structure, develop a narrative form (the *novella*), a structured sequence (the time-frame of the ten days and the ten stories within each), ultimately an "order," when, in the end, what was supposed to be represented, four levels removed and almost safely further down, was chaos, death, the coming apart of the social and symbolic orders as a result of the plague. Unfortunately, not many in the scholarship have emphasized this aspect, which I consider fundamental. But before turning to the impact of the Black Death, let

22 See Freud 120.

23 See for example Hortis 174–7 et infra, who underscores Bocccaccio's near contempt for the "sciocchi" who are often equated with the *profanum vulgus*, in short with the plebs he has, by the time of the *Genealogie*, left behind. However, this brings out by contrast the heterogeneity of the characters present in the *Decameron*, who hail from all walks of life, as we will remark below.

me gloss what I mean by the four levels removed we have to telescope through, and expand on the earlier levels of analysis proposed above:

A) *a real person*, historically documented to have existed, namely Giovanni Boccaccio, who before the greatest calamity ever known to humankind up to that point in time, a pandemic that devoured about a third of Europe's population within months according to some sources,[24] decides to *write about it*.[25] Though referential in the Introduction, this already sets up one level of distance between *res* and *verba*. Boccaccio is the narrator, an alter "I" directs us to what follows.
B) *fictional accounts*, however realistic the inner frame of reference, in what is called the *Decameron*, a work of the imagination within a tradition. These accounts must be articulated with reference to the metalanguage of the genres of the period, amply studied and which demand adherence to certain codes (and breaking or altering them is still a play with, and within, those institutions).
C) ten fictitious *characters*, the storytellers who rule over each of the ten days, tell "stories" *about other people* after having been "cast" to control the narration *within* the narration, and therefore impact the economy of the language, the sub-genres employed, the tenor of the actions, the range of the ideas expressed. Their electing to leave the city and hide in a mansion that is safe from the chaos and death also signals the erecting of a further barrier, another moat to isolate the blight all around (even if, factually, the writing may have taken place a year or two after 1348).[26]
D) *characters who represent people* in various contexts and situations, some imagined and some retrieved from hearsay, some from mythological and geographical accounts and some perhaps based

24 On the cruciality of this epochal event for the subsequent development of Florentine society, which sets the course for the rise of the *signorie*, see Najemy, *History of Florence* 145–9 et infra; for the broader implications for the entire European world, which will take nearly a century to recover, see McNeill 134–81 and 195–6.

25 I find the older scholarship, such as that of Bergin, no longer tenable: "As a nineteenth-century critic perceptively wrote: 'Between his ambitious poems of his youth and the learned works of his mature years Boccaccio grants himself a moment of relaxion and child-like mischief'" (286). "Perceptive"? This is akin to saying that after Hurricane Katrina a survivor in New Orleans decides to write fairy tales just to "relax."

26 See Branca, *Boccaccio: The Man*; Battaglia Ricci, *Boccaccio*; and Armstrong, Daniels, and Milner for reconstructions of the years just preceding and just following the writing of the *Decameron*.

on events and accidents the author may have witnessed first-hand during his many travels and stays in different locales. These are given a voice, greatly inspired by oral speech so as to lend more "realism"[27] to their actions and situations.

What we have are *thrice removed narrators/retellings*. This narratological distancing[28] constitutes, in a way, a "safer" way to refer explicitly to what was under everyone's eyes but was not duly acknowledged as symptomatic of a great sudden collapse of society, not in the abstract, but concretely, as it impacted *everything*: the people who were not dying had descended, within a few months, to a pre-civilized interregnum, as we had read in the Introduction. A reminder of this sneaks through at the end of the Sixth Day, when Dioneo prepares for his rule, and wants to focus on some titillating if unsettling aspects of women's behaviour. There is some opposition to that topic, but in justifying his choice, Dioneo says:

> Or non sapete voi che, per la perversità di questa stagione, li giudici hanno lasciati i tribunali? le leggi, così le divine come le umane, tacciono? e ampia licenzia per conservar la vita è conceduta a ciascuno? (VI.Concl.9)
>
> [Are you not aware that because of the chaos of the present age, the judges have abandoned the courts, the laws of God and man are in abeyance, and everyone is given ample licence to preserve his life as best he may?] (McWilliam 515)

Indeed, at a time where sheer survival is at stake, Dioneo counters that this is no time to be prudish, that is, hold up some veneer of modesty: "chi sapesse che voi vi cessaste da queste ciance ragionare alcuna volta forse suspicherebbe che voi in ciò non foste colpevoli, e per ciò ragionare non ne voleste" [VI.Concl.13; if it ever came out that you avoided this kind of light chat, people might well suspect that your refusal to do so was tantamount to an admission of guilt; 412].

27 Battaglia Ricci, *Boccaccio* 139.

28 What I call "levels" may also be thought of as "concentric circles" of analysis, as Eugenio Giusti, in *Dall'amore cortese*, does in his rich and revealing reading of some of Boccaccio's works. Giusti emphasizes the built-in critique of his narrative strategies, and his aim at getting a message through the several circles of understanding. See in particular 125–71. One element that I consider brilliant is that Boccaccio is practically ironizing about the ironic, thus eliminating the long-standing tradition of identifying narrator with author.

What were people, and relations among them, like before *Yersinia pestis* hit the Italian peninsula?[29] When all is lost and gone, and people of all stripes are ruined and in constant terror, and what remains is set back years, eons, what do we see? The author of medieval romances could not even begin to say by engaging yet again the earlier genres and their idealized fictions, though we know that by the mid-1340s he was in a different cast of mind. With the arrival of the plague, everything is questioned, everything is up for a rethinking, a reframing, a desperate search for something that would make sense. Facing the unknown and still broaching somehow the full panoply of human reality as it teetered on the edge of this judgment day, the author will pen down sketches, snapshots of situations, anecdotes, micro-récits. In a comic mode.[30]

But what emerges through the comic is that many aspects of the human condition are not so noble after all. Within that frame, the chosen rhetoric is that of humour. I believe the critique of established orders of society, as filtered through humour, is about, first, the long-entrenched violence and presumptuousness of local and regional barons and princes and kings (later in part berated in *De casibus virorum illustrium*); next, the everyday hypocrisies and abuses of the representatives of the various monastic orders and of the Church in general; and finally, the decay of the courtly code.[31] Let us recall that humour is rebellious, it is not resigned, and if it makes hostility acceptable it doesn't cancel the presence of that which is critiqued. Let us also recall that, unlike the comic in general, which can be perceived spontaneously, as something we may encounter even when we are by ourselves, humour is intentional, as the actors, throughout the *Decameron*, devise the "beffa"

29 McNeill refers to it by its older name, *Pasteurella pestis* (164–80).

30 For a general picture of humour in the Middle Ages, see Verberckmoes; and loci in Kleinhenz, ed.

31 See on this Olson, *Courtesy Lost* 56–97, who makes a clear case for a Boccaccio bent on reforming the tradition of *cortesia* to include the new mixed society, the "gente nuova" that had emerged during the author's lifetime. As a set of patterns and norms for social exchange, *cortesia*'s long-entrenched and multifaceted aspects – think of the different meaning it had in Dante's time – need to be contextualized for the changing environment and thus be historicized (7–15) in order to grasp how Boccaccio attempted to broaden its semantic-symbolic range (53–5). This will bear on the underlying ethics of the characters in the sixth tale, but of course also on all of his oeuvre, especially after the 1350s.

whether through action or through words.[32] This element of choice, of exercising judgment, especially present in the Sixth Day when people "give as good as they get," should be explored further, as a topos within and across the novelle, for they indicate that each person, for better or for worse, is capable of dealing with the ostracizing and threatening environment, though often elects to do something at the expense of someone else. We mentioned earlier that the day is under the sign of temperance, which means of proper judgment. The fact is that the plague practically cleared the field of canonical forms of reflection and habitual forms of interpersonal relations. Thus, the social forces that determined the scale of values of the citizenry, and effected a control over them, were suddenly pulled off their anchors. The temperance that assures us of the stability of a given set of mores and adhesion to norms, thus ensuring a predictable, safe social intercourse, is upended: judgment is now about survival, about "me," about getting by, and when possible or necessary, "giving it to them." Rather than direct invective, however, when the destructive forces came from "nowhere," and even God couldn't answer the call for help, the author's choice was to work through exempla, which are in rhetoric what demonstrations are in logic.[33]

Even within these three major areas of critical engagement – the nobility, the Church, and the weight of literary tradition as embodied in the paradigmatic genres[34] – which have been abundantly researched and written upon, what strikes one about the typologies of the individual *novellas* is that not only those in power but even common folk can be, and indeed are, capable of genuine vile and immoral acts, treachery, betrayals, cunning, lying, reciprocal tricking, and injuring, shaping their language-in-use, the pragmatics of the rhetorical act, to suit whatever end is proximate and desired. The good gestures by some

32 According to Aaron Smuts, there are three major types of humour, each expressing an entirely different aspect of the personality: *incongruity*, which harks back to Kant, is when humour is a response to logical impossibility, to irrelevance; *superiority*, which harks back to Hobbes, is when humour arises from a sense of glory and superiority over others; and *relief* theories, associated with Freud, wherein humour is basically a safety valve, escape from repression. What is of relevance here is that in the *novella* we find manifestations of all three kinds.

33 See Carravetta, *Elusive Hermes* 80, 186, et infra for a more detailed and documented version of this argument.

34 Giusti, in *Dall'amore cortese*, underscores the constant "meta-critical" aspect of Boccaccio's writing, which consistently breaks through the established topoi he inherited.

king or sultan or local landlord sound eerily improbable, possible but not likely. In VI.1, Oretta basically tells the knight to shut up, that he is pretentious. In VI.2, Cisti the baker reminds Master Geri of his manners, or lack thereof, of his insensitivity to consider the needs and values of those a station or two below him. Again, a critique of the sclerosis of behaviour patterns of an upper class. In VI.3, Nonna de' Pulci shuts up the bishop by another indirect quip, with the underlying context being that he, an eminence in the hierarchy of the Church, would assume he can take such liberties and even make such allusions. In VI.4, Chichibio gets away with his having broken the barrier of proper behaviour suited to his standing in the hierarchy by means of a quip which signals not so much that Currado is ultimately generous and forgiving as that the latter relieves his own tension by the realization, offered through laughter at the simplistic justification of the missing leg, that perhaps in the (his) real world there are more serious problems at hand. In VI.5, Giotto's retort to Forese's superficial but also offensive observation about the connection between reputation and talent and the looks of a person is doubly violent in its cutting sarcasm, a case of tit for tat, but this is where humour once again reveals its tension and barely suppressed agonism, for in fact we can assume that Forese and Giotto did not like each other at all. Unlike what happens in the parallel situation in VI.9, with Cavalcanti's own supercilious retort, the repartee did not have to be explained. In VI.7, Filippa is supposed to exemplify how saying the right thing, mustering the correct articulation of her case, "can save your life," except that it is so unrealistic that such a situation may actually happen, or have happened especially in those centuries, that one must laugh at the very idea that an adulterous woman could pull that off. In this case, humour may indirectly highlight that people's behaviour is informed also, and sometimes in large part, by their projections, which is to say their daydreaming, their utopias: standard constructs whose mechanisms are not so different from those that create humour to fend off a reality that's just overpowering. In VI.8 there is nothing transcendental to uncover, other than the fact that some people use words but don't know what they are saying, and when required to apply them to their own behaviour or values, they simply "don't get it." If one is thick, then let it be. We may laugh at Fresco's niece, but perhaps because we are relieved that we don't have one of those in our family.

Thus, despite the humour and the jokes and the pranks and the witticism, the *Decameron* is, at a deeper level, no human comedy at all, but rather a profound philosophical exploration of an existentially dramatic human condition. As noted above, Boccaccio in the *Decameron* is not "reporting" what is happening during the plague, beyond the few pages in the Introduction. As often in literature, different levels of speech coexist simultaneously,[35] but in order to get to the bottom of the human condition on the verge of what must have been experienced and consciously registered as a biblical punishment like the flood, or an impending Apocalypse, with the consequent creation of a newer and even poorer because diseased portion of the population that did not have any chance of being reintegrated into any society,[36] he resorts to the exempla of so many "parables," tesserae of a huge illustrative mosaic of what has preceded the falling apart of the social order and disintegration of human values. And although the logical structure of the entire work has been duly and persuasively studied, to the point that, given its numerological frame, and the entrenched deploy at the time of symbolisms and off-the-shelf allegorical frames of significations,[37] there is an inner tension or force to disrupt this selfsame coherence.

Thus, the humour borne by the linguistic exchanges represents ultimately an amoral response to a world whose demands for a morality are in shambles, foregrounding their contingency, the near impossibility for a normative ethic which is not subject to the foibles of a constantly changing human calculus, and in a way exposing, not some hidden human nature, but the ominous presence of the absence of such a thing. This is an inauspicious yet plausible hypothesis if we recall that the rest of the stories that bracket Day Six make palpable the fact – not to speak of innumerable other ones from the other days and almost independently

35 See, for example, the fine reading of the entire Sixth Day by Oesch-Serra. However, where the author seeks to explain the witticism as "resolving a conflict that often finds its origins in the social diversification of the protagonists" (4, with reference to works by Bosetti and Paolella), I try instead to see how the resolution is no more than a temporary truce, a moment of reprieve until the next story. But the conflict remains.

36 See on this Foucault's *Madness and Civilization*, and the prodromes that led to the creation of the outcast, the institutional "reject," those who later ended up on the *stultifera navis*.

37 I am thinking of Kirkham's interpretation, whereby "for all its wit and spice, the jokesters and philanderers among its population, the *Decameron* is a microcosm founded on the principle of reason" (*Sign of Reason* 13). In a different take, Nobili concurs on the strong presence of a logical apparatus in Boccaccio's early works but holds that he veers towards the scholastics much more than, in part following Muscetta, the logicians such as Ockham. Battaglia Ricci argues that Boccaccio wrote "against" both religious people and the philosophical elite (*Boccaccio*). On the relevance of Ockham for the changing intellectual climate in the 1320–40 period, where an actual "paradigm shift" was occurring, see Leff 32–92; Stump 251–69; and Moody 409–53.

of the "frame" within which they were ordered and narrated – that beneath the guise of the wit, the quirky remarks, the double-entendres, equivocations, hilarious escapes, and tongue-in-cheek exploits of some of the characters within each story – again, three times removed from the inexplicable doom of the *actualitas* of the years in which they were penned – there lurks a profound sadness about the human condition *tout court*, about the unredeemable fate of an existence which, stripped of any belief in transcendence, is left only with the immanence of providing for sheer survival, with getting lunch or singing a song or having sex one more time, as if it were the last time, for self and world.

This is some serious humour Boccaccio bequeathed us. He is disclosing the modern human being, a raucous and pretentious actor, but one keenly aware that existence is contingent, situational, and all values built on top of that will forever wobble, as an instability is lodged into the very possibility of organizing a society. A new epoch was about to begin in Italian and European culture, with the marks of severe tensions among the classes, among competing ideas about being human and about what an ideal person, an ideal society, would be like. Humanism has had the most travailed beginnings.

7 The Tale of Madonna Filippa (VI.7)

BERNARDO PICICHÉ

Quid est enim civitas nisi iuris societas?
[For what is a State except an association or partnership in justice?]

(Cicero, *De republica* I.49)

Quod omnes tangit, ab omnibus comprobetur
[What touches all must be approved by all]

(*Codex Iustinianus* 5.59.5.2)

Le leggi deono esser comuni e fatte con consentimento di coloro a cui toccano
[Laws should be common to all and made with the consent of those whom they concern]

(*Decameron* VI.7.13)[1]

Nolite dare Sanctum canibus
[Do not give what is holy to the dogs]

(Matthew 7:6)

… debbolo io gettare a' cani?
[… shall I toss it to the dogs?]

(*Decameron* VI.7.17)

Boccaccio's rubric to the seventh story of the Sixth Day reads: *"Madonna Filippa, dal marito con un suo amante trovata, chiamata in giudicio, con una pronta e piacevol risposta sé libera e fa lo statuto modificare"*

1 The quotations of *Decameron* are from the 1985 critical edition by Vittore Branca. The English translations are my own when not otherwise indicated.

[VI.7.1; Madonna Filippa's husband discovers her with her lover. Summoned to court, she is acquitted thanks to her witty and pleasant reply, and she amends the law]. It is perhaps true that the laughter of Voltaire was more effective than the tears of Rousseau, yet meaning hidden behind laughter can be difficult to detect. This is apparently the case of the *novella* of Madonna Filippa. The present reading argues that this short tale is more than facetious entertainment. Its protagonist, Filippa, should not be viewed as a jester, but rather as a critical piece within the intellectual design of the *Decameron*, inasmuch as Boccaccio is offering here both a juridical and an ethical statement. The juridical statement decries any normative practice that is unreasonably harsh on people. The ethical statement reaffirms the dignity of *amor profano*. Two major polemics are in evidence in this story: one against abusive laws in general (not necessarily those concerning women only), and one against Dante's treatment of Francesca da Rimini. In addition, the aforementioned two major arguments seem to be closely flanked by Boccaccio's partisan Florentine propaganda against the citizens of Prato, as well as by the author's desire for a rematch with the Neapolitan nobility of blood.

The significance of this *novella* has often been overlooked, perhaps in part because the legal education of Boccaccio, acquired at the University of Naples,[2] has been rarely mentioned as a source for his writings until very recently. Kenneth Pennington hinted at the importance of the legal *forma mentis* for understanding this tale in 1977, but never followed up his brief "note" with a more substantial reading of the tale. Legal thought indeed has a much more considerable impact on medieval writers and intellectuals than is usually credited, even if important inroads are currently being made in this subfield.[3]

2 See Branca, *Boccaccio: The Man* 31–3.

3 Since I first presented the research for this *lectura* at the American Boccaccio Association's special triennial conference in 2013 at Georgetown University, there has been very little work on Boccaccio *giurista*. Recently, work on literature and the law is becoming more popular in Boccaccio studies. See, for example, Steinberg. This *novella* in particular would be a natural focal point for legal studies of Boccaccio's literary imagination, as Pennington's 1977 "Note" outlines. Recent studies from this perspective include, for example, Brody; Barsella, "Il riso"; and Korneeva. I was only able to consult Brody's interesting 2019 article at a very late stage of revision for the Press. She also notes the paucity of scholarship on this story. For other readings of VI.7, see Giannetto; and Morosini, "Bone eloquence." For ideas on this *novella* in broader thematic readings of Day Six, see Bosetti; Meier, "Day Six"; and Mineo.

One might be drawn to consider the story of Madonna Filippa as simply a burlesque *intermezzo*, led by the comedic scene at the very opening of the day. The servants Licisca and Tindaro provoke their masters' hilarity by means of their salacious remarks on the alleged libertine mores of women. The amusement of the refined audience at Licisca's words generates for a moment an intersection of two social classes and two sets of ethical values. Similarly, Filippa, herself, brings together the *grand dame* and the plebeian because she blends courtly ethos with popular common sense, the dignity of classical heroines with vernacular quips. The brigade manages to tolerate the servants' trivial behaviour in the Introduction to the Sixth Day because it comes from individuals with no knowledge of decorum. In the end, however, Elissa, the queen of the day, brusquely stops the squawking of Licisca: "con un mal viso le 'mpose silenzio e comandolle che più parola né romor facesse" [VI.Intro.7; She frowned, imposed silence on her, and bade her utter no further word or sound]. Filippa cannot be similarly silenced. On the one hand, she is a "Madonna" that is, a woman of high rank; on the other, Boccaccio needs her to vouchsafe his polemical assertions. Filippa's twofold nature breaks with the traditional contraposition between angel woman and the "other," as for instance sanctioned in Dante's *Vita nuova*: "Donne che sono gentili e che non sono pure femine" [XIX.1; Women who are gentle and not merely female]. The former alone "hanno intelletto d'amore" [XIX.2; have intelligence of Love]. Here Filippa confounds this commonplace: she knows true Love, yet she is also "femina" because she exudes joyful carnality and proudly cheats on her husband. A true Decameronian character, Filippa exalts the mundane within the spiritual. Her quips stand as a monument to Boccaccio's penchant for *docere delectando*, teaching while amusing.[4]

Boccaccio's contemporaries presumably grasped the references hidden in the address uttered by Filippa in front of the judge. The sociopolitical debates that enflamed Italy during the juridical revival of the thirteenth and fourteenth centuries, along with the interplay among

4 Ovid is the model, of course, but also the mores that Boccaccio apprehended in Naples. The director Pier Paolo Pasolini understood it, when he attributed a Neapolitan voice to his adaptation of the *Decameron*. Pasolini, however, applied the "Neapolitanness" of the *Decameron* exclusively to episodes of brilliant frauds, street urchins, and salaciousness. Nevertheless, the Angevin capital represented for Boccaccio also a beacon of aristocratic values such as decorum, honour, selflessness, largesse, hospitality, and the *bon mot*. Values that at time clash with the now outdated vision of the *Decameron* solely as an "epic of the merchants."

Roman, canon, and common laws during this period, are important subtexts for understanding this *novella*. Elena Ceva Valla's 1950 glosses on this tale are a good example of how the semantic density of this short story has been missed in traditional readings: "La legge accusata di illegalità nella audace e cinica autodifesa di una adultera orgogliosa delle sue azioni." [2:437; Law is accused of illegality, in the audacious and cynical self-defence of an adulteress, proud of her own actions].[5]

Novella VI.7 presents then a case of cuckoldry with a husband who finds his guilty wife in the act, quite like the story of the *garzone* of Perugia described in V.10. However, while the latter shows almost immediately its humorous finale, the events involving Filippa provide the audience with some pathos before reaching the non-obvious resolution. The situation appears tragic initially: although honour killing was banned in Prato as the narrator acknowledges, adulteresses could be sentenced to death judicially.[6] The laws on this matter in the medieval city of Prato are lost, so no positive evidence confirms the narrator's story. Nevertheless, surviving Italian *statuti* report that a death sentence could have been a possibility.[7] Fortunately for Filippa, on the Sixth Day of the *Decameron*, queen Elissa declares that discussion shall turn upon "chi, con alcun leggiadro motto tentato, si riscotesse, o con pronta risposta o avvedimento fuggì perdita, pericolo o scorno" [V.Concl.3; those who, on being provoked by some verbal pleasantry, have returned like for like, or who, by a prompt retort or shrewd manoeuvre, have avoided danger, discomfiture, or ridicule]. Hence, Filippa is "fortunate" that Boccaccio did not situate her in less rosy days. Otherwise, we would be mourning her, as we do Lisabetta, Simona, Salvestra, and many infelicitous female lovers. Instead, Day Six favours the happy end: the climax of tension turns upside down and Filippa is acquitted among general jubilation. In addition, she even causes the laws of Prato to be modified.

---

5 Ceva Valla was generally very liberal in her political views, to the point of fighting as a militant partisan against Fascism.

6 For honour killing, see Frederick II's *Liber Augustalis* 3:8.1. The same Frederick II appears in the *Decameron* V.6, contemplating the idea of committing a murder of passion. See also Bellomo; and Piciché.

7 See, e.g., Menesto et al. On adultery specifically, see *Statuto* 1346 (97), in Menesto et al. 614. See also Bellomo 57: "Gli uomini potevano respingere con 12 giuramenti l'accusa di adulterio per una donna, altrimenti avrebbero potuto ucciderla" [Men could reject the accusation of adultery against a woman after twelve solemn oaths, or they could kill her]. There is evidence of use of the death penalty for female adultery in Cremona (statutes of 1387 c. 109, ed. 1578, p. 39), Bellona (statutes of 1428, ed. 1525, fol. 82r–v), and Bergamo (9.72, ed. 1490, fol. 143v).

Filippa's paradoxical remarks during her trial do not constitute merely a witticism, but a defence of *amor profano,* in an exemplary case of interplay between law and literature. The juridical *Stimmung* of the story is foreshadowed immediately through the terminology of the authorial synopsis: "statute," "court," "trial," and "amends the law." Consequently, the legal lens should constitute a primary hermeneutical tool for this story. A cautionary note here: Filippa gets away so easily from troubles because *she is a literary character*. Had she stood in front of a real judge, her fate would not have been so mild. Therefore, readings of this story as a kaleidoscope of the judicial system of medieval Prato confuse literature with reality.[8] Literature lives independently from the disciplines that it touches (in this case the legal one), conscious of its partiality and attitude to alter reality.

In the synopsis, Boccaccio mentions an adulteress, a trial, and a resounding *bon mot* which leads to a resolution. Since the *bon mot* represents the common denominator among the stories of the Sixth Day, Filippa's witty final remark cannot be taken as a specific trait of the tale. We remain then with an *adulteress* and a *trial* to decipher the sense of the narration. The circumstance that Filippa is a woman of high rank represents a not insignificant detail. As the established literary tradition dating back to Aristotle prescribed, buffoonery and primordial appetites linger in characters belonging to the lower classes, like Peronella (VII.2) and the characters who opened the Sixth Day. Since aristocratic characters, on the contrary, are supposed to wrestle with existential issues, Filippa's words, those pronounced by a *madonna* (or *donna*),[9] hint to the audience that a deeper meaning must be expected. If the setting of a trial is not tantamount to signifying "seriousness" in and of itself (since plays often presented mock trials), Boccaccio also mentions here a change of the *statute*. The demand for amendments of the law casts this story into the dialectic between tradition and innovation that occupies an important role in the *Decameron*. Boccaccio is stirring public opinion on socio-legal issues both through and within the limits of literary discourse. As Giuseppe Mazzotta notes, since Boccaccio is not writing a philosophical-juridical treatise, "it would be foolhardy to expect from the *Decameron* ... analytic overview of the principles and operations of the law." Yet the law court acts as "the arena where social

8 For example, see Kannowski. I thank Paola Gambarota for helping with the translation of this article.

9 For the use of the term Madonna, see Totaro 20.

and moral values are sanctioned in the theatrical space" (Mazzotta, *World at Play* 214).[10]

The tension between positive law (i.e., the laws put in place by human legislators) and the existence of objective criteria of justice has always troubled jurists. The relation between abstract principles of justice and the specific parameters to adopt in concrete cases responds to the question: what constitutes a *fair* application of the law? Cicero had already warned against strict applications of the law that create substantial injustice (*summus jus, summa iniuria*). Likewise, Boccaccio is aware of this problematic issue. In the *Decameron* he alludes to it more than once, for instance in III.7, when Emilia reproves the "cieca severità delle leggi" [16; the blind severity of laws]. Filippa's case prompts yet another reflection on law and justice, against norms created and applied "with no compassion" (from *cum patior*: "to suffer together").

The events that happened to Madonna Filippa are narrated by Filostrato. The name of the narrator, meaning "frustrated in love," and the arguments of Licisca, suggested to some that this is a tale of resentment against women, portrayed as inclined to lasciviousness and infidelity. Such an interpretation is problematic, given closer examination, because the *Decameron* is not the *Corbaccio*. Boccaccio's last work definitely rants against the female gender, although it could be argued that the *Corbaccio* is just coping with the literary trope *An uxor ducenda*. The *Decameron* reverberates with respect and sympathy for the value of women from the *Proemio* onward. From a philological perspective, there is no support for reading malevolence against women in this story. Filostrato introduces Filippa as a "gentil donna" and her merits are highlighted at the very beginning of the narration: "bella cosa è in ogni parte saper ben parlare, ma io la reputo bellissima quivi saperlo fare dove la necessità il richiede" [VI.7.3; it is an entirely beautiful thing to know how to talk well, but even more beautiful I deem to be able to talk well when it is necessary]. What is Filippa really talking about, camouflaged behind her unconventional tones? She is advocating for recognition of the dignity of a profound love that human beings feel towards other humans. In doing so, she epitomizes a longing for a kind of moral innovation, if not for revolution (in the Proudhonian terms of non-structural changes versus structural changes). In fact, if one compares Filippa's story to the

---

10 "Light stories" can contribute to stirring public opinion: much as in movies such as *Guess Who's Coming to Dinner* or *Divorzio all'italiana* did in the 1960s, so, too did they in the Middle Ages.

fate of the more famous adulteress in *Inferno* 5, one realizes that Boccaccio's character is defending not only all women who feel true love, but one in particular: Francesca da Rimini. Filippa's defence of human love is able to persuade the human judge. On the contrary, Francesca's self-defence, poetically expressed by the famous anaphora ("love …"), did not convince the divine Arbiter. Boccaccio, Filostrato, and Filippa are here to challenge such interpretation of divine laws. They propose an ethos of worldly love that works *with*, and not *against*, the love due to God. Let's go back to the story:

> E durante questo statuto avvenne che una gentil donna e bella e oltre a ogni altra inamorata, il cui nome fu Madonna Filippa fu trovata nella sua propria camera una notte da Rinaldo de' Pugliesi suo marito nelle braccia di Lazzarino de' Guazzagliotri, nobile giovane e bello di quella terra, il quale ella quanto se medesima amava (VI.7.5)

> [When the statute was still in vigour, a gentle, young, and beautiful woman, deeply in love, more than any other woman ever was, happened to be found by her husband, Rinaldo de Pugliesi, in the arms of her lover, Lazzarino de Guazzagliotri, noble and young gentleman of that city, whom she loved as much as she loved her own person]

Filippa is portrayed as "gentle," with all the density of meaning that this term entails in medieval literature. She is the "most enamoured of the women." Her beloved is worthy of her love. The reference to Francesca's "cor gentile cui amor ratto s'apprende" (Dante, *Inf.* 5.100), the gentle heart that is quickly taken by true love, appears obvious.[11] Boccaccio can sympathize overtly with his adulterous character because he is not judging her from a theological perspective, but from that of the laws of worldly love. The very incipit of the *Decameron* – "Comincia il libro chiamato Decameron, cognominato prencipe Galeotto" [Proem.1; Here Beginneth the Book Called Decameron and Surnamed Prince Galahalt; trans. Payne] – immediately evokes the words of Francesca da Rimini: "Galeotto fu 'l libro" [Dante, *Inf.* 5.137; A Galeotto was the book].[12] In the episode of Francesca, the reader/listener of *Inferno* 5 perceives Dante's sympathy for the lovers through the poetical imagery describing them (e.g., "quali colombe," or like doves, l. 82) and the

11 See Matrone 56–7. Quotations and translations of Dante's *Commedia* are from Hollander's facing-page edition and translation.

12 See Levine; and Battaglia Ricci, *Ragionare nel giardino.*

rhythmical structure of the verses. Yet Dante, unlike Boccaccio, must condemn Francesca in order to be consistent with the moral frame of the *Comedy* – also because Francesca allegorically symbolizes the dangers of misreading.[13] The tale of Filippa is not the first time that Boccaccio questions religious inanities, as in the tale of Ferondo's Purgatory (III.8),[14] or in Panfilo's Introduction to the first tale, where a distinction is made between human justice and divine justice, insinuating the doubt (expressed also in the *Divine Comedy*) that humans too often arrogantly believe that they understand divine will.

The narrator informs us that in the city of Prato – the setting of the tale – "fu già uno statuto, nel vero non men biasimevol che aspro" [VI.7.4; there was, then, a statute in truth no less blameworthy than cruel; trans. Payne 307]. As mentioned earlier, statutes are the laws that organized the medieval city. *Statuti* constituted the bulk of common law, the ensemble of local customs blended with the Roman-Byzantine laws (*jus civile* or *corpus juris civilis*) and the papal canon (*jus canonicum* or *corpus juris canonici*). Filostrato reports that the statute of Prato, "senza alcuna distinzione far, comandava che così fosse arsa quella donna che dal marito fosse stata con alcun suo amante trovata in adulterio, come quella che per denari con qualunque altro uomo stata trovata fosse" [VI.7.4; with no distinction, prescribed to burn alive both wives caught with their lovers by their husbands and women who practised love for money].[15] In this passage, the clause "senza alcuna distinzione" indicates the narrator's reproach to the legislators of Prato for ignoring the "due" distinction between women in love and prostitutes. The *incipit* of the tale already foreshadows a sort of pledge to rethink the nature of female adultery (the only one punished by the law), if motivated by love: "La donna, che di gran cuore era sì come generalmente esser soglion quelle che innamorate son da davvero" [VI.7.9; the woman (Filippa) had a big heart, as is the case in women who know what real love is]. Contempt for interest-driven intercourse versus the exaltation of noble love, worldly yet spiritual and conducive to transcendence, dates back at least to the Minoans, and later the Greeks. Translated by the medieval poets into Christianized heterosexuality, the concept constitutes the backbone of the *amor cortese* embodied by Filippa.

---

13 See Valesio.

14 See Eisner, "Tale of Ferondo's Purgatory."

15 Some English translations for this passage misinterpret the mercenary reasons as an attenuation of the gravity of the crime, rather than an aggravation.

In order to instil sympathy towards Filippa, Boccaccio introduces Rinaldo, Filippa's husband, as a petty and ungenerous man. A certain ambiguity surrounds Rinaldo's reaction. On the point of committing an honour killing, Rinaldo stops, as "di se medesimo dubitava" [VI.7.6; he began to doubt himself]. It is hard to interpret this sentence in Italian, let alone to translate it fully into English. Literarily these words mean "he doubted himself." Does this indicate that Rinaldo halts his murderous intention for fear of the laws of Prato that forbade vendettas? Or, given that his reluctance in killing is not dictated by emotional attachment to his wife, as the reader will soon find out, is Boccaccio hinting that such a man is so faint-hearted that has not even the stamina to defend his own honour with his own hands? Gianciotto Malatesta, Francesca's husband, at least acted in alignment with the code of feudal honour. Whatever interpretation one chooses, contempt apparently surrounds a husband who wishes the death of his wife. The misfortune of the god Vulcan should have taught something to Rinaldo. Rather than getting indignant at the adultery, in fact, the Olympic deities ridiculed the cuckold who summoned them to shame his wife Venus and her lover Mars. Similarly, Rinaldo will be scorned twice: for his cuckoldry made public, and for succumbing in a trial that seemed to promise an easy victory. Discretion is the golden rule in matters of honour, as Sicilian Argisto Giuffredi warns in the sixteenth century.[16]

As we saw, the tale begins by decrying the barbaric laws of Prato. The initial tone seems intended to arouse disapproval towards this statute and the people who produced it. Rhetorically it paves the way for the final climactic moment of Filippa's victory in the name of a superior justice. Nevertheless, the execration of the laws of Prato likely entails more than a simple rhetorical preparation for the final *coup de théâtre*. Prato is not far from Florence. In the tale, the city appears still as an independent state. When Boccaccio writes, however, this independence is drawing near its end. Prato will become part of the Florentine territory in 1351. In a desperate attempt to preserve her autonomy from aggressive neighbours, Prato had previously proclaimed herself a vassal of the king of Naples, Robert of Anjou. This choice would prove to be infelicitous, since Robert's successor, Queen Joanna, would eventually sell the city to Florence for 17,500 florins (not even a huge sum).[17] In the same year in which Prato lost her independence, Boccaccio led a Florentine

16 See Piciché 27–9 and 105–6.
17 See Castellani.

diplomatic envoy to Naples to negotiate the sale of Prato. The story of Madonna Filippa must have been written before or soon after this event, if one considers reliable the generally agreed upon timeframe of 1351–3 as the completion date of *Decameron*. The coincidence here rings a bell. Was Boccaccio's intensity in denouncing "the cruel laws" of Prato dictated by political reasons? Not only did the annexation of Prato occur during the lifetime of Boccaccio, he in fact contributed to the realization of this event. Was the writer playing the ancient stratagem of demonizing the enemy, by depicting them as barbarous and ferocious? Is Boccaccio using literature as a way to legitimize the Florentine oppression of her neighbour? The preamble on the harsh laws of Prato would work rhetorically to defame the rival city. A new piece to the hermeneutical mosaic ought to be added then: the tale of Madonna Filippa might represent a literary reinforcement of the diplomatic and military actions against Prato. This third interpretation is somehow encouraged by Branca's commentary on the already mentioned V.10 concerning Count Vincioli. Count Vincioli, a historical figure in Perugia, was, in Boccaccio's account, a homosexual, albeit married. When he finds his wife in bed with a young working-class man, rather than killing both, he opts for sharing the young lover with his wife. Branca comments: "Perugia è scelta per questo episodio infamante [sic] sia per rivalità commerciali, sia per il diffuso blasone di sodomia riservato ai suoi abitanti" [note 7; Perugia is chosen for this shameful episode both for the commercial rivalry with Florence and the notorious sodomite reputation of its inhabitants]. One could add to Branca's comment that the reputation of Perugia was perhaps also tied to the parody of *dolce stil novo* in homoerotic terms developed by some Perugian poets.[18] Branca exhibits certainty that the rivalry with Perugia pushed Boccaccio to "defame" a prominent citizen of Perugia as a homosexual. In the times of Boccaccio (and Branca, seemingly), stigmatizing a grandee of a city as not conventionally heterosexual was tantamount to shaming the entire city. If the illustrious scholar's reasoning is correct, Boccaccio does not hesitate to attack the personality of the leaders of the cities that are rival to Florence. Hence, we find a sodomite in Perugia and a cruel coward in Prato.

Thus far, we have proposed three keys to reading the tale of Madonna Filippa. The first key is juridical: Boccaccio using his background as jurist to articulate his plot. The second key is ethical: the episode as

18 See Dall'Orto.

a rebuke to Dante's moral condemnation of Francesca da Rimini. The third key is political: Boccaccio's anti-Prato propaganda.

Count Vincioli was a historical leader of Perugia, even if we know nothing about his alleged homosexuality. The de Puglisi family also historically existed in Prato, although there are no records of a Rinaldo or a Filippa. Lazzarino, Fillippa's lover, belongs to the prestigious family Guazzagliotri (also Guazzalotri) who ruled Prato and whose *palazzo* is still standing. The names Lazzarino and Zarino were recurrent in this family.[19] Lazzarino is an off-screen presence in the story. We know that he possesses noble qualities and is deeply loved by Filippa. Nevertheless, he shows up in the narration only in the mention that Filostrato makes of him enjoying the delight of love with Filippa. We imagine him embracing Filippa when Rinaldo arrives. After that, we know nothing else of him. Did Lazzarino run away wearing his breeches on his head, like another clandestine lover, a prioress, in *Decameron* IX.2? Did he try to fight for his life? Did he beg for pardon or did he take all fault upon himself in the attempt to save Filippa? Was he really as much in love with Filippa as Filippa was with him? Boccaccio does not delve into Lazzarino's soul or dress code. Filippa's lover is even more marginal than Francesca's. Paolo is at least physically present next to Francesca, silently crying. The similarity of passive masculine roles and the assignation of the active role to the female characters reinforce the idea that this story is singularly focused on the episode of Paolo and Francesca, albeit with a diametrically opposed end.

In the tale, the judge ("podestà") demonstrates compassion for Filippa. Various may be the reasons for the lenient judge's conduct. The first, insinuated by the narrator, is Filippa's pretty appearance ("bellissima"). Such a motivation would echo the plot of *novella* IV.10 in which a judge uses his position of power to satisfy his own pleasure. The story of Madonna Filippa, however, carries such semantic power that the benevolence of the judge cannot be reduced to mere lust, unlike the case in IV.10. Whatever other reasons might have influenced the judge, it is a fact that his conduct was also dictated by professional deontology, or duty, inasmuch as judges were bound to resolve such cases in the most lenient way, in accordance with the principle *in dubio, pro reo* (in case of

19 Gino Capponi mentions the Guazzagliotri family in *Storia della Repubblica di Firenze* 260. Capponi reports that before the annexation of Prato seven members of this family were invited to Florence with deceit and beheaded in the name of reasons of state. Why does Boccaccio speak highly of this particular member of the family? Perhaps as a way to reconcile the survivors to Florence after the annexation?

doubt, one must deliberate favourably to the accused). Moreover, several extant city statutes (which we must presume to be similar to the lost one of Prato) prescribed that the "podestà" (executive power that also handled the judiciary) urge harmony between husband and wife by inviting the litigants to pursue "pace, riposo, et perpetuo amore" [*Antichi statuti di Quarrata*, XII; Peace, rest, and perpetual love]. The rule – still mandatory in Italian divorce law – obliges judges and lawyers to try reconciliation first. The trial procedure described in the story corresponds with what in Alberto Gandino's essay *Tractatus de Maleficiis* is defined as "per denuntiationem," a hybrid figure between accusatory and inquisitorial procedures in which, if the accuser cannot prove, the accused is absolved (*actore non probante, reus absolvitur*).[20] This permits us to understand the behaviour of the judge in realistic terms. In the description of the procedure, the tale largely reflects the actual legal rules of the time; yet not so much as to be taken as an example of how the judiciary power worked in the Middle Ages. The judge implicitly suggests to Filippa what to do to save her life: "ma ciò far [i.e., condannarti] non posso se voi nol confessate" [VI.7.12; I cannot do that [i.e., condemn you], if you do not confess]. Gandino dedicates several pages to the procedure *per exceptionem* that the judge might use *contra accusatorem*, against the plaintiff. In such cases, the judge tries to impede a punishment by dismantling the accusation. The statute of the town of Quarrata prescribed that the plaintiff should pay a fine of five liras, if the accusation could not be proven. Clearly, a pecuniary fine for Rinaldo would have been a much less gruesome resolution than the immolation of Filippa!

Boccaccio knew these legal conundrums. He uses his competence in jurisprudential matters to buttress the discourse that remained close to his heart: the defence of worldly love. This defence drives him to turn Filippa into a hero, who shows "grande animo" [VI.7.11; great spirit], as demonstrated by her own words – "secondo che le sue parole testimoniavano" [VI.7.11; as her words bore witness] – and actions.

For most of the tale, the words uttered by Filippa are reported in indirect discourse. The narrator tells us that Filippa goes to the trial accompanied by many noble persons who implore her to escape, and that she disdains the idea, in a clear evocation of the last days of Socrates. Finally, Filippa speaks in the first person:

> Messere, egli è vero che Rinaldo è mio marito e che egli questa notte passata mi trovò nelle braccia di Lazzarino, nelle quali io sono, per buono e

20 See Dezza 15.

> per perfetto amore che io gli porto, molte volte stata, né questo negherei mai. (VI.7.13)
>
> [Sir, it is true that Rinaldo is my husband and that he found me in the arms of Lazzarino last night, as I have been many times motivated by the good and perfect love that I feel for him. I would never deny this.]

Thus, in addition to having rejected the advice of good friends to run away, she refuses to listen to the sympathetic words of the judge who invited her not to confess. She defies everyone for her right to love. At the same time, she proclaims the pure nature of her love, which she portrays as good and perfect – another echo of the classical world, precisely the conception of *kalokagathìa*, or natural pairing of beauty and goodness. Filippa has no intention of repudiating her feelings, whatever consequence this will bring to her. This is her *petitio principii*: no one should dare to consider her true love as a crime! In her fortitude, she resembles those famous women of classical antiquity whose biographies Boccaccio himself will pen in *De mulieribus claris*.

A fourth key element for deciphering Boccaccio's tale of Madonna Filippa is that of class. The protagonist acts as the champion of the courtly love of the troubadours by offering a living testimony of the sentiment expressed centuries earlier by a patroness of such a creed of love, the Countess of Die: that is, each woman, even the most honest, has the right to love, if she is truly in love. There is something odd, however, in Boccaccio's choice of speaker. Troubadours spring from a courtly environment. In Italy, the paradigm of such a society flourished in the South. This culture was still very much alive at the court of Naples, whose monarchs were the Provençal Anjou family, when Boccaccio lived there. Why did Boccaccio decide to assign the representation of courtly love to a woman who, although of high rank, does not belong to the traditional courtly class? Filippa does not live in a feudal castle, or in an urban court. She comes from the Italian aristocracy of central and northern Italy that did not disdain to meddle with business and "subiti guadagni" [*Inf.* 16.73; sudden profits], to use Dante's words. Her speeches show a pragmatism more akin to mercantile common sense than to courtly language. So, why Filippa? As we know, Boccaccio felt ultimately estranged from the court of Naples because of his mercantile and illegitimate birth. Might this story represent also a personal rebuttal to that blood nobility that was so gracious and affable until he came to dream of marriage with one of them? Filippa then would prove to the Caracciolos, Capece Minutolos, Del Balzos, Brancaccios, and so forth that the urban mercantile oligarchy is also able to harbour noble ideals. Social resentment, then, would constitute the fourth interpretative point.

The juiciest part of the tale comes just as the trial proceeds to its climax. After her bold confession, Filippa adds to the judge: "ma come io sono certa che voi sapete, le leggi deon essere comuni e fatte con il consentimento di coloro a cui toccano" [VI.7.13; as I am sure that you are aware, the laws must be issued with the approval of the subjects]. Cruel laws against adultery do not respect this premise, she continues, because women's opinions were not consulted before writing this law. Filippa remarks that this is an inconvenience not only for women but also for the entire population, because women can satisfy more men than the latter can satisfy the former. Branca notes that such argument was very dear to Boccaccio (note 22). True, but there is more here. The serious thesis expressed by Boccaccio is not how much women can satisfy a society with their sexual generosity. Filippa is making a precise reference to a topic that the judge is supposed to know. As Pennington first noticed, Filippa is paraphrasing one of the pillars of Roman law, the so-called *quod omnes tangit*, or QUOT, principle: "Quod omnes tangit, ab omnibus comprobetur" [*Codex Iustinianus* 5.59.5.2; What touches all must be approved by all].[21] The principle, modified to *quod dei tangit*, appeared also in the recent (at the time of Boccaccio) *Decretales* by Pope Boniface VIII (VI.V.12.29). Madonna Filippa's denial would have been enough to declare the accusation false, with no need to mention this principle. Why does Boccaccio want Filippa to paraphrase the language of jurists? Certainly, it would be anachronistic to transform Filippa into a medieval suffragette who fights for the rights of women in the city of Prato. Filippa's defence of the right of women to decide about the laws that concern women was probably meant to be a provocative paradox. Her arguments evoke the theses *per absurdum* that in the Middle Ages were commonly used as pedagogical devices in the classrooms of law. The teachers proposed provocative *quaestiones* to spur the class to debate. This method was commonly used even by rigorous thinkers like William of Ockham. The case of a woman defending the right of women could just as easily be put there as a form of paradoxical mockery. Boccaccio is probably not advocating for an improbable recognition of women's rights to vote. Nevertheless, through Filippa, he is voicing a general sentiment of innovation that was permeating the legal community in Italy, and that urged a more democratic approach in the administration of cities.

21 See Pennington 903.

Towards the end of the narrative, Filippa asks her husband whether she has ever left him deprived of love. At this point, Rinaldo's masculine pride is tweaked. He is quick to confirm that, indeed, his wife has always satisfied his needs. Thus, the poor fool opens the way to Filippa's final counter-attack:

> se egli [Rinaldo] ha sempre di me preso quello che gli è bisognato e piaciuto, io che doveva fare o debbo di quel che gli avanza? debbolo io gittare a' cani? non è egli molto meglio servirne un gentile uomo che piú che sé m'ama, che lasciarlo perdere o guastare? (VI.7.17)
>
> [If he (Rinaldo) has always enjoyed what he needed, what should I do with the amount of love that I still harbour in my heart? Shall I toss it to the dogs? Better to please a gentle young man who really loves me, rather than wasting the abundance of my love!]

The Pratesi – like the aforementioned gods of Olympus – burst into general laughter. And Rinaldo turns into a laughingstock.

Boccaccio is not afraid to refer to saints in his puns. Filippa's words are less of a saucy quip than they may look. They hide a quotation from nothing less than the Gospel: "Nolite dare Sanctum canibus" [Matthew 7:6; Do not give what is holy to the dogs].[22] After her witty, albeit blasphemous, remark, Filippa is acquitted and acknowledged in triumph. Boccaccio continues the tale by saying that Filippa was acclaimed "quasi dal fuoco resuscitata" [VI.7.19; almost as if she had been resuscitated from fire], which could be an allusion to the miraculous resuscitation from the fire of St Januarius, the protector of the city of Naples. Filippa's victory is complete: her case will constitute a precedent that will lead to the amendment of the cruel statute, perhaps – implicitly – after the Florentine conquest.

In conclusion, it is perhaps useful to think of the tale of Madonna Filippa as a palimpsest. Firstly, Filippa personifies a heartfelt defence of worldly love. Her success stands as Francesca's posthumous rehabilitation. In addition, the juridical subtext veiled behind Filippa's aphorisms calls for a more democratic society. At the same time, Boccaccio is also voicing Florentine propaganda against Prato and his personal animosity against the blood nobility of Naples who rejected him. Finally, the story of Madonna Filippa offers a prime example of how legal discourse can serve literature, and vice versa.

---

22 For the text of the Vulgate Bible, I have used Weber and Gryson's *Biblia Sacra Vulgata*.

8 The Tale of Cesca and the Mirror (VI.8)

AILEEN A. FENG

"Ma ella, più che una canna vana e a cui di senno pareva pareggiar Salamone, non altramenti che un montone avrebbe fatto intese il vero motto di Fresco, anzi disse che ella si voleva specchiar come l'altre. E così nella sua grossezza si rimase e ancor vi si sta."

Decameron VI.8.10

[But the girl, whose head was emptier than a hollow reed even though she imagined herself to be as wise as Solomon, might have been a carcase of mutton for all she understood of Fresco's real meaning, and she told him that she intended to look in the mirror just like any other woman. So she remained as witless as before, and she is still the same to this day.]

(466; translation amended)[1]

Can you teach a woman to stop being vain? In a mere fifty-seven lines of text, Boccaccio explores this question in *Decameron* VI.8, the story of Fresco da Celatico's attempt to correct gendered-female vices in his niece Cesca. The majority of the short *novella* comprises the narrator

1 This chapter was originally written during my Lila Wallace–Reader's Digest 2016–17 fellowship year at Harvard University's Villa I Tatti in Florence, Italy. It has greatly benefited from the many conversations I had with other fellows, as well as visiting professors, including Albert R. Ascoli, Marco Faini, John Gagné, Cory M. Gavito, Emanuele Lugli, and Paola Ugolini. A special thanks to Albert R. Ascoli, Marco Faini, Faith Harden, and Gur Zak for their comments on an early draft, to the two anonymous readers for the University of Toronto Press, and to David Lummus for being an exemplary editor of this volume. All citations of the *Decameron* are taken from Branca's 1976 edition for *Tutte le opere*. English translations are from McWilliam. Throughout this chapter I have changed McWilliam's translation of "specchio/specchiarsi" from "glass/to look in the glass" to "mirror/to look in the mirror."

Emilia's description of Cesca's negative attributes, including the vices of vanity, pride, and envy. As characteristic of Day Six – a day dedicated to the use of a "leggiadro motto" [verbal pleasantry] to prevent a "perdita o pericolo o scorno" [loss, danger, ridicule] – the main action of the narrative focuses on the clever dialogue between the two protagonists Fresco and Cesca. When Cesca returns home early on a feast day, she explains to her bewildered uncle that she cannot bear to be around such unpleasant people as the Florentines she encounters on the street. Disgusted by her haughtiness, Fresco hopes to correct her behaviour by telling her that if she cannot stand the sight of unpleasant people she should never again look in the mirror ("non ti specchiar giammai"; VI.8.9). As we see in the epigraph, Cesca completely misses the lesson and responds that she will continue to look at herself in the mirror as all women do ("si voleva specchiar come l'altre"). The narrative thus hinges on the different gendered uses of the mirror. Whereas Fresco hopes the mirror will serve as a truth-bearing and corrective object, in the hands of his niece it becomes a symbol of female vanity. Indeed, his "piacevol motto" (VI.8.4) concerning the mirror fails to bring about any change in his niece. And so Emilia tells us at the end of the *novella* that Cesca remains vacuous like a reed, vain, and ignorant, her pride further amplified by the false self-estimation of her intelligence as on par with that of the biblical Solomon.[2]

The story of Cesca and her mirror has not attracted much sustained critical attention compared to the other stories told during Day Six.[3] One could argue that the dialogue is not as witty a repartee as what we find in Madonna Oretta (VI.1), or that we lack the belly-laughing humour of Chichibio and his crane (VI.4), the linguistic cleverness of Madonna Filippa (VI.7), or the more complex metanarratives of the Giotto (VI.5), Cavalcanti (VI.9), and Frate Cipolla (VI.9) *novelle*. In the story of Cesca and her mirror we instead find a *novella* that includes two examples of the required "leggiadro motto," neither of which

---

2 In his forthcoming *lectura* of *Decameron* IX.9 for this series, Albert R. Ascoli has made a convincing argument for reading Solomon as Emilia's alter-ego, noting: "Emilia not only appropriates the authoritative figure of Solomon in support of her exemplary illustration of male governance of women, but also aligns herself with key, heterogeneous, elements of the Solomonic tradition, including both a claim to special wisdom concerning the legal, customary and natural basis of gendered hierarchies and the deployment of allegorical interpretation to transform an erotic proverb into a 'moral' lesson [in *Dec.* IX.9]" ("Solomon and Emilia").

3 For analyses of this *novella*, see Cervigni; Cuomo 260; Giusti, "La novella di Cesca"; Morosini, "Bone eloquence" 8; and Van der Voort. See also note 7 below.

particularly elicits humour or completes the thematic task of the day. That is, Fresco's clever remark is lost on Cesca and fails to bring about change, and Cesca's retort comes at the expense of the female sex (i.e., all women are vain). Indeed, the *novella* closes with Cesca seemingly proving the truth-value of medieval misogynist tropes about women: they are naturally vain and proud and cannot "unlearn" these, or other, vices. On the surface, then, Emilia's *novella* would appear to defy the thematic rule of Day Six.[4] But, if we shift our primary focus from understanding how the Cesca *novella* works within the narrative constraints of Day Six to what it says about female vice and virtue instead, we can appreciate how Cesca and her mirror fit into Boccaccio's broader engagement with the question of female exemplarity throughout his career.[5] From the narrative poem *Filostrato* (c. 1335), to Boccaccio's experimentation with medieval misogyny in the *Corbaccio* (1350s; traditionally dated 1355),[6] and the highly influential Latin treatise on women *De mulieribus claris* (1374), the image of the mirror holds a significant place in Boccaccio's writings on female virtue and vice. *Decameron* VI.8 is thus one part of a longer theorization about female worth, a small contribution to what will eventually become known as the *querelle des femmes*.[7] The story of Cesca – like the other works mentioned above – plays on what we might call "gendered mirrorings": mirrors that reflect gender-specific traits codified in medieval literature.[8] These gendered mirrorings appear in two distinct manners:

---

4 For the ways in which the Cesca *novella* does not follow Pampinea's theme, see Bosetti; and Markulin.

5 Current scholarship is moving towards viewing Boccaccio's works as part of a continuum rather than maintaining the traditional divisions between vernacular-Latin, pre-/post-1350 meeting with Petrarch, etc. See especially Daniels, "Boccaccio's Narrators"; and Filosa, *Tre studi*.

6 Most scholars have traditionally dated the *Corbaccio* as 1355. See Sapegno, Introduzione, in Boccaccio, *Corbaccio* [1977]; Hauvette; Hollander, *Boccaccio's Last Fiction*; Della Torre; Torraca. Exceptions are Giorgio Padoan, who dates it 1366 ("Sulla datazione del *Corbaccio*"), and Marco Veglia, who dates it even later to c. 1367 (*Il corvo* 38).

7 Scholarship on the broader *querelle des femmes* is vast. I would highlight the following studies, which discuss Boccaccio's place in the longer historical debate and whether or not *De mulieribus claris*, especially, is "pro-woman" or not: Benson, chapter 1; Cox, *Women's Writing*, Introduction; Filosa, *Tre studi*; Kolsky, *Genealogy of Women* and *Ghost of Boccaccio*; and Shemek.

8 Narcissus is one of the most frequently evoked myths concerning vanity and reflections (mirroring). While he is not traditionally depicted with an actual mirror, it is worth noting that his male pride and beauty often associate him with women. For an analysis of the use of the Narcisuss myth to feminize the courtly lover in the highly influential *Roman de la Rose*, see Lochrie.

mirrors as objects, and the text as a mirror of exemplarity *in bono* and *in malo*. For Fresco, the mirror symbolizes truth and a means towards opening his niece's eyes to her despicable character so that she may overcome her female vices. His lesson fails, however, because Cesca conflates his mirror of truth with the mirror of vanity, using her reflection as proof positive of her superiority. While Cesca might not have learned the intended lesson, by situating *Decameron* VI.8 within other literary engagements with the "woman question" – both Boccaccio's and his medieval predecessors' – we will be able to better understand the *novella* and its place in the intellectual history of Boccaccio's evolving theorization about female exemplarity.

~

The word "specchio" appears at only two moments in the *Decameron*, both related to the narrator Emilia: first during her so-called "mirror of beauty" love song in the Conclusion of Day One, and then in the Cesca story of Day Six, where it is associated with female vanity. In the first case, as the *brigata* is winding down from their first day of storytelling, the queen of the day Pampinea calls upon Emilia to sing a song, which, we are told, she delivers "amorosamente" (I.Concl.17):

> Io son sì vaga della mia bellezza,
> che d'altro amor già mai
> non curerò né credo aver vaghezza.
> Io veggio in quella, ognora mi specchio,
> quel ben che fa contento lo 'ntelletto:
> né accidente nuovo o pensier vecchio
> mi può privar di sì caro diletto.
> Quale altro dunque piacevole oggetto
> potrei veder gia mai
> che mi mettesse in cuor nuova vaghezza? (I.Concl.18–19)
>
> [In mine own beauty I take such delight
> That to no other love could I
> My fond affections plight.
> Since in my mirror I always spy
> Beauty enough to satisfy the mind,
> Why seek out past delights, or new ones try
> When all content within my mirror I find?
> What other sight so pleasing to mine eyes
> Is there that I might see
> Which further I could prize?] (69)

The opening verses of the song oscillate between two forms of love: self-love and love of another person. Emilia's enamourment with her own image seems to prevent her from finding another object of affection ("piacevol oggetto"). The use of repetition creates a kind of mirroring that is then symbolized by Emilia's actual mirror. She repeats "vaga/vaghezza" [delight] to describe her response to her own beauty ("mia bellezza"), which is reflected in her admission that "ognora mi specchio" [I always look at myself in the mirror]. Self-love becomes cyclical: she looks in the mirror every hour, repeatedly falling in love with her own image. She thus continually places herself – her beauty – in competition with external objects of desire, with her own image always prevailing. Her love song is directed at herself and her image, which looks forward to Cesca's love of her own image.[9] While both Emilia and Cesca represent vanity, although in her song Emilia loves her own image, she does not ultimately disdain the sight of others as Cesca does in Day Six.

The parallel mirror imagery between Emilia's song and her Day Four *novella* has been the subject of much scholarship. For the purposes of our argument here, Timothy Kircher's analysis of Boccaccio's philosophy and its relation to contemporary mendicant traditions is most pertinent. He has argued that Emilia's use of mirrors "exposes an inadequacy in the exemplum-tradition, especially in its rhetorical power, a power more than verbal in 'mov[ing] people to good works'" (*Poet's Wisdom* 137).[10] That is, Emilia's references to the mirror elucidate the contemporary crisis in the mendicant exemplum tradition: the conflict between sermonizing and an increased awareness of clerical frailty. For Kircher, then, the "specchio" of Emilia's song and Day Six *novella* is most meaningfully understood in comparison to the religious-moral *speculum* of the Church. While compelling, Kircher's reading narrowly limits exemplarity to religious examples. I would argue that the "specchio" functions within another evolving tradition of moral exemplarity, yet one that is specifically gendered female and tied to the notion

9 Paola Ugolini has suggested to me that Emilia's song might be a parody of Lia in *Purgatorio* 27.103–5: "Per piacermi a lo specchio, qui m'addorno; / ma mia suora Rachel mai non si smaga / dal suo miraglio, e siede tutto giorno" [To be pleased at my reflection I adorn myself, / but my sister Rachel never leaves her mirror, / sitting before it all day long]. For the text and translation of Dante's *Purgatorio*, I have used Hollander.

10 See also Kircher's earlier article, "Modality of Moral Communication." Other studies that have emphasized the contemplative aspects of Cesca's mirror are Smarr 179–80 and 200; and Hollander, "Struggle for Control" 270–1 and 293–4. For the important link between mirrors and music, see Beck.

of female worth. In both instances of the mirror, female vice informs its symbolic function in the *Decameron*. In *Decameron* VI.8 we see this in the manner in which Cesca is defined against both her uncle and other women, specifically through gendered mirroring. Before beginning her story, Emilia provides the *brigata* with a brief synopsis of her tale: "lo sciocco error d'una giovane … con un piacevol motto corretto da un suo zio, se ella da tanto stata fosse che inteso l'avesse" [VI.8.4; the foolish error of a young woman, and how it was corrected by an amusing remark of her uncle's, though she was far too dense to appreciate its significance; 465]. From the onset we know that the *novella* will revolve around a behavioural lesson delivered by an uncle to his niece. As Emilia begins her story, we note two examples of mirroring, involving male and female models:

> Uno adunque, che si chiamò Fresco da Celatico, aveva una sua nepote chiamata per vezzi Cesca: la quale, ancora che bella persona avesse e viso, non però di quegli angelici che già molte volte vedemmo, sé da tanto e sì nobile reputava, che per costume aveva preso di biasimare e uomini e donne e ciascuna cosa che ella vedeva, senza avere alcun riguardo a se medesima, la quale era tanto più spiacevole, sazievole e stizzosa che alcuna altra, che a sua guisa niuna cosa si potea fare; e tanto, oltre a tutto questo, era altiera, che se stata fosse de' Reali di Francia sarebbe stata soperchio. (VI.8.5)

> [There was once a certain gentleman called Fresco da Celatico, and he had a niece whose pet-name was Cesca. Whilst she had a good figure and a pretty face (though it was far from being one of those angelic faces that we not infrequently come across), she had such a high opinion of herself and gave herself so many airs that she fell into the habit of criticizing everything and everyone she ever set eyes upon, never thinking for a moment of her own defects, even though she was the most disagreeable, petulant, and insipid young woman imaginable, and nothing could be done to please her. Moreover, her pride was so enormous that even in a scion of the French royal family it would have been excessive.] (465)

From the first introductory line, the narrator Emilia begins to play around with the notion of likeness and mirroring, comparing Cesca to male and female models. First, Cesca is defined in comparison to her uncle. The protagonists are called by gendered, diminutive versions of the same name: Fr(anc)esco and (Fran)Cesca. The pun implies likeness, which is reinforced by the second mention of their blood relation: Cesca is "una sua nepote," a repetition of the earlier detail from the synopsis that her error would be corrected by "un suo zio." Furthermore, the minor detail that she was "nicknamed" Cesca – "chiamata *per vezzi* Cesca" (emphasis added) – strengthens the rapport, since it ambiguously implies that she might have been named after her uncle.[11] We thus see how Cesca's initial introduction is framed by her uncle's identity. We are led to believe that she is the mirror-image of her uncle, even though we know from Emilia's initial description of Cesca that the uncle would eventually be the morally superior of the two. Despite the similitude between the names, and the repetitive references to their shared lineage, Emilia has already given away the ending to the story. That is, Fresco and Cesca are, in the end, quite dissimilar. Fresco is introduced as someone who will attempt to model exemplary behaviour to his female counterpart, Cesca, who will eventually fail to learn from him. We therefore see a failed mirroring between male and female behaviour.

The second example places the figure of Cesca in dialogue with idealized women of the Trecento lyric tradition. Emilia's initial description of Cesca's beauty defines it against that of angelic women: "bella persona avesse e viso, non però di quegli angelici che già molte volte vedemmo" [she had a good figure and a pretty face (though it was far from being one of those angelic faces that we not infrequently come across)]. This specific characterization of her beauty recalls the figure of the Trecento lyrical *donna angelicata*, beginning with the poetry of Guinizzelli, Dante, and the *stilnovisti*, and then continuing in a highly codified manner with Petrarch. In the *stilnovista* tradition, the figure of the angelic, female beloved is divorced from terrestrial associations in her refiguration as the poet's conduit to God. In Dante's *Vita nova*, for example, Beatrice is often referred to as an angel and raised above the stature of other mortal women. In the first chapter of the *libello*, when the nine-year-old Beatrice appears to Dante for the first time, he claims that at that moment Amore [Love] "mi comandava molte volte che io cercasse per vedere questa *angiola* giovanissima" [I.9; commanded me to seek out this very young *angel*; emphasis added].[12] As Louise G. Clubb has noted, this religious elevation of the woman is what Boccaccio parodies throughout the *Decameron*: "Of all the stilnovist concepts the most foreign to Boccaccio's thinking is that of the *donna angelicata*. He allows

11 A further level of ambiguity here is the alternative meaning of "per vezzi," which could also mean that she was named as such because of her bad habits. Indeed, in Emilia's second use of this term later in the *novella*, "vezzi" will refer explicitly to Cesca's behaviour.

12 All references to the *Vita nova* are taken from volume 1 of *Opere* [2011]. Translations are mine.

that a lady may be pure and her behavior circumspect, but he will not promote her to the rank of angel or praise her for more than human virtue" (190).[13] In Petrarch's poetry, as well, the figure of his beloved Laura is defined by an other-worldly, celestial beauty and mystique such that she too is compared to an angel. Petrarch directly links this portrait of the beloved to his poetics, as for example in *Rerum vulgarium fragmenta* 170, "Lasso me ch'i' non so in quale parte pieghi" [Alas, I do not know where to turn], where the *donna angelicata* becomes a figure of poetic inspiration.[14] In the final stanza, in particular, he explicitly describes Laura's beauty as "angelic":

> Tutte le cose di che 'l mondo è adorno
> uscir buone de man del mastro eterno,
> ma me che così a dentro non discerno
> abbaglia il bel che mi si mostra intorno
> et s' al vero splendor giamai ritorno
> l'occhio non po star fermo,
> così l'à fatto infermo
> pur la sua propria colpa, et non quel giorno
> ch' i' volsi in ver l'angelica beltade
> "Nel dolce tempo de la prima etade." (41–50)

> [All things with which the world is beauteous came forth good from the hand of the eternal Workman: but I, who do not discern so far within, am dazzled by the beauty that I see about me, and if I ever return to the true splendor, my eye cannot stay still, it is so weakened by its very own fault, and not by that day when I turned toward her angelic beauty: "In the sweet time of my first age."]

Petrarch distinguishes between the beauty of the terrestrial world created by the "ma[e]stro eterno" [God] and Laura's beauty, also created by God but more akin to the celestial beauty of the angels. Indeed, throughout the *Rerum vulgarium fragmenta* Laura's "angelica beltade" [angelic beauty] is unique, one of several traits that separate her from other

13 Millicent Marcus has also discussed Boccaccio's ironic use of *stilnovist* tropes in the Cimone *novella* (V.1). See Marcus, "Sweet New Style Reconsidered."

14 This also distinguishes Laura from Beatrice. While Dante's beloved comes to symbolize the divine, Laura remains in-between. All citations and English translations from Petrarch's *Rerum vulgarium fragmenta* are taken from Durling's 1976 edition and translation, *Petrarch's Lyric Poems*.

women. She exists on a plane between the human and the divine, and in this poem Petrarch explicitly highlights the literariness of Laura's beauty as poetic inspiration. That is, each stanza of the longer *canzone* ends with a citation from the poetry of earlier great poets (Arnaut Daniel, Guido Calvacanti, Dante, Cino da Pistoia), but Petrarch closes the *canzone* with the incipit of his own *Rerum vulgarium fragmenta* 23 ("Nel dolce tempo de la prima etade"), subsequently including himself in the lineage of renowned vernacular amatory poets. Thus, when Emilia describes Cesca as beautiful but not like "quegli angelici che già molte volte vedemmo" [[one of] those angelic faces that we not infrequently come across], she defines her against the literary portrait of a Trecento beloved, while also devaluing the uniqueness of this kind of angelic beauty: we have seen them, she says, "già molte volte" [not infrequently].

Emilia's claim that angelic faces are present throughout Florence is an important detail because it recalls Boccaccio's earlier critique of the idealized portrait of the *donna angelicata* in the *mezza-novella* of Filippo Balducci (IV.Intro.12–29). In this lengthy authorial intervention, Boccaccio implicitly challenges the model of desire and beauty that was based on the *donna angelicata* figure. After the death of his wife, Balducci retreats with his young son to a "piccola celletta" [small cell] on Monte Asinaio where they live out their lives in devotion and prayer. Years later, when the son finally accompanies his father to Florence on errands, he is amazed by what he sees, especially a group of women en route to a wedding. Having never before seen women, he asks his father what they are and is told that they are "papere" [goslings] and, most importantly, "male cose" [evil things]. The son replies to his father, "Elle son più belle che gli agnoli dipinti che voi m'avete più volte mostrati" [IV.Intro.28; They are more beautiful than the painted angels that you have taken me to see so often; 287]. Although Balducci tried to shield his son from worldly things, and tried to stymie his son's desire by calling women by a different name, he learns that "più aver di forza la natura che il suo ingegno" [29; his wits were no match for Nature; 287].

The *ingegno-Natura* [wit-Nature] dyad of the Balducci *mezza-novella* applies to the game of semiotics he plays on his son, as well as to the distinction between artistic representations of women and "real" women. This is indeed a major theme in the Day Four Introduction, as we see when Boccaccio teases out the metaliterary implications of the story by turning his attention to the relationship between the Muses and human women:

> le Muse son donne, benché le donne quel che le Muse vagliono non vagliano, pure esse hanno nel primo aspetto simiglianze di quelle, sì che, quando per altro non mi piacessero, per quello mi dovrebber piacere;

senza che le donne già mi fur cagione di comporre mille versi, dove le Muse mai non mi furono di farne alcun cagione. Aiutaronmi elle bene e mostraronmi comporre que' mille. (IV.Intro.36)

[The Muses are ladies, and although ladies do not rank as highly as Muses, nevertheless they resemble them at first sight, and hence it is natural, if only for this reason, that I should be fond of them. Moreover, ladies have caused me to compose a thousand lines of poetry in the course of my life, whereas the Muses never caused me to write any at all. It is true that they have helped me, and shown me *how* to write those thousand lines.] (289; translation amended)

The relationship between Balducci's painted angels and Florentine women finds its analogy in Boccaccio's distinction between the Muses and real women. If in Petrarch's poetry his beloved-muse Laura is modelled on angels, for example, Boccaccio finds inspiration in real women, arguing that the Muses are modelled on women and not vice versa. On the metaliterary level, the Day Four Introduction pits Boccaccio's *Decameron* and the representation of women therein against the idealized *donne angelicate* of the Trecento lyric tradition of his predecessors.[15] This metaliterary backdrop informs Emilia's description of Cesca's beauty and general character: she is "real" and not idealized.

This distinction between Cesca and women with angelic faces is the starting point for the less than idealized moral portrait of the female protagonist. Where we might expect to see the virtues of a Dantean Beatrice or Petrarchan Laura, we instead find a list of vices:

sé da tanto e sì nobile reputava, che per costume aveva preso di biasimare e uomini e donne e ciascuna cosa che ella vedeva, senza avere alcun riguardo a se medesima, la quale era tanto più spiacevole, sazievole e stizzosa che alcuna altra, che a sua guisa niuna cosa si potea fare; e tanto, oltre a tutto questo, era altiera, che se stata fosse de' Reali di Francia sarebbe stata soperchio. (VI.8.5)

[she had such a high opinion of herself and thought herself so noble that she fell into the habit of criticizing both men and women, and anything she ever set eyes upon, never thinking for a moment of her own defects, even though she was the most disagreeable, petulant, and insipid young woman imaginable, and nothing could be done to please her. Moreover,

15 Boccaccio had already made such a distinction in the *Proemio*, where he claimed to be writing about and for real women.

her pride was so enormous that even in a scion of the French royal family it would have been excessive.] (465)[16]

Within the overall negative description of Cesca, the vice of pride stands out through repetition, since this particular vice is at the foundation of her most despicable attributes: she criticizes everyone (*invidia*), is unaware of her defects (pride), and is more proud than a French royal (pride). In the first example, Cesca's habit of speaking ill of others ("biasimare") recalls Andreas Capellanus's maxim about female *invidia* in the final book of *De amore* (*Liber tertius: De reprobatione amoris*):

> Invida quoque mulier omnis generali regula invenitur, quia semper mulier in alterius feminae pulchritudine zelo consumitur et rerum felicitate privatur ... Nec enim facile posset femina reperiri, cuius unquam noverit parcere lingua vel detractionis verba tacere. Et in hoc mulier omnis suas per omnes credit attollere laudes et propriam accrescere famam, si aliarum insistat laudibus derogare, quae res manifeste cunctis demonstrat modicum in mulieribus dogma vigere. (342–3)
>
> [That every woman is envious [invida] is also found to be a general rule, because a woman is always consumed with jealousy [zelo] over another woman's beauty, and she loses all pleasure in what she has ... It is not easy to find a woman whose tongue can ever spare anybody or who can keep from words of detraction. Every woman thinks that by running down others she adds to her own praise and increases her own reputation – a fact which shows clearly to everybody that women have very little sense.] (202)[17]

According to Capellanus's passage, *invidia* and jealousy (*zelo*) are founded upon pride and vanity, with the inclination to lower another woman's reputation stemming from the desire to maintain one's sense of superiority. Female beauty is both the basis of comparison and the source of ill will among women. Capellanus's general rule about women's natural inclination towards these vices is exemplified in the figure of Cesca, who "sì nobile reputava" [had such a high opinion of herself].[18] Her high

16 Translation amended from "[she] gave herself so many airs" and "she fell into the habit of criticizing everything and everyone."

17 Latin citations of Capellanus are taken from *Andrea Capellani regii Francorum De amore libri tres*. English translations of Capellanus are from Parry, *Art of Courtly Love*.

18 Cesca's misplaced belief in her "nobility" also serves as another example of a Boccaccian parody of the stilnovist *donna angelicata*, since in that tradition love had an ennobling power (i.e., nobility is not inherited).

self-estimation goes hand in hand with her constant critiques of others. The point is strengthened by the second example of Cesca's inability to see her own defects while cutting down others: her pride blinds her to reality. Although pride is a gender-neutral vice, in the *novella*, as in Capellanus, it is described as a particularly destructive vice in women. We see this in the third example, where Cesca is compared to the "Reali di Francia": "e tanto, oltre a tutto questo, era altiera, che se stata fosse de' Reali di Francia sarebbe stata soperchio" [VI.8.5; Moreover, her pride was so enormous that even in a scion of the French royal family it would have been excessive; 502].[19] Emilia's presentation of Cesca echoes medieval misogynist texts which often rely on rhetorical devices like *amplificatio* to catalogue the vices and general defects of the female sex. Thus, the description of Cesca's vices increases incrementally in degree of negativity towards a hyperbolic statement. While female vanity is not directly evoked in this initial description of Cesca, Emilia provides the listener/reader with just enough information for him/her to recall the subtexts and fill in what is missing. She also further highlights the vices of female pride and vanity through the abrupt manner in which she closes her listing of Cesca's faults: "Ora, lasciando stare molti altri suoi modi spiacevoli e rincrescevoli" [VI.8.7; Now, leaving aside her many other tiresome and disagreeable mannerisms; 465]. By passing over in silence Cesca's other vices, Emilia reveals female pride and vanity to be the most despicable of them all, and the ones that are most integral to the *novella* and Cesca's character.

Although in Emilia's initial description of Cesca, cited above, she says that "per costume aveva preso di biasimare e uomini e donne" [she fell into the habit of criticizing both men and women], when the *novella* transitions from description to the (brief) dialogue between Fresco and Cesca, we see in the character's own words that she is particularly critical of other women. When her uncle asks why she has returned home early, Cesca replies:

> Al quale ella tutta cascante di vezzi rispose: "Egli è il vero che io me ne sono venuta tosto, per ciò che io non credo che mai in questa terra fossero

19 It is important to note that Boccaccio uses almost exactly the same wording of this analogy in the *Corbaccio*. There, the Spirito describes his ex-wife's false *gentilezza* as "ed è tanta la sua vanagloria e la pompa che ella fa di questa sua gentilezza, che in verità a quelli di Baviera o a' Reali di Francia o a qualunque altri, se altri più se ne sanno antichi e le cui opere sieno state gloriose, sarebbe soperchio" [61; The vainglory and ostentation that she takes in this nobility of hers is so great that, in truth, it would be excessive for those of Bavaria, the royal house of France, or for any others, if any others are known to be more ancient or whose deeds to be more glorious; 50]. For the text of the *Corbaccio* I have used Ricci's 1977 edition and for the translation I have used Casell.

> e uomini e femine tanto spiacevoli e rincrescevoli quanto sono oggi, e non passa per via uno che non mi spiaccia come la mala ventura; e io non credo che sia al mondo femina a cui più sia noioso il vedere gli spiacevoli che è a me, e per non vedergli così tosto me ne sono venuta." (VI.8.8)

> ["The truth is," Cesca replied, affecting a thoroughly world-weary air, "that I have come home early because I doubt whether I have ever seen such a tiresome and disagreeable set of people as the ones who walk our streets today. Every man and woman that I meet is utterly repellent to me, and I don't believe there is a woman in the world who is so upset by the sight of horrid people as I am. So I came home early to spare myself the torment of looking at them."] (465)

While in this passage Cesca believes herself to be superior to Florentine men and women ("uomini e femine"), she presents the intolerance of seeing these "spiacevoli" as a specifically female problem when she clarifies that she doesn't believe that "sia al mondo *femina* a cui più sia noioso il vedere gli spiacevoli" [there is a *woman* in the world who is so upset by the sight of horrid people; emphasis added]. The juxtaposition of "uomini e femine" as objects of disdain, and "femina" as the sex most sensitive to the "spiacevoli," generalizes the *novella* to one focused on female-gendered behaviour. Cesca's point would have been strengthened had she said that there was not *anyone* – gender neutral – in the world more disgusted by the sight of horrid people. Instead, she presents the kind of disgust she feels as an emotion uniquely felt by women.

Cesca's gesture at a vice common to the female sex serves as a turning point in the *novella*, where Cesca's despicable behaviour and attitude are normalized and presented as typically "female." As we saw in the epigraph to this chapter, Fresco attempts to teach his niece a lesson using witty language:

> Alla qual Fresco, a cui li modi fecciosi della nepote dispiacevan fieramente, disse: "Figliuola, se così ti dispiaccion gli spiacevoli, come tu di', se tu vuoi viver lieta non ti specchiar giammai." Ma ella, più che una canna vana e a cui di senno pareva pareggiar Salamone, non altramenti che un montone avrebbe fatto intese il vero motto di Fresco, anzi disse che ella si voleva specchiar come l'altre. E così nella sua grossezza si rimase e ancor vi si sta. (VI.8.9–10)

> [Whereupon Fresco, who found the fastidious airs of his niece highly distasteful, said to her: "If you can't bear the sight of horrid people, my girl, I advise you, for your own peace of mind, to never look at yourself in the mirror." But the girl, whose head was emptier than a hollow reed even though

> she imagined herself to be as wise as Solomon, might have been a carcase of mutton for all she understood of Fresco's real meaning, and she told him that she intended to look in the mirror just like any other woman. So she remained as witless as before, and she is still the same to this day.] (465–6)

The switch from Fresco's first-person delivery of the lesson to Emilia's third-person use of indirect discourse to recount Cesca's reply presents the anecdote about female vanity as an embedded lesson within the *novella* about the nature of the female sex. The emphasis shifts from Cesca's perspective about women's natural inclination towards vanity to the narrator Emilia delivering a final lesson or moral to the story. That Cesca would continue to look into the mirror "come l'altre" – *altre* gendered female – is reported as a fact, much in the manner of the final line of the narrative, which reports that Cesca has remained in her "grossezza" [ignorance] even today. This oscillation between direct and reported speech, further complicated by Emilia's excursus on Cesca's reply, provides a nuanced version of one aspect of what F. Regina Psaki has called "voicing gender" in the *Decameron*. Psaki has noted, "Part of the liveliness of misogynous diatribes results from the ventriloquism by which these texts render the logorrhea and manipulativeness of women's speech. Long 'quotations' of women's speech are part of the toolbox of Juvenal and Ovid, as well as of Walter Map and Jean de Meun" ("Voicing Gender" 112). In VI.8 we see something similar at play, though the female narrator Emilia authorizes the trope of female vanity in a way that reads as more "authentic" than it would when ventriloquized by a male voice.

In this final scene we see how the mirror functions differently for the male and female protagonists, leading to two separate witty lessons within the *novella*. For Fresco, the mirror represents truth. His attempt to correct the vices of pride and vanity in his niece rests in her ability to see her true self reflected in the mirror.[20] But his lesson fails on two levels. First, Cesca is unable to pick up on the wittiness of his statement because she lacks intellect – she is "più che una canna vana" [emptier

20 Ascoli has read the Cesca *novella* as a crucial bridge between the Giotto (VI.5) and Cavalcanti (VI.9) *novelle*, arguing that "Il suo [di Cesca] desiderio di 'specchiarsi come l'altre' emerge come una parodica letteralizzazione della metafora primaria della filosofia – lo specchio interiore che dà nome all'attività favorita da Guido [Cavalcanti], quella della 'speculazione'. Inoltre, come la dimensione intelletuale dell'arte di Giotto si riconnette allor speculare filosofico di Guido, così lo specchio letterale invocato da Fresco e poi da Cesca richiama il potere della sua arte di restituire tale e quale una perfetta immagine della realtà terrena" ("Auerbach fra gli epicurei" 151).

than a hollow reed] – although she believes she is as wise as Solomon. Second, for Cesca the mirror is merely a tool, a means towards an end (beauty). Hers is a mirror of vanity that reflects what she values most and simultaneously symbolizes (for the reader, her uncle, and Emilia the narrator) her greatest vice. Her witty yet ignorant retort comes at the expense of the female sex, particularly since it is presented as a fact by the female narrator Emilia. For Cesca, all women are vain and highly value beauty. We thus see how Fresco's lesson about female exemplarity, his attempt to teach his niece how not to be vain and proud, is pitted against the exemplarity *in malo* of Cesca and her fixation on female vice. The *novella* itself becomes a story about the failure of exemplarity.[21] Cesca becomes a prototype for the kind of unexemplary female figure that we already see in Boccaccio's earlier work the *Filostrato*, the *Corbaccio*, and then, especially, the later *De mulieribus claris*, where exemplarity is taught through both positive (*in bono*) and negative (*in malo*) models. Thus while *Decameron* VI.8 might be short, it is an important middle ground in Boccaccio's longer intellectual engagement with the question of female exemplarity. When we read it as such, we are better able to appreciate the significance of Cesca and her mirror, as shall be examined in the next section.

~

The *Filostrato* offers us a glimpse into one of Boccaccio's earliest engagements with notions of female exemplarity that will eventually come to full fruition in *De mulieribus claris*. Most striking is the symbol of the mirror, used as a gendered contrast that, I would argue, serves as an early literary prototype for the mirror scene in *Decameron* VI.8. Considered one of Boccaccio's "youthful" works, and written around 1335, the *Filostrato* is set against the backdrop of the Trojan War and follows the tragic story of Troiolo, a young Trojan warrior who falls in love with Criseida, is eventually betrayed by her, and then, finally, is killed in battle by Achilles.[22] In Canto VIII, the last canto dedicated to the main narrative action, Troiolo sees proof of Criseida's betrayal (about which he had previously dreamt): his brother Deifobo brings back from war the Greek Diomede's clothing upon which is set the brooch that Troiolo had earlier gifted to Criseida. Vowing to kill Diomede, he rushes into

21 See especially Hampton, for an analysis of the problematic relationship between exemplary figures, history, and early modern moral and political action.

22 Both Chaucer and Shakespeare will later imitate this story.

battle, only to be slain by Achilles (VIII.28). After describing Troiolo's death, Boccaccio turns to his (male) readers in an aside that occupies the final five octaves of this canto (VIII.29–33). Here, Boccaccio advises the "giovinetti" [young men] to learn from the mistakes of Troiolo narrated in the previous seven cantos of the work. In the first three octaves of the aside, Boccaccio sets up a gendered mirroring between his direct address to men and a description of women that replicates commonly evoked misogynist tropes. In both instances, the image of the mirror anchors his message. He begins in octave 29 by instructing young men to mirror themselves in Troiolo in order to learn from his mistakes:

> O giovinetti, ne' quai con l'etate
> surgendo vien l'amoroso disio,
> per Dio vi priego che voi raffreniate
> i pronti passi all'appetito rio,
> e *nell'amor di Troiol vi specchiate,*
> il qual dimostra suso il verso mio;
> per che, se ben col cuor gli leggerete
> non di leggieri a tutte crederete. (VIII.29, emphasis added)

> [O youths, in whom amorous desire springs up as your age increases, I pray you in the name of God check your eager steps towards the illicit desire and see yourselves mirrored in the love of Troilus, which my verse has set forth. For, if you read with right feeling, you will not easily put your trust in all women.] (124)[23]

The use of the verbs "surgere" ("surgendo") and "raffrenare" ("raffreniate") in the first two verses of Boccaccio's address to a male audience creates a distinction between uncontrollable emotion and calculated reason. "Surgere" emphasizes the overwhelming rise of amorous desire ("amoroso desio"), while the imperative "raffreniate / i pronti passi all'appetito rio" [check your eager steps towards the illicit desire] stresses rationality as Boccaccio instructs his readers not to give in to this swelling passion, but to rein it in and control it. The juxtaposition of these two oppositional verbs highlights the tension underlying Boccaccio's use of "appetito rio" – literally an illicit hunger or appetite – to

23 Original Italian citations are taken from Branca's 1964 edition for *Tutte le opere*. English translations are from Gordon's 1964 version (*Story of Troilus*). Translation amended from "evil passion" and "see yourselves imaged."

describe sensual and sexual longing.[24] Like the "sorgere-raffrenare" coupling, "appetito rio" recognizes the natural, uncontrollable status of desire, but also gestures at one's ability to control it. In this manner, Boccaccio attributes a pedagogical value to the tragic love story, which he makes explicit in his second use of the imperative mood: "nell'amor di Troiol vi specchiate" [see yourselves mirrored in the love of Troilus]. By seeing themselves in the figure of Troiolo, Boccaccio hopes his male readers will avoid the pitfalls of love and not give in to the kind of desire that led to his protagonist's downfall. The mirror thus becomes a symbol of reason for men, Troiolo an exemplum *in malo* meant to teach the "giovinetti" how not to act. What is reflected in the mirror-text is negative potentiality that could be avoided if the male reader were to heed Boccaccio's warning not to trust "tutte" (all women).

While Boccaccio's closing "tutte" gestures at two distinct groups of women – some trustworthy, others not – in the next two octaves (VIII.30–1) we see that all women are universalized into the figure of the "giovan donna" [young woman], who stands in for everywoman and, as we shall see, serves as a prototype for Cesca in the *Decameron*:

Giovan donna, e mobile e vogliosa
è negli amanti molti, e *sua bellezza*
estima più ch'allo specchio, e pomposa
ha vanagloria di sua giovinezza,
la qual quanto piacevole e vezzosa
è più, cotanto più seco l'apprezza;
virtù non sente né conoscimento,
volubil sempre come foglia al vento.
E molte ancor *perché d'alto lignaggio*
discese sono, e sanno annoverare
gli avoli lor, si credon che vantaggio
deggiano aver dell'altre nell'amare,
e pensan che costume sia oltraggio,
torcere il naso, e dispettose andare;
queste schifate ed abbiatele a vili,
ché *bestie son, non son donne gentili.* (VIII.20–31, emphasis added)

[A young woman is inconstant and desirous of many lovers, and *she rates her beauty more highly than does the mirror,* and has exulting pride in her

24 This tension between the (sexual) "appetito" and rationality is a theme picked up on by Boccaccio's later imitators, particularly Bandello. See especially Ugolini.

youth; and the more she thinks of it the more pleasing and charming she finds it. Ever unsteady as a leaf in the wind, she cares not for virtue or reason. // And many women, too, *because they come out of noble family and can tell over their ancestors, think that they should be preferred before others in love*; and *they consider courtesy a thing to be scorned and turn up their noses and carry themselves haughtily*. Avoid these and deem them vile, for *they are beasts, not noble ladies*.] (124, emphasis added)

In this description of the vices of women, the mirror is evoked twice, both implicitly and explicitly. The incipit of Octave 30 – "Giovan donna" – falsely mirrors the hortatory "O giovinetti" that opened the aside to the young male readers in Octave 29. At first glance, it might appear that Boccaccio is invoking a male and female audience,[25] but the lack of hortatory address in Octave 30 signals the transition between addressing his male audience and then focusing their attention on the vices of women, making the "giovan donna" the object of investigation. The list of female vices is again reminiscent of the tropes popularized by Capellanus in *De amore*, including those about female vanity, pride, promiscuity, and inconstancy. While Boccaccio does not stray from the highly codified misogynist tradition he inherited, what is remarkable in these two octaves is how he sets the stage for the figure of Cesca who will appear in the *Decameron* some twenty years later. That is, the four sets of details highlighted in the above passage will later become defining characteristics of Cesca in *Decameron* VI.8. If we examine the descriptions side by side, we notice striking similarities. First, the mirror in the hands of the "giovan donna" does not function as a pedagogical tool. Whereas the "giovinetti" were instructed to see themselves mirrored in Troiolo in order to learn from his mistakes, here the "giovan donna" is unable to see the truth about her beauty in her mirror. Instead, she believes herself to be more beautiful than what is actually reflected in the mirror ("sua bellezza / estima più ch'allo specchio"). This is precisely the same reason for which Fresco's lesson falls short in *Decameron* VI.8: he hopes that Cesca will see her defects in the mirror, but she only sees beauty. And like the "giovan donna" of the *Filostrato* she sees a

25 The question of gendered audiences is a complicated issue in Boccaccio's oeuvre. Despite the pseudo-female addressee (Filomena) of the *Filostrato* and historical addressee (Andrea Acciaiuoli) of *De mulieribus claris*, there is little historical evidence to support a female readership of Boccaccio's works until the Quattrocento. See especially Daniels, "Boccaccio's Narrators" 36–51. For a detailed study of the circulation of the text in Latin and various vernaculars, see Daniels, *Boccaccio and the Book*, chapter 4.

self-inflated reflection of her beauty. So not only does the mirror not teach her better behaviour, it actually deceives her.

Second, in Octave 31 of the *Filostrato* Boccaccio hints at the problem of social class and the privileges assumed by women in this respect. Boccaccio notes that some women "perché d'alto lignaggio / discese sono, e sanno annoverare / gli avoli lor, si credon che vantaggio / deggiano aver dell'altre nell'amare" [because they come out of noble family and can tell over their ancestors, think that they should be preferred before others in love]. Pride in noble lineage leads this category of women to estimate themselves higher than others in matters of love (i.e., in choice of mate). While there is no indication in *Decameron* VI.8 that Cesca derives from nobility, Boccaccio recalls her *Filostrato*-prototype when he claims that Cesca "tanto ... era altiera, che se stata fosse de' Reali di Francia sarebbe stata soperchio" [VI.8.5; her pride was so enormous that even in a scion of the French royal family it would have been excessive; 465]. The Cesca passage gestures at both social class and pride and it further highlights her inflated sense of self. In this manner, Cesca surpasses her *Filostrato* model in her hypothetical ability to outshine French royals in this particular vice.

Third, in the *Filostrato* these same women "pensan che costume sia oltraggio, / torcere il naso, e dispettose andare" [they consider courtesy a thing to be scorned and turn up their noses and carry themselves haughtily]. The image of a woman going about town with her nose turned up is precisely how Cesca is described in the *Decameron*: "E quando ella andava per via sì forte le veniva del cencio, che *altro che torcere il muso non faceva*, quasi puzzo le venisse di chiunque vedesse o scontrasse" [VI.8.6; And whenever she walked along the street, *she was continually wrinkling up her snout in disgust*, as though a nasty smell was assailing her nostrils every time she saw or met anyone; 465, emphasis added].[26] In both descriptions, female vanity and pride are symbolized by the haughty image of the woman with upturned nose. In Cesca's case, Boccaccio specifically refers to her nose as a "muso" – an animal's snout. This change combines both the haughty air of the women in the *Filostrato* passage and the final line of Octave 31, where the "giovinetti" [young men] are instructed to avoid women because "bestie son, non son donne gentili" [they are beasts, not noble ladies]. In both the *Filostrato* and *Decameron* VI.8 women are thus dehumanized in

26 I have changed "muso" from "nose" to "snout" to better reflect the original Italian and the animal imagery discussed below.

their association with animals, their pride and vanity presented as base qualities. In the case of Cesca, the description of her nose as a "snout" ("muso"), combined with her bestial behaviour, is further underscored by Emilia's initial description of her beauty, examined earlier: "ancora che bella persona avesse e viso, non però di quegli angelici che già molte volte vedemmo [she had a good figure and a pretty face (though it was far from being one of those angelic faces that we not infrequently come across)]. As previously noted, Emilia's distinction between "bella" [beautiful] and "angelica" [angelic] is an important one, as it characterizes Cesca's beauty in reference to the archetypical *donna angelicata* of the Trecento lyric. Thus, not only is Cesca *not* like Dante's Beatrice or Petrarch's Laura – beautiful in physical aspect and morality – she is a beast.[27] Furthermore, the animal imagery ties Cesca's disparagement of others to Boccaccio's use of "mordere" in the Introduction to Day Four, where he defends himself and his work against his detractors. There, before embarking upon the *mezza-novella* of Filippo Balducci, Boccaccio claims: "tutto da' morsi della 'nvidia … lacerato" [IV.Intro.4; I am all ripped to shreds by envy's bites; my translation], and closes his aside with the subjunctive "per che tacciansi i morditori …" [IV.Intro.4; let the biters be silent; my translation], creating an analogy between his critics and biting dogs.[28] In the cases of both Boccaccio's detractors and Cesca as a disparager of others (but especially women), *invidia* forms the basis of the biting critiques, as it were.

As we have now seen in both the *Filostrato* and *Decameron* VI.8, the mirror functions differently in the hands of male and female characters: for men it signals reason and truth, while for women, female vanity and a misguided perception of beauty. The mirror as symbol of female vanity also recurs in the *Corbaccio* (1355) – Boccaccio's last work in the vernacular, and an explicitly misogynist work composed around the

27 Capellanus also compares women to dogs, though specifically in reference to their speech: "Est et omnis femina virlingosa, quia nulla est, quae suam noverit a maledictis compescere linguam, et quae pro unius ovi amissione die tota velut canis latrando non clamaret et totam pro re modica viciniam non turbaret" [352; Every woman is also loud-mouthed, since not one of them can keep her tongue from abuses, and if she loses a single egg she will keep up a clamor all day like a barking dog, and she will disturb the whole neighborhood over a trifle; 207].

28 In her reading of Day Six, Franziska Meier has argued, "Despite several reminiscences of courteousness, Elissa, from the beginning, makes it clear that the 'motto' serves as a weapon and that its tit for tat nature is very similar to the biting of animals, especially dogs" ("Day Six" 292). For an engaged analysis of dog imagery in the representation of contamination and contagion through the non-human, see Stoppino.

time of the *Decameron*.[29] The *Corbaccio* is a first-person narrative consolation to men who have been abandoned by their lovers, written in the voice of a man who was mistreated by a widow. It recounts a dream vision in which the widow's first husband (lo Spirito) exposes the evils of both the widow and women in general, counselling the narrator to swear off women altogether. Within the Spirito's excursus on the nature of women, he explores the issue of the perception of female beauty and female vanity in more explicit terms than we find in either the *Filostrato* or the Cesca *novella*. He tells the lover:

> se tu teco medesimo riguardare avessi voluto quanta sia la vanità delle femine, di quello ti saresti ricordato che tu molte volte hai già detto, cioè che gloriandosi elle sommamente d'essere tenute belle, e per essere facciano ogni cosa, e *tanto più loro essere paia quanto più si veggiono riguardare, più fede al numero de' vagheggiatori dando che al loro medesimo lo specchio.* (78–9, emphasis added)

> [had you, yourself, wished to ponder how great is the vanity of women, you would have understood that your gaze was not disagreeable but very dear to her, and you would have remembered what you have said many times in the past: that is, *since they pride themselves on being thought beautiful and do everything to be so, the more they see themselves looked at the more beautiful they believe they are, trusting more in the number of oglers than in their very mirrors.*] (64, emphasis added)

In this passage, there is a twofold problem of perception. First, women use the glances of others as a kind of mirror that reflects female vanity

29 Prudence Allen has argued that the *Corbaccio* is not misogynistic but rather a "meta-satire that satirizes satires about women" (214). The question of whether or not the *Corbaccio* is, indeed, misogynist has recently been addressed by a few literary scholars. F. Regina Psaki has said that it is "intended to be irresistibly funny, but also that it is a joke not on women, but rather on misogyny, and on the nexus of pseudo-intellectualism and masculine privilege that orients misogynous discourse" ("Boccaccio's *Corbaccio*" 105). See also Barricelli; Giusti, "*Il Corbaccio*"; Hollander, *Boccaccio's Last Fiction*; and Veglia, *Il corvo*. For an analysis of the intersections between Boccaccio's use of Juvenal's *Sixth Satire* in the *Corbaccio* and *Decameron*, see Filosa, "Modalità di contatto." For the French influence on the *Corbaccio*, see Peruzzi. For a more general reading of the intersections of French and Italian misogynist literature, see especially Psaki, "Traffic in Talk." Jason Houston has made a convincing argument for reading the *Corbaccio* against Ovid's *Ibis* in order to understand more fully Boccaccio's use of invective, particularly during a "period of bitter political disaffection" with Niccolò Acciaiuoli in 1362–3 (103).

and thus increases female pride. They perceive themselves as more beautiful depending on the "numero de' vagheggiatori" [number of oglers] that look at them. Second, women put more credence in this "mirror" than in what they see reflected in the actual "specchio." Any defect or blemish they might see is effaced by their interpretation of the gaze of others. This is similar to what we see in the punchline of *Decameron* VI.8, when Cesca is unable to see her true despicable nature in the mirror and understands the mirror to be merely a grooming tool that enables her to compete with other women; thus, her retort that she "si voleva specchiar come le altre" [VI.8.10; intended to look [at herself] in the mirror just like any other woman]. In all three cases – the *Filostrato*, *Decameron* VI.8, and the *Corbaccio* – the mirror imagery signals a problem of perspective: what an external observer sees as compared to what women see in the mirror. And in all cases, the mirror fails to teach women any sort of truth that would lead them towards self-realization or change.

~

Although the *Filostrato*, *Decameron*, and *Corbaccio* are not explicitly concerned with the issue of female exemplarity, they are all linked by gendered mirrorings and an excursus on female vanity and pride. By the time we reach *De mulieribus claris* (1374), where the express aim is to create a catalogue of historical women to serve as both positive and negative models for contemporary women, we see a shift in Boccaccio's treatment of women and mirrors.[30] In his Latin compendium of 106 biographies, "speculum" [mirror] appears only once: in the biography dedicated to the exemplary female artist Marcia, Daughter of Varro (*De Martia Varronis* [LXVI], 274–7).[31] Unlike the previous examples that we have examined, in the hands of Marcia the mirror takes on a positive symbolic function tied to the female intellect and artistry rather than vanity. From the onset of the biography, Boccaccio emphasizes the positive moral attributes of Marcia, particularly chastity and constancy, virtues he claims Marcia prioritized through her own free will. Praise of her high morality frames her accomplishments in art when

---

30 For general, critical studies of *De mulieribus claris*, in addition to those mentioned in note 7 above, see Franklin; Jordan, "Boccaccio's In-Famous Women" and *Renaissance Feminism*; Filosa, "Petrarca, Boccaccio e le *mulieres clarae*" and "Boccaccio tra storia"; Sciacovelli.

31 All references to *De mulieribus claris* are taken from *Famous Women*, Brown's 2001 facing-page Latin and English edition/translation for the I Tatti Renaissance Library.

Boccaccio writes, "Verum etsi hac tamen commendabili constantia plurimum hec laudanda sit Martia, non minus tamen ingenii viribus et artificio manuum commendanda est" [par. 3–4; Although Marcia deserves great commendation for her laudable constancy, she is to be praised no less for her intellectual ability and her manual dexterity; 275]. The detail concerning Marcia's "ingenium" [intellectual ability] is particularly important because it emphasizes her intellect as a driving force behind her art. Thus, when Boccaccio explicitly addresses her art and introduces the mirror, Marcia has already been introduced as a woman whose morality and intellect are exemplary:

> Fuerunt insuper diu eius artis insignia, sed, inter alia, eius effigies, quam adeo integer, lineaturis coloribusque servatis et oris habitu, in tabula, *speculo consulente*, protraxit, ut nemini coetaneo quenam foret, ea visa, verteretur in dubium. (par. 6, emphasis added)
>
> [Specimens of Marcia's art survived for a long time. Among them was a self-portrait which she painted on a panel *with the aid of a mirror*. She rendered the color, features, and expression of the face so faithfully that none of her contemporaries who saw it had trouble identifying the subject of the painting.] (275–7, emphasis added)

When Marcia gazes into the mirror she sees her true self, signalling that her mirror is a mirror of truth. It also symbolizes introspection, since she is able to then translate what she sees into a visual medium that truthfully represents her being. Boccaccio emphasizes this with the detail that the likeness was such that her contemporaries – i.e., those who had seen her – could easily identify her in the painting. Unlike the cases of the women in the *Filostrato* and *Corbaccio* or even Cesca, Marcia does not suffer from the problem of perception that led her literary predecessors towards female vanity and pride. Indeed, Boccaccio reminds the reader of her moral superiority when he continues, "et inter ceteras, ut ad singulares eius mores deveniamus, ei fuisse mos precipue asserunt, seu pinniculo pingeret seu sculperet celte, mulierum ymagines sepissime facere, cum raro vel nunquam, homines designaret" [par. 7; As regards her unique moral sensitivity, we are told among other things that, whether she was painting or sculpting, it was her practice to reproduce especially images of women, and those of men rarely if ever; 277]. As Stephen Kolsky has argued, "Marcia's rejection of male artistic values and of men themselves in her art is suggestive of a conscious difference explored in her representations of women. They are depicted as subjects rather than the naked objects of desire" (*Genealogy of Women* 153–4).

Boccaccio's source text for his biography is the few lines devoted to Iaia of Cyzicus (Marcia) in the section of Pliny's *Historia naturalis* (Book XXXV) that is dedicated to women artists. Yet, what we note in comparing Boccaccio's version to Pliny's is that Boccaccio has added the details concerning her chastity, constancy, and intellect. In Pliny, the biography is brief:

> Iaia Cyzicena, perpetua virgo, M. Varronis iuventa Romae et pencillo pinxit et cestro in ebore imagines mulierum maxime et Neapoli anum in grandi tabulia, suam quoque imaginem ad speculum. Nec ullius velocior in picture manus fuit, artis vero tantum, ut multum manipretiis antecederet celeberrimos eadem aetate imaginum pictores Sopolim et Dionysium, quorum tabulae pinacothecas inplent. (XXXV.40.147–8)

> [When Marcus Varro was a young man, Iaia of Cyzicus, perpetual virgin, painted pictures with the brush at Rome (and also drew with the *cestrum* or graver on ivory), chiefly portraits of women, as well as a large picture on wood of an Old Woman at Naples, and also a portrait of herself, done with a looking-glass. No one else had a quicker hand in painting, while her artistic skill was such that in the prices she obtained she far outdid the most celebrated portrait painters of the same period, Sopolis and Dionysius, whose pictures fill galleries.] (368–9)[32]

Boccaccio repeats several key details from Pliny's description – Marcia was a portrait artist, used a mirror for her self-portrait, and surpassed Sopolis and Dionysius in skill – but he takes the detail that she was a "perpetua virgo" [perpetual virgin] and amplifies the moral connotations associated with this detail. He refers to her "commendabili costantia" [laudable constancy], "mentis integritate" [purity of mind], and "singulares ... mores" [unique morals], as well as to her overall modesty and purity. In doing so, he imbues the mirror with moral and introspective qualities lacking in the original Plinian passage. This transforms Marcia from one example within a list of accomplished female artists to a female moral exemplum.[33]

---

32 For the text and translation of Pliny's *Historia naturalis* I have used Rackham's Loeb edition. I have translated "perpetua virgo" as "perpetual virgin" instead of Rackham's "who never married."

33 Gur Zak has pointed out to me that Boccaccio's association of mirroring and painting here looks forward to Leon Battista Alberti's later claim in *De Pictura* (1540) that Narcissus was the inventor of painting.

Marcia also stands out as the only woman – either positive, negative, or of ambiguous moral status – to be explicitly described with a mirror in the entire *De mulieribus claris*. Although Boccaccio includes several lessons about the vice of female vanity in his compendium, the mirror of vanity does not appear in any of those biographies. Instead, the only mirror present is a positive symbol of introspection, while female pride and vanity are represented through other symbols depending on the individual biography.[34] It is worth noting that in later manuscript miniatures of *De mulieribus claris* Marcia is regularly depicted with a mirror in hand.[35] When read in this light, Marcia and her mirror serve as a corrective to the Cesca story, not to mention Emilia (in her love song) and the women of the *Filostrato* and *Corbaccio*. In *Decameron* VI.8, Cesca gazes at herself in the mirror and is unable to see past vanity in order to better herself. Marcia, however, uses the mirror as a tool for introspection and art. From her moral beauty emerges art. She becomes an exemplary figure in a way that Fresco had hoped would happen to his young, vain niece. But as we have seen, his lesson fails and Cesca remains as vacuous and vain at the end of the *novella* as she was in the beginning. Whereas Marcia's moral beauty is independent of the male gaze, Cesca's moral turpitude is dependent on it, as well as the female gaze.

~

I opened this essay with a question: Can you teach a woman to stop being vain? It is the question that guides *Decameron* VI.8 and that gives insight into Boccaccio's more general approach to female vice and exemplarity over his career, and especially in *De mulieribus claris*. Indeed, the Cesca *novella* is structured similarly to the biographies that make up *De mulieribus claris*: we are presented with her genealogy, a

---

34 While not an exhaustive list, I would highlight only a few examples of biographies and their respective symbols of female pride and vanity: Semiramis (II) and her hair comb/braids (and implicitly, the mirror); Arachne (XVIII) and her loom; Cleopatra (LXXXVIII) and her wanton eyes.

35 Although an analysis of manuscript illuminations of Marcia's biography is beyond the scope of this chapter, I would highlight two French manuscripts held in the Bibliothèque nationale de France where she is depicted with a mirror: *Livre que fist Jehan BOCACE de Certalde des cleres et nobles femmes, lequel il envoia à Audice de Accioroles de Florence, contesse de Haulteville*, ca. 1403, BnF Ms.Fr.12420, fol. 101v; and *De Claris mulieribus, traduction anonyme en français Livre des femmes nobles et renommees*, BnF Ms.Fr. 598, fol. 100v. For a study of the miniatures in several manuscripts of *De mulieribus claris*, see especially Gathercole; and Frugoni.

description of her reputation, a defining action, and a final moral lesson delivered by an authoritative voice. Cesca, like many women in the Latin compendium, falls into the category of an example *in malo* whose behaviour should not be imitated by others. While her story does not necessarily follow the theme of *Decameron* Day Six, it does follow and elucidate the development of Boccaccio's broader intellectual history of writing about female exemplarity. When we read this *novella* as a middling point between the *Filostrato, Corbaccio,* and *De mulierbus claris* we are able to understand and appreciate it, since it highlights the potential failure of language to correct the vices of women. In her landmark study *The Concept of Woman*, Prudence Allen included Boccaccio as a foundational writer who contributed to a philosophical understanding of women. In her study she examined only texts that "used a philosophical method of discourse of logical reading" (4). While Allen considers *De mulieribus claris* within this category, she presents it in isolation from Boccaccio's other works, which do not – at least explicitly – follow the strict definition of the method she is examining. As I hope to have shown here, it is important to see how Boccaccio's theory of female exemplarity evolved over his career, and how he explored the question of female worth through multiple literary genres.

Nearing the end of his career, Boccaccio makes explicit in the dedication of *De mulieribus claris* to Andrea Acciaiuoli that his intent is not only to document "famous" women in history but also to urge her (and other women) to emulate "facinorum preteritarum mulierum" [8; the deeds of past women], and not the deeds of men. Indeed, this is reminiscent of Fresco's mirror of truth, which is a kind of male, humanist/misogynist mirror, where non-conforming women are seen as ugly, morally or otherwise. The text is thus presented as a kind of mirror of good and bad female behaviour, much like the stated intent of the *Filostrato* that we examined above. In her very meticulous three case studies of *De mulieribus claris*, Elsa Filosa has argued that Boccaccio was the first European author to describe "real" women, not only in the Latin biographies but also in the *Decameron*. She writes:

> Unlike the idealized women of many post-classical writers, Boccaccio's female characters are creatures made of flesh and bone, not mere metaphorical representations. I would like to propose an analysis of *De mulieribus claris* as a revolutionary work, capable of creating a new way of representing women in literature, and to show how this work creates a rupture in the stereotypical representation of female figures by casting them in a new perspective, more intimately psychological and

more human, besides being – if you will – humanist. (*Tre studi*, 141–2; my translation)[36]

For Filosa, the women described by Boccaccio are truer representations of reality than anything we find in earlier literature. They are portraits of real, rather than idealized, women and they defy stereotypes. Indeed, Boccaccio claims this very thing in the Introduction to *Decameron* Day Four with the Filippo Balducci *mezza-novella* and aside about his current and future detractors. The "stereotypes" about women to which Filosa refers are the idealized ones that led to the figure of the *donna angelicata*. But it is worth noting that an integral part of breaking from these idealized portraits is exposing women's faults, as we have seen in the Cesca *novella*, *Filostrato*, and the *Corbaccio*. By tracing Boccaccio's use of the "specchio" with regards to exemplarity, we see that widely circulated, negative stereotypes about women paradoxically rendered his female characters – like Cesca – more "real." Cesca suffers from the gendered-female vices about which Boccaccio's predecessors had written, and the various uses of gendered mirroring highlight this.[37] Language fails to convert her to a morally upstanding exemplar, but at the end of the *novella* she does not suffer any consequences other than remaining in her own ignorance. Within the *novella*, she symbolizes the failure of exemplary literature to do precisely what it sets out to do: better the lives of its readers. While Boccaccio will not fully theorize the relationship between language, gender, and exemplarity until *De mulieribus claris* some twenty years later, the Cesca *novella* anticipates that final project and all of its ambitions.

36 "A differenza delle donne idealizzate di molti scrittori del periodo post-classico, i personaggi femminili di Boccaccio sono creature in carne ed ossa, non mere rappresentazioni metaforiche. Si vorrebbe proporre un'analisi del *De mulieribus claris* come un lavoro rivoluzionario, capace di creare un nuovo modo di rappresentare le donne in letteratura, e dimostrare come quest'opera crei un punto di rottura nella rappresentazione stereotipica delle figure femminili, proiettandole in una nuova prospettiva più intimamente psicologica e più umana, oltre che – se si può dire – umanistica."

37 Although beyond the scope of this chapter, the figure of Cesca and her mirror counters Dante's great-great grandfather Cacciaguida's description of twelfth-century Florence in *Paradiso* 15.112–14 (trans. Mandelbaum 109): "Bellincion Berti vid'io andar cinto / di cuoio e d'osso, e venir da lo specchio / la donna sua sanza 'l viso dipinto" [I saw Bellincione Berti girt / with leather and with bone, and saw his wife / come from her mirror with her face unpainted]. Within this frame, Cesca represents the downfall of Florentine society and women (which Dante earlier lamented in his lengthy diatribe against them in *Purgatorio* 23).

A final observation: there is a level of irony in this *novella* surrounding the mirroring between Cesca, "women" as a category, and the female narrator Emilia, or, to speak of it discursively, between the *novella*, the *cornice* of the *Decameron*, and misogynist literature. That Emilia is the narrator of this particular *novella* about female vices and women's inability to surpass them further validates the tropes in her depiction of Cesca. First, Emilia herself oscillates between the idealized portrait of a *donna angelicata* during her "mirror of beauty" love song at the Conclusion of Day One. She is both a sighing, amorous woman and a narcissist. Second, the bulk of her *novella* in Day Six is dedicated to her description of Cesca's faults, with little text dedicated to the dialogue or outcome of the *novella*. In the end, we see Emilia participating in and embodying one of the most damning of the female vices presented – deriding other women – that the *novella* presents as one of its object of study.[38] In the same way that Cesca "proves" the validity of the medieval misogynist tropes described in the *novella*, and its subtexts, so too does Emilia. Indeed, her female voice authorizes the "real" portrait of women that Boccaccio presents in the *Decameron*, flaws and all. Thus, in the end, both Cesca and her storyteller Emilia simultaneously validate and challenge long-held beliefs about women, making *Decameron* VI.8 another example of Boccaccio's great ability to toe the line between pro-woman and misogynist literature.[39]

---

38 Ascoli has astutely noted that "As gender theorist she [Emilia] is self-subverting, advancing a theory of female incompetence that undermines her authority to articulate such a theory" ("Solomon and Emilia").

39 In her reading of *De mulieribus claris*, Deanna Shemek has highlighted this aspect of Boccaccio's writing as profoundly humanist, noting that although the humanists were responsible for extolling women's virtues in writing and educating the first generations of women writers, "the humanist fascination with women also betrayed anxieties about the security of male supremacy, especially as women rose increasingly to positions of real agency and power. Boccaccio's *De mulieribus claris*, remarkably, is both feminist and misogynist. In this sense, it may be considered a quintessentially humanist work" (204).

9 The Tale of Cavalcanti's Leap (VI.9)

MARIA LETTIERO
(TRANSLATED BY NICOLE GOUNALIS)

"A' quali Guido, da lor veggendosi chiuso, prestamente disse: Signori, voi mi potete dire a casa vostra ciò che vi piace'; e posta la mano sopra una di quelle arche, che grandi erano, sì come colui che leggerissimo era, prese un salto e fusi gittato dall'altra parte, e sviluppatosi da loro se n'andò."

(*Decameron* VI.9.12)

[Finding himself surrounded, Guido promptly replied: "Gentlemen, in your own house you may say whatever you like to me." Then, placing a hand on one of the tombstones, which were very tall, he vaulted over the top of it, being very light and nimble, and landed on the other side, whence, having escaped from their clutches, he proceeded on his way.]

(468)[1]

Animated by Boccaccio's pen, Guido di Messer Cavalcante de' Cavalcanti, "leggiadrissimo e costumato uom parlante" [VI.9.12; an exceedingly charming and sophisticated man, with a marked gift for conversation; 467], abandons the image of the tormented and suffering poet and swiftly takes on a proud and sarcastic tone. Placing his hand on the tombstone,[2] the distinguished poet takes a leap, crossing the boundary

---

1 This essay emerged from a series of conversations with Professor L. Rino Caputo, whom I thank kindly for his rich and novel suggestions regarding both the analytic and critical-methodological dimensions of my work. For the text of this *novella*, I have used Branca's 1976 edition for the Accademia della Crusca. For the English translation, I have used McWilliam.

2 On the term for tombstone, "arca," see Watson, "Architettura e scultura": "Nell'uso normale del xiii e xiv secolo, 'arca' è degenerata, dalla sua originale nobile funzione, che indicava l'arca del patto divino o la nave di Noè, al significato di una semplice

between life and death, good and evil, order and disorder, God and not-God, and, finally, between disorientation and the return to a sound sense of morality. It is precisely this memorial stone (ὅρος) – or border stone – which excludes and circumscribes: it constitutes the "artificial" side of demarcation, as a street, a grave, or even a temple does, in the way these were used in Greece from the classical era through the late Roman Empire. With his witty and enigmatic response, the Florentine poet demonstrates the extent to which the restrictive borders of the self anticipate a path of intellectual redemption once the threshold is crossed.

The symbolic image of lightness typified by the leap – Calvacanti "being very light and nimble" – takes on, according to Italo Calvino, an emblematic quality in the figure of the poet-philosopher, who hovers with his slender legs balanced on the gravestone. Referring to the witticism Boccaccio attributes to Cavalcanti – "Gentlemen, in your own house you may say whatever you like to me" – Calvino explicates not so much the fact that the death of the body can be defeated by whoever

cassa o una cassaforte, un sinonimo di 'cassa' o di 'cassone,' in una fase del linguaggio molto più avanzata. Dante trasforma il significato domestico di 'arca' nell'*Inferno*, X, usandolo per indicare le tombe degli arcieretici, come il padre di Guido, Cavalcante, imprigionati in 'arche di marmo.' Descrivendo i sarcofagi, fatti come casse, del Battistero, il Villani riprende l'accezione dantesca della parola, come fa il Boccaccio, sia qui sia più tardi nelle *Esposizioni* quando glosserà l' 'arca' di Dante per darle uno speciale significato di oggetto rettangolare simile a una cassa usata per contenere i cereali ... Il commento del Boccaccio su Dante, letto pubblicamente ancora molto tempo dopo che il *Decameron* aveva cominciato ad essere conosciuto tra il pubblico, presenta un'altra e abbastanza notevole digressione sulle tombe, la loro forma, e i termini che le descrivono" [In the normal usage of the thirteenth and fourteenth centuries, in a more advanced phase of language development, "arca" had deviated from its original elevated meaning, in which it indicated the Ark of the Covenant or Noah's Ark, to mean a simple chest or safe, as a synonym for a crate or a large case. Dante transforms the household meaning of "arca" in *Inferno* 10, using it to refer to the tombs of the arch-heretics imprisoned in "arche di marmo" (tombstones of marble), like that of Guido's father, Cavalcante. Describing the coffins, made in the shape of chests from the Baptistery, Villani repurposes the word in Dante's sense, as does Boccaccio, who does so here as well as later in the *Expositions*. There, he glosses Dante's "arca" to give it the special significance of a rectangular object similar to a chest used to store grain ... Boccaccio's commentary on Dante, widely read even long after the *Decameron* had begun to be known among the public, presents another, rather notable digression on the tombs, their shape, and the terminology used to describe them].

elevates themselves through intellectual speculation, but rather the visual image Boccaccio evokes through the liberation of the leap itself:[3]

> Se volessi scegliere un simbolo augurale per l'affacciarsi al nuovo millennio, sceglierei questo: l'agile salto improvviso del poeta-filosofo che si solleva sulla pesantezza del mondo, dimostrando che la sua gravità contiene il segreto della leggerezza, mentre quella che molti credono essere la vitalità dei tempi, rumorosa, aggressiva, scalpitante e rombante, appartiene al regno della morte, come un cimitero d'automobili arrugginite ... Un tema niente affatto leggero come la sofferenza d'amore, viene dissolto da Cavalcanti in entità impalpabili che si spostano tra anima sensitiva e anima intellettiva, tra cuore e mente, tra occhi e voce. (*Lezioni* 16–17)

> [Were I to choose an auspicious image for the new millennium, I would choose that one: the sudden agile leap of the poet-philosopher who raises himself above the weight of the world, showing that with all his gravity he has the secret of lightness, and that what many consider to be the vitality of the times – noisy, aggressive, revving and roaring – belongs to the realm of death, like a cemetery for rusty old cars ... A theme by no means "light," such as the sufferings of love, is dissolved into impalpable entities that move between sensitive soul and intellective soul, between heart and mind, between eyes and voice.] (*Six Memos* 12–13)

If the gravity and weight of the world contain "the secret of lightness," as Calvino claims, then the denunciation of spiritual death which Guido advances surely bears the influences of the death that permeates the world and, above all, of the ethical and moral degradation of the city of Florence. The plague narrated in the Introduction to the First Day of the one hundred tales of the *Decameron* takes on a symbolic role, representing an imposing allegory for the moral degradation of a people tortured by the epidemic and in the throes of the crisis of an entire civilization, that of the late medieval period.[4]

---

3 Giovanni Villani describes Cavalcanti in this way in his *Nuova Cronica*: "era come filosofo, virtudioso uomo in più cose, se non ch'era troppo tenero e stizzoso [VIII.42; he was like a philosopher, a virtuoso in many things, if not also too sensitive and quick-tempered].

4 This tale has attracted the attention of many critics and intellectuals, among whom Calvino is by now the most well known internationally. I also discuss below the readings of Pound and Jolles, among others. Both Calvino and Jolles, as Martin Eisner notes, are "oddly faithful to Boccaccio" in their allegorical readings of the tale as figuring a cultural shift (*Boccaccio and the Invention* 104). Major critical readings of the tale from a more pre-modern perspective include Barański; Durling; Forni, *Adventures in Speech* 76–69; Gorni, "Guido Cavalcanti"; Inglese 199–225; Parodi; Stone 107–21; Velli; and Watson, "On Seeing." More recently, on the political aspects of the tale's representation of Cavalcanti as read in relation to the *Esposizioni*, see Olson, "Resurrecting." For a reading in the light of Boccaccio's MS Chigi L.V. 176, see Eisner, *Boccaccio and the Invention* 103–10. See also Olson, "'Concivus meus.'"

The boundary that Boccaccio proposes to cross is that between a life lived in the midst of the mental and physical decay caused by the pandemic and an existence which could depict, as on a stage, a more real form of life, filling in the gaps in order to enjoy them more fully. In this spirit Boccaccio composes his work of art, the *Decameron*, crossing the *limen*, or threshold, and losing himself in the pleasure of the maze of a reconstructed reality. Boccaccio took narrative refuge in a *locus amoenus*,[5] both a garden and the space of interiority and outward appearances, which served as an antidote to the horror generated by the bubonic plague; this place protects his young protagonists from the apocalypse of ordinary life. The garden-microcosm, for the *brigata*, becomes the Author's methodological map for overcoming the limits of consciousness: from the recuperation of the lightness of existence, desire, instinct, and passion, to the life of the spirit, as it is tied to the mind and to cognition.

It is erudition which ignites both in the Author of the *Decameron*, and therefore in Cavalcanti, the flame of perception of the other; erudition understood not as the sterile vaunting of knowledge acquired in one or more fields, but as inquiry into original truths, be they hidden or opposed to received wisdom. Guido marks the profound abyss between those who know – therefore real men – and the masses, revealing the absolute distance between the two groups. Only a select few can gain access to the abstract forms of the intellect; any possible rational knowledge is denied to the brutes. For this reason, aware that science cannot be popularized, the poet-philosopher signals his detachment from the men of the *brigata* through his remarks.[6] In this way Guido affirms his superiority to the unsophisticated men, who, after this episode, refrain from bothering him further. Cavalcanti's philosophy also emerges through the well-known *canzone* "Donna me prega" [A lady asks me], in which no intellectual redemption is allowed to those without knowledge or to those who are base-hearted:

Ond'a presente canoscente chero,
per ch'io no spero ch' om di basso core

5 In Greek and Latin texts, *locus amoenus*, or "pleasant place," connotes an idea of nature and its harmonious relationship with humankind. The topos of nature's *amoenitas* also betrays its relationship to the term *amor*. In fact, many believed that the *locus amoenus* was a place conducive to love in which one experienced all pleasure. For a more in-depth consideration of the relationship between the *locus amoenus* and the garden, see Samson; and Battaglia Ricci, *Ragionare nel giardino*.

6 For an interpretation of the social dynamics related to the concept of the *brigata* in the literary imagination of the thirteenth and fourteenth centuries, see Barolini, "Sociology of the 'Brigata.'"

a tal ragione porti canoscenza:
ché senza natural dimostramento
non ho talento di voler provare
là dov' e' posa, e che lo fa creare,
e qual sia sua vertute e sua Potenza. (ll. 5–11)[7]

[Whence I now demand a knowledgeable interlocutor, because I do not expect that a man of a lowly heart have any knowledge of this topic: since without natural demonstration, I have no intention to prove where [love] resides, or what creates it, or the quality of its virtue and power.]

To interpret the *canzone*, likely among poetry's most difficult from a philosophical point of view, Cavalcanti needs an expert, wise reader, one who has access to the tools of natural philosophy and who understands and displays similar argumentation. Cavalcanti is not only the first great "psychologist of the emotions" and of mental states transformed into words through an "absolute rhythm" (Pound, *Sonnets* xii, xxi).[8] He is also the poet of love experienced as irrational passion, more endured than sought after. He shows himself to be one who is activating a theoretical process of creating knowledge, interpreting human ideas and putting them into words – and thereby into the phenomena of signs – in an era characterized by a "high degree of semioticity" (Zumthor 30).[9]

---

7 For Cavalcanti's poem, I have used the text in *Antologia della poesia italiana*, ed. Segre and Ossola, 404–9. The citation indicates the page and line numbers. The translation is by David Lummus.

8 Ezra Pound's astute claim was based on the idea of poetry as a "sort of inspired mathematics, which gives us equations, not for abstract figures, triangles, squares, and the like, but for the human emotions" (*Spirit of Romance* 14). See also the fifth chapter of *The Spirit of Romance* (87–100). He saw in Calvacanti's poetry "no rhetoric, but always a true description, whether it be of pain itself, or of the apathy that comes when the emotions and possibilities of emotion are exhausted" (*Sonnets* xii). Years later, in 1932, amid many difficulties, Pound's personal and formidable Italian edition of Cavalcanti's *Rime* would be born, "rappezzata fra le rovine" [cobbled together among the ruins], as the subtitle reads on the frontispiece. See Pound, ed., *Rime*.

9 Zumthor's full declaration is worth citing in its entirety: "We can no longer fail to take certain things into account: the high degree of semioticity of a culture – the Middle Ages – which thought of itself as an immense network of signs; the fact that the conventional character of medieval art implies a near-Platonic comprehension of the Chain of Resemblances, proceeding from absolute Identity to perfect Otherness."

For this reason the "thinker" is not understood by the "common herd,"[10] who see in him an introverted and solitary figure. His speculations "erano solo in cercare se trovar si potesse che Iddio non fosse" [VI.9.9; were exclusively concerned with whether it could be shown that God did not exist; 467]. And this is why "Guido alcuna volta speculando molto abstratto dagli uomini divenia" [VI.9.9; his passion for speculative reasoning occasionally made him appear somewhat remote from his fellow beings; 467]. He seems to be aware of the impact of this depth on the level of form, creating a greater knowledge of reality, as Barthes realizes that the colour aquamarine "comes from the reflection of its depth onto its surface, and it is there that one must walk, not in the sky or in the abyss."[11] Cavalcanti's enigmatic philosophical claim – "Signori, voi mi potete dire a casa vostra ciò che vi piace" [VI.9.12; Gentlemen, in your own house you may say whatever you like to me; 468][12] – paired with the athletic gesture of

---

10 This concept could be considered antithetical to that expressed, for example, by Montaigne, Rabelais, and Pascal. See D'Ambrosio: "l'intellettuale non si sente depositario assoluto della verità, ma la sa cogliere nel popolo, nel momento in cui aiuta la gente a pensare meglio. Quando, cioè, offre alla gente strumenti adeguati per elaborare quanto ha già intuito, svolgendo così quella funzione maieutica di socratica memoria. È allora molto importante – si direbbe in termini gramsciani – che gli intellettuali si confondano nella società civile, ne diventino e se ne sentano parte integrante" [140; the intellectual does not consider himself the absolute repository of the truth, but rather knows how to grasp the truth from within the people, in the moment in which he helps them to think better. When, in other words, he offers the people tools suitable for explaining what they have already intuited, performing in this way the midwife function that we see in Socrates. It is, therefore, very important – to put it in Gramscian terms – that intellectuals are part of civil society, that they become and see themselves as one of its integral parts].

11 "vient du reflet de son fond sur sa surface, et c'est là qu'il faut se promener, et non dans le ciel ou dans les abîmes" (Barthes, "Réflexion" 60).

12 The remark is linked to the *incipit* of Psalm 48.12 in the Latin Vulgate with regard to the binomial pairing "tomb-house": "Sepulchra eorum domus illorum in aeternum" [their tomb-houses shall continue forever]. As Rossi notes, the difference between the Psalm and Cavalcanti's remark is substantial: the tombs in the Psalm can accommodate the learned and the foolish (Psalm 48:11–12 in the Latin Vulgate: "Et videbit sapientes morientes; simul insipiens et stultus peribunt et reliquent alienis divitias suas. Sepulchra eorum domus illorum in aeternum; tabernacula eorum in progeniem et progeniem, etsi vocaverunt nominibus suis terras suas" [And he will see the wise will die; the senseless and the foolish will die and will leave their riches to strangers. Their tombs will remain their houses forever; their tents for generations, even if they had called their lands with their own names]), and the eternity in question is related to the mortal destiny of all people, while "le arche indicate da Cavalcanti sono dimora esclusiva della brigata e non la sua" [the tombs indicated by Cavalcanti are exclusively home to the *brigata*, and not to him]. See Rossi 503–5.

the leap over the tomb and over the gravestones of San Giovanni, embodies the entanglement of the perceptible and the intelligible, the obscured and the visible, and the signifier and signified. The apparently cryptic nature of the words is undone and therefore fixed by the astute decoding performed by Messer Betto, who interprets for the *brigata*:

> Gli smemorati siete voi, se voi non l'avete inteso: egli ci ha onestamente e in poche parole detta la maggior villania del mondo, per ciò che, se voi riguarderete bene, queste arche sono le case de' morti, per ciò che in esse si pongono e dimorano i morti; le quali egli dice che son nostra casa, a dimostrarci che noi e gli altri uomini idioti e non letterati siamo, a comparazion di lui e degli altri uomini scienziati, peggio che uomini morti, e per ciò, qui essendo, noi siamo a casa nostra. (VI.9.14)
>
> [You're the ones who are out of your minds, if you can't see what he meant. In a few words he has neatly paid us the most back-handed compliment I ever heard, because when you come to consider it, these tombs are the houses of the dead, this being the place where the dead are laid to rest and where they take up their abode. By describing it as our house, he wanted to show us that, by comparison with himself and other men of learning, all men who are as uncouth and unlettered as ourselves are worse off than the dead. So that, being in a graveyard, we are in our own house.] (468)

Following Betto's interpretation, Guido's comment recalls, in a certain sense, Seneca's sentence: "Otium sine litteris mors est et hominis vivi sepultura" [*Ad Lucilium* 82.3; Leisure without study is death; it is a tomb for the living man; 243]. The analogy is clear through the direct relationship between men who are "illiterate" = "dead" = "buried alive." Cavalcanti's positioning of himself beyond the threshold confirms the profound distance between "uncouth and unlettered" men who are "worse off than the dead" and cultured "men of learning."

Boccaccio's deep sensibility grasps the great limits of humankind, expressed through Guido's words: he exorcises the death of the body and, above all, the death of the intellect, the part of the soul capable of knowing and judging. Regarding the clear boundary that exists between intellectual wealth and poverty, we can find a connection with V.S. Naipaul's caustic opening sentence: "The world is what it is; men who are nothing, who allow themselves to be nothing, have no place in it" (Naipaul 3). Each word of this sentence appears as a provocation which "crowns" humankind with his own fears and accentuates his distaste for the loser. If by "nothing" – in Cavalcanti's case – we mean "intellectually nothing," this refers to him who is incapable of crossing the boundary: the "idiota" [uncouth man], useless and deeply alone, because he is not intellectually and spiritually regenerated. This is Boccaccio's veiled but incisive message; he does not suggest any of the truths that may await humankind, once he has overcome the limits of his singular existence. For this reason, it would be unwise to consider Boccaccio's vision of the world an absolute one. His "voice" is only one of the many that can be heard in the story, alongside those of other characters.

That Cavalcanti's *facezia*, or witticism, in the *Decameron* may derive from Petrarch's *Rerum memorandarum* is worthy of note:

> Dinus quidam concivis meus, qui etate nostra gratissime dicacitatis adolescens fuit, casu preteriens per loca frequentissima sepulcris, aliquot sibi notos senes illic confabulantes comperit; qui ut iocandi peritum irritarent, iocari simul omnes – ut est etas illa loquacior – et manibus etiam apprehendere ceperunt. Ille se proripiens hoc unum omnibus respondit: "Iniquum hoc loco certamen; vos enim ante domos vestras animosiores estis"; senio scilicet eorum et vicinie mortis alludens. Nec prius intellectus est, quam eo ex oculis ablato cimiterium circumspicientes, quas ille domos loqueretur perpenderunt. Innumerabilia dixit ad hunc modum, que apud nos vulgo etiam nota sunt; hoc enim loco non iocos eius prosequi, sed nomen attingere propositum fuit. (2.60)

> [A fellow citizen of mine named Dino, who in our time was a young man of most agreeable biting wit, was by chance passing through a place full of tombs and ran into some old men whom he knew who were chatting there. Thinking that they would provoke that expert joker, they all began at once to make fun of him – since that age is more talkative – and to grab him with their hands. Pulling himself away, Dino responded one thing to all of them: "In this place the competition is unfair, for you are more courageous in front of your own houses," alluding of course to their old age and to their nearness to death. And it was not understood sooner than, when Dino moved off, they had looked around at the cemetery and understood what homes he was talking about. Dino said innumerable things of this kind, which are known in our city even to the multitude. But I did not intend to describe in detail his jokes here, only to mention his name.]

Petrarch's Dino, who appears to coincide with the Florentine doctor Dino del Garbo,[13] is the author of the Latin commentary on Cavalcanti's

13 Dino del Garbo died, according to Filippo Villani, on 30 September 1327. The transcription of the gloss on Cavalcanti's poem probably dates to the decade 1360–70.

canzone "Donna me prega."[14] Boccaccio puts his transcription of the erudite Latin commentary alongside Guido's *canzone* in the vernacular.[15] The genius of Boccaccio's rewriting within a Florentine setting emerges from a comparison of the Latin and vernacular texts. According to Guglielmo Gorni, Boccaccio "transforms the petulant *senes* into a *brigata* of young *viveurs*. He redeems the offensive and scornful tone of the protagonist's Latin response, making it into an enigmatic, metaphysically-inflected comment. The most conspicuous change is that Petrarch attributed the remark not to Guido, but to a Dino who is his 'fellow citizen.'"[16] Gorni makes clear that, in this "repurposing" of Petrarch's text, Boccaccio "becomes the author, rather than the annotator, of this celebrated text by reformulating the story and changing its provenance."[17] Rossi, on the other hand – in his careful selection of the sources for, and antecedents of, Cavalcanti's remark – starts from the conviction, supported by Petrarch's own admission, that Boccaccio never knew the *Rerum memorandarum libri*, or specifically the section "De facetiis ac salibus illustrium."[18] It is for this reason that Rossi maintains

> the idea of an autonomous reworking of patrimony from the oral tradition, which would function as a common source for the two authors. … At the same time, at least minimal points of contact are recognizable with the *Decameron* tale: the scenario (meeting in a place filled with tombs) and the sequence of events (the introduction of the character; meeting with a group of provocateurs; remark; understanding of the comment) are the

14 The title of the Latin commentary is "Scriptum super cantilena Guidonis de Cavalcantibus." See 29r of MS Chigi L.V.176 of the Biblioteca Apostolica Vaticana. It is difficult to locate the printed version, published in Venice in 1498: "De natura et motu amoris venereis cantio cum enarratione Dini de Garbo."

15 Both come together in the Dante and Petrarch anthology in MS Chigi L.V. 176, c. 29r, which can be found as a reproduction from the manuscript in Eisner, *Boccaccio and the Invention* 99.

16 "muta i *senes* petulanti in una brigata di giovani *viveurs*; riscatta la replica del protagonista dal tono offensivo e sprezzante che è nell'originale latino facendone una battuta enigmatica, di portata metafisica. La variante più cospicua è che il Petrarca attribuiva il motto non già a Guido, ma a un Dino 'concivis meus'" (Gorni, "Guido Cavalcanti" 39–40).

17 "nel riformulare l'aneddoto e nel cambiarne la paternità passerebbe dal chiosatore all'autore del celebre testo" (Gorni, "Guido Cavalcanti" 40).

18 Begun in Provence and continued during Petrarch's second stay in Parma (1343–5), the *Rerum memorandarum libri* was known only after his death and remained unfinished after the fourth book. In "'Concivus meus,'" Olson also maintains that Boccaccio did not know Petrarch's version of the story.

> same as in *Decameron* VI.9 … Even the formulation of the remark is similar ("vos enim ante *domos vestras* animosiores estis," "voi mi potete dire a *casa vostra* ciò che vi piace") … The two texts, as far as has been verified, are independent, and therefore the episode in the *Rerum memorandarum libri* is not a source for the *Decameron* VI.9, but, perhaps, an autonomous parallel generated by a shared inspiration.[19]

For Rossi, the significant difference between the remark in the *Decameron* and Petrarch's "witticism" is that Dino's sentence is an "irreverent, exaggerated, Tuscan-style comment, while Guido's is an implicit declaration of intellectual superiority."[20] Dino del Garbo's gloss has been a fundamental resource for Cavalcanti scholars: Ezra Pound, Maria Corti, and Guido Favati have examined the content of Cavalcanti's *canzone* by looking at Boccaccio's manuscript copy.[21] Martin Eisner's ideas on Pound add to this understanding. For Pound, the intellectual superiority reflected in Cavalcanti's leap becomes a motivation for further archival research: "Boccaccio's image of Cavalcanti leaping over the tomb not only provided Pound with a model for his own intellectual superiority, but also stimulated the archival research that eventually led to Pound's discovery of the commentary that Boccaccio had transcribed" (*Boccaccio and the Invention* 96).

André Jolles, a Dutch scholar with a predilection for Boccaccio, interprets Guido's gesture – an unprecedented action, which does not appear in the preceding version of the anecdote attributed by Petrarch to Dino del Garbo – as the "first sign of the Renaissance consciously understood as a new life."[22] Jolles studies and interprets Cavalcanti's proposition, which marks the divide between two opposing visions of the world: that of the Florentine gentlemen, and that of the poet-philosopher

---

19 "l'idea di un'autonoma ripresa dal patrimonio di tradizione orale, che fungerebbe da fonte comune per i due letterati … Tuttavia si possono riconoscere alcuni minimi punti di contatto con la novella decameroniana: la situazione (l'incontro in una zona piena di sepolcri) e la sequenza dei fatti (presentazione del personaggio; incontro col gruppo dei provocatori; motto; comprensione della battuta) sono le stesse del *Dec.* VI.9 … Anche la formulazione del motto è prossima ('vos enim ante *domos vestras* animosiores estis', 'voi mi potete dire a *casa vostra* ciò che vi piace') … I due testi sono, per quanto è dato verificare, indipendenti, pertanto l'episodio dei *Rerum memorandarum libri* non costituisce uno spunto per *Dec.* VI.9, ma forse solo un autonomo parallelo generato da una suggestione condivisa" (Rossi 503–4).

20 "battutaccia irriverente alla toscana, quella di Guido è una implicita dichiarazione di superiorità intellettuale" (Rossi 504).

21 See Favati; and Corti. On Pound, see note 8 above.

22 "primo segno di un Rinascimento cosciente inteso come nuova vita" (Jolles 55).

"conscious of the fact that one era has ended behind him, while another is opening before him."[23] This idea, with regard to the content of Guido's witticism, can be compared with a letter Jolles writes to Johan Huizinga on 25 October 1920: "Do you remember the ninth tale of the sixth day of the *Decameron*? The story of Guido Cavalcanti and the Florentine gentlemen? It seems to me that here we have a good example of what the *Stilnovo* poets could have conceived regarding the word 'renaissance.' The word by itself had not yet made its appearance in history, but the concept already existed: Guido is the one who is 'alive,' while the others are 'dead.'"[24] Gabriele Fichera seems to share Jolles's conception of the leap, understood as a break in history – in other words, a separation – that will lead to the attainment of autonomy and to the passage into a greater order, so to speak. He writes,

> As the Cavalcanti of the witticism breaks away, through his verbal leap, from the mere facticity of the once-living dead, to reposition himself in a qualitatively superior intellectual domain, so Jolles indicates the presence of a decisive hermeneutical break between history and poetry, which yet again repositions the particular event, irrelevant in and of itself, within a gradual structure, within which we can recognize a progression.[25]

In this way, Cavalcanti, full of passion for poetry and science, is reborn through his verbal leap, himself passing into a greater order. With regard to leaps, historical periodization, and depth of thinking, Jolles writes: "Historical subdivisions are like the rungs of a ladder, along which we have cautiously descended into the vortex of the past."[26]

23 "cosciente del fatto che un'epoca si è chiusa dietro di lui, mentre un'altra si è aperta" (Jolles 47).

24 "Ricordi la novella nona della sesta giornata del *Decameron*? L'aneddoto di Guido Cavalcanti e dei cavalieri fiorentini? Mi pare che qui si abbia un bell'esempio di ciò che i poeti dello Stilnovo potevano pensare riguardo alla parola 'rinascimento.' La parola in sé deve ancora fare la sua apparizione nella storia, ma il concetto esiste già: Guido è il 'vivo,' mentre gli altri sono 'morti'" (Huizinga 309).

25 "Come il Cavalcanti della facezia si stacca col suo salto verbale dalla mera fattualità dei vivi già defunti, per ricollocarsi in un dominio intellettuale qualitativamente superiore, cosi Jolles indica la presenza di uno scarto ermeneutico decisivo fra storia e poesia, che ricolloca ancora una volta l'avvenimento particolare, di per sé irrilevante, in una struttura graduale, nella quale riconosciamo una progressione" (Fichera 131–2).

26 "Le suddivisioni storiche sono come pioli di una scala, lungo i quali siamo discesi con cautela nel vortice del passato" (Jolles 99).

Immediately after this remark, he adds: "Now that the depth has been sounded, those who aren't suffering from vertigo can risk the leap."[27]

The most profound sense of the *inventio* of Cavalcanti's remark is demonstrated by the synthetic introduction to the tale of the solitary *stilnovo* poet transcribed by Francesco Pandolfini in the years 1487–8: "Eam [fabellam] enim si diligenter perspexeris indoctos viros a doctis quam pictos homines a vivis distare cognoveris" [Pirovano 568; For if you diligently examine that story, you will see that unlearned men stand apart from learned men just like painted men do from living men].[28] The wise translator judges the ninth tale of the Sixth Day "cum iocis facetijsque tum gravitate quocunque summo homine dignam" [Pirovano 568; worthy not only of jokes and jests but also of gravity for whatever great man]. The depiction of Guido here, according to Donato Pirovano,

> places itself halfway between that of the humanist haughtily detached from the common people, and that of the Ciceronian *vir facetus*. In fact, choosing VI.9, Pandolfini intends to present an ideal model of the man of letters and the intellectual humanist, as an example of the distance between the learned and the ignorant (a gap deemed enormous and insurmountable) ... In this way he projects tensions and aspirations onto Cavalcanti that actually belong to his own activities as a young student and to his own time.[29]

Another testimony to Guido's talents and thought is presented by Giacomo da Pistoia, *magister* of medicine at the University of Bologna, who dedicates his work *Quaestio disputata de felicitate* to Cavalcanti.[30]

---

27 "Ora che la profondità è stata misurata, coloro che non soffrono di vertigini possono arrischiare il salto" (Jolles 99).

28 *Decameron* VI.9, translated into Latin by Francesco Pandolfini and found in the miscellaneous manuscript Riccardiano 2995, has been published in Pirovano.

29 "si configura a metà strada tra quello dell'umanista snobisticamente staccato dal volgo e quello del ciceroniano *vir facetus*. Infatti scegliendo la VI 9, Pandolfini intende presentare un modello ideale di uomo di studio e di intellettuale umanista, come un esempio della distanza tra dotti e ignoranti (distacco ritenuto enorme e incolmabile) ... In tal modo proietta sul personaggio Cavalcanti tensioni e aspirazioni che sono proprie della sua giovanile attività studentesca e del suo tempo" (Pirovano 570).

30 In reference to the dedication, sent to Guido Cavalcanti in Florence by Giacomo da Pistoia, on folio 194r of MS 110, Biblioteca Comunale e dell'Accademia Etrusca, Cortona, see Kristeller, *Studies* 536. As Kristeller rightly emphasizes, the dedication does not validate the belief that Guido Cavalcanti was a disciple of Giacomo, but nevertheless attests to the existence of a direct relationship between the Tuscan poets of the *dolce stil novo* and the philosophers of the *facoltà delle Arti* at the University of Bologna. See Kristeller, "Philosophical Treatise" 439.

Giacomo addresses to Guido his treatise on the Aristotelian path to happiness, a path that consists in liberating oneself from obstacles ("impedimenta," or passions that push one towards the pleasures of the flesh, towards recognition and wealth) and, step by step, ascending the ladder of philosophy, which leads to the full life of the intellect.[31] As Irene Zavattero has written: "The theme of the damaging effect of the *passiones* in general could constitute, therefore, the point of contact, the common interest, and perhaps the motivation behind the dedication to the Florentine poet."[32] The year the treatise was composed can be dated to between 1290 and 1300, a date which coincides with the death of the poet-philosopher.

Giacomo's wish is that Guido may know how to put into practice the philosophical model of the good life, lived according to the intellect. Boccaccio too does not hesitate to observe this same virtuosity:

> Tralle quali brigate n'era una di messer Betto Brunelleschi, nella quale messer Betto e' compagni s'erano molto ingegnato di tirare Guido di messer Cavalcante de' Cavalcanti, e non senza cagione: per ciò che, oltre a quello che egli fu un de' miglior logici che avesse il mondo e ottimo filosofo naturale (delle quali cose poco la brigata curava). (VI.9.7–8)

> [Among these various companies, there was one that was led by Messer Betto Brunelleschi, into whose ranks Messer Betto and his associates had striven might and main to attract Messer Cavalcante de' Cavalcanti's son, Guido. And not without reason, for … he was one of the finest logicians in the world and an expert natural philosopher (to none of which Betto and his friends attributed much importance).] (467)

The statement – "he was one of the finest logicians in the world" – echoes the words of Dante: "Forse / tu non pensavi ch'io loico fossi" [*Inf.* 27.122–3; Perhaps you did not think I was a logician!].[33] It functions as a way for Boccaccio to present Messer Cavalcanti as an astute rational mind, an esteemed logician, and an excellent natural philosopher. Guido avails himself of arts such as dialectic, rhetoric, mathematics,

31 On the work by Jacobus de Pistorio, *Quaestio de felicitate*, see Zavattero 402–4.

32 "Il tema degli effetti dannosi delle *passiones* in generale potrebbe costituire, quindi, il punto di contatto, l'interesse comune e forse il motivo della dedica al poeta fiorentino" (Zavattero 375).

33 For the text of the *Inferno* I have used the 1996 edition and translation by Durling and Martinez.

natural philosophy, and metaphysics: speculative disciplines to help facilitate the attainment of "mental happiness." The same philosophical principle belongs to Dante when he refers to Aristotle at the beginning of the *Convivio*:

> Sì come dice lo Filosofo nel principio della Prima Filosofia, tutti li uomini naturalmente desiderano di sapere. La ragione di che puote essere [ed] è che ciascuna cosa, da providenza di prima natura impinta, è inclinabile alla sua propia perfezione; onde, acciò che la scienza è ultima perfezione della nostra anima, nella quale sta la nostra ultima felicitade, tutti naturalmente al suo desiderio semo subietti. (I.1)
>
> [As the Philosopher says at the beginning of the First Philosophy, all men by nature desire to know. The reason for this can be and is that each thing, impelled by a force provided by its own nature, inclines towards its own perfection. Since knowledge is the ultimate perfection of our soul, in which resides our ultimate happiness, we are all therefore by nature subject to a desire for it].[34]

If the highest form of perfection consists in knowledge and wisdom, which make humankind worthy and happy, then the Author of the *Decameron* takes as an example the personality of the keen wordsmith – a point of reference both for poets of Boccaccio's time and for those to come – in order to contrast the tragedy of the death of the body with that of the soul. According to Boccaccio, only a person who doubts and who interrogates herself can truly comprehend, avoiding the acceptance of dogmatic and indisputable truths. In this way, Boccaccio seems to bring to fruition the narrative intention contained in Cavalcanti's discourse, giving it, through the elegance of his poetry, a wonderful springboard from which to "vault" beyond the limit, *per visibilia ad visibilia*.

34 For the text of the *Convivio* I have used Vasoli's 1979 edition. For the English translation, I have used the Lansing translation, originally published in 1990 and now available online. On the possibility of presences of the *Convivio* in the *Decameron*, see Arduini; Ferreri; and Forni, "Boccaccio tra Dante e Cino."

10 The Tale of Frate Cipolla (VI.10)

CORMAC Ó CUILLEANÁIN

Boccaccio scholarship shines countless points of light on Frate Cipolla's tale. While piggybacking on that critical heritage, the present essay will mostly shadow the structure of a typical Dante *lectura*: a progressive journey through *Decameron* VI.10, rather than a definitive analysis that might stray too far from the reading experience, sidestepping risky confrontations with the text while foregrounding the critic's reflective judgment. Some critical "findings" may, however, be flagged right now: the story's emphasis on narration as performance; the canny sequencing of its revelations; its playful allegiance to Dante; its challenge to our ability to tell truthiness from fakery; its compulsive creativity regarding names and things. This latter point, universally acknowledged, will be explored here partly through the creative responses of translators, as they grapple with Boccaccio's storytelling techniques.

Our expedition will run into some features that might strike a naïve modern reader as alien. We will evaluate these elements in both realistic and strategic terms, commenting on story structure, visualizing "performance" elements and audience reactions, while also sketching some broader contexts. This exploratory approach does not claim to break new ground – indeed it involves some bad faith, as everyone who studies the *Decameron* will have picked up critical perspectives that (happily) guide what we notice when revisiting a favourite text. But a "fresh" rereading may yield the occasional surprise. *Decameron* VI.10 is justly famed for celebrating the creative power of unmediated eloquence, yet can seem strangely tongue-tied: important interactions are narrated without "live" dialogue – the two tricksters planning their theft (VI.10.14); Cipolla warning his servant to mind his belongings (VI.10.20); Guccio's pick-up lines (VI.10.22–4); Cipolla eulogizing the Angel Gabriel (VI.10.34). Moreover, Cipolla's first direct speech, advertising his relic-show (VI.10.9–12), is kept relatively grey and boring (the better to set off his final technicolour outburst). Less surprisingly, some key themes, contradictions, and core imagery – up versus down, flying versus roasting, wings versus grease, angel versus animal – will be seen to flow seamlessly between main plot and subplot.

First, a little context. To use a crass commercial metaphor: if the Sixth Day were a shopping mall, this final tale would be its anchor tenant. Before reaching it, the reader will experience expectations, appetites, disappointments. The day has been meagre – a mere thirty pages for the Introduction and first nine stories, whereas the Fifth Day had taken seventy-one pages to reach that same point.[1] Settings have been Tuscan, or even Florentine, which may be reassuring,[2] but one does miss the freewheeling travel of earlier days. There hasn't been a great build-up; the position of some stories could be swapped without loss. The witticisms and retorts that populate the tales have naturally been brief, with one-dimensional quips or put-downs providing most of the punchlines. Some can seem flat (VI.5.15) or offensive (VI.8.9), with failure to accept even the nastiest rebuke being classified as stupidity.[3] Even more puzzling is Guido Cavalcanti's insult, which, although undeniably elegant, is so obscure as to require an explanatory coda (VI.9.14) – going against our assumption that jokes like these are instantaneous, needing no explication.[4] In each tale, the scene is deftly drawn, the cultural contexts fascinating, the closing lines neatly choreographed – yet, when all is said and (not) done, anecdotal tales like these are a one-shot form. And in many cases (the third and seventh stories being notable exceptions) the modern reader might feel that nothing much is at stake.

Of course, that is a misreading. Medieval Italian culture valued sharpness of wit very differently, and the Florentines had their own angle on

---

1 These page counts are taken from Rebhorn's translation: Boccaccio, *Decameron* [2013], 472–501 and 388–458.

2 See Cottino-Jones, *Order from Chaos* 105.

3 Fresco's niece Cesca is awarded the IQ of a sheep for failing to "understand" her uncle's sexist insult (VI.8.10), while Forese (VI.5.15) is chastened by Giotto's uncouth reply to his awkward compliment. The cultural convention of accepting rebukes, even from inferiors, is widespread in the *Decameron* (e.g., I.4.21, I.8.16, I.9.6, IX.2.15), and clearly amounts to a core value in the book's model of civility. These and other points are taken from a widely forgotten study, Ó Cuilleanáin, *Religion and the Clergy*. See chapter 6, "Cipolla's Sermon," esp. 182–4. The present reading will downplay the religious structures and significance of the Cipolla story, thus avoiding too much repetition from that book.

4 "Humor can be dissected, as a frog can, but the thing dies in the process" (White 243). Boccaccio's explanation manages to keep Guido's quip alive by poking fun at stupid people who try to understand it. But immediacy of impact has been lost.

its importance. An episode from Salimbene's *Chronicle*, famously cited by Erich Auerbach, shows how central to their self-image was their appreciation of sharp humour, even when directed against themselves.[5] David Wallace points out how vital the questions of skill and intelligence, especially among public servants, could be for the survival and prosperity of Florence (93).[6] And the value of verbal humour is not just political but also aesthetic, perhaps even spiritual: the *Novellino*, which includes some vulgar, disrespectful, or obscene sayings, opens with a quotation from Christ (Matthew 12:34: "out of the abundance of the heart the mouth speaketh"), which underpins the beauty and value of the book's "fiori di parlare, di belle cortesie e di belli risposi" [17; flowers of speech, lovely courtesies and responses].[7] Even when recording unworthy quips, verbal intelligence is a God-given faculty, and God should be praised as we embark upon our task.[8]

In this light, even the spavined "leggiadro motto" [VI.1.2; graceful witty saying] that inaugurates the Sixth Day has inherent value; that tale has been much admired, and critics including Getto, Baratto, Almansi, and Fido have pointed out its significant concern with the art of narrative and the proper place of fiction in a civilized society, as epitomized by the ladies and gentlemen of the *Decameron* frame story.[9] And yet, as the day wears on, we may feel short-changed. Approaching the end, the reader, accustomed to the copiousness of earlier days, may feel that this time around we've had a succession of short recitatives, but now it's time for a proper aria. Other images also spring to mind: the Sixth Day as a series of short skips leading up to a soaring pole vault, or a series of *amuse-bouches* followed by a solid main course, or the capstone that solidifies, protects, and retrospectively validates the structure of lower stones in an architectural structure. These metaphors are admittedly fanciful, though perhaps preferable to a shopping mall.

5 A Franciscan friar has fallen on icy ground, and local Florentines have gathered, not to help but to mock. On being asked if he would like something placed under him, he replies, "Yeah – your wife," and the Florentines bless him as one of their own. See Auerbach 215. On the callousness of medieval humour, see Brewer xviii.

6 This, Wallace convincingly suggests, provides a civic rationale even for the crude forms of physical trickery represented in *Decameron* VIII.5 and VIII.9.

7 For the text and translation of the *Novellino*, I have used Consoli's dual-language edition.

8 Compare Panfilo's pious words bookending the first story of the *Decameron* (I.1.2 and 91).

9 See Getto 141; Baratto, *Realtà e stile* 74–6; Almansi, *Writer as Liar* 23; Fido, "Boccaccio's *Ars Narrandi*" 239.

Another "structural" cause of heightened anticipation is the identity of the last tale's narrator. Dioneo made his mark in the First Day, lowering the tone with his *novella* of the lusty monk, the abbot, and the girl, and later negotiating his right to tell a story outside the set theme of each day, speaking every time as the last contributor (I.4; I.Concl.12–14). Using these privileges, he has regaled the company with earthy tales including the judge's wife and the lusty pirate (II.10), the simple girl and the lusty hermit (III.10), and a bisexual romp from Apuleius (V.10). Can he rise to the challenge and cap the elegant witticisms of the Sixth Day? And will he manage to keep it clean? (Yes: his tale will focus on religion, money, cookery, and trickery, with sex taking a back seat.)

As things turn out, Dioneo's role will prove to be pivotal for the wider *Decameron*. In the Conclusion to Day Six, speaking as the incoming "king" of the storytelling group, Dioneo will pick up the topics that disrupted the Sixth Day's Introduction – an indecent squabble between servants who have staged "a brief eruption from the kitchens below" (Milner, "Boccaccio's *Decameron*" 89) – to launch a new line of tales concerning deception and trickery between spouses, dominating the Seventh and Eighth Days. He will defend the propriety of his choice by several arguments, including the sorry state of the world and, crucially, the distinction between word and deed (VI.Concl.8–12). That same overarching theme of trickery (combined with the motif of servants as embodiments of the lower life) is used within the Cipolla story, pitted against the Sixth Day's main theme of quick-tongued wit: Dioneo's tale will in fact portray a clever trick (*beffa*) eclipsed and obliterated by a monstrously expanded display of verbal wit (the *motto* theme) unfurled by the story's clerical hero.

And so we begin. First comes the story's rubric, which immediately reveals that Cipolla promises to display the Angel Gabriel's feather, while cannily concealing the fact that this feather belongs to a parrot.[10] The text starts with a brief flurry of praise for the previous tale, which Dioneo silences. He promises that today he will break his habit of departing from the set theme. Complimenting the previous narrators, he sets out his own plot: a friar's quick wit will nullify a trick played on him by two young men. Nor should it weigh upon the ladies if he stretches himself a little in the telling, in order to tell the whole story properly, given that the sun is still high in the sky.

10 We'll learn this detail much later, at VI.10.26.

"Nè vi dovrà esser grave" (VI.10.4) can be glossed simply as "it shouldn't annoy you," but for present purposes I have deliberately rendered "grave" in terms of weight, with a sexual connotation, as Boccaccio will use that image in his authorial defence of the whole book (Author's Conclusion, 22–3), and as Dioneo himself used it in the story of the abbot and the monk (I.4.1, 18). By alluding to the time available, he implicitly reproves the brevity of the preceding stories, and hints that he may redress the deficient length of the Sixth Day.

So far, so normal: the prevailing pattern of Decameronian storytelling, with its preparatory scene-setting or theorizing, is being followed, acknowledging the thematic continuity of the book, the presence of an audience, and the applicability of stories to wider social values, as well as hinting at the basic opposition that will power the *novella*. All of which leads into the initial situation that the central action of the story will transform.[11]

The first word of the real beginning is "Certaldo." Geography, real and imaginary, will be crucial to this tale, and Certaldo is the author's hometown. Disappointingly, perhaps, we are still confined to Tuscany. As the story unfolds, we'll discover that the town is largely populated (like so many writers' hometowns) by ignorant yokels. One may even suspect some authorial irony in the narrator's suggestion (VI.10.5) that his listeners have perhaps heard of the place, and his claim that it was once inhabited by wealthy and noble men. Into this setting he parachutes a predatory travelling preacher, Frate Cipolla ("Friar Onion"), of the Order of St Anthony, who comes once yearly to gather "le limosine fatte loro dagli sciocchi" [VI.10.6; the alms given by fools], as St Anthony is known as a protector of livestock.[12] The name and order are emblematic: Certaldo was famous for its onions, while the order was widely regarded as corrupt and – more to the point – had been denounced for fraudulent sermonizing by Dante, using imagery of pigs and fat: "Di questo ingrassa il porco sant'Antonio, / e altri assai che sono ancor più porci" [*Par.* 29.124–5; Pigs of Saint Anthony grow fat on these – / and many others, too, still bigger pigs].[13] The friar's

11 The terms "basic opposition" and "initial situation" are borrowed from Cottino-Jones, "Observations on the Structure."

12 The Order is named not for St Anthony of Padua (a Franciscan) but for the desert father St Anthony the Great, whose iconography included a pig.

13 For Dante's *Paradiso*, I have used the edition and translation by Kirkpatrick. This passage stuck in Boccaccio's mind; another quotation from *Paradiso* 29 surfaces at *Decameron* VI.10.39.

motivation for visiting Certaldo is also stated in "foodie" terms: "per ciò che buona pastura vi trovava" [VI.10.6; because it was such good grazing ground], as Musa and Bondanella aptly translate (109). Pasture for sheep to graze is exactly the image that Dante had used to express what a proper preacher should give his congregation, whereas the prating of the friars leaves the faithful (whom Dante characterizes as "pecorelle" [little sheep]) "pasciute di vento" [fed on wind] rather than wholesome food (*Par.* 29.107). Frate Cipolla seeks not to provide good grazing for others, but to snaffle it himself. His values are animal, not spiritual. Money is metaphorically edible.

There follows (VI.10.7) a physical description of the friar (small, red-haired, cheery), and a sketch of his character (good company, quick-tongued, pseudo-erudite, extravagantly eloquent, a supreme networker). His eloquence is not exemplified, but we are told that his excellent off-the-cuff speech-making would make him sound, to the uninitiated, like Cicero or Quintilian.

Next, the timescale narrows, signalling a move towards the "inciting incident."[14] Cipolla is making his regular August visit (the date will prove doubly significant) to Certaldo. Celebrating Sunday mass for the villagers, he interrupts the service to advertise his forthcoming show:

> Signori e donne, come voi sapete, vostra usanza è di mandare ogni anno a' poveri del baron messer Santo Antonio del vostro grano e delle vostre biade, chi poco e chi assai, secondo il podere e la divozion sua, acciò che il beato santo Antonio vi sia guardia de' buoi e degli asini e de' porci e delle pecore vostre; e oltre a ciò solete pagare, e spezialmente quegli che alla nostra compagnia scritti sono, quel poco debito che ogni anno si paga una volta. Alle quali cose ricogliere io sono dal mio maggiore, cioè da messer l'abate, stato mandato, e per ciò, con la benedizion di Dio, dopo nona, quando udirete sonare le campanelle, verrete qui di fuori della chiesa là dove io al modo usato vi farò la predicazione, e bascerete la croce; e oltre a ciò, per ciò che divotissimi tutti vi conosco del barone messer santo Antonio, di spezial grazia vi mostrerò una santissima e bella reliquia, la quale io medesimo già recai dalle sante terre d'oltremare: e questa è una delle penne dell'agnol Gabriello, la quale nella camera della Vergine Maria rimase quando egli la venne ad annunziare in Nazarette. (VI.10.9–11)

14 The "inciting incident" is an element from McKee 181–207. Its function is to disrupt an existing balance and propel a new story. McKee's blueprint fits neatly with Cottino-Jones's views on the structure of the *Decameron novella*, cited above (note 11).

[Gentlemen and ladies, it is, as you know, your custom to send every year to the poor of our patron the Baron St Anthony some of your corn and your oats. One person gives a little, another gives a lot, according to his means and his devoutness, so that the blessed St Anthony may keep watch over your cows and your asses and your pigs and your sheep. Besides this you always pay – especially those of you that are members of our confraternity – that small subscription which is payable once a year. To collect these sums I have been sent here by my superior – I mean by my Lord Abbot; and so, with the blessing of God, you must come here in the afternoon, when you hear the bells ring, and gather outside the church, where I will preach you a sermon in the usual fashion, and you will kiss the cross. Moreover, as I know you all to be great devotees of our lord St Anthony, as a special favour I am going to show you a very holy and precious relic, which I myself brought back long ago from the Holy Land beyond the seas. This relic is one of the Angel Gabriel's feathers, which were left behind in the Virgin Mary's bedroom when he came to her in Nazareth for the Annunciation.] (452)[15]

Coming from Cipolla, whose prodigious speech-making powers have been proclaimed, this announcement is frankly disappointing – although wide-awake readers may possibly recall the Annunciation parody from the tale of Frate Alberto (IV.2). Cipolla insists on the tedious regularity and legitimacy of his customary mission: "vostra usanza è" [it is your custom] … "ogni anno" [every year] … "solete pagare" [you always pay] … "io sono stato mandato" [I have been sent] … "al modo usato" [in the usual fashion]. What could be more normal, apart from his choice of relic? And even that does not strike such a strange note: miracles and wonders are the everyday stock of medieval religion.

Normality is about to be breached, however, as the church congregation includes "due giovani astuti molto, chiamato l'uno Giovanni della Bragoniera e l'altro Biagio Pizzini" [VI.10.13; two very sharp young men, one called Giovanni della Bragoniera and the other Biagio Pizzini]. Amused by the friar's outlandish relic, they hatch a cunning plan. While Cipolla is out to lunch, Biagio will distract his servant and Giovanni will steal the feather, just to see what the friar will say when he finds it gone. (The feather comes from a parrot's tail, but we don't know that yet, so I will refrain from revealing it.)

15 All references to the text of the *Decameron* are from Vittore Branca's 1992 reprint of his 1980 edition. Uncredited translations are taken from my own 2004 translation of the *Decameron*, which is based on John Payne's 1886 translation.

Historically, the Bragoniera and Pizzini were families living in Certaldo.[16] Structurally, the names are superfluous, and interchangeable. These are two wily lads: that's all we need to know. In a "serious" modern novel they would lack consistency, but they fit nicely in the *Decameron*, where characters "are described inasmuch as their specific characteristics are functionally involved with the actions they will be performing" (Cottino-Jones, "Observations" 386). Their essential feature is simply their number: they supply the classic motif of "due giovani" deciding to play some sort of trick ("beffa") on Cipolla.[17]

Although the Sixth Day has hitherto confined itself to clever speech, this final story will combine two distinct forms of humour that animate the *Decameron*: the verbal and the physical, the *motto* and the *beffa* (witty saying, practical joke), both essential manifestations of that variegated intelligence which has been seen as one of the guiding values of the book.[18] Consistently with the general theme of the day, the *motto* will emerge triumphant – and what a *motto*!

The *beffa* conceived by Giovanni and Biagio proceeds as planned, except that there is no need to distract the friar's servant, who is perfectly capable of distracting himself.

Here comes that great Caliban figure, Guccio Imbratta, Frate Cipolla's servant. Monstrously fat, ugly, and greasy, Guccio is a compendium of basic urges, and on this Sunday morning he has spotted a suitable target for his attentions, in the person of Nuta, the hideously carnal kitchen maid in the inn where his master is lodging. So Guccio swoops down to the kitchen and sits by the fire (although this is August, as the narrator points out), and starts to boast (and presumably roast).[19]

Unlike the "due giovani," this essential ancillary character is presented as a sort of rhetorical joint venture between Dioneo the narrator and Cipolla the protagonist. From the narrator we learn of Guccio's three aliases – Balena, Imbratta, Porco – which call forth a profusion of

16 See Branca's note in Boccaccio, *Decameron* [1992] 762n8.

17 See Ó Cuilleanáin, *Religion and the Clergy* 190, for exponents of the "due giovani" motif in nine other tales of trickery from the *Decameron*.

18 See, for example, McWilliam's remarks in his introduction to Boccaccio, *Decameron* [1995] cix–cxiv. On some vital differences between *motto* and *beffa*, see Fontes.

19 These characters' names have grotesque associations in the *Decameron*: Branca points out (Boccaccio, *Decameron* [1992] 763n5) that Guccio (Arriguccio) previously appeared as a gravedigger in the tragic tale of Simona and Pasquino (IV.7.24). Nuto and Nuta (Benvenuto/Benvenuta) are names associated with degraded and indigent peasant life (III.1.7; VIII.2.40).

responses from translators,[20] but then Cipolla jumps in with his justly celebrated catalogue of his servant's failings, laid out in rhythmic triads:

> Il fante mio ha in sé nove cose tali che, se qualunque è l'una di quelle fosse in Salamone o in Aristotile o in Seneca, avrebbe forza di guastare ogni lor vertú, ogni lor senno, ogni lor santità. Pensate adunque che uom dee essere egli, nel quale né vertú né senno né santità alcuna è, avendone nove! (VI.10.16)
>
> [My servant's got nine habits so bad that if just one of them were found in Solomon or Aristotle or Seneca, it would be enough to ruin all their worth, all their wit, all their sanctity. Think, then, what a man this must be, in whom there is neither worth nor wit nor sanctity, but he has all nine of them!]

Asked to elaborate (and one presumes that his verbal solos are well known to "la sua brigata" – his cronies[21] – who may or may not include Giovanni and Biagio), Cipolla continues to invade the narrator's space as he reprises his oft-recited description:

> Dirolvi: egli è tardo, sugliardo e bugiardo; negligente, disubidente e maldicente; trascutato, smemorato e scostumato; senza che egli ha alcune altre teccherelle con queste, che si taccion per lo migliore. (VI.10.17)

Hainsworth's dactylic translation captures the energy: "He's sluggish and sloppy and lying, he's feckless, malicious and trying, and he's dopey and loutish and mentally dying. That's forgetting a few other blemishes better not mentioned" (*Tales from the Decameron* 192).[22] Cipolla's performance tells us that in this particular tale, rhythm and cadence may trump semantic meaning. He continues more conversationally, laying out some necessary plot points, particularly Guccio's susceptibility to womankind:

> E quel che sommamente è da rider de' fatti suoi è che egli in ogni luogo vuol pigliar moglie e tor casa a pigione; e avendo la barba grande e nera

20 Rebhorn (Boccaccio, *Decameron* [2013] 504) offers Whale, Slob, Pig. Peter Hainsworth calls him Gucky Whaleblubber, Mucky Gucky, Guck the Pig: Giovanni Boccaccio (Boccaccio, *Tales from the Decameron* 192). For Guido Waldman he is The Whale, Porky, Mucky Pup (Boccaccio, *Decameron* [1993] 406).

21 The *brigata* or micro-society is the group that embodies civilized living in the *Decameron*, so "cronies" may be too disrespectful a translation for Cipolla's merry companions. Or not.

22 For other fine translations of this passage by John Florio (possibly), and by J.G. Nichols, see Ó Cuilleanáin, "Translating Boccaccio" 215.

> e unta, gli par sí forte esser bello e piacevole, che egli s'avisa che quante femine il veggano tutte di lui s'innamorino, e essendo lasciato, a tutte andrebbe dietro perdendo la coreggia. (VI.10.18)

> But what's most ridiculous about him is that wherever he goes he's always fixing to marry a wife and rent him a house, for despite his big black greasy beard, he thinks he's so desperately handsome and winning that he's convinced any female who sees him must instantly fall in love with him. If you let him, he'd run after them all till he lost track of his trousers.

In passages like these, Boccaccio's exuberant comic writing creates a powerful atmosphere of playfulness which is not just funny but also strategic, as it ties the verbal presentation of characters (with their richly allusive names and over-egged descriptions) into the extravagant verbal creativity of Cipolla's final speech. Profusion, rather than exact meaning, is the point. The translators underline this with their free colloquial responses to Boccaccio's text.

Guccio's greasy beard and indiscriminate tomcatting make a perfect narrative bridge to greasy smoky Nuta, whom we have yet to meet. As a book about the structures and mechanisms of human interaction, the *Decameron* often works on contrasting images. Binary oppositions, as already noted, form an essential part of this story. Guccio and Nuta are at the bottom of the seesaw.

So far, we've had two kinds of verbal performance from Cipolla: his pedestrian announcement hypnotically persuading those dumb villagers that giving him money is a regular, natural part of their year, and now these two outbursts of creative description, painting Guccio's character for his cronies and for us readers. The first of the two Guccio descriptions, citing Solomon, Aristotle, and Seneca, harks back to his own associations with Cicero and Quintilian, while both descriptions echo the overlapping triads associated with his servant's three alternative names. In his great final speech we will see Cipolla's ability to make his genial rhythmic rhetoric work also on the dull audience that he has previously lined up. Savvy and stupid will be equally satisfied.

As the story is designed as a crescendo of rhetorical performances, it made strategic sense to start Cipolla off at a modest scale of eloquence and then ramp up the level of bombast. As the narrator, Dioneo, steps back in to provide the next description, he seems already to have been infected by Cipolla's verbal exuberance:

> A costui, lasciandolo all'albergo, aveva frate Cipolla comandato che ben guardasse che alcuna persona non toccasse le cose sue, e spezialmente le

sue bisacce, per ciò che in quelle erano le cose sacre. Ma Guccio Imbratta, il quale era piú vago di stare in cucina che sopra i verdi rami l'usignuolo, e massimamente se fante vi sentiva niuna, avendone in quella dell'oste una veduta, grassa e grossa e piccola e mal fatta, con un paio di poppe che parean due ceston da letame e con un viso che parea de' Baronci, tutta sudata, unta e affumicata, non altramenti che si gitti l'avoltoio alla carogna, lasciata la camera di frate Cipolla aperta e tutte le sue cose in abbandono, là si calò. (VI.10.20–1)

[Fra Cipolla, on leaving Guccio at the inn, had ordered him to take good care that nobody touched his gear, and especially his saddlebag, which contained the sacred things. But Guccio loved being in kitchens more than nightingales love perching on green boughs – especially if he knew there was some serving-wench there, and he had seen in the kitchen of the inn a gross fat cookmaid, low-sized and shapeless, with a pair of tits like two baskets of manure and a face like one of the Baronci clan, all sweaty and greasy and smoky. So he left Fra Cipolla's chamber and all his gear to look after themselves, and swooped down on the kitchen like a vulture landing on a fresh carcass.]

Again we note some thematic and narrative bridges. The images of Guccio as both nightingale and vulture ("usignuolo," "avoltoio") link him to the angel-parrot of Cipolla's promised relic (although we still haven't heard about that parrot). The omnivorous range of Guccio's repertoire of associations (whale, filth, pig, nightingale, vulture), conveyed through his protean nicknames, will link to the extravagant variety of Cipolla's imagined relics. In another intertextual twist, the nightingale in the green branches is a sly reminder of the "nightingale" that performed so nicely on Caterina's balcony, one hot summer night (V.4.29–30), but also, more significantly, it's an ironic *hommage* to Guido Guinizzelli's refined celebration of noble love in his canzone, "Al cor gentil reimpara sempre amore, / come l'ausello in selva a la verdura" [ll. 1–2; Love always makes its way to the noble heart, as the bird in the woods makes its way to the green branches].[23]

Nuta's sweat, grease, and smoke, suggestive of cured meat, link her thematically back to Guccio's greasy beard, and forward to Cipolla's final, somewhat tasteless, revelation of the holy coals of St Lawrence, doused by the body fluids of the roasted saint (VI.10.51). But Nuta is an incidental character.

---

23 For the text of Guinizzelli's *canzone*, I have used the edition in Contini's *Poeti del duecento* 2:460–4.

As he sits by the fire, Guccio wears "un suo cappuccio sopra il quale era tanto untume, che avrebbe condito il calderon d'Altopascio" – a hood of sorts, smeared with enough grease to season the great cauldron of Altopascio (VI.10.23) – yet another culinary reference, Altopascio being a town near Lucca where the monks make soup for the poor twice weekly; helpfully, its name recalls the verb "pascere" (to feed) and "pastura," which we saw earlier.[24] His torn, patched doublet is "glazed with filth around the neck and under the armpits" (VI.10.23; Boccaccio, *Decameron*, trans. Rebhorn, 505),[25] so this garment too could presumably be pressed into service for soup. And the manure baskets (par. 21; "due ceston da letame") to which Nuta's bosom is ungallantly compared move us even further into the processes of food consumption and digestion. Rural love, among the poor, comes down to grease and dung.

Guccio's filthy doublet, we learn, is spotted with "piú macchie e di piú colori che mai drappi fossero tartereschi o indiani" [VI.10.23; more multicoloured splotches than you'd see on the embroidered cloths of Tartary or India] – directly echoing Dante's description of Gerione, that "filthy image of fraud" (*Inf.* 17.7; "sozza imagine di froda"), who flew the explorers down to Malebolge (where images of cooking and sewage also abound).[26] Like the previously mentioned echoes of *Paradiso* 29, this is a creative endorsement of Dante's view: Guccio is indeed a "sozza imagine."[27]

His speeches to Nuta (VI.10.22) are not presented directly, but Dioneo's summary includes some phrases that sound like verbatim quotations – for example, "de' fiorini piú di millantanove" [squillions in the bank] – channelling his babbling tones as he assures her of his

24 See Branca's note in Boccaccio, *Decameron* [1992] 765n8. See also *Paradiso* 29.107 and *Decameron* VI.10.6. Note that the hoods of preaching friars are nests for devils in *Paradiso* 29.118.

25 This is Rebhorn's translation of "un suo farsetto rotto e ripezzato e intorno al collo e sotto le ditella smaltato di sucidume."

26 See Boccaccio, *Decameron* [1992] 766n1. See also *Inf.* 17.7 and 16ff; 18.112–14; and 21.55–7.

27 Agreement and admiration do not preclude parody, either of Guinizzelli or of Dante. Gerione's spiritual filthiness is rather magnificent; Guccio's grime is not. Likewise Nuta, all "grassa e grossa," may look like the Baronci (VI.6.13–14), whom Tateo saw as Michele Scalza's joking adoption of Dante's conviction (*Convivio* IV, Canzone, ll. 65–70) that antiquity of lineage confers equal nobility on all. Nuta's squat fleshy rotundities are not thereby ennobled, despite Ghismonda's ultra-serious arguments (IV.1.39) about our communal descent from the same ancestral "massa di carne" (literally "stock of flesh"). Literary allegiance allows for contrary creations deriving from the same source. See Tateo 162–3.

wealth, standing, and intentions. He speaks grandly, like the Lord of Châtillon ("siri di Ciastiglione"), but his bluster is mere wind and (unlike Cipolla's) comes to nothing.

More stage business follows, performed without directly recorded speech (VI.10.25–9). Guccio being otherwise engaged, Giovanni and Biagio enter Cipolla's bedroom unopposed, and find the friar's bag containing a parrot feather (at last we learn its provenance), which they correctly identify as Cipolla's fake relic of the Angel Gabriel. At that time, the soft refinements of Egypt had not yet made much headway against the simple lifestyle of Tuscan peasants – and here Dioneo primly laments the decadence of Italy today– so there is no fear the stout peasants of Certaldo will know anything of parrots. Removing the feather, the two young men gratuitously replace it with some lumps of coal, and leave the inn, waiting expectantly to see what Cipolla will say.

This, then, is Cipolla's challenge. Unlike other Sixth Day protagonists, he is not responding to a story, a quip, or an accusation. His words will be deployed against a physical trick: *motto* versus *beffa*.

Meanwhile, news of the great relic has spread. Cipolla has lunch and a siesta. Waking to find that a capacity crowd has gathered in the citadel to see the feather, he sends a message to Guccio to come up to the top of the town with bags and bells. With an effort ("con fatica"), Guccio uproots himself from the kitchen, and from Nuta – both attractions being given equal mention.[28] Painfully bloated from drinking too much water, he climbs the main street with slow steps ("con lento passo"), gasping for breath ("ansando") and on Cipolla's instructions starts ringing the bell loudly, at the church door.

The loudness ("forte incominciò le campanelle a sonare") may be just another index of Guccio's endearing enthusiasm, but why the references to effort, slowness, wheeziness, bloating? The answer again lies in Dante. Physically, Guccio embodies the ills of fleshly living at ground level, far from the sphere of angels or parrots, but, in literary terms, this description echoes an image from the depths of Dante's Malebolge, where Mastro Adamo, forger of florins, bloated with dropsy, describes his longing for fresh water and confesses his sin (*Inf.* 30.49–129). Injury and disease are among the punishments there, and Guccio's physical condition here suggests a similar link (poetic, cultural, not logical) between bad morals and bad health. And all this time, Guccio has not been permitted to voice a single phrase of Boccaccio's text.

---

28 See VI.10.32. Agricultural meanings for *divellere* include *uproot, pull up, eradicate,* and Guccio's rooted existence may be almost as vegetable as it is animal.

Yet more stage business, this time from Cipolla: After some initial preaching, with "many words" (unreported) to set the scene, he solemnly recites the *Confiteor* (unquoted), has two torches lit, bares his head by drawing back his hood (another chance to mention the "cappuccio," which will be smuggled in again at VI.10.51), gently unwinds the cloths that wrap the relic-box, speaks more words (unspecified) in praise of the Angel and the relic. Only then does he open the box, and see the coals.

At this moment of truth, the reader gets a glimpse into Cipolla's mind. It is a calculating, but surprisingly generous and forgiving mind. Seeing the box full of coals,

> non sospicò che ciò Guccio Balena gli avesse fatto, per ciò che nol conosceva da tanto, né il maladisse del male aver guardato che altri ciò non facesse, ma bestemmiò tacitamente sé, che a lui la guardia delle sue cose aveva commessa, conoscendol, come faceva, negligente, disubidente, trascurato e smemorato. Ma non per tanto, senza mutar colore, alzato il viso e le mani al cielo, disse sí che da tutti fu udito: "O Idio, lodata sia sempre la tua potenzia!" (VI.10.35–6)
>
> [he did not suspect Guccio Balena of having played him this trick, as he knew he would not have been clever enough; nor did he curse him for having kept a careless watch against others doing it; but silently he cursed himself for having entrusted his things to the care of Guccio, knowing, as he did, how lawless and uncouth and gawky and awkward he was. Nevertheless, without changing colour, he raised his eyes and hands to heaven and said so that everyone could hear him: "O God, praised be your power for ever!"]

These are the first directly quoted words we have heard since Cipolla's description of Guccio's habits, several pages previously (VI.10.19). Cipolla shuts the box, turns to the people. He has not missed a beat. His exclamation to God and his ancillary gestures (raising, shutting, turning) follow seamlessly from the seven earlier stages of his theatrical buildup. His inner reflections, which have taken no time at all, lead him to launch into the torrential speech through which he recreates the pedigree and provenance of those lumps of coal as an authentic relic, one of many acquired on his mythical journey in the days of his youth through Eastern parts where the sun does shine – a relic, in truth, no less credible than the one originally promised.

Space does not allow a full examination of Cipolla's great speech; my concern has been to highlight the sequence of moves that shape the story as a whole. Fine analyses of the speech, its purposes, contents, techniques, and contexts, can be found,[29] while numerous scholarly annotations explicate the complicated puns whereby Cipolla, playing with place names, rattles off Florentine districts that sound like far-flung places, thus entertaining the two feather-snatchers with a Joycean circuit of Florence while simultaneously hornswoggling the credulous folk of Certaldo with delusions of long-distance travel.

English translations, striving to match his unchained virtuosity, are particularly illuminating about Cipolla's creativity and his audience control techniques.[30] One example: his invented "Patriarch of Jerusalem," "Nonmibiasmete Sevoipiace" (VI.10.43), is translated literally by Musa and Bondanella as "Blamemenot Ifyouplease." Rebhorn (508) and Nichols almost agree on "Dontblameme Ifyouplease," while McWilliam offers "Besokindas Tocursemenot" (475). But Hainsworth's solution, "Lord High Shurrup Orelse" (196), although not quite literal, is doubly successful in capturing different desiderata for the Patriarch's English name: mispronounceable enough to slip by the congregation, but sharp enough to warn Giovanni and Biagio not to betray him at this delicate stage of the proceedings.[31] And it reminds us that diverse elements in Cipolla's monologue are deliberately aimed at distinct segments of his audience.[32]

---

29 See especially Usher, "Frate Cipolla's 'Ars Praedicandi.'"

30 McWilliam's *Decameron* provides copious notes on Cipolla's allusions (474–6 and 843–5). Hainsworth and Rebhorn helpfully explain some special effects requiring translation.

31 Such a warning is appropriate: in the Second Day, the jester and contortionist Martellino, while perpetrating a religious fraud, was betrayed by the laughter of a fellow-Florentine who suddenly recognized him (II.1.14); he then was beaten, tortured, and very nearly killed. At the end of Cipolla's tale, we'll learn that Giovanni and Biagio "avevan tanto riso che eran creduti smascellare" [VI.10.55; had laughed so hard they thought their jaws would break: Boccaccio, *Decameron* (2013) 510]. When exactly did this laughter happen? Pluperfect laughter is recurrent in the *Decameron*. The ladies of the *cornice* are sometimes recorded as *having* laughed (e.g., III.Concl.1; IV.Concl.1; IX.Concl.1; etc.), although that laughter is never noted while a tale is being told. An ill-timed guffaw from Giovanni and Biagio, during Cipolla's sermon, could represent a clear and present danger to the preacher. So: "shut up or else!"

32 The point (necessarily tentative) is prompted by Hainsworth's translation, combined with Francesco Ciabattoni's intriguing suggestion that Cipolla is surreptitiously rebuking his negligent servant, when he says he would never entrust his relics to anyone ("Boccaccio's Miraculous Art" 169). This "ironic wink," Ciabattoni suggests, is addressed both to Guccio and to the pranksters. Another "wink," Cipolla's reference (VI.10.39) to friars living in "Menzogna" – "Liarland," says McWilliam (474) – and spending money "senza conio," echoes Dante's denunciation of St Anthony's friars, who pay their way in "moneta senza conio" [*Par.* 29.126; currency that bears no stamp]. Who's winking at whom, here? Giovanni and Biagio don't look like Dante readers. This has to be Boccaccio the author winking at you the reader.

His essential trick is to situate his two fake relics – the feather which was promised, the coals which were given – amid a host of equally unlikely relics that he saw in the (fictitious) collection of the Patriarch of Jerusalem, including the Holy Ghost's finger, a fingernail from one of the Cherubim, and some rays of the star that appeared to the Three Wise Men. He continues:

> E per ciò che io liberamente gli feci copia delle piagge di Monte Morello in volgare e d'alquanti capitoli del Caprezio, li quali egli lungamente era andati cercando, mi fece egli partefice delle sue sante reliquie: e donommi uno de' denti della santa Croce, e in una ampolletta alquanto del suono delle campane del tempio di Salomone e la penna dell'agnol Gabriello, della quale già detto v'ho, e l'un de' zoccoli di san Gherardo da Villamagna (il quale io, non ha molto, a Firenze donai a Gherardo di Bonsi, il quale in lui ha grandissima divozione) e diedemi de' carboni, co' quali fu il beatissimo martire san Lorenzo arrostito; le quali cose io tutte di qua con meco divotamente le recai, e holle tutte. (VI.10.46–7)

> [And as I made him a free gift of the Black Mountain Slopes, translated into the vulgar tongue, not to mention some chapters of the Book of Billygoat which he had long been wishing to collect, he gave me a share in his holy relics. He presented me with some of the teeth of Holy Cross, and a sample of the sound of the bells of Solomon's Temple in a bottle, and the feather of the Angel Gabriel which I already mentioned to you, and one of the clogs of St Gherardo da Villamagna – which not long ago in Florence I gave to Gherardo di Bonsi, who has a particular devotion to that saint – and he also gave me some of the coals over which the most blessed martyr St Lawrence was roasted. All of these things I devoutly brought home with me and I still have them all.]

The coals, listed last, are more feasible than some of these other outlandish relics. St Lawrence really did get roasted; there could be physical leftovers. Cipolla still has to link the coals to his present visit, which he does by explaining that (a) the feather and coals are kept in similar boxes, (b) he mixed up the two boxes, (c) this was the will of God, because (d) St Lawrence's feast day is 10 August – two days hence. Now the full significance of the date swims into focus, and we finally grasp Cipolla's triumphant leap of association: Coal → Lawrence → August – QED! And if we thought Guccio's proximity to the fire in Nuta's kitchen was just about sweat and body odour, we now know it as a foretaste of Laurentian cookery.

Scattered throughout the sermon are snippets of pseudo-scientific information to edify the peasants. These are another sideways nod to

Dante, who had condemned intellectual showmanship in sermons, specifically mentioning "il porco sant'Antonio," meaning Cipolla's order.[33] The "science" is intercut with veiled jokes about sodomy to amuse his two young friends.[34] Now this ability to speak simultaneously to different audience groups, the educated and the ignorant, is an essential skill for the effective preacher. The Augustinian Alexander of Ashby had recommended that a preacher should mix profound allegories for his erudite hearers with lighter tales for the simpler sort: there has be something for everyone.[35] Cipolla, in his own perverse way, is following that approach. And he does know his audience.[36]

Some structural points enhance the sermon's claims to realism. Firstly, Cipolla begins not from the feather but from a tale of his own youthful travels; his complex progression from the familiar to the exotic creates a sort of personal guarantee while, crucially, buying him time to think through the tricky question of the relic's authenticity. The recital of his European and Levantine travels may thus be more extravagantly surreal than he had planned, given that his first speech to the peasants (VI.10.9–11) had stressed the powers of St Anthony rather than the extraordinary nature of the relic.

Secondly, he launches into this account of his travels without any involuntary hesitation. We learn of one thought that flashed through his mind – "could Guccio have done this?" – but there's no hint of the other obvious question: "what now?" This controlled transition makes his speech all the more convincing to the listeners, all the more creative to the readers as it grows out of itself through associations of sound and sense and wordplay. Against this, we note that he had previously (VI.10.11) promised a relic brought back from "oltre mare" [overseas],

33 In *Paradiso* 29.85–105, Dante attacks the use of pseudo-scientific speculation from the pulpit where "inventions" and "fables" displace the humble preaching of Gospel truths, the propagation of which has cost so much blood (presumably the blood of the martyrs as well as of Christ). In his *Corbaccio*, Boccaccio offers a comparable rant (*Corbaccio* [1993] 30–1).

34 The sodomy jokes (Monte Morello, Caprezio, zoccoli etc.) are explained by McWilliam, Hainsworth, Rebhorn, and Nichols in their notes.

35 See Kemmler 71; and Murphy 313.

36 Writing of Madonna Filippa's "legal" defence (VI.7), Roberta Morosini invokes the distinction between proving and arguing: proof envisages a universal listener representing *homo sapiens*, while argumentation addresses a real audience, defined by the circumstances of the communication. See Morosini, "Bone eloquence" 2. The standing of relics is inextricably bound up with their provenance, discovery, and effects; Cipolla's personal tale of discovery and his assurances regarding the relics' efficacy (VI.10.48) combine to parody proof while enacting persuasion.

implying that some kind of travelogue would be included in the sermon; therefore his glorious improvisation may be partly an adaptation of existing memes.

Several other strands might have been worth developing at this point – the treatment of body parts; the confusion of solids, liquids, sounds, and abstract qualities; the techniques of comic inversion whereby expectation and logic are subverted. Instead I will throw down some places, names, and entities (real and imagined) scattered not just through the final speech but throughout the story.

Places: Certaldo Valdelsa Toscana Nazarette Altopascio Ciastiglione Egitto Toscana Vinegia Porcellana Borgo de' Greci Garbo Baldacca Parione Sardigna Braccio di San Giorgio Truffia Buffia Menzogna Abruzzi India Pastinaca Ierusalem San Lorenzo Monte Morello Firenze …

People or entities: Santo Antonio Cipolla Tulio Quintiliano Gabriello Vergine Maria Giovanni Biagio Guccio Balena Guccio Imbratta Guccio Porco Lippo Topo Salamone Aristotile Seneca Baronci Nuta Idio Maso del Saggio Nonmibiasmete Sevoipiace Antonio Caprezio Santa Croce Spirito Santo San Francesco Gherubini Verbum Caro Salomone Gabriello Gherardo da Villamagna Gherardo di Bonsi Patriarca San Lorenzo Dio San Lorenzo …

No wonder the peasants are confused. Even the modern reader, propped up by footnotes, may struggle to sort out the barrage of references, some real, some coded, some invented, some ambivalent, some almost duplicated, some presumably misheard, some seemingly meaningless. The mutability of language swirls names and places into a litany of echoes: young Cipolla visits the mythical lands of Truffia and Buffia (VI.10.39), brings home a relic of Gherardo da Villamagna which he gives to Gherardo di Bonsi. These rapid-fire convergent-divergent pairs of names create confusion, and therefore mystery, which serves the preacher's purpose. Millicent Marcus draws particular attention to Cipolla's technique of reducing language to pure sound, with "Truffia" and "Buffia" featuring as "jabberwocky combinations of *trucco* and *beffa* which ricochet off each other like *abracadabra*" (*Allegory of Form* 70). Quite.

Although many exotic-sounding places (Porcellana, Vinegia, Borgo de' Greci, Garbo, Baldacca, Parione) have been shown to refer to parts of Florence,[37] the first literal reference to "Firenze" only comes in towards the end of the place names (VI.10.46). Whether or not Cipolla

37 See Boccaccio, *Decameron* [1992] 768–9n8.

comes from Florence, his duping of the rustics of Certaldo certainly embodies some core values of that great city. Within the *Decameron*, an ideal image of Florence may well be "la città dell'uomo armoniosa e razionale" [Ramat 9; the city of man, harmonious and rational].[38] A harsher aspect of that same civic identity is the disdain that citizens feel for rustic simpletons.[39] Might it therefore be significant that the name attached to the relic that finally wraps up Cipolla's puzzle, San Lorenzo, is also that of a church in Florence? As is Santa Croce, whose tooth figured in the relic collection? And Santo Spirito, almost named in "il dito dello Spirito Santo" (VI.10.45)? Should we imagine these too as hidden toponyms, Florentine allusions designed to be caught by that sophisticated duo, Giovanni and Biagio? Does Cipolla catch their eye as he calls out these words? Unanswerable questions, but they help us visualize an essential factor in all of this: Cipolla's hybrid audience, Boccaccio's uncertain readership.

Another key place, Rome, is not mentioned at all. Lawrence (patron saint of cooks) was a Roman martyr roasted alive by the Emperor Valerian. A humorous man, he asked his executioners to flip him over on the gridiron, as he was done enough on one side. Cipolla's graphic reference to the form of his martyrdom – "i carboni co' quali esso fu arrostito … i benedetti carboni spenti dall'omor di quel santissimo corpo" [VI.10.51; the coals over which he was roasted … the blessed coals that were doused by the bodily fluids of that most holy man] – risks reminding listeners of exactly where it took place. Isn't Cipolla skating on thin ice here? Surely the people of Certaldo would wonder how this quintessentially Roman relic could fetch up in Jerusalem?[40]

The point is, they don't. They're too stupid, too bounded by their humdrum existence. Never having been "away," unable to spot geographical or historical contradictions, they're dazzled by Cipolla's parade of real and fake place names. They have an existential need to believe. Also, they dimly recognize a religious genre in which the sequential naming of far-flung places creates a virtual sense of spatial ownership (this land is your land), just as the *Decameron* reader recognizes VI.10

38 Ramat argues that the storytellers' retreat from plague-stricken Florence is an attempt to reconstruct the city of man.

39 David Wallace mentions the "enduring rustic simplicity and credulity against which Florentine urbanity defines and exercises itself," referring to the arch-victim Calandrino, all of whose stories show his "strong impulse to leave the house and head for the countryside" (95).

40 Ditto the clogs of St Gherardo, from little Villamagna, near Florence (VI.10.46).

as another version of the "novelle 'di viaggio'" ["travelling" tales] that first appeared in the Second Day under the rubric of Fortune. Pegoretti brilliantly maps the maritime misadventures of Alatiel (II.7), the exile of the Count of Antwerp (II.8), and other tales, culminating in Cipolla's *itinerarium* to the Holy Land.[41] When it comes to creative travel writing, fake pilgrimage trumps real shipwreck, real exile.

The extravagant geography of the tale has reached a suitably comic conclusion. The Sixth Day, which began with a kitchen eruption (VI. Intro.4), is drawing towards its end in a welter of kitchen-centred imagery. The grease of Guccio's filthy clothes, in that intermediate scene with Nuta, has come home to roost among the coals drenched in the sweat of a roasted Roman.

The story ends with an outrageous extension of the joke: Cipolla marks his hearers' clothing with the coals, which he has now invested with a worthless fire insurance guarantee (VI.10.52–4), before meeting the two tricksters for a friendly reconciliation, involving the return of the stolen feather and mention of its equally profitable exposition next year in Certaldo. No po-faced coda explaining "the joke" is required.

Needless to say, Cipolla is one of the most widely discussed heroes in the *Decameron*, a master of language and narration comparable to his soulmate Ciappelletto (I.1). As Millicent Marcus observes, their two tales together constitute "a revelation of the storyteller's art at its most powerful and perverse" (*Allegory of Form* 66). This is achieved partly through the explicit separation of the tales' audiences into two main groups, the gullible populace versus the wised-up eavesdroppers; the latter already know the underlying facts of the case, and enjoy the narration as pure literary artifice.[42] We readers may hope to do the same, unless the protean changeability of narrative voices, and the babbling cascade of alternative facts, have managed to loosen our grip on reality.

---

41 See Pegoretti 85, 98, 102, and 113. On Boccaccio's geographical horizons, see Morosini, ed. *Boccaccio geografo*.

42 Franco Fido remarks on the two types of listener in *Decameron* I.1 and VI.10: "The second … hidden listener (the two Florentine brothers, the two pranksters who stole the parrot feather), recognizes the story as fiction, that is, as literature" ("Tale of Ser Ciappelletto" 72).

Bibliography

Primary Sources

Aberdeen Bestiary. Aberdeen University Library MS 24. http://abdn.ac.uk/bestiary [accessed 14 February 2021].

Alighieri, Dante. *Convivio*. Edited by Cesare Vasoli. In *Opere Minori*, vol.1, part 2, edited by Domenico De Robertis, Gianfranco Contini, and Cesare Vasoli. Milan and Naples: Ricciardi, 1979.

– *Il Convivio (The Banquet)*. Translated by Richard H. Lansing. Garland Library of Medieval Literature, Ser. BN, 1990. https://digitaldante.columbia.edu/text/library/the-convivio/ [accessed 14 February 2021].

– *Convivio*. Edited by F. Brambilla Ageno. 3 vols. Florence: Le Lettere, 1995.

– *De vulgari eloquentia*. Edited and translated by Stephen Botterill. Cambridge: Cambridge University Press, 1996.

– *The Divine Comedy of Dante Alighieri. Paradiso*. Translated by Allen Mandelbaum. New York: Bantam Books, 1984.

– *The Divine Comedy of Dante Alighieri. Volume I: Inferno*. Edited and translated by Robert M. Durling. Introduction and notes by Ronald L. Martinez and Robert M. Durling. Oxford: Oxford University Press, 1996.

– *The Divine Comedy (Inferno, Purgatorio, Paradiso)*. Translated by Robert Hollander and Jean Hollander. 3 vols. New York: Random House, 2002–7.

– *The Divine Comedy of Dante Alighieri. Volume 2: Purgatorio*. Translated by Robert M. Durling. Edited by Ronald L. Martinez and Robert M. Durling. Oxford: Oxford University Press, 2003.

– *The Divine Comedy 3: Paradiso*. Translated and edited by Robin Kirkpatrick. London: Penguin Books, 2007.

– *Opere. Volume primo. Rime, Vita nova, De vulgari eloquentia*. Milan: Mondadori, 2011.

– *La vita nuova*. Edited by Michele Barbi. Florence: Società Dantesca Italiana, 1960.

Ambrose of Milan. *Exameron*. In *Opera*. Edited by Carol Schenkl. CSEL 32.1. Vienna, 1897.

Andreas Capellanus. *Andrea Capellani regii Francorum De amore libri tres*. Edited by E. Trojel. Hanau: Libraria Ganiana, 1892.

– *The Art of Courtly Love*. Translated by John Jay Parry. New York: Columbia University Press, 1990.

Anthony of Padua. *Sermones dominicales et festivi*. Edited by Beniamino Costa et al. 3 vols. Padua: Centro studi antoniani: Edizioni Messaggero, 1979.

Gli antichi statuti di Quarrata. Edited by Maria Cristina Monti. Florence: Tipografia Nuova Castello, 1996.

Antologia della poesia italiana. Vol. I. Duecento–Trecento. Edited by Cesare Segre and Carlo Ossola. Turin: Einaudi-Gallimard, 1997.

Apuleius, *Metamorphoses*. Edited and translated by J. Arthur Hanson. 2 vols. Cambridge, MA: Harvard University Press, 1989–96.

Aristotle. *The Complete Works of Aristotle*. Edited by Jonathan Barnes. 2 vols. Princeton: Princeton University Press, 1984.

Augustine. *De doctrina christiana*. Edited by Joseph Martin. *CCSL* 32. Turnhout: Brepols, 1962.

– *The De Haeresibus of Saint Augustine: A Translation with an Introduction and Commentary*. Edited and translated by Rev. Liguori G. Müller, OFM. Washington, DC: Catholic University of America Press, 1956.

– *Enarrationes in Psalmos*. Edited by Eligius Dekkers and Johannes Fraipont. 3 vols. Turnout: Brepols, 1990.

– *In Iohannis evangelium tractatus CXXIV*. Edited by Radbodus Willems. Turnout: Brepols, 1990.

Avianus. *Fabulae Aviani*. In *Minor Latin Poets*, vol. 2, edited and translated by J. Wright Duff and Arnold M. Duff, 680–749. Cambridge, MA: Harvard University Press, 1934.

Bacon, Roger. *Roger Bacon and the Origins of Perspectiva in the Middle Ages: A Critical Edition and English Translation of Bacon's "Perspectiva" with Introduction and Notes*. Edited by David C. Lindberg. Oxford: Clarendon Press, 1996.

Il bestiario toscano. Edited by Milton Stahl Garver and Kenneth McKenzie. In "Il Bestiario toscano secondo la lezione dei codici di Parigi e di Roma." *Studi romanzi* 8 (1912): 1–100 (17–94).

Biblia Sacra Vulgata. Edited by Robert Weber and Roger Gryson. 5th ed. Stuttgart: Deutsche Bibelgesellschaft, 2007.

Boccaccio, Giovanni. *Boccaccio on Poetry*. Translated by Charles G. Osgood. New York: Liberal Arts Press, 1956.

– *Boccaccio's Expositions on Dante's* Comedy. Translated by Michael Papio. Toronto: University of Toronto Press, 2009.

– *Il Codice Chigiano L.V. 176 autografo di Giovanni Boccaccio*. Facsimile edition. Edited by Domenico De Robertis. Rome: Archivi, 1974.

– *Corbaccio*. Edited by Pier Giorgio Ricci. Turin: Einaudi, 1977.
– *The Corbaccio or the Labyrinth of Love*. Translated by Anthony K. Casell. 2nd ed., revised. Binghamton, NY: Medieval and Renaissance Texts and Studies, 1993.
– *Corbaccio*. Edited by Giorgio Padoan. In *Tutte le opere*, vol. 5, pt. 2. Milan: Mondadori, 1994.
– *The Decameron or Ten Days' Entertainment of Boccaccio*. London: Chatto & Windus, 1904.
– *The Decameron of Giovanni Boccaccio*. Translated by J.M. Rigg. London, 1921. *Decameron Web*. https://www.brown.edu/Departments/Italian_Studies/dweb/texts/DecIndex.php?lang=eng [accessed 14 February 2021].
– *The Decameron of Giovanni Boccaccio*. Translated by John Payne. New York: Random House, 1931.
– *The Decameron of Giovanni Boccaccio*. Translated by Richard Aldington. 2 vols. London: Elek Bestseller Library, 1959.
– *Decameron*. Edited by Vittore Branca. Edizione critica secondo l'autografo hamiltoniano. Florence: Accademia della Crusca, 1976.
– *Decameron*. Edited by Vittore Branca. In *Tutte le opere*, vol. 4. Milan: Mondadori, 1976.
– *The Decameron. A New Translation; 21 Novelle; Contemporary Reactions; Modern Criticism*. Selected, translated, and edited by Mark Musa and Peter E. Bondanella. New York: W.W. Norton, 1977.
– *Decameron*. Edited by Vittore Branca. Milan: Mondadori, 1985.
– *Decameron*. Edited by Vittore Branca. 2 vols. Turin: Einaudi, 1992.
– *The Decameron*. Translated by Guido Waldman, with introduction and notes by Jonathan Usher. Oxford: Oxford University Press, 1993.
– *The Decameron*. 2nd ed. Translated with an introduction and notes by G.H. McWilliam. London: Penguin, 1995.
– *Decameron: A New English Version by Cormac Ó Cuilleanáin Based on John Payne's 1886 Translation*. Ware, Herts.: Wordsworth Editions, 2004.
– *Decameron*. Translated by J.G. Nichols. Richmond, Surrey: Oneworld Classics, 2008.
– *Decameron*. Edited by Maurizio Fiorilla. Rome: Istituto della Enciclopedia Italiana, 2011.
– *Decameron*. Edited by Amedeo Quondam, Maurizio Fiorilla, and Giancarlo Alfano. Milan: BUR, 2013.
– *The Decameron*. Translated and with an introduction by Wayne A. Rebhorn. New York: W.W. Norton, 2013.
– *De Claris mulieribus, traduction anonyme en français Livre des femmes nobles et renommees*, BnF Ms.Fr. 598, fol. 100v. http://gallica.bnf.fr/ark:/12148/btv1b84521932/f210.item [accessed 14 February 2021].
– *Epistole e lettere*. Edited by Ginetta Auzzas. In *Tutte le opere*, vol. 5, pt. 1. Milan: Mondadori, 1992.

– *Esposizioni sopra la Comedia di Dante*. Edited by Giorgio Padoan. In *Tutte le opere*, vol. 6. Milan: Mondadori, 1965.
– *Famous Women* [*De mulieribus claris*]. Edited and translated by Virginia Brown. I Tatti Renaissance Library. Cambridge, MA: Harvard University Press, 2001.
– *Filostrato*. Edited by Vittore Branca. In *Tutte le Opere*, vol. 2. Milan: Mondadori, 1964.
– *Genealogia deorum gentilium*. Edited by Vittorio Zaccaria. In *Tutte le opere*, vols. 7–8. Milan: Mondadori, 1998.
– *Genealogy of the Pagan Gods*. Vol. 1: Books 1–V. Translated by Jon Solomon. I Tatti Renaissance Library. Cambridge, MA: Harvard University Press, 2011.
– *Livre que fist Jehan BOCACE de Certalde des cleres et nobles femmes, lequel il envoia à Audice de Accioroles de Florence, contesse de Haulteville*, ca. 1403, BnF Ms.Fr.12420, fol. 101v. http://gallica.bnf.fr/ark:/12148/btv1b10509080f/f210.image [accessed 14 February 2021].
– *The Story of Troilus as told by Benoît de Sainte-Maure, Giovanni Boccaccio, Geoffrey Chaucer, Robert Henryson*. Translated by R.K. Gordon. New York: E.P. Dutton and Co., 1964.
– *Tales from the Decameron*. Translated, introduced, and with notes by Peter Hainsworth. London: Penguin Books, 2015.
– *Teseida delle nozze d'Emilia*. Edited by Alberto Limentani. In *Tutte le Opere*, vol. 2. Milan: Mondadori, 1964.
– *Teseida delle nozze d'Emilia*. Edited by Edvige Agostinelli and William Coleman. Florence: SISMEL, 2015.
– *Tutte le opere di Giovanni Boccaccio*. Edited by Vittore Branca. 10 vols. Milan: Mondadori, 1964–98.
– *Lo Zibaldone Boccaccesco mediceo laurenziano plut. XXXI-8*. Florence: Olschki, 1915.
Bono Giamboni. *Il libro de' Vizî e delle Virtudi*. Edited by Cesare Segre. Turin: Einaudi, 1968.
Capponi, Gino. *Storia della Repubblica di Firenze*. 2nd ed. vol. 1. Florence: Barbera, 1876.
Cicero. *De oratore*. Translated by Edward W. Sutton and Harris Rackham. 2 vols. Cambridge, MA: Harvard University Press, 1948.
– *On the Republic. On the Laws* [*De republica. De legibus*]. Translated by Clinton W. Keyes. Cambridge, MA: Harvard University Press, 1928.
Codex Iustinianus. Vol. 2. Ed. Paul Kreuger. *Corpus iuris civilis*. Berlin: Weidmann, 1895.
Esopo toscano dei frati e dei mercanti trecenteschi. Edited by Vittore Branca. Venice: Marsilio, 1989.
Fabliaux du Moyen âge. Edited and translated by Jean Dufournet. Paris: Flammarion, 1998 [repr. 2014].

"Florilegium Casinense. Ex Codice XXIV: Hymni Sacri, Vitae Sanctorum, et alia." In *Bibliotheca Casinensis seu Codicum Manuscriptorum qui in tabulario Casinensi asservantur. Series per paginas singillatim enucleata notis characterum speciminibus ad unguem exemplatis aucta cura et studio Monachorum Ordinis S. Benedicti Abbatiae Montis Casini. Tomus Primus*, 235–83. Ex Typographia Casinensi, 1873.

Geoffrey of Vinsauf. *Poetria Nova*. Translated by Margaret F. Nims. Toronto: Pontifical Institute of Mediaeval Studies, 1967.

Gregory the Great. *Epistolarum libri XIV*. In *PL* 77, cols 431–1328. Paris, 1849.

– *Moralia in Iob*. Edited by Paolo Siniscalco. 3 vols. Rome: Città Nuova Editrice, 1992–7.

Guido da Pisa. *Expositiones et glose; Declaratio super "Comediam" Dantis*. Edited by Michele Rinaldi and Paola Locatin. Rome: Salerno, 2013.

Guinizzelli, Guido. *Rime*. In *Poeti del duecento*, edited by Gianfranco Contini, 2 vols, vol. 2, 450–84. Milan and Naples: Riccardo Ricciardi, 1960.

Hugh of St Victor. *De scripturis et scriptoribus sacris*. In *PL* 175, cols 9–28.

Humbert of Romans. *Liber de eruditione praedicatorum*. In Humbert of Romans, *De vita regulari*, edited by Joachim Berthier. 2 vols. Rome: Befani, 1888.

Isidore of Seville. *Etymologiae sive origines*. Edited by Wallace M. Lindsay. 2 vols. Oxford: Clarendon Press, 1911 [repr. 1989].

– *The Etymologies of Isidore of Seville*. Translated by Stephen A. Barney, W.J. Lewis, J.A. Beach, and Oliver Berghof. Cambridge: Cambridge University Press, 2006.

The Justinian Code. Edited by John W. Snyder. Kansan City, MO: Kansas City School of Law, 1949.

Latini, Brunetto. *I libri naturali del "Tesoro" emendati colla scorta de' codici, commentati e illustrati da Guido Battelli*. Florence: Successori Le Monnier, 1917.

– *La Rettorica*. Edited by Francesco Maggini. Florence: Le Monnier, 1968.

– *Tresor*. Edited by Pietro Beltrami et al. Turin: Einaudi, 2007.

Livy. *Ab urbe condita*. Vol. 1. Edited by Robert S. Conway and Carol F. Walters. Oxford: Clarendon Press, 1955.

Lucan. *The Civil War (Pharsalia)*. Edited by Jeffrey Henderson. Translated by James D. Duff. Cambridge, MA: Harvard University Press, 1928.

Macrobius. *Saturnalia*. Edited by Robert A. Kaster. Oxford: Clarendon Press, 2011.

Martial. *Epigrams*. Edited and translated by D.R. Shackleton Bailey. 3 vols. Cambridge, MA: Harvard University Press, 1993.

Matthew of Vendôme. *Ars versificatoria*. In *Opera*, vol. 3, edited by Franco Munari. Rome: Edizioni di storia e letteratura, 1977.

Nicholas of Autremont. *Exigit ordo executionis*. Edited by Reginald O'Donnell. *Mediaeval Studies* 1 (1939): 179–267.

Il Novellino. Edited by Alberto Conte. Rome: Salerno, 2001.
The Novellino or One Hundred Ancient Tales: An Edition and Translation Based on the 1525 Gualteruzzi Editio Princeps. Edited and translated by Joseph P. Consoli. New York: Garland Publishing, 1997.
Ovid. *Metamorphoses*. Vol. 1. Edited by G.P. Gould. Translated by Frank J. Miller. Loeb Classical Library. Cambridge, MA: Harvard University Press, 1984.
Peter Aureol. *Scriptum in libros sententiarum*. Edited by Eligius Buytaert. 2 vols. St Bonaventure: Franciscan Institute, 1952–6.
Peter of Limoges. *Tractatus moralis de oculo*. In *Johannis Pithsani archiepiscopi Canthuariensis ordinis fratrum minorum liber de oculo morali foeliciter incipit*. Augsburg: A. Sorg, 1475.
Petrarca, Francesco. *Petrarch's Lyric Poems. The Rime sparse and Other Lyrics*. Translated and edited by Robert M. Durling. Cambridge, MA: Harvard University Press, 1976.
– *Rerum memorandarum libri*. Edited by Giuseppe Billanovich. Edizione Nazionale delle Opere di Francesco Petrarca. Florence: Sansoni, 1943.
Pico della Mirandola. *On the Dignity of Man and Other Works*. Translated by C. Glen Wallis. Indianapolis: Bobbs-Merrill, 1965.
Pirovano, Donato. "Due novelle del Boccaccio (*Dec.* VI 9 e VII 7) tradotte in latino da Francesco Pandolfini." *Giornale Storico della Letteratura italiana* 175 (1998): 556–76.
Pliny, the Elder. *Historia naturalis Vol. IX*. Translated by H. Rackham. Cambridge, MA: Harvard University Press, 1938.
– *Naturalis historia*. 12 vols. London: Heinemann, 1938–63.
Quintilian. *Institutio Oratoria*. Vol.1. Translated by H.E. Butler. Cambridge, MA: Harvard University Press, 1920–2.
– *Institutio oratoria*. Edited and translated by Donald A. Russell. 4 vols. Cambridge, MA: Harvard University Press, 2001.
– *Institutiones oratoriae*. Edited by Michael Winterbottom. 2 vols. Oxford: Clarendon Press, 1970.
Seneca. *Epistles*. Translated by Richard M. Gummere. 3 vols. London: Heinemann, 1917–25.
Thomas Aquinas. *Catena aurea in quatuor Evangelia. Expositio in Matthaeum*. Edited by Roberto Busa. Turin: Marietti, 1953.
– *Summa contra gentiles*. Edited by Paul Marc et al. 3 vols. Turin: Marietti, 1961.
– *Summa Theologiae*, vol. 36 Prudence (2a 2ae. 47–56). Translated by Thomas Gilby et al. London: Blackfriars; New York: McGraw-Hill, 1964–76.
– *Super Evangelium S. Ioannis lectura*. Edited by Roberto Busa. Turin: Marietti, 1952.
– *Super Evangelium S. Matthaei lectura*. Edited by Roberto Busa. Turin: Marietti, 1951.

Uguccione da Pisa. *Derivationes*. Edited by Enzo Cecchini and Guido Arbizzoni. 2 vols. Florence: SISMEL–Edizioni del Galluzzo, 2004.

L'ultima forma dell'"Ottimo commento." Chiose sopra la "Comedia" di Dante Allegieri fiorentino tracte da diversi ghiosatori. Inferno. Edited by Claudia Di Fonzo. Ravenna: Longo, 2008.

Villani, Giovanni. *Nuova Cronica*. Edited by Giuseppe Porta. Parma: Guanda, 1991.

Virgil. *Eclogues. Georgics. Aeneid: Books 1–6*. Translated by H. Rushton Fairclough. Revised by G.P. Goold. Loeb Classical Library 63. Cambridge, MA: Harvard University Press, 1916.

William of St Amour. *De Pharisaeo*. In *Opera omnia*. Constance [for Paris]: Alithophilos, 1632. 7–16.

Secondary Sources

Akbari, Suzanne C. *Seeing through the Veil: Optical Theory and Medieval Allegory*. Toronto: University of Toronto Press, 2004.

Albers, Irene. "The Passions of the Body in Bocaccio's *Decameron*." *MLN* 125.1 (January 2010): 26–53.

Alfano, Giancarlo. "Giornata V. Scheda introduttiva." In Boccaccio, *Decameron*, edited by Quondam, Fiorilla, and Alfano, 803–31 [2013].

– "Giornata VI. Scheda introduttiva." In Boccaccio, *Decameron*, edited by Quondam, Fiorilla, and Alfano, 949–74 [2013].

Allen, Prudence. *The Concept of Woman. Volume II: The Early Humanist Reformation, 1250–1500*. Grand Rapids and Cambridge: William B. Eerdmans Publishing Company, 2002.

Almansi, Guido. "Lettura della novella di Madonna Oretta." *Paragone* 23 (1972): 139–43.

– *The Writer as Liar: Narrative Technique in the "Decameron."* London: Routledge and Kegan Paul, 1975.

Alonzo, Giuseppe. "Motto e moneta: le vie del riscatto della donna." *ACME: Annali della Facoltà di Lettere e Filosofia dell'Università di Milano* 61 (2008): 87–121. http://www.ledonline.it/acme [accessed 14 February 2021].

Andrei, Filippo. *Boccaccio the Philosopher: An Epistemology of the Decameron*. Cham: Palgrave Macmillan, 2017.

– "The *Motto* and the Enigma: Rhetoric and Knowledge in the Sixth Day of the *Decameron*." *Heliotropia* 10 (2013): 17–36.

Arduini, Beatrice. "Il ruolo di Boccaccio e di Marsilio Ficino nella tradizione del *Convivio* di Dante." In Filosa and Papio, *Boccaccio in America*, 95–103 [2012].

Armstrong, Guyda. "Boccaccio and Dante." In Armstrong, Daniels, and Milner, *The Cambridge Companion to Boccaccio*, 121–38.

– "Boccaccio and the Infernal Body: The Widow as Wilderness." In *Boccaccio and Feminist Criticism*, edited by Thomas C. Stillinger and F. Regina Psaki, 83–104. Chapel Hill, NC: Annali d'Italianistica, 2006. [*Annali d'Italianistica* 8 (2006)].

– "Fat Is a Feminist Issue: Female Greed in the *Corbaccio*." In *L'italiano a tavola: Linguistic and Literary Traditions*, edited by Anna Laura Lepschy and Arturo Tosi, 17–26. Perugia: Guerra, 2010.

– "Heavenly Bodies: The Presence of the Divine Female in Boccaccio." *Italian Studies* 60.2 (2005): 1–13.

– "Towards a Spatial Early Modern Translation Studies." *InTRAlinea*. Special Issue: Transit and Translation in Early Modern Europe, edited by Donatella Montini, Iolanda Plescia, Anna Maria Segala, and Francesca Terrenato (2019). http://www.intralinea.org/specials/article/2352 [accessed 14 February 2021].

Armstrong, Guyda, Rhiannon Daniels, and Stephen J. Milner. "Boccaccio as Cultural Mediator." In Armstrong, Daniels, and Milner, *The Cambridge Companion to Boccaccio*, 3–19. [2015].

Armstrong, Guyda, Rhiannon Daniels, and Stephen J. Milner, eds. *The Cambridge Companion to Boccaccio*. Cambridge: Cambridge University Press, 2015.

Arrighi, Vanna. "Gianfigliazzi, Corrado." In *Dizionario biografico degli italiani*, vol. 54, 355–7. Rome: Istituto della Enciclopedia italiana, 2000.

Ascoli, Albert R. "Auerbach fra gli epicurei: dal canto X dell'*Inferno* alla VI giornata del *Decameron*." *Moderna* 11 (2009): 135–52.

– "Boccaccio's Auerbach: Holding the Mirror Up to *Mimesis*." *Studi sul Boccaccio* 20 (1991–2): 377–97.

– *Dante and the Making of a Modern Author*. Cambridge: Cambridge University Press, 2008.

– *A Local Habitation and a Name: Imagining Histories in the Italian Renaissance*. New York: Fordham University Press, 2011.

– "Pyrrhus' Rules: Playing with Power from Boccaccio to Machiavelli." *MLN* 114.1 (1999): 14–57. [In *A Local Habitation and a Name*, 80–117.]

– "Solomon and Emilia, or the King and I: A Reading of *Decameron* 9.9." In *The "Decameron" Ninth Day in Perspective*, edited by Susanna Barsella and Simone Marchesi. Toronto: University of Toronto Press, forthcoming.

Auerbach, Erich. *Mimesis: The Representation of Reality in Western Literature*. Translated by Willard R. Trask. Princeton: Princeton University Press, 1953.

Austin, J.L. *How to Do Things with Words*. 2nd ed. Cambridge, MA: Harvard University Press, 1975.

Barański, Zygmunt G. "'Alquanto tenea della oppinione degli Epicuri': The *auctoritas* of Boccaccio's Cavalcanti (and Dante)." In *Mittelalterliche*

Novellistik im europäischen Kontext, edited by Mark Chinca, Timo Reuvekamp-Felber, and Christopher Young, 280–325. Berlin: Erich Schmidt Verlag, 2006.

Barański, Zygmunt G., and Lino Pertile, eds. *Dante in Context*. Cambridge: Cambridge University Press, 2015.

Barasch, Moshe. *Theories of Art. I. From Plato to Winckelmann*. New York and London: Routledge, 1985.

Baratto, Mario. *Realtà e stile nel "Decameron."* 3rd ed. Rome: Editori Riuniti, 1999.

– "Struttura narrativa e messaggio ideologico." In *Il Testo moltiplicato: Lettura di una novella del "Decameron,"* edited by Mario Lavagetto, 41–60. Parma: Pratiche Editrice, 1982.

Bàrberi-Squarotti, Giorgio. "La 'cornice' del Decameron o il mito di Robinson." In *Da Dante al Novecento. Studi critici offerti dagli scolari a Giovanni Getto nel suo ventesimo anno di insegnamento universitario*, edited by Giovanni Getto, 111–58. Milan: Mursia, 1970.

Barilli, Renato. "Semiologia e retorica nella lettura del *Decameron*." *Il Verri* 35–6 (1970): 27–48.

Barolini, Teodolinda. *Dante and the Origins of Literary Culture*. New York: Fordham University Press, 2006.

– "'Le Parole son femmine e i fatti sono maschi': Toward a Sexual Poetics of the *Decameron* (*Decameron* II 10)." *Studi sul Boccaccio* 21 (1993): 175–97. Rpt. in Barolini, *Dante and the Origins*, 281–303.

– "Sociology of the 'Brigata': Gendered Groups in Dante, Forese, Folgore, Boccaccio – from 'Guido, i' vorrei' to Griselda." *Italian Studies* 67.1 (2012): 4–22.

– "The Wheel of the *Decameron*." *Romance Philology* 34.4 (May 1983): 521–38. Rpt. in Barolini, *Dante and the Origins*, 234–44.

Barricelli, Jean-Pierre. "Satire of Satire: Boccaccio's *Corbaccio*." *Italian Quarterly* 18 (1975): 95–111.

Barsella, Susanna. "The Myth of Prometheus in Boccaccio's *Decameron*." *MLN* 119, supplement (2004): S120–S141.

– "Il riso dei padri: Il caso di madonna Filippa (*Dec.* VI 7)." *Humanistica* 4.2 (2009): 13–22.

Barthes, Roland. "Réflexion sur le style de *L'Étranger*." In *Œuvres complètes*, vol. 1, 60–3. Paris: Seuil, 1994.

Bartuschat, Johannes. "'Non pur Policleto, ma la natura'. Perfezione dell'arte e perfezione della natura in Dante e Boccaccio." In *Studi sul canone letterario del Trecento*, edited by Johannes Bartuschat and Luciano Rossi, 79–98. Ravenna: Longo, 2003.

Battaglia Ricci, Lucia. *Boccaccio*. Rome: Salerno Editrice, 2000.
– "*Exemplum* e novella." In *Letteratura in forma di sermone. I rapporti tra predicazione e letteratura nei secoli XIII–XVI*, edited by Ginetta Auzzas et al., 281–99. Florence: Olschki, 2003.
– "Leggere e scrivere novelle tra '200 e '300." In *La novella italiana*, vol. 2, 629–55.
– "'Una novella per esempio'. Novellistica, omiletica e trattatistica nel primo trecento." *Studi sul Boccaccio* 28 (2000): 106–24.
– *Ragionare nel giardino. Boccaccio e i cicli pittorici del "Trionfo della morte."* Rome: Salerno, 1987.
– *Scrivere un libro di novelle. Giovanni Boccaccio autore, lettore, editore*. Ravenna: Longo, 2013.
Bausi, Francesco. "Gli spiriti magni: filigrane aristoteliche e tomistiche nella decima giornata del *Decameron*." *Studi sul Boccaccio* 27 (1999): 205–53.
Beck, Eleanora M. "Mirrors and Music in the *Decameron*." *Heliotropia* 7.1–2 (2010): 81–103.
Bejczy, István P. *The Cardinal Virtues in the Middle Ages: A Study in Moral Thought from the Fourth to the Fourteenth Century*. Leiden: Brill, 2011.
Bellomo, Manlio. "La condizione giuridica della donna nel Medievo." In *Né Eva, né Maria. Condizione femminile e immagine della donna nel Medievo*, edited by Michela Pereira, 55–63. Bologna: Zanichelli, 1981.
Belting, Hans. *Das Bild und sein Publikum im Mittelalter: Form und Funktion früher Bildtafeln der Passion*. Berlin: Mann, 1981.
Benson, Pamela J. *The Invention of the Renaissance Woman: The Challenge of Female Independence in the Literature and Thought of Italy and England*. University Park: Pennsylvania State University Press, 1999.
Bergin, Thomas. *Boccaccio*. New York: Viking Press, 1981.
Bériou, Nicole. "La Confession dans les écrits théologiques et pastoraux du XIII siècle: médication de l'âme ou démarche judiciaire." In *L'Aveu: antiquité et moyen âge*, 261–82. Rome: École française de Rome, 1986.
Bertini, Ferruci. "La commedia elegiaca." In *Lo spazio letterario del Medioevo*, edited by Guglielmo Cavallo and Piero Boitani, 5 vols., vol. 1, part 2, 217–30. Rome: Salerno, 1992–.
Bisanti, Armando. *Le favole di Aviano e la loro fortuna nel Medioevo*. Florence: SISMEL, Edizioni del Galluzzo, 2010.
– "Una fonte probabile della novella di Chichibio." *Esperienze letterarie* 22.2 (1997): 47–58.
Boitani, Piero. *Chaucer and the Imaginary World of Fame*. Cambridge: D.S. Brewer, 1984.

Bosetti, Gilbert. "Analyse 'structurale' de la sixième journée du *Decameron*." *Studi sul Boccaccio* 7 (1975): 141–58.

Boskoff, Priscilla S. "Quintilian in the Late Middle Ages." *Speculum* 27.1 (January 1952): 71–8.

Branca, Vittore. *Boccaccio: The Man and His Works*. Translated by R. Monges. New York: New York University Press, 1976.

– *Boccaccio Medievale*. Florence: Sansoni, 1970.

Branca, Vittore, ed. *Boccaccio visualizzato: narrare per parole e per immagini fra Medioevo e Rinascimento*. 3 vols. Turin: Einaudi, 1999.

Brewer, Derek. *Medieval Comic Tales*. 2nd ed. Woodbridge: D.S. Brewer, 1996.

Broadie, Alexander. *Introduction to Medieval Logic*. Oxford: Clarendon Press, 1993.

Brody, Annelise Morani. "Madonna Filippa: A Model of Polyamory in the *Decameron*." *MLN* 134 supplement (September 2019): S78–S89.

Brown, Katherine. *Boccaccio's Fabliaux: Medieval Short Stories and the Function of Reversal*. Gainesville: University Press of Florida, 2014.

Brundage, James A. "The Teaching and Study of Canon Law in the Law Schools." In *The History of Medieval Canon Law in the Classical Period, 1140–1234*, edited by Wilfried Hartmann and Kenneth Pennington, 98–120. Washington, DC: Catholic University of America Press, 2008.

– "Vultures, Whores, and Hypocrites: Images of Lawyers in Medieval Literature." *Roman Legal Tradition* 1 (2002): 56–103.

Bruni, Francesco. *Boccaccio. L'invenzione della letteratura mezzana*. Bologna: Il Mulino, 1990.

Cahill, Spencer E. "Cross-Sex Pseudocommunication." *Berkeley Journal of Sociology* 26 (1981): 75–88.

Calvino, Italo. *Lezioni americane. Sei proposte per il prossimo millennio*. Milan: Mondadori, 2007.

– *Six Memos for the Next Millennium*. Translated by Patrick Creagh. Cambridge, MA: Harvard University Press, 1988.

Capaldi, Nicholas. *Art of Deception: An Introduction to Critical Thinking*. Amherst, NY: Prometheus Books, 2007.

Cape, Robert W. "Cicero and the Development of Prudential Practice at Rome." In *Prudence: Classical Virtue, Postmodern Practice*, edited by Robert Hariman, 35–66. University Park: Pennsylvania State University Press, 2003.

Carey, Sorcha. *Pliny's Catalogue of Culture: Art and Empire in the "Natural History."* Oxford and New York: Oxford University Press, 2003.

Carravetta, Peter. *The Elusive Hermes: Method, Discourse, Interpreting*. Aurora, CO: Davies Group, 2012.

Casagrande, Carla, and Silvana Vecchio. *I peccati della lingua*. Rome: Istituto della Enciclopedia Italiana, 1987.

Castellani, Antonio. "Il fiorino di Firenze, storia del 'dollaro del medioevo.'" *Il giornale della Numismatica* (19 January 2017). http://www.ilgiornaledellanumismatica.it/dossier-speciale-il-fiorino-di-firenze-breve-storia-del-dollaro-del-medioevo/ [accessed 14 February 2021].
Cerbo, Anna. *Metamorfosi del mito classico da Boccaccio a Marino*. Pisa: ETS, 2001.
Cerisola, Pier Luigi. "La questione della cornice nel *Decameron*." *Aevum* 49 (1975): 137–56.
Cervigni, Dino. "The *Decameron*'s Ballads and Emilia's Happy Song." In Cervigni, *Boccaccio's "Decameron,"* 131–71 [2013].
Cervigni, Dino, ed. *Boccaccio's "Decameron": Rewriting the Christian Middle Ages*. Chapel Hill: University of North Carolina Press, 2013 [*Annali d'Italianistica* 31 (2013)].
Ceva Valla, Elena, ed. *Decameron* by Giovanni Boccaccio. 2 vols. Milan: Rizzoli, 1950.
Charbonneau-Lassay, Louis. *Le bestiaire du Christ: la mystérieuse emblématique de Jésus-Christ*. Paris: Albin Michel, 2006 [1st ed. 1940].
Cherchi, Paolo. "The Inventors of Things in Boccaccio's *De genealogia deorum gentilium*." In *Petrarch and Boccaccio: The Unity of Knowledge in the Pre-Modern World*, edited by Igor Candido, 244–69. Berlin: De Gruyter, 2018.
– "Vernacular Literatures." In Barański and Pertile, *Dante in Context*, 371–88 [2015].
Chiappelli, Fredi. "Discorso o progetto per uno studio sul *Decameron*." In *Studi di italianistica in onore di Giovanni Cecchetti*, edited by Paolo Cherchi and Michelangelo Picone, 105–11. Ravenna: Longo, 1988.
Ciabattoni, Francesco. "Boccaccio's Miraculous Art of Storytelling: *Dec*. I.1, II.1 and VI.10." *Italica* 82.2 (Summer 2010): 167–78.
– "Musica sacra e musica profana nel *Decameron*." In Filosa and Papio, *Boccaccio in America*, 67–79 [2012].
Ciabattoni, Francesco, and Pier Massimo Forni, eds. *The "Decameron" Third Day in Perspective*. Toronto: University of Toronto Press, 2014.
Ciappelli, Giovanni. "Forese da Rabatta." In *Dizionario Biografico degli Italiani*, vol. 48, 794–5. Rome: Istituto della Enciclopedia Italiana, 1997.
Ciccuto, Marcello. "Il novelliere 'en artiste': strategie della dissimiglianza fra Boccaccio e Bandello." In *La novella italiana*, vol. 2, 771–93 [1989].
– "Un'antica canzone di Giotto e i pittori di Boccaccio." *Intersezioni* 16 (1996): 403–16.
Cioffari, Vincenzo. "The Conception of Fortune in the *Decameron*." *Italica* 17.4 (December 1940): 129–37.
Cirilli, Francesca. "Le ore del *Decameron*" ["'Tempo' e 'tempi' nel *Decameron*"]. *Testo e senso* 14 (2013). http://testoesenso.it/article/view/136 [accessed 14 February 2021].

Civitarese, Giuseppe. "Abjection and Aethetic Conflict in Boccaccio's [L]isabetta." *Journal of Romance Studies* 10.3 (2010): 11–25.

Clubb, Louise George. "Boccaccio and the Boundaries of Love." *Italica* 37.3 (September 1960): 188–96.

Cohen, Morris R., and Ernest Nagel. *An Introduction to Logic*. New York: Harcourt, Brace and World, 1962 [1934].

Cohn, Dorrit. "Metalepsis and Mise en Abyme." Translated by Lewis S. Gleich. *Narrative* 20.1 (2012): 105–14.

Coleman, William E. "*Teseida delle nozze d'Emilia*." In De Robertis et al., *Boccaccio autore e copista*, 89–93 [2013].

Conetti, Mario. "Il colasso dell'ordine giuridico e il diritto naturale nel *Decameron*." *Heliotropia* 12–13 (2015–16): 105–27.

Confalonieri, Luca Badini. "Madonna Oretta e il luogo del *Decameron*." In *L'arte dell'interpretare. Studi critici offerti a Giovanni Getto*, 127–43. Cuneo: L'Arciere, 1984.

Congar, Yves. "Bref historique des formes du 'magistère' et des ses relations avec les docteurs." *Revue des sciences philosophiques et théologiques* 60 (1976): 99–112.

Conte, Silvia. "'Lai' di gru e 'lai' di rondinella." *Linguistica e letteratura* 41 (2016): 111–29.

Cook, Eleanor. *Enigmas and Riddles in Literature*. Cambridge: Cambridge University Press, 2006.

Coomaraswamy, Ananda K. *Figures of Speech or Figures of Thought? The Traditional View of Art*. Edited by William Wroth. Bloomington: World Wisdom, 2007.

Copeland, Rita. "Medieval Rhetoric: An Overview." In *Encyclopedia of Rhetoric*, edited by Thomas O. Sloane, 469–79. Oxford: Oxford University Press, 2001.

Cornish, Alison. *Vernacular Translation in Dante's Italy: Illiterate Literature*. Cambridge: Cambridge University Press, 2010.

Corti, Maria. *La felicità mentale: Nuove prospettive per Cavalcanti e Dante*. Turin: Einaudi, 1983.

Cottino-Jones, Marga. "The Hiccuping Rhythm of Chichibio's Adventure: A Comic Farce." In Cottino-Jones, *An Anatomy of Boccaccio's Style*, 83–96. Naples: Cymba, 1968.

– "Observations on the Structure of the *Decameron* Novella." *Romance Notes* 15 (1973): 378–87.

– *Order from Chaos: Social and Aesthetic Harmonies in Boccaccio's "Decameron."* Washington, DC: University Press of America, 1982.

Coulter, Cornelia C. "Boccaccio's Knowledge of Quintilian." *Speculum* 33.4 (October 1958): 490–6.

Cox, Virginia. "Ciceronian Rhetoric in Italy, 1260–1350." *Rhetorica* 17 (1999): 239–88.

– "Ciceronian Rhetorical Theory in the *volgare*: A Fourteenth-Century Text and Its Fifteenth-Century Readers." In *Rhetoric and Renewal in the Latin West 1100–1540: Essays in Honor of John O. Ward*, edited by Constant J. Mews, Cary J. Nederman, and Rodney M. Thomson, 201–26. *Disputatio* 2. Turnhout: Brepols, 2003.

– *Women's Writing in Italy, 1400–1650*. Baltimore: Johns Hopkins University Press, 2008.

Cox, Virginia, and John O. Ward, eds. *The Rhetoric of Cicero in Its Medieval and Early Renaissance Commentary Tradition*. Leiden: Brill, 2006.

Creed, Barbara. "Horror and the Monstrous-Feminine: An Imaginary Abjection." In *Horror, The Film Reader*, edited by Mark Jancovich, 67–76. New York: Routledge, 2002.

Crombie, A.C. *Medieval and Early Modern Science*, vol. 2. Garden City, NY: Doubleday Anchor, 1963.

Crosby, Alfred W. *The Measure of Reality: Quantification and Western Society, 1250–1600*. Cambridge: Cambridge University Press, 1977.

Crum, Roger J., and John T. Paoletti, eds. *Renaissance Florence: A Social History*. Cambridge: Cambridge University Press, 2006.

Cuomo, Luisa. "Sillogizzare motteggiando e motteggiare sillogizzando: dal *Novellino* alla VI giornata del *Decameron*." *Studi sul Boccaccio* 13 (1981–2): 217–65.

Curtius, Ernst R. *European Literature and the Latin Middle Ages*. Princeton: Princeton University Press, 1953.

D'Addario, Arnaldo. "Adimari." In *Encicopedia dantesca*. https://www.treccani.it/enciclopedia/elenco-opere/Enciclopedia_Dantesca/ [accessed 14 February 2021].

Dall'Orto, Giovanni. "La cerchia perugina." In *L'omosessualità nella poesia volgare italiana, fino al tempo di Dante. Appunti*. http://www.giovannidallorto.com/saggistoria/poesia/poesia.html#perugini [accessed 14 February 2021].

D'Ambrosio, Rocco. *Istituzioni, persone e potere*. Soveria Mannelli: Rubbettino, 2004.

D'Andrea, Antonio. *Il nome della storia: studi e ricerche di storia e letteratura*. Naples: Liguori, 1982.

Daniels, Rhiannon. *Boccaccio and the Book: Production and Reading in Italy 1340–1520*. London: Legenda, 2009.

– "Boccaccio's Narrators and Audiences." In Armstrong, Daniels, and Milner, *The Cambridge Companion to Boccaccio*, 36–51 [2015].

– "Where Does the *Decameron* Begin? Editorial Practice and the Role of Rubrics." *Modern Language Review* 114.1 (January 2019): 52–78.

DeCoste, Mary-Michelle. "Filomena, Dioneo, and an Ass." *Heliotropia* 2 (2004): 59–68.

De Hamel, Christopher. *Medieval Craftsmen: Scribes and Illuminators*. London: British Museum Press, 1992 [repr. 2004].

De Lauretis, Teresa. "The Violence of Rhetoric." *Semiotica* 54 (1985): 31–51.

Delcorno, Carlo. "Appunti su Boccaccio lettore della Bibbia." *Studi sul Boccaccio* 47 (2019): 159–80.

– "Metamorfosi boccacciane dell''exemplum.'" In Delcorno, *"Exemplum" e letteratura tra medioevo e rinascimento*, 265–94. Bologna: Il Mulino, 1989.

Della Cagna, Chiara. "Echi della similitudine delle gru di Lucano (*Pharsalia*, V, 709–16) nella *Commedia* di Dante." *Linguistica e letteratura* 15.1–2 (2015): 69–93.

Della Torre, Armando. *La giovinezza di Giovanni Boccaccio, 1313–1341*. Città di Castello: Lapi, 1905.

Delumeau, Jean. *Sin and Fear: The Emergence of Western Guilt Culture, 13th–18th Centuries*. Translated by Eric Nicholson. New York: St Martin's Press, 1990.

Denery, Dallas G. *Seeing and Being Seen in the Later Medieval World: Optics, Theology and Religious Life*. Cambridge: Cambridge University Press, 2005.

Derbes, Anne. *Picturing the Passion in Late Medieval Italy*. Cambridge: Cambridge University Press, 1996.

De Robertis, Teresa, et al., eds. *Boccaccio autore e copista*. Firenze, Biblioteca Medicea Laurenziana, 11 ottobre 2013–11 gennaio 2014. Florence: Mandragora, 2013.

Dezza, Ettore. *Lezioni di storia del processo penale*. Pavia: Pavia University Press, 2013

Didi-Huberman, Georges. "The Molding Image: Genealogy and the Truth of Resemblance in Pliny's *Natural History*, Book 35, 1–7." In *Law and the Image: The Authority of Art and the Aesthetics of Law*, edited by Costas Douzinas and Lynda Nead, 71–88. Chicago and London: University of Chicago Press, 1999.

Doering, Pia C. "Madonna Filippa chiamata in giudizio. Diritto naturale e diritto posisitivo nel *Decameron*." In Ferracin and Venier, *Giovanni Boccaccio*, 435–47 [2014].

Durling, Robert M. "Boccaccio on Interpretation: Guido's Escape (*Decameron* VI.9)." In *Dante, Petrarch, Boccaccio: Studies in the Italian Trecento in Honor of Charles S. Singleton*, edited by Aldo S. Bernardo, 273–304. Binghamton, NY: Medieval and Renaissance Texts and Studies, 1983.

Eckstein, Nicholas. "Neighborhood as Microcosm." In Crum and Paoletti, *Renaissance Florence*, 219–39 [2006].

– "Prepositional City: Spatial Practice and Micro-Neighbourhood in Renaissance Florence." *Renaissance Quarterly* 71 (2018): 1235–71.

Eco, Umberto. *The Aesthetics of Thomas Aquinas*. Translated by Hugh Bredin. Cambridge, MA: Harvard University Press, 1988.

– *Art and Beauty in the Middle Ages*. Translated by Hugh Bredin. New Haven: Yale University Press, 1986.

Eco, Umberto, et al. "On Animal Language in the Medieval Classification of Signs." In *On the Medieval Theory of Signs*, edited by Umberto Eco and Marmo Constantino, 3–41. Amsterdam: John Benjamins, 1989.

Eisner, Martin. *Boccaccio and the Invention of Italian Literature: Dante, Petrarch, Cavalcanti, and the Authority of the Vernacular*. Cambridge: Cambridge University Press, 2013.

– "The Tale of Ferondo's Purgatory (III.8)." In Ciabattoni and Forni, *The "Decameron" Third Day in Perspective*, 150–69 [2014].

Elukin, Jonathan. "Judaism: From Heresy to Pharisee in Early Medieval Christian Literature." *Traditio* 57 (2002): 49–66.

Emison, Patricia A. *Creating the "Divine" Artist from Dante to Michelangelo*. Leiden and Boston: Brill, 2004.

Evans, Gillian R. *Getting It Wrong: The Medieval Epistemology of Error*. Leiden: Brill, 1998.

Falaschi, Enid. "Giotto: The Literary Legend." *Italian Studies* 27 (1972): 1–27.

Fanini, Barbara. "Chichìbio o Chichibìo?" *Accademia della Crusca*. 26 November 2012. https://accademiadellacrusca.it/it/consulenza/chichìbio-o-chichibìo/746 [accessed 14 February 2021].

Favati, Guido. "La glossa latina di Dino del Garbo a 'Donna me prega' del Cavalcanti." *Annali della Scuola Normale di Pisa* 2nd series 21 (1952): 70–103.

Fenzi, Enrico. "'Sollazzo' e 'leggiadria'. Un'interpretazione della canzone dantesca *Poscia ch'Amor*." *Studi danteschi* 63 (1991): 191–280.

Ferracin, Antonio, and Matteo Venier, eds. *Giovanni Boccaccio: tradizione, interpretazione e fortuna. In ricordo di Vittore Branca*. Udine: Forum, 2014.

Ferreri, Rosario. "Appunti sulla presenza del *Convivio* nel *Decameron*." *Studi sul Boccaccio* 19 (1990): 63–77.

Fichera, Gabriele. "Il salto di Jolles fra gli stili del *Decameron*: dalla cornice alle novelle, e viceversa." *Cahiers d'études italiennes* 23 (2016): 125–35. http://cei.revues.org/3153 [accessed 14 February 2021].

Fido, Franco. "Boccaccio's *Ars Narrandi* in the Sixth Day of the *Decameron*." In *Italian Literature: Roots and Branches: Essays in Honor of Thomas Goddard Bergin*, edited by Giose Rimanelli and Kenneth John Atchity, 225–42. New Haven: Yale University Press, 1976. Rpt. in *Il regime delle simmetrie imperfette: studi sul "Decameron,"* 73–89.

– *Il regime delle simmetrie imperfette. Studi sul "Decameron."* Milan: Franco Angeli, 1988.
– "Silenzi e cavalli nell'eros del *Decameron.*" *Belfagor* (1983): 79–84.
– "The Tale of Ser Ciappelletto (I.1)." In Weaver, *The "Decameron" First Day in Perspective*, 59–76.
Filosa, Elsa. "Boccaccio tra storia e invenzione: dal *De fide uxorum erga viros* di Valerio Massimo al *De mulieribus claris.*" *Romance Quarterly* 54.3 (2007): 219–30.
– "'Decameron' 7: Under the Sign of Venus." In Cervigni, *Boccaccio's "Decameron,"* 314–53.
– "Modalità di contatto tra *Decameron* e *Corbaccio*: Giovenale nella novella di Madonna Sismonda (Dec. VII 8)." *MLN* 122.1 (January 2007): 123–32.
– "Petrarca, Boccaccio e le *mulieres clarae*: dalla *Familiare* 21:8 al *De mulieribus claris.*" *Annali d'Italianistica* 22 (2004): 381–93.
– "The Tale of the King and the Groom." In Ciabattoni and Forni, *The "Decameron" Third Day in Perspective*, 2–43 [2014].
– *Tre studi sul "De mulieribus claris."* Milan: LED, 2012.
Filosa, Elsa, and Michael Papio, eds. *Boccaccio in America*. Ravenna: Longo Editore, 2012.
Fioretti, Francesco. "Il 'girone dei poeti' e la teoria del *dolce stil.*" In Fioretti, *Ethos e leggiardria: lo Stilnovo dialogico di Dante, Guido e Cino da Pistoia*, 61–102. Rome: Aracne, 2012.
Fiorilla, Maurizio. Introduction to *Decameron*, by Giovanni Boccaccio, xv–lix. Rome: Istituto della Enciclopedia Italiana, 2011.
Flasch, Kurt. *Poesia dopo la peste. Saggio su Boccaccio.* Bari: Laterza, 1995.
Fontes, Anna. "Le thème de la 'beffa' dans le Décaméron." In *Formes et significations de la "Beffa" dans la littérature italienne de la Renaissance*, edited by André Rochon, 2 vols., vol. 1, 11–44. Paris: Université de la Sorbonne Nouvelle, 1972.
Forni, Pier Massimo. *Adventures in Speech: Rhetoric and Narration in Boccaccio's "Decameron."* Philadelphia: University of Pennsylvania Press, 1996.
– "Boccaccio tra Dante e Cino." *Quaderni d'Italianistica* 16.2 (1995): 179–95.
– *Retorica del reale nel "Decameron."* Florence: Le Lettere, 1988.
– "The Tale of the King of Cyprus and the Lady of Gascony (I.9)." In Weaver, *The "Decameron" First Day in Perspective*, 207–21.
Foucault, Michel. *Madness and Civilization*. New York: Anchor Books, 1966.
Franklin, Margaret. *Boccaccio's Heroines: Power and Virtue in Renaissance Society*. Burlington, VT: Ashgate, 2006.
Freedberg, David. *The Power of Images: Studies in the History and Theory of Response*. Chicago: University of Chicago Press, 1989.
Freedman, Alan. "Il cavallo del Boccaccio: Fonte, struttura e funzione della metanovella di Madonna Oretta." *Studi sul Boccaccio* 9 (1975–6): 225–41.

Freud, Sigmund. *The Joke and Its Relation to the Unconscious*. Translated by J. Crick. New York: Penguin, 2002.

Frugoni, Chiara. "La donna nelle immagini, la donna immaginata." *Il Medioevo* (1991): 424–57.

Garver, Eugene. *Aristotle's Rhetoric: An Art of Character*. Chicago: University of Chicago Press, 1994.

Gathercole, Patricia M. "Illuminations on the French Manuscripts of Boccaccio's *De mulieribus claris*." *Italica* 42.3 (1965): 213–17.

Gattoweb. Edited by Pär Larson and Elena Artale. http://gattoweb.ovi.cnr.it [accessed 14 February 2021].

Gaylard, Susan. "The Crisis of Word and Deed in *Decameron* V, 10." In *The Italian Novella*, edited by Gloria Allaire, 33–48. New York: Taylor and Francis, 2003.

Genette, Gérard. *Narrative Discourse: An Essay in Method*. Translated by Jane E. Lewin. Ithaca: Cornell University Press, 1972.

Getto, Giovanni. *Vita di forme e forme di vita nel "Decameron."* 4th rev. ed. Turin: Petrini, 1986.

Giannetto, Nella. "Madonna Filippa tra 'Casus' e 'Controversia'. Lettura della novella VI 7 del *Decameron*." *Studi sul Boccaccio* 31 (2004): 81–100.

Gilbert, Creighton. "La devozione di Giovanni Boccaccio per gli artisti e per l'arte." In Branca, *Boccaccio visualizzato*, vol. 1, 145–53 [1999].

Gittes, Tobias Foster. *Boccaccio's Naked Muse: Eros, Culture, and the Mythopoetic Imagination*. Toronto: University of Toronto Press, 2008.

– "Boccaccio's 'Valley of Women': Fetishized Foreplay in *Decameron* VI." *Italica* 76.2 (1999): 147–74.

Giusti, Eugenio L. "*Il Corbaccio*: Tra misoginia e comprensione." *Italiana 1988*: Selected Papers from the Proceedings of the Fifth Annual Conference of the American Association of Teachers of Italian (18–20 November 1988), Monterey, CA, edited by Albert N. Mancini, Paolo A. Giordano, and Anthony J. Tamburri. Rosary College *Italian Studies* 4 (1990): 51–62.

– *Dall'amore cortese alla comprensione*. Milan: CEA, 1999.

– "La novella di Cesca e 'intenderlo come si conviene' nella sesta giornata del *Decameron*." *Studi sul Boccaccio* 18 (1989): 319–46.

Gobyn, Saartje. "Textual Efficts of Metalepsis." *Narratology* 7 (2012): 120–38.

Goering, Joseph. "The Internal Forum and the Literature of Penance and Confession." In *The History of Medieval Canon Law in the Classical Period, 1140–1234*, edited by Wilfried Hartmann and Kenneth Pennington, 379–427. Washington, DC: Catholic University of America Press, 2008.

Gorni, Guglielmo. "'Gru' di Dante. Lettura di *Purgatorio* XXVI." *Rassegna europea di letteratura italiana* 3 (1994): 11–34.

– "Guido Cavalcanti nella novella del Boccaccio (*Decameron* VI, 9) e in un sonetto di Dino Compagni." *Cuadernos de Filologia Italiana* n° extraordinario (2001): 39–45. https://revistas.ucm.es/index.php/CFIT/article/view/CFIT0101220039A [accessed 14 February 2021].

Grassi, Luigi. "Il concetto di 'moderno' in rapporto a Giotto nella riflessione del pensiero critico del Trecento." In *Giotto e il suo tempo. Atti del Congresso internazionale per la celebrazione del VII centenario della nascita di Giotto*, 419–27. Rome: De Luca, 1971.

Green, Richard F. "Medieval Literature and Law." In *The Cambridge History of Medieval English Literature*, edited by David Wallace, 407–31. Cambridge: Cambridge University Press, 1999.

Grossvogel, Steven. *Ambiguity and Allusion in Boccaccio's "Filocolo."* Florence: Olschki, 1992.

Gualtieri, Teresa Flora Lucia. "Birds of Prey and the Sport of Falconry in Italian Literature through the Fourteenth Century: From Serving Love to Served for Dinner." PhD diss., University of Madison, WI, 2005.

Gulizia, Stefano. "Ambiguità della forma breve da Boccaccio all'Umanesimo." *Heliotropia* 3.1–2 (2005–6): 13–31.

Gullace, Giovanni. "Medieval and Humanistic Perspectives in Boccaccio's Concept and Defense of Poetry." *Mediaevalia* 12 (1986): 226–48.

Güntert, Georges. *Tre premesse e una dichiarazione d'amore: Vademecum per il lettore del "Decameron."* Modena: Mucchi Editore, 1997.

Hampton, Timothy. *Writing from History: The Rhetoric of Exemplarity in Renaissance Literature*. Ithaca: Cornell University Press, 1990.

Hankins, James. "Boccaccio and the Political Thought of Renaissance Humanism." In *A Boccaccian Renaissance: Essays on the Early Modern Impact of Giovanni Boccaccio and His Works*, edited by Martin Eisner and David Lummus, 3–35. Notre Dame: University of Notre Dame Press, 2019.

Hastings, Robert. *Nature and Reason in the "Decameron."* Manchester: Manchester University Press, 1975.

Hauvette, Henri. "Une confession de Boccacce: *Il Corbaccio*." *Bulletin Italien* 1 (1901): 3–21.

Hollander, Robert. *Boccaccio's Dante and the Shaping Force of Satire*. Ann Arbor: University of Michigan Press, 1997.

– *Boccaccio's Last Fiction: "Il Corbaccio."* Philadelphia: University of Pennsylvania Press, 1988.

– "The Struggle for Control among the 'novellatori' of the *Decameron* and the Reason for Their Return to Florence." *Studi sul Boccaccio* 39 (2011): 243–314.

– "'Utilità' in Boccaccio's *Decameron*." *Studi sul Boccaccio* 15 (1985–6): 215–33.

Honess, Claire. "Feminine Virtues and Florentine Vices: Citizenship and Morality in *Paradiso* XV–XVII." In *Dante and Governance*, edited by John Woodhouse, 102–20. Oxford: Oxford University Press, 1997.

– *From Florence to the Heavenly City: The Poetry of Citizenship in Dante*. Italian Perspectives 13. London: Legenda, 2006.

Hortis, Attilio. *Studj sulle opera latine del Boccaccio*, vol. 1. Trieste: Julius Dase, 1879 [rpt. Adelmo La Polla, 1981].

Houston, Jason. *Building a Monument to Dante: Boccaccio as Dantista*. Toronto: University of Toronto Press, 2010.

Huizinga, Johan. *Briefwisseling*. I. Edited by Léon Hanssen, Wessel E. Krul, and Anton Van Der Lem. Utrecht and Antwerp: Veen-Tjeenk Willink, 1989.

Inglese, Giorgio. *L'intelletto e l'amore. Studi sulla letteratura italiana del Due e Trecento*. Florence: La Nuova Italia, 2000.

Jolles, André. "La facezia di Guido Cavalcanti." In *I travestimenti della letteratura. Saggi criticie teorici (1897–1932)*, edited by Silvia Contarini, 44–56. Milan: Mondadori, 2003.

Jordan, Constance. "Boccaccio's In-Famous Women: Gender and Civic Virtue in the *Mulieribus Claris*." In *Ambiguous Realities: Women in the Middle Ages and Renaissance*, edited by Carole Levin and Jeanie Watson, 25–47. Detroit: Wayne State University Press, 1987.

– *Renaissance Feminism: Literary Texts and Political Models*. Ithaca: Cornell University Press, 1990.

Kahn, Victoria. *Rhetoric, Prudence, and Skepticism in the Renaissance*. Ithaca: Cornell University Press, 1985.

Kannowski, Bernd. "Giovanni Boccaccio und die Juristerei. Rechtshistorische Aspekte des Dekameron." In *Von den Leges Barbarorum bis zum ius barbarum des Nationalsozialismus. Festschrift für Herman Nehlsen zum 70 Geburtstag*, edited by Hans-Georg Hermann et al., 48–59. Cologne: Böhlau, 2008.

Keen, Catherine. *Dante and the City*. Stroud: Tempus, 2003.

Kemmler, Fritz. *"Exempla" in Context: A Historical and Critical Study of Robert Mannyng of Brune's Handlyng Sinne*. Studies and Texts in English 6. Tübingen: Narr, 1984.

King, Margaret L. *Women of the Renaissance*. Chicago and London: University of Chicago Press, 1991.

Kircher, Timothy. "The Modality of Moral Communication in the *Decameron*'s First Day, in Contrast to the Mirror of the Exemplum." *Renaissance Quarterly* 54 (2001): 1035–73.

– *The Poet's Wisdom: The Humanists, the Church, and the Formation of Philosophy in the Early Renaissance*. Leiden and Boston: Brill, 2006.

Kirkham, Victoria. "An Allegorically Tempered *Decameron.*" *Italica* 62 (1985): 1–23.
– "Morale." In *Lessico critico decameroniano*, edited by Renzo Bragantini and Pier Massimo Forni, 249–68. Turin: Bollati Boringhieri, 1995.
– *The Sign of Reason in Boccaccio's "Decameron."* Florence: Olschki, 1993.
Kirkham, Victoria, Michael Sherberg, and Janet Levarie Smarr, eds. *Boccaccio: A Critical Guide to the Complete Works*. Chicago: University of Chicago Press, 2013.
Klapisch-Zuber, Christiane. "La femme et la lignage florentin (xive–xvie siècles)." In *Persons in Groups: Social Behaviour as Identity Formation in Medieval and Renaissance Europe*, edited by Richard Trexler, 141–53. Binghamton: Center for Medieval and Early Renaissance Studies, 1985.
– *La maison et le nom: Stratégies et rituels dans l'Italie de la Renaissance*. Paris: Editions de l'Ecole des Hautes Etudes en Sciences Sociales, 1990.
– *Women, Family and Ritual in Renaissance Italy*. Translated by Lydia Cochrane. Chicago and London: University of Chicago Press, 1985.
Kleinhenz, Christopher, ed. *Medieval Italy: An Encyclopedia*. London: Routledge, 2003.
Kolsky, Stephen. *The Genealogy of Women: Studies in Boccaccio's "De mulieribus Claris."* New York: Peter Lang, 2003.
– *The Ghost of Boccaccio: Rewritings on "Famous Women" in Renaissance Italy*. Turnhout: Brepols, 2005.
Korneeva, Tatiana. "Law and Women's Rights in Boccaccio's *Decameron*: Madonna Filippa vs. Antigone." *Comparatio* 4.2 (2012): 225–38.
Kriesel, James C. *Boccaccio's Corpus: Allegory, Ethics, and Vernacularity*. Notre Dame: University of Notre Dame Press, 2018.
– "The Genealogy of Boccaccio's Theory of Allegory." *Studi sul Boccaccio* 36 (2009): 197–226.
– "The Marvelous between Dante and Boccaccio." *Traditio* 73 (2018): 213–54.
Kristeller, Paul Oskar. "A Philosophical Treatise from Bologna Dedicated to Guido Cavalcanti: Magister Jacobus de Pistorio and his *Quaestio de felicitate*." In *Medioevo e Rinascimento. Studi in onore di Bruno Nardi*, vol. 1, 425–63. Florence: Sansoni, 1955.
– *Studies in Renaissance Thought and Letters. Vol. 3*. Storia e letteratura. Raccolta di Studi e Testi, 178. Rome: Edizioni di storia e di letteratura, 1993.
Kristeva, Julia. *Powers of Horror: An Essay on Abjection*. Translated by Leon S. Roudiez. New York: Columbia University Press, 1982.
Kuhns, Richard. *"Decameron" and the Philosophy of Storytelling: Author as Midwife and Pimp*. New York: Columbia University Press, 2005.
Ladis, Andrew. "The Legend of Giotto's Wit and the Arena Chapel." *Art Bulletin* 68 (1986): 581–96.
Larner, John. *Culture and Society in Italy, 1290–1420*. New York: Scribner, 1971.

A Latin Dictionary. Founded on Andrews's edition of Freund's Latin Dictionary. Revised, enlarged, and in great part rewritten by Charlton T. Lewis and Charles Short. Oxford: Clarendon Press, 1996.

Lausberg, Heinrich. *Literary Rhetoric*. Boston: Brill, 1998.

Layman, Beverly Joseph. "Boccaccio's Paradigm of the Artist and His Art." *Italian Quarterly* 13.51 (1970): 19–36.

Ledda, Giuseppe. "Animali nel *Paradiso*." In *La poesia della natura nella "Divine Commedia."* Atti del convegno internazionale di studi, Ravenna, 10 novembre 2007, edited by Giuseppe Ledda, 93–135. Ravenna: Centro conventuale dei frati minori conventuali [Longo Editore], 2009.

Leff, Gordon. *The Dissolution of the Medieval Outlook*. New York: New York University Press, 1976.

Legassie, Shayne A. "The Lies of the Painters: Artisan Trickery and the Labor of Painting in Boccaccio's *Decameron* and Sacchetti's *Trecentonovelle*." *Journal of Medieval and Early Modern Studies* 43 (2013): 487–519.

Levine, Peter. "Why Dante Damned Francesca da Rimini." *Philosophy and Literature* 23.2 (1991): 334–50.

The Liber Augustalis, or Constitutions of Melfi Promulgated by the Emperor Frederick II for the Kingdom of Sicily in 1231. Translated by James M. Powell. New York: Syracuse University Press, 1971.

Lochrie, Karma. *Covert Operations: The Medieval Uses of Secrecy*. Philadelphia: University of Pennsylvania Press, 1999.

Lorenzi, Cristiano. "*Farsaglia* volgarizzata." *Dizionario dei volgarizzamenti*. 2014. http://tlion.sns.it/divo [accessed 14 February 2021].

Lummus, David. "Boccaccio's Hellenism and the Foundations of Modernity." *Mediaevalia* 33 (2012): 101–67.

– "Boccaccio's Poetic Anthropology: Allegories of History in the *Genealogie deorum gentilium libri*." *Speculum* 87.3 (July 2012): 725–65.

– "The *Decameron* and Boccaccio's Poetics." In Amstrong, Daniels, and Milner, *The Cambridge Companion to Boccaccio*, 65–82 [2015].

– "Placing Petrarch's Legacy: The Politics of Petrarch's Tomb and Boccaccio's Last Letter." *Renaissance Quarterly* 70 (2017): 435–73.

Luperini, Romano, et al., eds. *La scrittura e l'interpretazione*. Edizione rossa (il nuovo). 6 vols. Palermo: Palumbo, 2011.

Macy, Gary. "Theology of the Eucharist in the High Middle Ages." In *Companion to the Eucharist in the Middle Ages*, edited by Ian Christopher Levy et al., 365–98. Leiden: Brill, 2011.

Marcus, Millicent. *An Allegory of Form: Literary Self-Consciousness in the "Decameron."* Stanford French and Italian Studies 18. Saratoga, CA: Anma Libri, 1979.

– "Cross-Fertilizations: Folklore and Literature in *Decameron* 4.5." *Italica* 66.4 (1989): 383–98.
– "Faith's Fiction: A Gloss on the Tale of Melchisedech (*Decameron* 1.3)." *Canadian Journal of Italian Studies* 2 (1978): 40–55.
– "The Sweet New Style Reconsidered: A Gloss on the Tale of Cimone (*Decameron* V, 1)." *Italian Quarterly* 21 (Summer 1980): 5–16.
Marino, Lucia. "Prometheus or the Mythographer's Self-Image." *Studi sul Boccaccio* 12 (1980): 263–73.
Markulin, Joseph. "Emilia and the Case for Openness in the *Decameron*." *Stanford Italian Review* 3 (1983): 183–99.
Martinez, Ronald L. "Calandrino and the Powers of the Stone: Rhetoric, Belief and the Progress of *Ingegno* in *Decameron* VIII.3." *Heliotropia* 1.1 (2003): 1–32.
– "The Pilgrim's Answer to Bonagiunta and the Poetics of the Spirit." *Stanford Italian Review* 4 (1983): 37–63.
– "*Scienze della Cittade*: Rhetoric and Politics in the Sixth day of the *Decameron*." *Mediaevalia* 34.1 (2013): 57–86.
Matrone, Marcella. *Per l'esegesi del Purgatorio XXIV, 37: "Gentucca."* Streetlib, 2016. Ebook.
Mazza, Antonia. "L'inventario della 'Parva libraria' in Santo Spirito e la biblioteca del Boccaccio." *Italia medioevale e umanistica* 9 (1966): 1–74.
Mazzotta, Giuseppe. "Boccaccio: The Mythographer of the City." In *Interpretation and Allegory: Antiquity to the Modern Period*, edited by Jon Whitman, 349–64. Leiden: Brill, 2000.
– "The *Decameron*: The Marginality of Literature." *University of Toronto Quarterly* 42.1 (1972): 64–85.
– *The World at Play in Boccaccio's "Decameron."* Princeton: Princeton University Press, 1986.
McKee, Robert. *Story: Substance, Structure, Style, and the Principles of Screenwriting*. London: Methuen, 1999.
McNamer, Sarah. *Affective Meditation and the Invention of Medieval Compassion*. Philadelphia: University of Pennsylvania Press, 2010.
McNeill, William H. *Plagues and Peoples*. New York: Anchor Books, 1998.
Meier, Franziska. "Day Six of the *Decameron*: Language's Polysemy or the Importance of Being Understood." In Cervigni, *Boccaccio's "Decameron,"* 289–313 [2013].
– "The *Novellino* or 'How to Do Things with Words': An Early Western Way of Using Language." *MLN* 125.1 (January 2010): 1–25.
Menesto, Enrico, Laura Andreani, Renzo Civili, and Rita Nanni, eds. *Amelia e i suoi Statuti medievali.* Atti delle giornata di studio (Amelia 15 marzo 2001). Spoleto: Centro Studi Sull'Alto Medievo, 2004.

Migiel, Marilyn. *A Rhetoric of the "Decameron."* Toronto: University of Toronto Press, 2003.

Milanese, Angela. "Affinità e contraddizioni tra rubriche e novelle del *Decameron.*" *Studi sul Boccaccio* 23 (1995): 89–111.

Milner, Stephen J. "Boccaccio's *Decameron* and the Semiotics of the Everyday:" In Armstrong, Daniels, and Milner, *The Cambridge Companion to Boccaccio,* 83–100.

– "Communication, Consensus and Conflict: Rhetorical Precepts, the *ars concionandi,* and Social Ordering in Late Medieval Italy." In Cox and Ward, *The Rhetoric of Cicero,* 365–408.

– "The Florentine Piazza della Signoria as Practiced Place." In Crum and Paoletti, *Renaissance Florence,* 83–103 [2006].

Mineo, Nicolò. "La sesta giornata del *Decameron* o del potere delle donne." *Rassegna europea di letteratura italiana* 3 (1994): 49–69.

Minnis, Alastair J. "Late-Medieval Discussions of *Compilatio* and the Rôle of the *Compilator.*" *Beiträge zur Geschichte der deutschen Sprache und Literatur* 101/3 (1979): 385–421.

– "*Nolens auctor sed compilator reputari*: The Late-Medieval Discourse of Compilation." In *La Méthode critique au Moyen Âge,* edited by Mireille Chazan and Gilbert Dahan, 47–63. Turnhout: Brepols, 2008.

Moody, Ernest A. *Studies in Medieval Philosophy, Science, and Logic.* Los Angeles: University of California Press, 1975.

Morosini, Roberta. "*Bone eloquence* e mondo alla rovescia nel discourso *semblable a la reisun* nella novella di Madonna Filippa (*Decameron* VI.7)." *Italica* 77.1 (Spring 2000): 1–13.

Morosini, Roberta, ed. *Boccaccio geografo: un viaggio nel Mediterraneo tra le città, i giardini e ... il "mondo" di Giovanni Boccaccio.* Florence: Mauro Pagliai, 2010.

Morreal, John, ed. *The Philosophy of Laughter and Humor.* Albany: SUNY Press, 1987.

Mouchet, Valeria. "Anguille, capponi, gru e galline: gli animali come vivande nelle novelle medievali." *Italianistica: Rivista di letteratura italiana* 33.3 (2004): 69–82.

– "Asini, gru e galline: breve indagine sugli animali del *Decameron.*" *Reinardus* 16 (2003): 133–64.

Murphy, James J. *Rhetoric in the Middle Ages.* Berkeley: University of California Press, 1974.

Muscetta, Carlo. *Boccaccio.* Bari: Laterza, 1972.

– "Introduzione alla VI giornata del 'Decameron.'" In *Ritratti e letture,* 195–211. Milan: Marzorati, 1961.

– *Ritratti e letture.* Milan: Marzorati, 1961.

Musumeci, Salvatore. "'How Does It Taste Cisti? Is It good?': Authentic Representations of Italian Renaissance Society and Wine Consumption in

Giovanni Boccaccio's *Decameron*." In *Authenticity in the Kitchen: Proceedings of the Oxford Symposium on Food and Cookery, 2005*, edited by Richard Hosking, 331–44. Devon: Prospect Books, 2006.

Naipaul, V.S. *A Bend in the River*. London: Penguin, 1980.

Najemy, John M. "Florentine Politics and Urban Spaces." In Crum and Paoletti, *Renaissance Florence*, 19–54 [2006].

– *A History of Florence, 1200–1575*. Malden, MA: Blackwell Publishing, 2006.

Nelson, Robert S., ed. *Visuality before and beyond the Renaissance*. Cambridge: Cambridge University Press, 2000.

Newhauser, Richard. Introduction. In Peter of Limoges, *The Moral Treatise on the Eye*, xi–xxxiii. Toronto: Pontifical Institute of Mediaeval Studies, 2012.

Nirenberg, David. "Discourses of Judaizing and Judaism in Medieval Spain." *La corónica* 41 (2012): 207–33.

Nissen, Christopher. *Ethics of Retribution in the "Decameron" and the Late Medieval Italian Novella*. New York: Mellen Press, 1993.

Nobili, Sebastiana. "'Tu non pensavi ch'io loico fossi': Boccaccio e l'eredità della scolastica." *Studi sul Boccaccio* 39 (2011): 139–54.

La novella italiana. Atti del convegno di Caprarola, 19–24 settembre 1988. 2 vols. Rome: Salerno editrice, 1989.

Nussmeier, Anthony. "Boccaccio e il *De vulgari eloquentia* fra il codice Toledano 104.6 e il codice Chigiano L.V.176." In *Boccaccio 1313–2013*, edited by Francesco Ciabattoni, Elsa Filosa, and Kristina Olson, 249–57. Ravenna: Longo Editore, 2015.

Ó Cuilleanáin, Cormac. "Man and Beast in the *Decameron*." *Modern Language Review* 75.1 (1980): 86–93.

– *Religion and the Clergy in Boccaccio's "Decameron."* Rome: Edizioni di Storia e Letteratura, 1984.

– "Translating Boccaccio." In Armstrong, Daniels, and Milner, *The Cambridge Companion to Boccaccio*, 203–18.

Oesch-Serra, Cecilia. "Il motto di spirito: istruzioni per l'uso: appunti per una lettura pragmatica della VI giornata del *Decameron*." *Versants* 17 (1990): 3–16.

Olson, Kristina M. "'Concivus meus': Petrarch's *Rerum memorandarum libri* 2.60, Boccaccio's *Decameron* 6.9, and the Specter of Dino del Garbo." *Annali d'italianistica* 22, *Francis Petrarch and the European Lyric Tradition* (2004): 375–80.

– *Courtesy Lost: Dante, Boccaccio, and the Literature of History*. Toronto: University of Toronto Press, 2014.

– "The Language of Women as Written by Men: Dante, Bocacaccio and Gendered Histories of the Vernacular." *Heliotropia* 8–9 (2011–12): 51–78.

– "Resurrecting Dante's Florence: Figural Realism in the *Decameron* and *Esposizioni*." *MLN* 124.1 (January 2009): 45–65.

Orvieto, Paolo. "Boccaccio mediatore di generi o dell'allegoria d'amore." *Interpres* 2 (1979): 7–104.
Padoan, Giorgio. "Mondo aristocratico e mondo comunale nell'ideologia e nell'arte di Giovanni Boccaccio." *Studi Sul Boccaccio* 2 (1964): 81–216.
– "Sulla datazione del *Corbaccio*." *Lettere italiane* 15 (1963): 1–27.
Palumbo, Matteo. "'I motti leggiadri' nella sesta giornata del *Decameron*." *Esperienze letterarie* 33.3 (2008): 3–23.
Panebianco, Beatrice, et al., eds. *Letterautori: percorsi ed esperienze letterarie*. Expanded edition. 3 vols. Bologna: Zanichelli, 2011.
Parkes, Malcolm B. "The Influence of the Concepts of *Ordinatio* and *Compilatio* on the Development of the Book." In *Medieval Learning and Literature: Essays Presented to R.W. Hunt*, edited by Jonathan J.G. Alexander and Margaret T. Gibson, 115–41. Oxford: Clarendon Press, 1975.
Parodi, Ernesto G. "La miscredenza di Guido Cavalcanti e una fonte del Boccaccio." *Bullettino della società dantesca* 22 (1915): 37–47.
Pastore Stocchi, Manlio. "Giovanni Boccaccio: La 'Genealogia deorum gentilium,' Una novità mitografica." In *Il mito nella letteratura italiana*, vol. 1, edited by Gian Carlo Alessio, 229–46. Brescia: Morcelliana, 2004.
Payen, Jean Charles. "La Pénitence dans le contexte culturel des XIIe et XIIIe siècles: des doctrines contritionistes aux pénitentiels vernaculaires." *Revue des sciences philosophiques et théologiques* 61 (1977): 399–428.
Pegoretti, Anna. "'Di che paese se' tu di ponente?': cartografie boccacciane." *Studi sul Boccaccio* 39 (2011): 83–113.
Pennington, Kenneth. "A Note to *Decameron* 6.7: The Wit of Madonna Filippa." *Speculum* 52.4 (October 1977): 902–5.
Peruzzi, Simonetta Mazzoni. *Medioevo francese nel "Corbaccio."* Florence: Le Lettere, 2001.
Petoletti, Marco. "Scheda 58." In De Robertis et al., *Boccaccio autore e copista*, 336–7.
Petrini, Mario. *Nel giardino di Boccaccio*. Trieste: Del Bianco Editore, 1986.
– *Ragionare nel giardino*. Udine: Edizioni Del Bianco, 1986.
Petrolini, Giovanni. "'Voi non l'avrí da mi, madonna Brunetta, voi non l'avrí da mi' (*Dec.* VI, 4, 8): una 'contrafacture' di 'Donna Lombarda'?" *Critica letteraria* 10/37.4 (1982): 711–18.
Piciché, Bernardo. *Argisto Giuffredi. Gentiluomo borghese nel vicereame di Sicilia*. Rome: Euroma–La Goliardica, 2006.
Picone, Michelangelo. "Dal fabliau alla novella: il caso di Chichibìo (*Decameron* VI.4)." In *La Nouvelle: Formation, codification et rayonnement d'un genre médiéval*. Actes du colloque international de Montreal (McGill University, 14–16 October 1982), edited by Michelangelo Picone et al., 111–22. Montreal: Plato Academy Press, 1983.

– "Leggiadri motti e pronte risposte: la sesta giornata." In *Introduzione al "Decameron,"* edited by Michelangelo Picone and Margherita Mesirca, 163–85. Florence: Cesati, 2004.

Pirotta, Nino. *Music and Culture in Italy from the Middle Ages to the Baroque: A Collection of Essays.* Cambridge, MA, and London: Harvard University Press, 1984.

Pistolesi, Elena. "Il *De vulgari eloquentia* di Giovanni Boccaccio." *Giornale storico della letteratura italiana* 131.2 (2014): 161–99.

Pound, Ezra. *Sonnets and Ballate of Guido Cavalcanti.* London: Stephen Swift and Co., 1912.

– *The Spirit of Romance.* London: Peter Owen, 1910.

Pound, Ezra, ed. *Rime, edizione rappezzata fra le rovine*, by Guido Cavalcanti. Genoa: Marsano, 1932.

Psaki, F. Regina. "Boccaccio's *Corbaccio* as a *Secret* Admirer." *Heliotropia* 7.1–2 (2010): 105–32.

– "Giving Them the Bird: Figurative Language and the 'Woman Question' in the *Decameron* and the *Corbaccio.*" *Studi sul Boccaccio* 41 (2013): 207–37.

– "The Traffic in Talk about Women: Cultural Traffic in Medieval Texts and Medieval Studies." *Journal of Romance Studies* 4.3 (2004): 13–34.

– "Voicing Gender in the *Decameron.*" In Armstrong, Daniels, and Milner, *The Cambridge Companion to Boccaccio*, 101–17 [2015].

– "Women in the *Decameron.*" In *Approaches to Teaching Boccaccio's "Decameron,"* edited by James H. McGregor, 79–86. New York: Modern Language Association of America, 2000.

– "'Women Make All Things Lose Their Power': Women's Knowledge, Men's Fear in the *Decameron* and the *Corbaccio.*" *Heliotropia* 1.1 (2003): 33–48.

Quondam, Amedeo. "Introduzione." In Boccaccio, *Decameron*, edited by Quondam, Fiorilla, and Alfano, 5–65 [2013].

Ramat, Rafaello. "Indicazioni per una lettura del 'Decameron.'" In *Scritti su Giovanni Boccaccio*, edited by Sergio Gensini, 7–19. Florence: Società Storica della Valdelsa [Olschki], 1964.

Richardson, Brian. "Onomastica boccacciana. 'La moglie di Sicofante.'" *Lingua nostra* 34 (1973): 42–4.

Ricketts, Jill. *Visualizing Boccaccio: Studies on Illustrations of "The Decameron," from Giotto to Pasolini.* Cambridge: Cambridge University Press, 2011.

Righini, Pietro. *L'acustica per il musicista. Fondamenti fisici della musica.* Padua: Zanibon, 1994.

Robins, William. "The Case of the Court Entertainer: Popular Culture, Intertextual Dialogue, and the Early Circulation of Boccaccio's *Decameron.*" *Speculum* 91.2 (2017): 1–35.

Rossi, Luca Carlo. "Sul motto di Cavalcanti in *Dec.* VI 9." In *L'antiche e le moderne carte: studi in memoria di Giuseppe Billanovich*, edited by Antonio Manfredi and Carla Maria Monti, 499–517. Rome and Padua: Antenore, 2007.

Ruffini, Marco. "Boccaccio e l'immagine mimetica." *Critica del testo* 16 (2013): 307–22.

Ruggiero, Guido. "Mean Streets, Familiar Streets, or the Fat Woodcarver and the Masculine Spaces of Renaissance Florence." In Crum and Paoletti, *Renaissance Florence*, 295–310 [2006].

Russo, Luigi. *Letture critiche del "Decameron."* Bari: Laterza, 1967.

– *Novelle scelte del "Decameron."* Florence, Sansoni, 1943.

Samson, Alexander. *Locus amoenus: Gardens and Horticulture in the Renaissance.* Malden: Wiley-Blackwell, 2012.

Sanguineti-White, Laura. *La scena conviviale e la sua funzione nel mondo del Boccaccio.* Florence: Olschki, 1983.

Sapegno, Natalino. "Giovanni Boccaccio." In *Dizionario biographico degli italiani*, Treccani, 1968. https://www.treccani.it/biografico/elenco_voci/ [accessed 14 February 2021].

Savelli, Giulio. "La misura del privilegio: il vino di Cisti Fornaio." In *Soavi sapori della cultura italiana* (Atti del 13. Congresso dell'A.I.P.I, Verona-Soave 27–29 agosto 1998), edited by Bart Van den Bossche, Michel Bastiansen, and Corinna Salvadori Lonergan, 189–95. Florence: Cesati, 2000.

Scaglione, Aldo. *Nature and Love in the Late Middle Ages: An Essay on the Cultural Context of the "Decameron."* Berkeley: University of California Press, 1963.

Schaber, Bennet. "The Aesthetics of Deception. Giotto in the Text of Boccaccio." In *Postmodernism across the Ages*, edited by Bill Readings and Bennet Schaber, 47–62. Syracuse: Syracuse University Press, 1993.

Schnapp, Jeffrey T. "A Commentary on Commentary in Boccaccio." *South Atlantic Quarterly* 91 (1992): 813–34.

Sciacovelli, Antonio Donato. "Dal *De viris illustribus* al *De mulieribus claris.*" *Verbum* 7 (2005): 263–79.

Scott, John A. *Understanding Dante.* Notre Dame: University of Notre Dame Press, 2004.

Serafini-Sauli, Judith. "The Pleasures of Reading: Boccaccio's *Decameron* and Female Literacy." *MLN* 126.1 (January 2001): 29–46.

Shemek, Deanna. "Doing and Undoing: Boccaccio's Feminism (*De mulieribus claris*)." In Kirkham, Sherberg, and Smarr, *Boccaccio*, 195–204 [2013].

Smarr, Janet Levarie. *Boccaccio and Fiammetta: The Narrator as Lover.* Urbana: University of Illinois Press, 1986.

Smuts, Aaron. "Humor." *The Internet Encyclopedia of Philosophy.* https://www.iep.utm.edu/ [accessed 17 May 2020].

Spackman, Barbara. "*Inter musam et ursam moritur*: Folengo and the Gaping "Other" Mouth." In *Refiguring Women: Perspectives on Gender and the Italian Renaissance*, edited by Marilyn Migiel and Juliana Schiesari, 19–34. Ithaca: Cornell University Press, 1991.

Spani, Giovanni. "Il vino di Boccaccio: Usi e abusi in alcune novelle del *Decameron*." *Heliotropia* 8–9 (2011–12): 79–98.

Speca, Anthony. *Hypothetical Syllogistic and Stoic Logic.* Leiden: Brill, 2001.

Stefanelli, Ruggiero. *Boccaccio e la poesia.* Naples: Loffredo, 1978.

Steinberg, Justin. "Mimesis on Trial: Legal and Literary Verisimilitude in Boccaccio's *Decameron*." *Representations* 139 (2017): 118–45.

Stewart, Pamela. "La novella di Madonna Oretta e le due parti del 'Decameron.'" *Yearbook of Italian Studies* (1973–5): 27–39.

– *Retorica e mimica nel "Decameron" e nella commedia del Cinquecento.* Florence: Olschki, 1986.

Stillinger, Thomas C. "The Language of Gardens: Boccaccio's 'Valle delle donne.'" *Traditio* 39 (1983): 301–21.

– *The Song of Troilus: Lyric Authority in the Medieval Book.* Philadelphia: University of Pennsylvania Press, 1992.

Stone, Gregory B. *The Ethics of Nature in the Middle Ages: On Boccaccio's Poetaphysics.* New York: St Martin's Press, 1998.

Stoppino, Eleonora. "Contamination, Contagion and the Animal Function in Boccaccio's *Decameron*." *Critica del testo* 17.3 (2014): 93–114; special issue on *Contaminazione/Contaminazioni*, edited by Maria Luisa Meneghetti and Stefano Resconi.

Strocchia, Sharon T. "Gender and the Rites of Honor in Italian Renaissance Cities." In *Gender and Society in Renaissance Italy*, edited by Judith C. Brown and Robert C. Davis, 39–60. London and New York: Longman, 1998.

– "Theaters of Everyday Life." In Crum and Paoletti, *Renaissance Florence*, 55–80 [2006].

Stump, Eleonore. *Dialectic and Its Place in the Development of Medieval Logic.* Ithaca: Cornell University Press, 1989.

Symonds, John A. *Giovanni Boccaccio as Man and Author.* New York: AMS Press, 1968 [London 1895].

Szittya, Penn R. *The Antifraternal Tradition in Medieval Literature.* Princeton: Princeton University Press, 1986.

Tachau, Katherine. *Vision and Certitude in the Age of Ockham.* Leiden: Brill, 1988.

Tang, Chenxi. "The Transformation of the Law of Nations and the Re-invention of the Novella: Legal History and Literary Innovation from Boccaccio's *Decameron* to Goethe's *Unterhaltungen deutscher Aus-gewanderten.*" *Goethe Yearbook* 19 (2012): 67–92.

Tavoni, Mirko. "Linguistic Italy." Translated by James Cotton. In Barański and Pertile, *Dante in Context*, 243–59 [2015].

Tateo, Francesco. *Boccaccio.* Bari: Laterza, 1998.

TLIO (*Tesoro della Lingua Italiana delle Origini*). Online edition. Edited by Pär Larson and Paolo Squillacioti. Rome: Consiglio Nazionale delle Ricerche-Opera del Vocabolario Italiano, 1997–present. http://tlio.ovi.cnr.it/TLIO [accessed 14 February 2021].

Testaferri, Ada. "Motto di spirito e potere eversivo di Chichibio." *Quaderni d'Italianistica* 12.2 (1991): 223–30.

Todorov, Tzvetan. *Grammaire du "Décaméron."* Paris: Mouton, 1969.

Tomas, Natalie. "Did Women Have a Space?" In Crum and Paoletti, *Renaissance Florence*, 311–28 [2006].

Torraca, Francesco. *Per la biografia di Giovanni Boccaccio.* Milan, Rome, and Naples: Albrighi e Segati, 1912.

Totaro, Luigi. *Ragioni d'amore. Le donne del "Decameron."* Florence: Firenze University Press, 2005.

Trexler, Richard. *Public Life in Renaissance Florence.* Ithaca: Cornell University Press, 1991.

Ugolini, Paola. "L'adulterio e la rappresentazione della donna nelle *Novelle* di Matteo Bandello." *Matteo Bandello. Studi di letteratura rinascimentale* 3 (2010): 175–200.

Usher, Jonathan. "'Desultorietà' nella novella portante di Madonna Oretta (*Decameron* VI, 1) e altre citazioni apuleiane nel Boccaccio." *Studi sul Boccaccio* 29 (2001): 67–104.

– "Frate Cipolla's 'Ars Praedicandi' or a 'Récit du discours' in Boccaccio." *Modern Language Review* 88.2 (1993): 321–36.

– "Le rubriche del *Decameron.*" *Medioevo romanzo* 10 (1985): 391–418.

Valesio, Paolo. "Canto V. The Fierce Dove." In *Lectura Dantis: Inferno. A Canto-by-Canto Commentary*, edited by Allen Mandelbaum et al., 63–83. Berkeley and Los Angeles: University of California Press, 1998.

Van der Voort, Cok. "Convergenze e divaricazioni tra la prima e la sesta giornata del *Decameron.*" *Studi sul Boccaccio* 11 (1979): 207–41.

Veglia, Marco. *Il corvo e la sirena: cultura e poesia del "Corbaccio."* Pisa and Rome: Istituti Editoriali e Poligrafici Internazionali, 1998.

– *"La vita lieta." Una lettura del "Decameron."* Ravenna: Longo, 2000.

Velli, Giuseppe. "Seneca nel *Decameron.*" *Giornale storico della letteratura italiana* 168 (January 1991): 321–34.

Verberckmoes, John. "What about Medieval Humour? Some Historiography." In *Risus Mediaevalis*, edited by H. Braet, G. Latré, and W. Verbeke, 1–9. Leuven: Leuven University Press, 2003.

Viladesau, Richard. *The Beauty of the Cross: The Passion of Christ in Theology and the Arts, from the Catacombs to the Eve of the Renaissance*. Oxford: Oxford University Press, 2006.

Volpato, Simone. "Note sul vocabolario dei mercanti-scrittori." *Studi sul Boccaccio* 26 (1996): 131–63.

von Dobschütz, Ernst. *Christusbilder. Untersuchungen zur christlichen Legende.* Leipzig: Hinrichs, 1899.

Wallace, David. *Giovanni Boccaccio: "Decameron."* Cambridge: Cambridge University Press 1993.

Ward, John O. *Ciceronian Rhetoric in Treatise, Scholion, and Commentary*. TSO 58. Turnhout: Brepols, 1995.

– "Rhetorical Theory and the Rise and Decline of *Dictamen* in the Middle Ages and Early Renaissance." *Rhetorica* 19 (2001): 175–223.

Watson, Paul F. "Architettura e scultura e senso della narrazione: Guido Cavalcanti e le case dei morti." In Branca, *Boccaccio visualizzato*, vol. 1, 75–84 [1999].

– "The Cement of Fiction: Giovanni Boccaccio and the Painters of Florence." *MLN* 99 (1984): 43–64.

– "On Seeing Guido Cavalcanti and the Houses of the Dead." *Studi sul Boccaccio* 18 (1989): 301–18.

Watt, J.A. "Dante, Boniface VIII and the Pharisees." In *Post Scripta: Essays on Medieval Law and the Emergence of the European State in Honor of Gaines Post*, edited by Joseph R. Strayer and Donald E. Queller, 201–15. Rome: Libreria Ateneo Salesiano, 1972.

Weaver, Elissa B., ed. *The "Decameron" First Day in Perspective*. Toronto: University of Toronto Press, 2004.

White, E.B. "Some Remarks on Humor." In *Essays of E.B. White*, 243–9. New York: Harper and Row: 1977.

Wippel, John F. "Metaphysics." In *The Cambridge Companion to Aquinas*, edited by Normann Kretzmann and Eleonore Stump, 85–127. Cambridge: Cambridge University Press, 1993.

Wofford, Susanne L. "The Social Aethetics of Rape: Closural Violence in Boccaccio." In *Creative Imitation: New Essays on Renaissance Literature in Honor of Thomas M. Greene*, edited by David Quint, Margaret W. Ferguson, G.W. Pigman III, and Wayne A. Rebhorn, 189–238. Binghamton, NY: Medieval and Renaissance Texts and Studies, 1992.

Zafarana, Zelina. "Boccaccio di Chellino." In the *Dizionario biografico degli italiani*, Treccani 1968. https://www.treccani.it/biografico/elenco_voci/ [accessed 14 February 2021].

Zak, Gur. "Boccaccio and Petrarch." In Armstrong, Daniels, and Milner, *The Cambridge Companion to Boccaccio*, 139–54 [2015].

Zavattero, Irene. "La *Quaestio de felicitate* di Giacomo da Pistoia: un tentativo di interpretazione alla luce di una nuova edizione critica del testo." In *Le felicità nel medioevo*. Atti del Convegno della Società Italiana per lo studio del pensiero medievale (SISPM), edited by Maria Bettetini and Francesco D. Paparella, 355–409. Louvain and La-Neuve: FIDEM, 2005.

Ziolkowski, Jan M. "Mastering Authors and Authorizing Masters in the Long Twelfth Century." In *Latinitas Perennis. I. The Continuity of Latin Literature*, edited by Wim Verbaal et al., 93–118. Leiden: Brill, 2007.

– "Popular Culture." In Barański and Pertile, *Dante in Context*, 389–98 [2015].

Zumthor, Paul. *Speaking of the Middle Ages*. Translated by Sarah White. Lincoln: University of Nebraska Press, 1986.

Contributors

Guyda Armstrong is Senior Lecturer in Italian Studies and Director of the Centre for Digital Humanities at the University of Manchester. Her research focuses on Boccaccio and medieval Italian literature, and its transmission across languages, cultures, and media from the medieval period to the present day. She is the author of numerous articles on Boccaccio, Dante, Petrarch, and medieval Italian literature, and of the book *The English Boccaccio: A History in Books* (2013). She is the co-editor (with Rhiannon Daniels and Stephen J. Milner) of *The Cambridge Companion to Boccaccio* (2015), and the 2017 special issue of *Heliotropia, Locating Boccaccio*. She was also co-investigator (with Simon Gilson and Federica Pich) on the AHRC-funded *Petrarch Commentary and Exegesis in Renaissance Italy* (*PERI*) project (2017–19), for which she directed the Petrarch Digital Library, a collection of some eighty-five fully digitized editions of Petrarch printed between 1470 and 1650, available via Manchester Digital Collections.

Zygmunt G. Barański is Serena Professor of Italian Emeritus at the University of Cambridge and R.L. Canala Professor of Romance Languages and Literatures at the University of Notre Dame. He has published extensively on Dante, on medieval Italian literature, on Dante's fourteenth- and twentieth-century reception, and on twentieth-century Italian literature, film, and culture. His most recent book is *Dante, Petrarch, Boccaccio: Literature, Doctrine, Reality* (2020). For many years he was senior editor of *The Italianist*, and currently holds the same position with *Le tre corone*.

Giulia Cardillo is an assistant professor of Italian at James Madison University. Her research interests include the question of exegesis and readership in the works of Dante Alighieri and Giovanni Boccaccio, the relationship of literary to visual arts in the Renaissance, and the rewritings of the myth of Echo in Italian literature. She has published on Tasso and Michelangelo, and on the concept of *Terra Australis* in the Middle Ages. She is currently working on a monograph on the readers' role in Dante's *Commedia* and on a project on women's literary networks in the early modern period.

Peter Carravetta is a professor of philosophy at SUNY/Stony Brook. Critic, historian, poet, and translator, he has published nine books of cultural criticism and philosophy, including *Prefaces to the Diaphora: Rhetorics, Allegory, and the Interpretation of Postmodernity* (1991), *The Elusive Hermes: Method, Discourse, Interpreting* (2012), and *After Identity: Migration, Critique, Italian American Culture* (2017). He is also the author of eight collections of poetry, including *The Sun and Other Things* (1997), *L'infinito. Poesie 1972–2012* (2013), and *The Other Lives* (2014). He was the founder and director of *DIFFERENTIA review of italian thought* (9 vols. 1986–99), and translator of G. Vattimo and P.A. Rovatti's *Weak Thought* (2012). His recent work is focused on migration and on humanism.

Aileen A. Feng is an associate professor of Italian at the University of Arizona, where she is also Director of Italian Studies and a faculty affiliate in the Department of Gender and Women's Studies. She holds a BA in French and Italian from the University of Texas at Austin, an MA in Italian from the University of Notre Dame, and a PhD in Italian from the University of California, Berkeley. She has also been a Lila Wallace–Reader's Digest Fellow at Villa I Tatti, the Harvard University Center for Renaissance Studies in Florence, Italy. She has published extensively on late medieval and Renaissance Italian literature. She is the author of *Writing Beloveds: Humanist Petrarchism and the Politics of Gender* (2017), the co-translator (with Fabian Alfie) of *The Poetry of Burchiello (ca. 1404–1449): Deep-Fried Nouns, Hunchbacked Pumpkins, and Other Nonsense* (2017), and the co-editor (with Unn Falkeid) of *Rethinking Gaspara Stampa in the Canon of Renaissance Poetry* (2015).

Teresa Kennedy earned her PhD in Comparative Literature and Linguistics from the Catholic University of America in 1989. She is a professor of English, and has directed the Simpson Program in Medieval Studies at the University of Mary Washington in Fredericksburg, Virginia since 1991. Her main research interests include fourteenth-century English, Italian, and French literature and linguistics. She is currently working on a monograph, *Boccaccio and the Making of the Modern Reader*, and recent publications include an edited special issue, "Tra Amici:

Essays in Honor of Giuseppe Mazzotta" (with Theodore Cachey, Walter Stephens, and Zygmunt Barański), *MLN* 127.1 (January 2012), and "Boccaccio's Greek Philology" in *Through a Classical Eye: Essays in Honor of Winthrop Wetherbee*, edited by R.F. Yeager and A. Galloway (2009). Additionally, she served on the editorial board of *Exemplaria* (ex officio), and edited (with Barton Palmer) the *Routledge Medieval Authors* series. Her essay, "From Imitation to Invention: Chaucer's Journey from House of Fame to the Nun's Priest Tale," appears in *Chaucer and Italian Culture*, edited by Helen Fulton (2020).

James C. Kriesel is an associate professor of Italian at Villanova University. His research explores medieval ideas about the emotions, gender, and nature. He has also published on the Renaissance reception of Boccaccio and Dante. His monograph *Boccaccio's Corpus: Allegory, Ethics, and Vernacularity* appears in the University of Notre Dame Press's Devers Series in Dante and Medieval Italian Literature (2019).

Maria Lettiero holds degrees in pianoforte and harpsichord performance, as well as a *Laurea specialistica* in Musicology and *Beni Culturali* from the University of Rome "Tor Vergata" and a PhD in Italian literature from the European consortium between the University of Rome "Tor Vergata" and the University of País Vasco (Spain), with a dissertation titled "Il *Decameron* di Boccaccio: un 'salto' oltre confine tra *melos* e *verbum*." She is the author of *Le ottave di Boiardo nella cultura musicale del Cinquecento* (2011) and of several essays and reviews on musicology and literature. She teaches pianoforte and continues to collaborate on teaching and research projects in Lettere e Filosofia at "Tor Vergata." A professional musician, she also regularly performs and conducts choirs and orchestras.

David Lummus is the co-director of the Center for Italian Studies and the Devers Family Program in Dante Studies at the University of Notre Dame, where he is also a visiting assistant professor of Italian. He holds a BA *summa cum laude* in Classics and Italian from the University of Texas at Austin and an MA and PhD in Italian from Stanford University. He has published extensively on fourteenth-century Italian literature and culture. With Martin Eisner, he is co-editor of *A Boccaccian Renaissance: Essays on the Early Modern Impact of Giovanni Boccaccio and His Works* (2019). His monograph *The City of Poetry: Imagining the Civic Role of the Poet in Fourteenth-Century Italy* (2020) won the 2019 MLA Aldo and Jeanne Scaglione Publication Award for a Manuscript in Italian Literary Studies.

Cormac Ó Cuilleanáin is an emeritus professor at Trinity College Dublin. The author of *Religion and the Clergy in Boccaccio's Decameron* (1984), he has co-edited volumes including *Dante and the Middle Ages* (1995), *Patterns in Dante* (2005), *Translation and Censorship* (2009), and *Translation Right or Wrong* (2013). A former chairman of the Irish Writers' Centre, he has been active at various times as a translator and crime novelist. His new English version of the *Decameron*, based on John Payne's 1886 translation, was published in 2004, and he contributed the essay "Translating Boccaccio" to *The Cambridge Companion to Boccaccio* (2015). He is a Cavaliere dell'Ordine della Stella d'Italia, a former winner of the John Florio translation prize, an Honorary Member of the Irish Translators' and Interpreters' Association, and an Honorary Member of the American Boccaccio Association.

Bernardo Piciché is associate professor in the Department of World Studies at the Virginia Commonwealth University. He holds a law degree and an MA in International Studies from the University of Rome; literature degrees and MPhils from the Universities of Rome and Paris, and Yale University. At Yale he also earned his PhD in Italian Renaissance Literature. His areas of interest are Italian and comparative literature, film studies, the influence of Roman law on medieval literature, and Mediterranean Studies. His book *Argisto Giuffredi. Gentiluomo borghese nel vicereame di Sicilia* (2006) won the Premio Internazione di Poesia e Letteratura "Nuove Lettere" in 2007. In 2019, he edited and introduced the special issue of *Forum Italicum*, "Diritto e letteratura a dialogo nella tradizione italiana." His recent publications are on the sixteenth-century Italian poet Torquato Tasso; Italian Futurism; the painter Caravaggio in relation to macaronic literature; the Moorish writer Leo Africanus; the Turkish film director Erol Mintas; and the Mediterranean identity and Mediterranean Studies as a discipline.

Index

www.ingramcontent.com/pod-product-compliance
Lightning Source LLC
Chambersburg PA
CBHW030424310726
48979CB00009B/1601/J